COMMENTARY

ON

THE BOOK OF PSALMS

VOL. II

THE CALVIN TRANSLATION SOCIETY,

INSTITUTED IN MAY M.DCCC.XLIII.

FOR THE PUBLICATION OF TRANSLATIONS OF THE WORKS OF
JOHN CALVIN.

COMMENTARY

ON

THE BOOK OF PSALMS

BY JOHN CALVIN

TRANSLATED FROM THE ORIGINAL LATIN, AND COLLATED
WITH THE AUTHOR'S FRENCH VERSION,

BY THE REV. JAMES ANDERSON

VOLUME SECOND

WIPF & STOCK · Eugene, Oregon

Wipf and Stock Publishers
199 W 8th Ave, Suite 3
Eugene, OR 97401

Commentary on the Book of Psalms, Volume 2
By Calvin, John and Anderson, James
Softcover ISBN-13: 979-8-3852-1669-7
Hardcover ISBN-13: 979-8-3852-1670-3
eBook ISBN-13: 979-8-3852-1671-0
Publication date 2/13/2024
Previously published by Baker Book House, 2005

This edition is a scanned facsimile of the original edition published in 2005.

THE first part of this volume is translated by the REV. JAMES M'LEAN, Kirkwall, and the second, by the REV. GEORGE M'CRIE, Clola. The annotations have been drawn up by the REV. JAMES ANDERSON, to whom the general editorship of the work has been intrusted.

From the copiousness of CALVIN'S COMMENTARIES ON THE PSALMS, it has been found impracticable to complete the Work in less than Five Volumes; and to do justice to this valuable portion of his labours, it is of importance that it should not be hurried through the press. The Subscribers are, however, respectfully informed, that there will be no unnecessary delay, and that the whole is expected to be completed within the course of two years.

EDINBURGH, *June 1st*, 1846.

COMMENTARY

UPON

THE BOOK OF PSALMS.

PSALM XXXVI.

ALMOST all interpreters agree in supposing, that in this psalm David in general expresses his wonder and amazement at the goodness of God, because, in the exercise of his favour and mercy, he bears with the wicked, who, notwithstanding, basely contemn him. The opinion which I have formed is somewhat different. I think that the holy prophet, being grievously troubled and harassed by wicked and ungodly men, first complains of their depravity, and then seeks refuge in the infinite goodness of God, which extends not only to all men in general, but in a particular and special manner to his own children; and this he does in order to console, and, so to speak, take his breath, in the assurance that he shall at length be delivered since God is favourable to him. This is evident from the conclusion of the psalm, in which he arms and fortifies himself against all the assaults of the ungodly, by reflecting that he is safe under the protection of God.

¶ To the chief musician. A Psalm of David, the servant of Jehovah.

Why the appellation, *the servant of God*, is ascribed to David only in this place and in the eighteenth psalm, rather than elsewhere, cannot positively be ascertained, unless that having been victorious in a conflict, of all others the most difficult, he proved himself to be a valiant warrior and an invincible champion in the sight of God. We know how rare and singular a virtue it is, when ungodliness is prevailing without restraint, and when the shade of its obscurity darkens our spiritual vision, to look up, notwithstanding, by the eye of faith, to the providence of God, which, by disposing our minds to patience, may keep us constantly in the fear of God.

1. *Ungodliness saith to the wicked in the midst of my heart,*
   There is no fear of God before his eyes.
2. *For he flattereth himself in his own eyes, until his iniquity*
   be found to be hateful.[1]
3. *The words of his mouth are iniquity*[2] *and deceit; he hath*
   left off to understand that he may do good.
4. *He meditates* [or *devises*] *iniquity upon his bed; he setteth*
   himself in a way that is not good; and abhorreth not evil.

1. *Ungodliness saith to the wicked in the midst of my heart.* Commentators are not agreed as to the interpretation of the first verse. Literally it is, *The saying* [or *speech*] *of transgression,* or rather, *Transgression saith to the wicked.* As, however, the letter ל, *lamed*, is in Hebrew sometimes used for מן, *min*, some translate it thus, *Ungodliness or transgression speaketh of the wicked in my heart;* as if the prophet had said, I clearly perceive from the wickedness which the ungodly commit, that they are not influenced by the fear of God. But as there is no need to depart from the proper signification of the words, I rather agree with others in supposing that the language of the prophet is to this effect: The malice of the wicked, though seemingly hidden and unknown, speaks aloud in my heart, and I am a sure witness of what it says or suggests.

And, first, it is to be observed, that the prophet speaks not of outward faults, but penetrates even to the very source; as if he had said, Although the wicked cloak their malice with wily dissimulation, yet I know it so well that I seem to hear it speaking. It is indeed true, that as the ungodly and profane rush headlong into every kind of wickedness, as if they were never to be called to render up an account of it, the judgment which David here expresses may be formed even from their life; but his language is much more emphatic when he says, that the servants of God openly perceive the depravity of such persons hidden within the heart. Now David does not speak of the wicked generally, but of the abandoned

---

[1] "C'est, tant que chacun commence à avoir en haine l'iniquite d'iceluy."
—*Fr. marg.* "That is, so that every one begins to hate his iniquity."

[2] "Mensonge."—*Fr.* "Falsehood."

despisers of God. There are many who indulge in their vices, who, notwithstanding, are not intoxicated by the wretched infatuation which David here censures. But when a man becomes hardened in committing sin, ungodliness at length reduces him to such a state of insensibility, that, despising the judgment of God, he indulges without fear in the practice of every sin to which his depraved appetite impels him. A reckless assurance, therefore, in the commission of sin, and especially where it is associated with a contempt and scorn of every holy admonition, is, as it were, an enchantment of Satan, which indicates that the condition of such a person is indeed hopeless. And although true religion has the effect of keeping the hearts of the godly in the fear of God, and drives wicked thoughts far from their minds, yet this does not prevent them from perceiving and understanding in their hearts how the ungodly are agitated with horrible fury when they neither regard God nor are afraid of his judgments.

There is no fear of God before his eyes. David shows in these few words the end of all evil suggestions; and it is this, that the sense both of good and evil being destroyed or suppressed, men shrink from nothing, as if there were not seated in heaven a God, the Judge of all. The meaning therefore is, Ungodliness speaks in my heart to the wicked man, urging him to the extremity of madness, so that, laying aside all fear of God, he abandons himself to the practice of sin; that is to say, I know as well what the ungodly imagine in their hearts, as if God had set me as a witness or judge to unveil their hypocrisy, under the mask of which they think their detestable malice is hidden and deeply buried. When the wicked, therefore, are not restrained by the fear of God from committing sin, this proceeds from that secret discourse with themselves, to which we have referred, and by which their understanding is so depraved and blinded, that, like brute beasts, they run to every excess in rioting. Since the eyes are, as it were, the guides and conductors of man in this life, and by their influence move the other senses hither and thither, it is therefore said that men have the fear of God before their eyes when it regulates their lives, and by presenting itself to them on every side to which they may turn, serves like a bridle to restrain their appetites and passions. David, by using here a contrary form of expression, means that the ungodly run to every excess in licentiousness, without having any regard to God, because the depravity of their own hearts has completely blinded them.

2. *For he flattereth himself in his own eyes.* Here the Psalmist shows by their fruits or the marks of their character, that there is no fear of God among the wicked, seeing they take such pleasure in committing deeds of wickedness, that, although hateful in the sight of all other men, they still cherish the natural obstinacy of their hearts, and wilfully harden themselves in their evil course. First, he says that they nourish their vices by flatteries,[1] that they may not be dissatisfied with themselves in sinning. But when he adds,

[1] The verb חלק, *chalak*, which is rendered *flattereth*, signifies *to smooth*, and means here, that the wicked man described endeavours by plausible arguments to put a soft, smooth, and fair gloss on his wickedness, as if there were nothing repulsive and hateful about it, nothing amiss or blameworthy in it; and in this way he deceives himself. This is the sense expressed in the literal translation of Montanus, which seems very forcible: "Quoniam lenivit ad se in oculis ipsius, ad inveniendum iniquitatem suam ad odiendam."—"For he has smoothed over [or set a polish] to himself in his own eyes, with respect to the finding out of his iniquity, [that is, so as not to find it out,] to hate it." Horsley reads,

"For he giveth things a fair appearance to himself,
In his own eyes, so that he discovers not his own iniquity to hate it."

"He sets such a false gloss," says this critic, "in his own eyes, upon his worst actions, that he never finds out the blackness of his iniquity, which, were it perceived by him, would be hateful even to himself." The wicked in all ages have thus contrived to put a fair appearance upon the most unprincipled maxims and pernicious practices. It will be seen that Montanus' and Horsley's translation of the last clause of the verse gives a different meaning from that given by Calvin. The original text is somewhat obscure and ambiguous from its brevity; but it seems to support the sense given by these critics. The Hebrew is, למצא עונו לשנא, *limtso avono lisno, to find,* or *to, for,* or *concerning the finding of,* [the first word being an infinitive with the prefix ל, *lamed,*] *his iniquity to hate* [*it.*] "The prefix ל," says Walford, "cannot, I imagine, be translated with any propriety by *until.*" His rendering is,

"For he flattereth himself in his own sight,
That his iniquity will not be found to be hateful:"

That is, will not be viewed by others as the hateful thing which it really is. The original words will easily bear this sense as well as that given by Montanus and Horsley.

until their iniquity be found to be hateful, by these words he is to be understood as referring to their determined obstinacy; for the meaning is, that while they falsely flatter themselves, they proceed to such an extent in their evil course, that their iniquity becomes hateful to all men. Some translate the words thus: *So that he himself finds his own iniquity to be hateful;* and understand them as meaning, that the wicked persist in rushing headlong into sin without restraint, until, satiated or glutted with the indulgence of their depraved desires, they begin to loathe it: for even the most depraved are sometimes dissatisfied with themselves on account of their sinful conduct. The first interpretation is, however, the more natural, namely, that the wicked, though they are hateful to all men on account of their iniquity, which, when once discovered and made manifest, excites a general feeling of displeasure, are not affected by any displeasure against themselves, but, on the contrary, rather applaud themselves, whilst the people despise them, and abhor the wickedness of their lives. The prophet, therefore, condemns them for their infatuation in this, that while all others are offended at their disgraceful conduct, they themselves are not at all affected by it. As far as in them lies, they abolish all distinction between good and evil, and lull their conscience into a state of insensibility, lest it should pain them, and urge them to repentance. Certainly the infatuation here described ought to be the subject of our serious consideration, the infatuation which is manifested in this, that men who are given up to a reprobate mind, while they render themselves hateful in the sight of all other men, are notwithstanding destitute of all sense of their own sins.

3. *The words of his mouth are iniquity and deceit.* The two clauses of this verse may be understood as referring to the same thing, namely, that the wicked indulging in deceit and vanity, will not receive or admit the light of understanding. This, I apprehend, is the meaning of David. He reproves the wicked not merely for circumventing others by their wiles and stratagems, but especially because they are altogether destitute of uprightness and sincerity. We have already

said that the Psalmist is here speaking not of sinful and wicked men, in whose hearts there still remains some fear of God, but of the profane despisers of his name, who have given themselves up entirely to the practice of sin. He therefore says that they have always in their mouth some frivolous excuses and vain pretexts, by which they encourage themselves in rejecting and scoffing at all sound doctrine. He then adds, that they purposely suppress in themselves all knowledge or understanding of the distinction between good and evil, because they have no desire to become better than they are. We know that God has given understanding to men to direct them to do what is good. Now David says that the wicked shun it, and strive to deprive themselves of it, that they may not be constrained to repent of their wickedness, and to amend their lives. We are taught from this passage, that if at any time we turn aside from the path of rectitude, the only remedy in such a case is to open the eyes of our understanding, that we may rightly distinguish between good and evil, and that thus we may be led back from our wandering. When, instead of doing this, a man refuses instruction, it is an indication that he is in a state of depravity altogether desperate.

4. *He meditates iniquity upon his bed.* Here the sacred writer shows that the wickedness of the ungodly man is of a secret and very determined character. It sometimes happens that many, who otherwise are not disposed to wickedness, err and fall into sin, because occasion presents itself all on a sudden; but David tells us, that the wicked, even when they are withdrawn from the sight of men, and in retirement, form schemes of mischief; and thus, although there is not presented before them any temptation, or the evil example of others to excite them to it, they, of their own accord, devise mischief, and urge themselves to it without being impelled by any thing else. Since he describes the reprobate by this distinguishing mark of character, that *they devise mischief upon their beds,* true believers should learn from this to exercise themselves when alone in meditations of a different nature, and to make their own life the subject of examination, so that they

may exclude all evil thoughts from their minds. The Psalmist next refers to their stubbornness, declaring *that they set themselves in a crooked and perverse way;* that is to say, they purposely and wilfully harden themselves in doing evil. Finally, he adds the reason of their doing this: *They abhor not evil.* Wilfully shutting their eyes, they rush forward in their headlong course till they spontaneously yield themselves the slaves of wickedness. Let us now shortly state the contrast between the ungodly and the people of God, contained in the preceding verses. The former deceive themselves by flattery; the latter exercise over themselves a strict control, and examine themselves with a rigid scrutiny: the former, throwing loose the reins, rush headlong into evil; the latter are restrained by the fear of God: the former cloak or disguise their offences by sophistry, and turn light into darkness; the latter willingly acknowledge their guilt, and by a candid confession are brought to repentance: the former reject all sound judgment; the latter always desire to vindicate themselves by coming to the open light of day: the former upon their bed invent various ways of doing evil; the latter are sedulously on their guard that they may not devise or stir up within themselves any sinful desire: the former indulge a deep and fixed contempt of God; the latter willingly cherish a constant displeasure at their sins.

5. *O Jehovah! thy mercy is unto the heavens, and thy truth even unto the clouds.*
6. *Thy righteousness is as the mountains of God;*[1] *thy judgments are a great deep:*[2] *O Jehovah! thou preservest man and beast.*
7. *O God! how excellent*[3] *is thy loving-kindness! therefore, the children of men shall trust in the shadow of thy wings.*

[1] In the French version it is, " Comme hautes montagnes;"—" as the high mountains;" and in the margin Calvin states that the Hebrew is, " Montagnes de Dieu;"—" Mountains of God." The Hebrews were accustomed to describe things eminent, as Calvin observes in his exposition of the verse, by adding to them the name of God; as, " river of God," Ps. lxv. 9; " mount of God," Ps. lxviii. 15; " cedars of God," Ps. lxxx. 10; " the trees of the Lord," Ps. civ. 16. " The mountains of God," therefore, here mean *the highest mountains.*
[2] Lowth reads, " A vast abyss."   [3] Heb. how precious.

8. *They shall be abundantly satisfied with the fatness of thy house ; and thou shalt make them to drink of the river of thy pleasures.*

9. *For with thee*[1] *is the fountain of life ; and in thy light*[2] *shall we see light.*

5. *O Jehovah! thy mercy is unto the heavens.* Commentators think that David, after having described the great corruption and depravity which every where prevail in the world, takes occasion from thence to extol in rapturous praises the wonderful forbearance of God, in not ceasing to manifest his favour and good-will towards men, even though they are sunk in iniquity and crime. But, as I have already observed, I am of a somewhat different opinion. After having spoken of the very great depravity of men, the prophet, afraid lest he should become infected by it, or be carried away by the example of the wicked, as by a flood, quits the subject, and recovers himself by reflecting on a different theme. It usually happens, that in condemning the wicked, the contagion of their malice insinuates itself into our minds when we are not conscious of it; and there is scarcely one in a hundred who, after having complained of the malice of others, keeps himself in true godliness, pure and unpolluted. The meaning therefore is, Although we may see among men a sad and frightful confusion, which, like a great gulf, would swallow up the minds of the godly, David, nevertheless, maintains that the world is full of the goodness and righteousness of God, and that he governs heaven and earth on the strictest principles of equity. And certainly, whenever the corruption of the world affects our minds, and fills us with amazement, we must take care not to limit our views to the wickedness of men who overturn and confound all things; but in the midst of this strange confusion, it becomes us to elevate our thoughts in admiration and wonder, to the contemplation of the secret providence of God. David here enumerates four cardinal attributes of Deity, which, according to the figure of speech called *synecdoche,* include all the others, and

---

[1] " En toy."—*Fr.* " In thee."
[2] " Par ta clarte."—*Fr.* " By thy light."

by which he intimates, in short, that although carnal reason may suggest to us that the world moves at random, and is directed by chance, yet we ought to consider that the infinite power of God is always associated with perfect righteousness. In saying that the goodness of God is *unto the heavens,* David's meaning is, that in its greatness it is as high as the heavens. In the same sense he adds, *Thy truth is even unto the clouds.* The term *truth* in this place may be taken either for the faithfulness which God manifests in accomplishing his promises, or for the just and well regulated character of his government, in which his rectitude is seen to be pure and free from all deception. But there are many other similar passages of Scripture which constrain me to refer it to the promises of God, in the keeping and fulfilling of which he is ever faithful.

6. *Thy righteousness is as the mountains of God.* In this verse there is a commendation of God's righteousness, which the sacred writer compares to the high mountains, (this being the manner of the expression—" the mountains of God," for we know that the Hebrews were accustomed to distinguish by the appellation *divine,* or *of God,* whatever is excellent,) because his glory shines forth more clearly there. In the last place, it is said, that his *judgments are like a great and bottomless abyss.* By these words he teaches us, that to whatever side we turn our eyes, and whether we look upward or downward, all things are disposed and ordered by the just judgment of God. This passage is usually quoted in a sense quite different, namely, that the judgments of God far exceed our limited capacity, and are too mysterious for our being able to comprehend them; and, indeed, in this sense the similitude of an abyss is not inappropriate. It is, however, obvious from the context, that the language of the Psalmist is to be understood in a much more extensive sense, and as meaning, that however great the depth of wickedness which there is among men, and though it seems like a flood which breaks forth and overflows the whole earth, yet still greater is the depth of God's providence, by which he righteously disposes and governs all things. Whenever, therefore, our faith may be shaken by the confusion and disorder of human affairs, and when we are unable to explain the reasons of this

disorder and confusion, let us remember that the judgments of God in the government of the world are with the highest propriety compared to a great depth which fills heaven and earth, that the consideration of its infinite greatness may ravish our minds with admiration, swallow up all our cares, and dispel all our sorrows. When it is added in the end of the verse, *O Jehovah! thou preservest man and beast,* the meaning is to this effect, that since God vouchsafes to extend his providential care even to the irrational creation, much more does he provide for the wants of men. And, indeed, whenever any doubt may arise in our minds regarding the providence of God, we should fortify and encourage ourselves by setting before us this consideration, that God, who provides food for the beasts of the field, and maintains them in their present state, can never cease to take care of the human race. The explanation which some have given of the term *beasts,* interpreting it allegorically of beastly men, I regard as too forced, and reject it.

7. *O God! how precious is thy loving-kindness!* Some explain these words in this sense: That the mercy of God is precious, and that the children of men who put their trust in it are precious; but this is a sense too far removed from the words of the text. Others understand them as meaning, that the mercy of God is very great to the gods, that is to say, to the angels and the sons of men; but this is too refined. I am also surprised that the Jewish Rabbins have wearied and bewildered themselves, without any occasion, in seeking to find out new and subtile interpretations, since the meaning of the prophet is of itself perfectly evident; namely, that it is because the mercy of God is great and clearly manifested, that the children of men put their trust under the shadow of it. As David has hitherto been speaking in commendation of the goodness of God, which extends to every creature, the opinion of other commentators, who consider that David is here discoursing of the peculiar favour which God manifests towards his children, is in my judgment very correct. The language seems to refer in general to all the sons of men, but what follows is applicable properly to the faithful alone. In

order to manifest more clearly the greatness of divine grace, he thus speaks in general terms, telling us, that God condescends to gather together under his wings the mortal offspring of Adam, as it is said in Psalm viii. 4, " What is man, that thou art mindful of him ? and the son of man, that thou visitest him ?" The substance of the passage is this : The ungodly may run to every excess in wickedness, but this temptation does not prevent the people of God from trusting in his goodness, and casting themselves upon his fatherly care ; while the ungodly, whose minds are degraded, and whose hearts are polluted, never taste the sweetness of his goodness so as to be led by it to the faith, and thus to enjoy repose under the shadow of his wings. The metaphorical expression of *wings*, as applied to God, is common enough in Scripture.[1] By it God teaches us that we are preserved in safety under his protecting care, even as the hen cherishes her chickens under her wings ; and thus he invites us kindly and affectionately to return to him.

8. *They shall be abundantly satisfied with the fatness of thy house.* I have no doubt that by *the fatness of God's house* the prophet means the abundance of good things which is not designed for all men indiscriminately, but is laid up in store for the children of God who commit themselves wholly to his protection. Some restrict the expression to spiritual graces ; but to me it seems more likely, that under it are comprehended all the blessings that are necessary to the happiness and comfort of the present life, as well as those which pertain to eternal and heavenly blessedness. It ought, however, to be observed, that in the style of speaking which the prophet here employs, the use of earthly blessings is connected with the gracious experience of faith, in the exercise of which we can alone enjoy them rightfully and lawfully to our own welfare. When the ungodly glut themselves with the abun-

---

[1] " Frequens in Psalmis figura ab alio Cherubinorum Arcæ," &c. ; *i. e.* " A common figure in the Psalms, taken more immediately, in my opinion, from the wings of the Cherubim overshadowing the mercy-seat which covered the ark ; but more remotely from birds, which defend their young from the solar rays by overshadowing them with their wings. See Ps. xvii. 8 ; lvii. 1 ; lxi. 4 ; xci. 1, &c., and Deut. xxxii. 11."—*Bishop Hare.*

dance of God's benefits, their bodies indeed grow fat like the flesh of cattle or swine, but their souls are always empty and famished. It is the faithful alone, as I have said, who are satisfied with the goodness of God towards them, because it is to them a pledge of his fatherly love. The expression *meat* and *drink* denotes a complete and perfect fulness, and the term *river*[1] denotes an overflowing abundance.

9. *For with thee is the fountain of life.* The Psalmist here confirms the doctrine of the preceding verse, the knowledge of which is so profitable that no words can adequately express it. As the ungodly profane even the best of God's gifts by their wicked abuse of them, unless we observe the distinction which I have stated, it were better for us to perish a hundred times of hunger, than to be fed abundantly by the goodness of God. The ungodly do not acknowledge that it is in God they live, move, and have their being, but rather imagine that they are sustained by their own power; and, accordingly, David, on the contrary, here affirms from the experience of the godly, and as it were in their name, that the fountain of life is in God. By this he means, that there is not a drop of life to be found without him, or which flows not from his grace. The metaphor of *light*, in the last clause of the verse, is tacitly most emphatic, denoting that men are altogether destitute of light, except in so far as the Lord shines upon them. If this is true of the light of this life, how shall we be able to behold the light of the heavenly world, unless the Spirit of God enlighten us? for we must maintain that the measure of understanding with which men are by nature endued is such, that " the light shineth in darkness, but the darkness comprehendeth it not," (John i. 5;) and that men are enlightened only by a supernatural gift. But it is the godly alone who perceive that they derive their light from God, and that, without it, they would continue, as it were, buried and smothered in darkness.

[1] The words in the original are, נחל עדניך, *nachal adanecha*, *the river of thy Eden*, in which there is probably an allusion to the garden of עדן, Eden, and to the river which flowed through and watered it.

10. *Prolong*[1] *thy mercy to them that know thee, and thy righteousness to the upright in heart.*
11. *Let not the foot of pride come upon me, and let not the hand of the wicked remove me.*
12. *There the workers of iniquity are fallen: they are thrust down, and shall not be able to rise.*

10. *Prolong thy mercy to them that know thee.* David now sets himself to pray. And, first, he asks in general, that God would continue his mercy to all the godly, and then he pleads particularly in his own behalf, imploring the help of God against his enemies. Those who affirm that God is here said to prolong or extend his mercy because it is exalted above the heavens, indulge in a style of speaking too puerile. When David spake of it in such terms in a preceding verse, his intention was not, as I have already said, to represent the mercy of God as shut up in heaven, but simply to declare that it was diffused throughout the world; and here what he desires is just this, that God would continue to manifest, even to the end, his mercy towards his people. With the mercy of God he connects his righteousness, combining them as cause and effect. We have already said in another place, that the righteousness of God is manifested in his undertaking the defence of his own people, vindicating their innocence, avenging their wrongs, restraining their enemies, and in proving himself faithful in the preservation of their welfare and happiness against all who assail them. Now, since all this is done for them freely by God, David, with good reason, makes mention particularly of his goodness, and places it first in order, that we may learn to depend entirely upon his favour. We ought also to observe the epithets by which he describes true believers; first, he says, that *they know God;* and, secondly, that *they are upright in heart.* We learn from this that true godliness springs from the knowledge of God, and again, that the light of faith must necessarily dispose us to uprightness of heart. At the same time, we ought always to bear in mind, that we only know God aright when we render to him

[1] Heb. Draw out at length.

the honour to which he is entitled; that is, when we place entire confidence in him.

11. *Let not the foot of pride come upon me.* As I have observed a little before, the Psalmist here applies to his own circumstances the prayer which he had offered. But by including in his prayer in the preceding verse all the children of God, he designed to show that he asked nothing for himself apart from others, but only desired that as one of the godly and upright, who have their eyes directed to God, he might enjoy his favour. He has employed the expressions, *the foot of pride*,[1] and *the hand of the wicked*, in the same sense. As the wicked rush boldly to the destruction of good men, lifting up their feet to tread upon them, and having their hands ready to do them wrong, David entreats God to restrain their hands and their feet; and thus he confesses that he is in danger of being exposed to their insolence, abuse, and violence, unless God come speedily to his aid.

12. *There the workers of iniquity are fallen.* Here he derives confidence from his prayer, not doubting that he has already obtained his request. And thus we see how the certainty of faith directs the saints to prayer. Besides, still farther to confirm his confidence and hope in God, he shows, as it were, by pointing to it with the finger, the certain destruction of the wicked, even though it lay as yet concealed in the future. In this respect, the adverb *there*[2] is not superfluous; for while the ungodly boast of their good fortune, and the world applaud them, David beholds by the eye

---

[1] That is, the foot of the proud man, as the Chaldee translates it, the thing being put for the person in whom it is; a mode of expression of frequent occurrence in Scripture. Thus *deceit*, in Prov. xii. 27, is put for *a deceitful man*; *poverty*, in 2 Kings xxiv. 14, *for poor people*, &c. There seems to be here an allusion to the ancient practice of tyrants in treading upon their enemies, or in spurning those who offended them from their presence with their feet.

[2] Heb. שם, *sham*, *there*, that is, (pointing with the finger to a particular place,) see there! lo! the workers of iniquity are fallen. "It represents strongly before the eye," says Mudge, "the downfal of the wicked. Upon the *very spot* where they practise their treachery, they receive their downfal." A similar mode of expression occurs in Ps. xiv. 5.

of faith, as if from a watch-tower, their destruction, and speaks of it with as much confidence as if he had already seen it realised. That we also may attain a similar assurance, let us remember, that those who would hasten prematurely the time of God's vengeance upon the wicked, according to the ardour of their desires, do indeed err, and that we ought to leave it to the providence of God to fix the period when, in his wisdom, he shall rise up to judgment. When it is said, *They are thrust down,* the meaning is, that they are agitated with doubt, and totter as in a slippery place, so that in the midst of their prosperity they have no security. Finally, it is added, that they shall fall into utter destruction, so that it can never be expected that they shall rise again.

PSALM XXXVII.

This psalm, the title of which shows it to have been composed by David, contains most profitable instruction. Since the faithful, so long as they pursue their earthly pilgrimage through life, see things strangely confused in the world, unless they assuaged their grief with the hope of a better issue, their courage would soon fail them. The more boldly any man despises God, and runs to every excess in wickedness, so much the more happily he seems to live. And since prosperity appears to be a token of God's favour towards the ungodly, what conclusion, it may be said, can be drawn from this, but either that the world is governed by chance, and that fortune bears the sovereignty, or else that God makes no difference between the good and the bad? The Spirit of God accordingly confirms and strengthens us in this psalm against the assaults of such a temptation. However great the prosperity which the wicked enjoy for a time, he declares their felicity to be transient and evanescent, and that, therefore, they are miserable, while the happiness of which they boast is cursed; whereas the pious and devoted servants of God never cease to be happy, even in the midst of their greatest calamities, because God takes care of them, and at length comes to their aid in due season. This, indeed, is paradoxical, and wholly repugnant to human reason. For as good men often suffer extreme poverty, and languish long under many troubles, and are loaded with reproaches and wrongs, while the wicked and profligate triumph, and are regaled with pleasures, might we not suppose that

God cares not for the things that are done on earth? It is on this account that, as I have already said, the doctrine of this psalm is so much the more profitable; because, withdrawing our thoughts from the present aspect of things, it enjoins us to confide in the providence of God, until he stretch forth his hand to help those who are his servants, and demand of the ungodly a strict account of their lives, as of thieves and robbers who have foully abused his bounty and paternal goodness.

¶ A Psalm of David.

1. *Fret not thyself because of the wicked, and be not envious at the workers of iniquity:*
2. *For they shall soon be cut down like grass; and they shall wither as the green and tender herb.*
3. *Put thy trust in Jehovah, and do good; dwell in the land, and be fed in truth,* [or *faithfully.*[1]]
4. *And delight thyself in Jehovah, and he will give thee the desires of thy heart.*
5. *Roll* [or *devolve*] *thy ways on Jehovah, and trust in him, and he will bring it to pass.*
6. *And he will bring forth thy righteousness as the light, and thy judgments*[2] *as the noon-day.*

1. *Fret not thyself because of the wicked.* David lays down this as a general principle, that the prosperity of the wicked, in which they greatly rejoice, should on no account vex or disquiet the children of God, because it will soon fade away. On the other hand, although the people of God are afflicted for a time, yet the issue of their afflictions shall be such, that they have every reason to be contented with their lot. Now all this depends upon the providence of God; for unless we are persuaded that the world is governed by him in righteousness and truth, our minds will soon stagger, and at length entirely fail us. David then condemns two sinful affections of the mind, which are indeed closely allied, and the one of which is generated by the other. He first enjoins the faithful not to fret on account of the wicked; and, secondly, that they should

---

[1] " C'est, jouy des biens d'icelle en repos ferme et asseuré."—*Fr. marg.* "That is, enjoy the good things of it in quietness and security."

[2] " C'est, ton bon droict."—*Fr. marg.* "That is, thy just cause, or thy rectitude."

not indulge an envious spirit towards them. For, in the first place, when they see the wicked enjoying prosperity, from which it might naturally be supposed that God regards not the affairs of men, there is a danger lest they should shake off the fear of God, and apostatize from the faith. Then another temptation follows, namely, that the influence of the example of the wicked excites in them a desire to involve themselves in the same wickedness with them. This is the natural sense. The Hebrew words, אַל־תִּתְחַר, *al-tithechar,* which we have rendered, *Fret not thyself,* are by some translated, *Do not mingle thyself with.*[1] But this interpretation is too forced, and may be disproved by the context; for in the eighth verse, where mention is expressly made of *wrath* and *anger,* it would surely be absurd to interpret in another sense the same verb which immediately follows these two words, and which is there used in the same sense and for the same end as in this first verse. In the second place, the order which David observes is very natural; for when the prosperity of the wicked has irritated our minds, we very soon begin to envy them their happiness and ease. First, then, he exhorts us to be on our guard, lest a happiness which is only transitory, or rather imaginary, should vex or disquiet us; and, secondly, lest envy should lead us to commit sin. The reason by which he enforces this exhortation is added in the following verse: for if the wicked flourish to-day like the grass of the field, to-morrow they shall be cut down and wither. We need not wonder that this similitude is often to be met with in the sacred writings, since it is so very appropriate; for we see how soon the strength of the grass decays, and that when cast down by a blast of wind, or parched with the heat of the sun, even without being cut by the hand of man, it withers away.[2] In like manner, David tells us that the judgment of God, like a scythe in the hand of man, shall cut down the wicked, so that they shall suddenly perish.

[1] That is, do not enter into fellowship with.
[2] The fitness of this figure to express the transient and short-lived character of the prosperity of the wicked, will appear in a still more striking light when we take into consideration the great heat of the climate of Palestine.

3. *Put thy trust in Jehovah, and do good.* The inspired writer now goes on, in the second place, to say, that every thing in the end shall be well with the righteous, because they are under the protection of God. But as there is nothing better or more desirable than to enjoy the fostering and protecting care of God, he exhorts them to put their trust in him, and at the same time to follow after goodness and truth. It is not without good reason that he begins with the doctrine of faith, or trust in God; for there is nothing more difficult for men than to preserve their minds in a state of peace and tranquillity, undisturbed by any disquieting fears, whilst they are in this world, which is subject to so many changes. On the other hand, while they see the wicked becoming rich by unjust means, extending their influence, and acquiring power by unrestrained indulgence in sin, it is no less difficult for them steadily to persevere in a life of piety and virtue. Nor is it sufficient merely to disregard those things that are commonly sought after with the greatest eagerness. Some of the philosophers of antiquity were so noble-minded, that they despised riches unjustly acquired, and abstained from fraud and robbery; nay, they held up to ridicule the vain pomp and splendour of the wicked, which the common people look upon with such high admiration. But as they were destitute of faith, they defrauded God of his honour, and so it happened that they never knew what it was to be truly happy. Now, as David places faith first in order, to show that God is the author of all good, and that by his blessing alone prosperity is to be looked for; so it ought to be observed that he connects this with a holy life: for the man who places his whole confidence in God, and gives himself up to be governed by him, will live uprightly and innocently, and will devote himself to doing good.

Dwell in the land. This language is much more expressive than if he had promised that the righteous should dwell securely in the land.[1] It is just as if he had led them to the

---

[1] Some read, "Thou shalt dwell in the land." The Hebrew verb is in the imperative mood; but the imperative in Hebrew is sometimes used for the future of the indicative.—Glass. tom. i. can. XL. p. 285.

place, and put them in possession of it. Moreover, by these words he declares that they shall long enjoy it. They are, it is true, only strangers or sojourners in this world, yet the hand of the Lord is stretched forth to protect them, so that they live in security and peace. This David again confirms by the following clause, *Thou shalt be fed in truth.* Assured of the protection of God, he exhorts them to place entire and unsuspecting confidence in him. It is surprising to find how interpreters have wrested, and as it were mangled this clause, by the different meanings they have put upon it. Some take the verb *to feed* in an active signification; and others understand the expression *to feed on faith* as denoting to cherish within the heart the promises of God. Others are of opinion that David exhorts us to feed our brethren with faith by ministering to them the pure word of God, which is the spiritual food of the soul. Others render the term for *faith* in the sense of *sincerity*, so that the expression *to feed on faith* would signify to behave in an upright and honest manner among men. But the scope and connection of the passage necessarily require, and it is quite in accordance with the nature of the Hebrew language, that the verb רְעֵה, *re-eh*, should be taken in a passive signification, *Be fed.* This, too, is the opinion of the greater part of commentators, who, notwithstanding, afterwards differ in explaining its meaning. Some of them adopt the interpretation, that we are fed with faith, when the promises of God suffice us, and we are satisfied with them. Others give this explanation, *Feed thyself with the fruit of faith,* because God will indeed show that we have not believed his word in vain. Others explain it in this way, *Let truth be thy food,* and let nothing give thee greater pleasure than to converse sincerely and frankly with thy neighbours. There is still another interpretation which, although in some respects different, is similar to the preceding, namely, Live not upon spoil, but be content with lawful sustenance; that is to say, with that which is lawfully acquired.[1] It is certainly a shameful and disgraceful thing

---

[1] "C'est à dire, qui te vient loyaument."—*Fr.*

that so many learned men should have erred in a matter so plain and obvious.[1] Had not every one been led by his own ambition to seek for something new, the true and natural meaning of the prophet would have occurred at once, which is this, Dwell in the land, that thou mayest enjoy it in sure and lasting repose. The Hebrew word אמונה, *emunah*, not only signifies *truth* or *faith*, but also *secure continuance for a long period*. And who does not see that since the possession of the land was given to the righteous, this latter clause was added by way of exposition?

4. *And delight thyself in Jehovah.* This delight is set in opposition to the vain and deceitful allurements of the world, which so intoxicate the ungodly, that despising the blessing of God, they dream of no other happiness than what presents itself for the time before their eyes. This contrast between the vain and fickle joys with which the world is deluded, and the true repose enjoyed by the godly, ought to be carefully observed; for whether all things smile upon us, or whether the Lord exercise us with adversities, we ought always to hold fast this principle, that as the Lord is the portion of our inheritance, our lot has fallen in pleasant places,[2] as we have seen in Psalm xvi. 5, 6. We must therefore constantly recall to our minds this truth, that it can never be well with us except in so far as God is gracious to us, so that the joy we derive from his paternal favour towards us may surpass all the pleasures of the world. To this injunction a promise is added, that, if we are satisfied in the enjoyment of God alone, he will liberally bestow upon us all that we shall desire: *He will give thee the desires of thy heart.*

---

[1] Modern critics have varied as much in their interpretations of this clause of the verse as those who preceded Calvin, of whom he complains. For example, Ainsworth reads, "Thou shalt be fed by faith;" Archbishop Secker, "Thou shalt be fed in plenty;" Parkhurst, "Thou shalt be fed in security;" Dathe, "Tunc terram inhabitabis et secure vivas," assigning the reason for this translation to be, that "*pascere securitatem, sive si malis, in securitate,* nihil aliud est quam *secure vivere;*" and Gesenius reads, "Follow after truth," or, "seek to be faithful," deriving the verb from a root which signifies *to take delight in,* or *to follow after.*

[2] "D'autant que Dieu est la part de nostre heritage, que nostre lot est escheu en lieux plaisans."—*Fr.*

This does not imply that the godly immediately obtain whatever their fancy may suggest to them; nor would it be for their profit that God should grant them all their vain desires. The meaning simply is, that if we stay our minds wholly upon God, instead of allowing our imaginations like others to roam after idle and frivolous fancies, all other things will be bestowed upon us in due season.

5. *Roll*[1] *thy ways upon Jehovah.* Here David illustrates and confirms the doctrine contained in the preceding verse. In order that God may accomplish our desires, it behoves us to cast all our cares upon him in the exercise of hope and patience. Accordingly, we are taught from this passage how to preserve our minds in tranquillity amidst anxieties, dangers, and floods of trouble. There can be no doubt, that by the term *ways* we are here to understand all *affairs* or *businesses*. The man, therefore, who, leaving the issue of all his affairs to the will of God, and who, patiently waiting to receive from his hand whatever he may be pleased to send, whether prosperity or adversity, casts all his cares, and every other burden which he bears, into his bosom; or, in other words, commits to him all his affairs,—such a person *rolls his ways upon Jehovah.* Hence, David again inculcates the duty of hope and confidence in God: *And trust in him.* By this he intimates, that we render to him the honour to which he is entitled only when we intrust to him the government and direction of our lives; and thus he provides a remedy for a disease with which almost all men are infected. Whence is it that the children of God are envious of the wicked, and are often in trouble and perplexity, and yield to excess of sorrow, and sometimes even murmur and repine, but because, by involving themselves immoderately in endless cares, and cherishing too eagerly a desire to provide for themselves

---

[1] Calvin here gives the exact sense of the Hebrew verb בֹּל, *galal*. It literally signifies *to roll,* or *to devolve;* and in this passage it evidently means, Roll or devolve all thy concerns upon God; "cast thy burden upon him," as it is in Ps. lv. 22; "the metaphor being taken," says Cresswell, "from a burden put by one who is unequal to it upon a stronger man." But Dr Adam Clarke thinks that the idea may be taken from the camel who lies down till his load be rolled upon him.

irrespective of God, they plunge, as it were, into an abyss, or at least accumulate to themselves such a vast load of cares, that they are forced at last to sink under them? Desirous to provide a remedy for this evil, David warns us, that in presuming to take upon us the government of our own life, and to provide for all our affairs as if we were able to bear so great a burden, we are greatly deceived, and that, therefore, our only remedy is to fix our eyes upon the providence of God, and to draw from it consolation in all our sorrows. Those who obey this counsel shall escape that horrible labyrinth in which all men labour in vain; for when God shall once have taken the management of our affairs into his own hand, there is no reason to fear that prosperity shall ever fail us. Whence is it that he forsakes us and disappoints our expectations, if it is not because we provoke him, by pretending to greater wisdom and understanding than we possess? If, therefore, we would only permit him, he will perform his part, and will not disappoint our expectations, which he sometimes does as a just punishment for our unbelief.

6. *And he will bring forth thy righteousness as the light.* This David says, in order to anticipate the misgivings which often trouble us when we seem to lose our labour in faithfully serving God, and in dealing uprightly with our neighbours; nay, when our integrity is either exposed to the calumnies of the wicked, or is the occasion of injury to us from men; for then it is thought to be of no account in the sight of God. David, therefore, declares, that God will not suffer our righteousness to be always hid in darkness, but that he will maintain it and bring it forth to the light; namely, when he will bestow upon us such a reward as we desire. He alludes to the darkness of the night, which is soon dispelled by the dawning of the day; as if he had said, We may be often grievously oppressed, and God may not seem to approve our innocence, yet this vicissitude should no more disturb our minds than the darkness of the night which covers the earth; for then the expectation of the light of day sustains our hope.

7. *Be silent to Jehovah, and wait for him ; fret not because of the man who prospereth in his way, against the man who commits wickedness.*[1]
8. *Cease from anger, and forsake wrath: fret not thyself so as to do evil.*
9. *For the wicked shall be cut off; but those that wait upon Jehovah shall inherit the earth.*
10. *Yet a little while; and the wicked shall not be ; and thou shalt look upon his place, and shalt not find him.*
11. *But the meek shall inherit the earth,*[2] *and shall delight themselves in the abundance of peace.*

7. *Be silent to Jehovah.* The Psalmist continues the illustration of the same doctrine, namely, that we should patiently and meekly bear those things that usually disquiet our minds; for amid innumerable sources of disquietude and conflict there is need of no small patience. By the similitude of *silence,* which often occurs in the sacred writings, he declares most aptly the nature of faith ; for as our affections rise in rebellion against the will of God, so faith, restoring us to a state of humble and peaceful submission, appeases all the tumults of our hearts. By this expression,[3] therefore, David commands us not to yield to the tumultuous passions of the soul, as the unbelieving do, nor fretfully to set ourselves in opposition to the authority of God, but rather to submit peacefully to him, that he may execute his work in silence. Moreover, as the Hebrew word חוּל, *chul,* which we have rendered *to wait,* sometimes signifies to *mourn,* and sometimes to *wait,* the word הִתְחוֹלֵל, *hithcholel,* in this place is understood by some as meaning *to mourn moderately,* or *to bear sorrow patiently.* It might also be rendered more simply *to*

---

[1] "Ou, qui vient à bont de ses entreprises."—*Fr. marg.* "Or, who accomplishes his devices."

[2] "C'est, y auront leurs plaisirs avec grande prosperite."—*Fr. marg.* "That is, shall have their enjoyment in it with great prosperity."

[3] The Hebrew verb rendered *silent* is דם, *dom,* from which the English word *dumb* appears to be derived. The silence here enjoined is opposed to murmuring or complaining. The word is rendered by the Septuagint, ὑποτάγηθι, *be subject;* which is not an exact translation of the original term : but it well expresses the meaning ; for this silence implies the entire subjection of ourselves to the will of God.

mourn before God, in order that he might be a witness of all our sorrows; for when the unbelieving give way to doubt and suspense, they rather murmur against him than utter their complaints before him. As, however, the other interpretation is more generally received, namely, that David is exhorting us to hope and patience, I adhere to it. The prophet Isaiah also connects hope with silence in the same sense, (Isaiah xxx. 15.)

David next repeats what he had said in the first verse, *Fret not because of the man who prospereth in his way,* or who brings his ways to a happy issue; nor *against the man who behaveth himself wickedly,* or *who accomplishes his devices.* Of these two interpretations of this last clause, the latter is more in accordance with the scope of the psalm. I confess, indeed, that the word מְזִמּוֹת, *mezimmoth,* is commonly taken in a bad sense for fraud and stratagem. But as זָמַם, *zamam,* sometimes signifies in general *to meditate,* the nature of the Hebrew language will bear this meaning, that *to execute his devices* is of the same import as to effect what he has purposed. Now we see that these two things are connected, namely, *to dispose his ways according to his desires,* or *to prosper in his way,* and *to accomplish his devices.* It is a very great temptation to us and difficult to bear, when we see fortune smiling upon the ungodly, as if God approved of their wickedness; nay, it excites our wrath and indignation. David, therefore, not contented with a short admonition, insists at some length upon this point.

The accumulation of terms which occurs in the next verse, in which he lays a restraint as with a bridle upon anger, allays wrath and assuages passion, is not superfluous; but, as is necessary, he rather prescribes numerous remedies for a disease which it is difficult to cure. By this means, he reminds us how easily we are provoked, and how ready we are to take offence, unless we lay a powerful restraint upon our tumultuous passions, and keep them under control. And although the faithful are not able to subdue the lusts of the flesh without much trouble and labour, whilst the prosperity of the wicked excites their impatience, yet this repetition teaches us that we ought unceasingly to wrestle against them; for if we steadily persevere, we know that our endeavours shall not be in vain in the end. I differ from other commentators in the exposition of the last clause. They translate it, *at least to do evil;* as if David meant that we should appease our anger lest it should lead us to do mischief. But as the particle אך, *ach,* which they translate *at least,* is often used affirmatively in Hebrew, I have no doubt that David here teaches, that it cannot be otherwise than that the offence which we take at the prosperity of the wicked should lead us to sin, unless we speedily check it; as it is said in another Psalm, " God will break the cords of the ungodly, lest the righteous put forth their hands unto iniquity," (Ps. cxxv. 3.)

9. *For the wicked shall be cut off.* It is not without cause that he repeatedly inculcates the same thing, namely, that the happiness and prosperity which the ungodly enjoy is only a mask or phantom; for the first sight of it so dazzles our senses, that we are unable to form a proper estimate of what will be its issue, in the light of which alone we ought to judge of the value of all that has preceded. But the contrast between the two clauses of the verse ought to be observed. First, in saying that *the wicked shall be cut off,* he intimates that they shall flourish fresh and green till the time of their destruction shall arrive; and, secondly, in allotting the earth to the godly, saying, *They shall inherit the earth,* he means that they shall live in such a manner as that the blessing of God shall follow them, even to the grave. Now, as I have already said, the present condition of men is to be estimated by the state in which it will terminate. From the epithet by which he distinguishes the children of God, we learn that they are exercised by a severe conflict for the trial of their faith; for he speaks of them, not as *righteous* or *godly,* but as those that *wait upon the Lord.* What purpose would this waiting serve, unless they groaned under the burden of the cross? Moreover, the possession of the earth which he promises to the children of God is not always realised to them; because it is the will of the Lord that they should live as strangers and pilgrims in it; neither does he

permit them to have any fixed abode in it, but rather tries them with frequent troubles, that they may desire with greater alacrity the everlasting dwelling-place of heaven. The flesh is always seeking to build its nest for ever here; and were we not tossed hither and thither, and not suffered to rest, we would by and by forget heaven and the everlasting inheritance. Yet, in the midst of this disquietude, the possession of the earth, of which David here speaks, is not taken away from the children of God; for they know most certainly that they are the rightful heirs of the world. Hence it is that they eat their bread with a quiet conscience, and although they suffer want, yet God provides for their necessities in due season. Finally, although the ungodly labour to effect their destruction, and reckon them unworthy to live upon the earth, yet God stretches forth his hand and protects them; nay, he so upholds them by his power, that they live more securely in a state of exile, than the wicked do in their nests to which they are attached. And thus the blessing, of which David speaks, is in part secret and hidden, because our reason is so dull, that we cannot comprehend what it is to possess the earth; and yet the faithful truly feel and understand that this promise is not made to them in vain, since, having fixed the anchor of their faith in God, they pass their life every day in peace, while God makes it manifest in their experience, that the shadow of his hand is sufficient to protect them.

10. *Yet a little while, and the wicked shall not be.* This is a confirmation of the preceding verse. It might well have been objected, that the actual state of things in the world is very different from what David here represents it, since the ungodly riot in their pleasures, and the people of God pine away in sickness and poverty. David, therefore, wishing to guard us against a rash and hasty judgment, exhorts us to be quiet for a little while, till the Lord cut off the wicked entirely, and show the efficacy of his grace towards his own people. What he requires then on the part of the true believers is, that in the exercise of their wisdom they should suspend their judgment for a time, and not stop at every trifle, but

exercise their thoughts in meditation upon divine providence, until God show out of heaven that the full time is come. Instead, however, of describing them as *those who wait upon the Lord*, he now speaks of them as *the meek* ; and this he does not without good reason : for unless a man believe that God preserves his own people in a wonderful manner, as if they were like sheep among wolves, he will be always endeavouring to repel force by force.[1] It is hope alone, therefore, which of itself produces meekness ; for, by restraining the impetuosity of the flesh, and allaying its vehemence, it trains to equanimity and patience those who submit themselves to God. From this passage it would seem, that Christ has taken that which is written in Matthew, chap. v., verse 5. The word *peace* is generally employed in the Hebrew to denote the prosperous and happy issue of things ; yet another sense will agree better with this place, namely, that while the ungodly shall be agitated with inward trouble, and God shall encompass them on every side with terror, the faithful shall rejoice in the abundance of peace. It is not meant that they are exempted from trouble, but they are sustained by the tranquillity of their minds ; so that accounting all the trials which they endure to be only temporary, they now rejoice in hope of the promised rest.

12. *The wicked plotteth against the righteous, and gnasheth upon him with his teeth.*
13. *But the Lord[2] shall laugh at him ; for he seeth that his day is coming.*
14. *The wicked draw their sword, and bend their bow, to cast down the poor and needy, and to slay those that are of upright ways.*
15. *But their sword shall enter into their own heart, and their bow shall be broken.*

12. *The wicked plotteth against the righteous.* David here anticipates an objection which might have been taken to the preceding verse. Where, it might be said, can tranquillity

[1] " De se venger, et de rendre mal pour mal."—*Fr.* " To take revenge, and to render evil for evil."
[2] Dominus. Heb. אדני, Adonai.

and joy be found when the wicked are mad with rage, and plot every kind of mischief against the children of God? And how shall they cherish good hope for the future who see themselves surrounded with innumerable sources of death? David therefore replies, That although the life of the godly should be assailed by many dangers, yet they are secure in the aid and protection of God; and that however much the wicked should plot against them, they shall be continually preserved. Thus, the design of David is to obviate our fears, lest the malice of the ungodly should terrify us above measure, as if they had the power of doing with us according to their pleasure.[1] He indeed confesses that they are not only full of fraud, and expert in deceiving, but also that they burn with anger, and a raging desire of doing mischief, when he says, *that they plot mischief deceitfully against the righteous, and gnash upon them with their teeth.* But after making this statement, he immediately adds, that their endeavours shall be vain. Yet he seems to provide very coldly for our consolation under sorrow, for he represents God as merely *laughing.* But if God values highly our salvation, why does he not set himself to resist the fury of our enemies, and vigorously oppose them? We know that this, as has been said in Psalm ii. 4, is a proper trial of our patience, when God does not come forth at once, armed for the discomfiture of the ungodly, but connives for a time and withholds his hand. But as the eye of sense in such circumstances reckons that he delays his coming too long, and from that delay concludes that he indulges in ease, and feels no interest in the affairs of men, it is no small consolation to be able by the eye of faith to behold him laughing; for then we are assured that he is not seated idly in heaven, nor closes his eyes, resigning to chance the government of the world, but purposely delays and keeps silence because he despises their vanity and folly.

And lest the flesh should still murmur and complain, demanding why God should only laugh at the wicked, and not rather take vengeance upon them, the reason is added, that

---

[1] "Comme s'ils avoyent puissance de faire de nous à leur plaisir."—*Fr.*

he sees the day of their destruction at hand: *For he seeth that his day*[1] *is coming.* Whence is it that the injuries we sustain from the wickedness of man so trouble us, if it be not that, when not obtaining a speedy redress, we begin to despair of ever seeing a better state of things? But he who sees the executioner standing behind the aggressor with drawn sword no longer desires revenge, but rather exults in the prospect of speedy retribution. David, therefore, teaches us that it is not meet that God, who sees the destruction of the wicked to be at hand, should rage and fret after the manner of men. There is then a tacit distinction here made between God and men, who, amidst the troubles and confusions of the world, do not see the day of the wicked coming, and who, oppressed by cares and fears, cannot laugh, but because vengeance is delayed, rather become so impatient that they murmur and fret. It is not, however, enough for us to know that God acts in a manner altogether different from us, unless we learn to weep patiently whilst he laughs, so that our tears may be a sacrifice of obedience. In the meantime, let us pray that he would enlighten us by his light, for by this means alone will we, by beholding with the eye of faith his laughter, become partakers thereof, even in the midst of sorrow. Some, indeed, explain these two verses in another sense; as if David meant to say, that the faithful live so happily that the wicked envy them. But the reader will now perceive that this is far from the design of the prophet.

14. *The wicked draw their sword, and bend their bow.* David now goes on to say, that the ungodly, being armed with sword and bow, threaten with death the children of God; and this he does in order to meet the temptation which would otherwise overwhelm them. The promises of God do not have place in a time of quietness and peace, but in the midst of severe and terrible conflicts. And, therefore, David now

---

[1] "Day is often used," says Ainsworth, "for the time of punishment; as, 'the posterity shall be astonied at his day,' Job xviii. 20; 'Woe unto them, for their day is come,' Jer. l. 27. So 'the day of Midian,' Isa. ix. 4; 'the day of Jezreel,' Hos. i. 11; 'the day of Jerusalem,' Ps. cxxxvii. 7."

teaches us that the righteous are not deprived of that peace of which he had spoken a little before, although the wicked should threaten them with instant death. The sentence ought to be explained in this way: Although the wicked draw their swords and bend their bows to destroy the righteous, yet all their efforts shall return upon their own heads, and shall tend to their own destruction. But it is necessary to notice the particular terms in which the miserable condition of the righteous is here described, until God at length vouchsafe to help them. First, they are called *poor and needy;* and, secondly, they are compared to sheep devoted to destruction,[1] because they have no power to withstand the violence of their enemies, but rather lie oppressed under their feet. Whence it follows, that a uniform state of enjoyment here is not promised to them in this psalm, but there is only set before them the hope of a blessed issue to their miseries and afflictions, in order to console them under them. But as it often happens that the wicked are hated and treated with severity for their iniquity, the Psalmist adds, that those who thus suffered were *those who were of upright ways;* meaning by this, that they were afflicted without cause. Formerly he described them as *the upright in heart,* by which he commended the inward purity of the heart; but now he commends uprightness in the conduct, and in fulfilling every duty towards our neighbour; and thus he shows not only that they are unjustly persecuted, because they have done no evil to their enemies, and have given them no cause of offence, but also, that though provoked by injuries, they nevertheless do not turn aside from the path of duty.

In the 15th verse, David is not speaking of the laughter of God, but is denouncing vengeance against the ungodly, just as we have already seen in the second psalm, at the fourth verse, that although God, by conniving at the wicked, has often suffered them for a time to run to every excess in mirth and rioting, yet he at length speaks to them in his anger to overthrow them. The amount of what is stated is, that the ungodly should prevail so little, that the sword

---

[1] " De brebis destinees au sacrifice."—*Fr.*

which they had drawn should return into their own bowels, and that their bow should be broken in pieces.

16. *Better is the little of the righteous than the abundance of many wicked.*[1]
17. *For the arms of the wicked shall be broken; but Jehovah upholdeth the righteous.*
18. *Jehovah knoweth the days of the upright, and their inheritance shall be everlasting.*
19. *They shall not be ashamed in the season of adversity; and in the days of famine they shall be satisfied.*

16. *Better is the little of the righteous, &c.* This verse, without any sufficient reason, has been variously rendered. The word הָמוֹן, *hamon*,[2] which is rendered *abundance*, indeed, sometimes signifies a great multitude of men, and sometimes abundance of things; sometimes, too, an adjective of the plural number is joined to a substantive of the singular number. But those who wrest David's words to this sense, that a few righteous persons are better than a great multitude of the ungodly,[3] plainly destroy their import, and pervert the meaning of the whole sentence. Nor can I receive the explanation which others have given, that the little which the just man possesses is better than the great abundance of the wicked; for I see no necessity for connecting, contrary to the rules of grammar, the word הָמוֹן, *hamon*, which denotes *abundance*, with the word רַבִּים, *rabbim*, which signifies *many* or *great*, and not with the word רְשָׁעִים, *reshaim*, which means *wicked*. I have therefore no doubt that David here contrasts the limited possessions of one righteous man with the riches and wealth of many wicked men. The

---

[1] "Ou, aux grans qui sont meschans."—*Fr. marg.* "Or, to the great who are wicked."

[2] Ainsworth renders this word, "plenteous mammon," which, he remarks, "signifieth multitude, plenty, or store of riches, or any other thing." The Septuagint renders it *riches*. The English word *mammon* is derived from this Hebrew word.

[3] This is the view taken by Fry, who renders the words,
 "Better are the few of the JUST ONE,
 Than the great multitude of the wicked."
By the JUST ONE he understands Christ.

Hebrew word רבים, *rabbim,* however, which I have rendered *many,* may also be properly taken to denote persons of great authority and power. Certainly, it is not difficult to understand that David means to say, that although the wicked excel in this world, and are enriched with its possessions in great abundance and trust in their riches, yet the little which the just man possesses is far better than all their treasures. From this we learn, that David is here speaking, not so much of external grandeur and wealth, as of the secret blessing of God which truly enriches the righteous; for although they live from hand to mouth, yet are they fed from heaven as it were with manna; while the ungodly are always hungry, or else waste away in the very midst of their abundance.

To this also belongs the reason which is added in the next verse, namely, that there is nothing stable in the world except it be sustained by the power of God; but we are plainly told that *the righteous* only are *upheld by him,* and that *the power of the ungodly shall be broken.* Here again we see, that in order to form a right and proper estimate of true felicity, we must look forward to the future, or contemplate by the eye of faith the secret grace of God, and his hidden judgments. Unless we are persuaded by faith that God cherishes us in his bosom as a father does his children, our poverty will always be a source of trouble to us; and, on the other hand, unless we bear in mind what is here said concerning the wicked, that *their arms shall be broken,* we will make too great account of their present condition. But if this doctrine be deeply fixed in the hearts of the faithful, as soon as they shall have learned to rely upon the divine blessing, the delight and joy which they will experience from their little store shall be equal to the magnanimity with which they shall look down, as it were from an eminence, upon the vast treasures in which the ungodly glory. At the same time, we are here admonished, that whilst the ungodly rely upon their own strength, and proudly boast of it, we ought to wait patiently till God arise and break their arms in pieces. As for us, the best consolation which we could have in our infirmity is, that God himself upholds and strengthens us.

18. *Jehovah knoweth the days of the upright.*[1] It is not without good reason that David so frequently inculcates this doctrine, that the righteous are blessed because God provides for their necessities. We see how prone the minds of men are to distrust, and how much they are vexed by an excess of cares and anxieties from which they are unable to extricate themselves, while, on the other hand, they fall into another error in being more anxious regarding the future than there is any reason for; and yet, however active and industrious in the formation of their plans, they are often disappointed in their expectations, and not unfrequently fail altogether of success. Nothing, therefore, is more profitable for us than to have our eyes continually set upon the providence of God, which alone can best provide for us every thing we need. On this account, David now says, that *God knoweth the days of the righteous;* that is to say, he is not ignorant of the dangers to which they are exposed, and the help which they need. This doctrine we ought to improve as a source of consolation under every vicissitude which may seem to threaten us with destruction. We may be harassed in various ways, and distracted by many dangers, which every moment threaten us with death, but this consideration ought to prove to us a sufficient ground of comfort, that not only are our days numbered by God, but that he also knows all the vicissitudes of our lot on earth. Since God then so carefully watches over us for the maintenance of our welfare, we ought to enjoy, in this our pilgrimage on earth, as much peace and satisfaction as if we were put in full possession of our paternal inheritance and home. Because we are regarded by God, David from this concludes, that our inheritance is everlasting. Moreover, in declaring that those who are upright are thus carefully protected by God, he exhorts us to the sincere pursuit of truth and uprightness; and if we desire to be placed in safety under the protection of God, let us cultivate meekness, and reject with detestation this hellish proverb, "We must howl among wolves."

[1] " ' Depositeth the days of the upright,' lays them up in safety for them: for such is the original idea of ידע."—*Fry.*

19. *They shall not be ashamed in the season of adversity.* This verse also shows us, that the faithful have no right to expect such exemption as the flesh would desire from affliction and trial, but they are assured of deliverance in the end; which, though it be indeed obtained, yet it is of such a nature as can be realised only by faith. We must regard these two things as inseparably connected, namely, that as the faithful are mingled among the wicked in this world, so hunger and adversity are common to both. The only difference betwixt them is, that God stretches forth his hand towards his own people in the time of their need, while he abandons the ungodly, and takes no care of them. If it should be objected, that the wicked often fare sumptuously in the time of famine, and gratify all their desires, whilst the faithful are oppressed with poverty and want, I answer, that the fulness of which mention is here made consists chiefly in this, that the faithful, though they live sparingly, and often labour hard to acquire the means of subsistence, are nevertheless fed by God as truly as if they had a greater abundance of this world's goods than the ungodly, who greedily devour the good things of this life in all their variety and abundance, and yet are never satisfied. Besides, as I have elsewhere said, these temporal blessings are not always seen flowing in one uniform course. The hand of God is indeed always open, but we are straitened and limited in our desires, so that our own unbelief is no small hinderance to his liberality. Moreover, as our corrupt nature would soon break forth into excess, God deals with us more sparingly; and lest he might corrupt us by too great indulgence, he trains us to frugality by bestowing with a sparing hand what he was ready otherwise to lavish upon us in full abundance. And, indeed, whoever shall consider how much addicted we are to sensuality and pleasure, will not be surprised that God should exercise his own people with poverty and want. But although God may not bestow upon us what is necessary for our gratification, yet, unless our own ingratitude prevent us, we shall experience, even in famine and want, that he nourishes us graciously and liberally.

20. *For the wicked shall perish, and the enemies of Jehovah shall be consumed as the preciousness*[1] *of lambs; they shall be consumed into smoke.*[2]
21. *The wicked borroweth, and payeth not again; but the righteous is merciful, and giveth.*
22. *For those who are blessed by him shall inherit the earth; and those who are cursed of him shall be cut off.*

20. *For the wicked shall perish.* The causal particle כִּי, *ki*, which is here translated *for*, might also be rendered as if used adversatively by *but* or *although*, unless, perhaps, some would prefer to expound the sentence as of much higher import. But the preferable interpretation is, that there is here a contrast between the subjects spoken of, namely, that the righteous are satisfied in the time of famine, whereas the ungodly shall perish in the midst of their affluence; for, while they trust in their abundance, God brings them to nought by the use of means that are secret and hidden. In calling them the *enemies of Jehovah*, he teaches us, that they are justly overwhelmed by his vengeance, which they bring upon themselves by their own wickedness. When he says, that they *shall be consumed as the excellency of lambs*, this is understood by some to refer to the fat of them. But as יָקָר, *yakar*, signifies *excellency*, as I have said elsewhere, I have no doubt that this expression denotes the very best of lambs, and such as are of extraordinary fatness: and this is very suitable to the contrast here stated. We learn from this what another prophet likewise teaches, that the ungodly are fattened for the day of slaughter; so that the more sumptuously they shall have lived, the more suddenly shall their destruction come upon them. *To be consumed into smoke* is of the same import as *to vanish away quickly;* as if it had been said, There is no stability or substance in them. Those who understand the term יָקָר, *yakar*, to mean *fat*, explain this latter clause in this sense: that the wicked are consumed into smoke as

---

[1] " Ou, l'excellence, c'est, les agneaux plus beaux et plus gras."—*Fr. marg.* " Or, the excellency, that is, the finest and fattest lambs."
[2] " C'est, s'esvanouiront en brief."—*Fr. marg.* " That is, shall speedily vanish away."

fat melts or wastes away.¹ But the reader will see that the first interpretation is better.

21. *The wicked borroweth, and payeth not again.* Those are mistaken who suppose that the wicked are here blamed for their treachery in carrying off the goods of others by fraud and deception; and that, on the other hand, the children of God are commended for their kindness in being always ready to relieve the wants of their poorer brethren. The prophet rather extols, on the one hand, the blessing of God towards the godly; and declares, on the other, that the ungodly never have enough. The meaning therefore is, that God deals bountifully with his own people, that they may be able to aid others; but that the ungodly are always in want, so that their poverty leads them to have recourse to fraud and rapine. And were we not blinded by insensibility and indifference, we could not fail to perceive the many proofs of this which are daily presented to our view. However great the abundance of the ungodly, yet their covetousness is so insatiable, that, like robbers, they plunder right and left, and yet are never able to pay;² while God bestows upon his own people a sufficiency not only for the supply of their own ordinary wants, but also to enable them to aid others. I do not indeed deny, that the wicked are reproved for wasteful extravagance, by which they defraud their creditors of what is their due, and also that the righteous are praised for applying to a proper use the bounty of God; but the design of the prophet is to show the high value of the divine blessing. This is confirmed by the following verse, in which he illustrates the difference resulting from the blessing and the

¹ It is generally supposed that there is here an allusion to the sacrificial services of the former dispensation. Lambs were then offered in large numbers as burnt-offerings; and if the allusion is to these sacrifices, as is highly probable, the doctrine taught is, that as the fat of them melted away, and was wholly and rapidly consumed by the fire of the altar of burnt-offering, so the wicked shall melt away and be quickly consumed in the fire of Jehovah's wrath. The Chaldee paraphrases the last clause thus:—"They shall be consumed in the smoke of Gehenna," or of hell.

² "Comme escumeurs de mer sans jamais avoir de quoy satisfaire."—*Fr.* "Like pirates, without ever having any thing to pay."

curse of God. If then it is asked, whence the children of God are able to relieve the wants of the needy, and to exercise liberality towards them? and why it is that the ungodly are continually contracting debts from which they are never able to extricate themselves? David answers, that the former are blessed of the Lord, and that the latter are brought to utter ruin by his curse. Some expound the word מברכיו, *meborakayv,* actively, as if it were, *Those who bless the righteous shall possess,* &c.;[1] but this is constrained and absurd. The meaning is simply this, that whatever we need for the preservation and maintenance of life, and for the exercise of humanity towards others, comes to us neither from the heavens nor from the earth, but only from the favour and blessing of God; and that if he once withdraw his grace, the abundance of the whole world would not satisfy us.

23. *The footsteps of a man are directed by Jehovah, and he will delight* [or, *take pleasure*] *in his way.*
24. *Though he fall, he shall not be utterly cast down: for Jehovah upholdeth him with his hand.*
25. *I have been young, I am also become old; and yet I have not seen the righteous forsaken, nor his seed begging bread.*
26. *He is daily merciful, and lendeth, and his seed is for blessing.*

23. *The footsteps of a man are directed by Jehovah.* Some join together these two things, first, that the footsteps of the godly are ordered by the grace of God, since men do not in their own strength follow what is just and right, but only in so far as the Spirit of God directs them; and hence the second follows, namely, that God favours and approves what is his own. But David simply continues his commendation of the divine blessing towards the faithful, of whom this is especially worthy of being remembered, that whatever they undertake always has a favourable and happy result. At the same time, the reason why God crowns with prosperity and success all our efforts throughout the course of our life is to be observed, namely, because we attempt nothing which is

---

[1] " Comme s'il y avoit, Ceux qui beniront les justes, possederont," &c. —*Fr.*

not pleasing to him. For I consider the copula *and*, in the second clause of the verse, to be used instead of the causal particle *because*, and resolve the whole verse in this way: Because the way of the godly is acceptable to God, he directs their footsteps to a happy issue; so that the meaning is, As God sees that the faithful act conscientiously, and do not turn aside from the way which he has appointed, he blesses their efforts. And, certainly, since the prophet speaks generally—and yet it is certain that the faithful only are here spoken of—the second clause must necessarily be considered as spoken by way of exposition. Accordingly, the term *way* denotes their manner and course of living; as if he had said, that the godly have no other object in view but to frame their lives agreeably to the will of God, and to obey what he commands. The term *footsteps* I consider as referring to external success.

24. *Though he fall, he shall not be utterly cast down.* This verse has generally been interpreted proverbially, and as meaning, that though the righteous may fall into sin, his fall is not deadly; but this is not at all in accordance with the design of the prophet, who is discoursing of the happiness of the godly. The simple meaning is, that when God visits his servants with severe afflictions, he at the same time mitigates them that they may not faint under them;[1] as Paul declares, 2 Cor. iv. 9, "We are persecuted, but not forsaken; cast down, but not destroyed." Some say that the righteous are not utterly cast down, because they lose not their courage, but rather bear with invincible fortitude whatever burden is laid upon them. I readily admit that the reason why they are not overwhelmed is, that they are not so tender and delicate as to sink under the burden. I, however, understand the words in a more extensive sense, and explain them thus: That the miseries of the godly are so tempered with God's fatherly mercy, that they fail not under their burden, and even when they fall, sink not into destruction. From these words we learn that the godly,

[1] " Neither the text," says Dr Adam Clarke, " nor any of the versions, intimate that *a falling into sin* is meant; but a falling into *trouble, difficulty,*" &c.

although they serve God sincerely, and study to lead a blameless life, are not suffered to continue unmoved, and always in the same condition, but are often afflicted and cast down by various trials; and that the only difference between them and the unbelieving is, that their falls are not deadly. We know that if God smite the reprobate, though it be but very slightly, it becomes the cause of their final destruction. Solomon speaks still more expressly when he says, " For a just man falleth seven times, and riseth up again," (Prov. xxiv. 16 :) and by these words he teaches us, that the godly are not only subjected to frequent afflictions in this life, but that they are visited with daily trials, and yet are never forsaken of the Lord. We must also shortly observe, that even the slightest fall would be enough to destroy us utterly, did not God uphold us by his hand.

25. *I have been young, I am also become old.* The meaning of these words is not in the least doubtful, namely, that David, even when he was become an old man, had not seen any of the righteous, or any of their children, begging their bread. But here there arises a question of some difficulty with respect to the fact stated; for it is certain that many righteous men have been reduced to beggary. And what David here declares as the result of his own experience pertains to all ages. Besides, he refers in this verse to the writings of Moses, for in Deut. xv. 4, begging is reckoned among the curses of God; and the law, in that place, expressly exempts from it those who fear and serve God. How then does the consistency of this appear, that none of the righteous ever begged his bread, since Christ placed Lazarus among the most abject of them? (Luke xvi. 20.) I answer, that we must bear in mind what I have before said upon this subject, that with respect to the temporal blessings which God confers upon his people, no certain or uniform rule can be established. There are various reasons why God does not manifest his favour equally to all the godly in this world. He chastises some, while he spares others: he heals the secret maladies of some, and passes by others, because they have no need of a like remedy : he exercises the patience of some, according as he has given them the spirit of fortitude ;

and, finally, he sets forth others by way of example. But in general, he humbles all of them by the tokens of his anger, that by secret warnings they may be brought to repentance. Besides, he leads them, by a variety of afflictions, to fix their thoughts in meditation upon the heavenly life; and yet it is not a vain or imaginary thing, that, as is set forth in the Law, God vouchsafes earthly blessings to his servants as proofs of his favour toward them. I confess, I say, that it is not in vain, or for nought, that an abundance of earthly blessings, sufficient for the supply of all their wants, is promised to the godly. This, however, is always to be understood with this limitation, that God will bestow these blessings only in so far as he shall consider it expedient: and, accordingly, it may happen that the blessing of God may be manifested in the life of men in general, and yet some of the godly be pinched with poverty, because it is for their good. But if it happen that any of the faithful are brought to beggary, they should lift up their minds on high, to that blessed state in which God will largely recompense them for all that is now wanting in the blessings of this transitory life. We must also bear this in mind, that if God sometimes involve the faithful in the same punishments by which he takes vengeance upon the ungodly —seeing them, for example, affected with the same diseases, —in doing so there is no inconsistency; for although they do not come the length of contemning God, nor are devoted to wickedness, nor even act according to their own inclination, nor yield themselves wholly to the influence of sin like the wicked, yet are they not free of all blame; and, therefore, it need not surprise us though they are sometimes subjected to temporal punishments. We are, however, certain of this, that God makes such provision for his own people, that, being contented with their lot, they are never in want; because, by living sparingly, they always have enough, as Paul says, Philip. vi. 12, " I am instructed both to abound and to suffer need."

26. *He is daily merciful.* The Psalmist here repeats what he had already said, that the grace of God is a fountain of all blessings which can never be exhausted ; and, therefore, while it is displayed towards the faithful, they not only have

enough for the supply of their own wants, but are able also liberally to assist others. What he adds concerning *their seed* is variously expounded. That he is speaking of the children of the godly, there can be no doubt; and this is evident from the preceding verse. But when he says that they *shall be for blessing*,[1] some understand it as if he had said, They shall be the ministers of God's liberality: so that, according to them, the sense would be, that they shall follow the good example of their fathers in helping the poor, and in exercising liberality towards all men. But I fear that this exposition is too refined. Nor do I admit the interpretation which has been given by others, that the meaning is, that the grace of God shall be so signally manifested towards the children of the godly, that their names shall be employed in a form of prayer, when prosperity and success are prayed for. This mode of expression, I allow, is to be so understood in various places; but here, in my opinion, David designs nothing more than to extol the continuation of God's favour from the fathers to their children: as if he had said, God's blessing does not terminate with the death of the righteous man, but it extends even to his children.[2] And there is indeed no inheritance more certain to which our children may succeed us, than when God, receiving them in like manner into his fatherly favour, makes them partakers of his blessing.

27. *Depart from evil, and do good, and dwell for ever.*
28. *For Jehovah loveth judgment, and forsaketh not his meek ones: they shall be preserved for ever: and the seed of the wicked shall be cut off.*
29. *The righteous shall inherit the earth, and shall dwell for ever upon it.*

27. *Depart from evil, and do good.* In this verse David argues, that, in order to realise the blessedness of which he has

---

[1] This is also the reading of the Septuagint, Τὸ σπέρμα αὐτοῦ εἰς εὐλογίαν ἔσται.

[2] Ainsworth reads, "And his seed are in the blessing," and understands the words as meaning, that the children of the just man "are in the blessing, or are appointed to the blessing, as the heirs thereof," Gen. xxviii. 3; 1 Peter iii. 9; and that they have still abundance, notwithstanding the liberality of their parents; for "the blessing of the Lord maketh rich," Prov. x. 22.

spoken, we must abstain from all evil, perform the duties of humanity, and exert ourselves in doing good to our neighbours. This doctrine is at variance with the dictates of corrupt human nature; but it is, notwithstanding, certain that many of the troubles and distresses in which the whole human race are involved, proceed from no other cause than this, that every man respectively, in his own sphere, being given to injustice, fraud, extortion, and evil-dealing, contemptuously rejects the blessing of God. Thus, it is in consequence of the barriers which men throw in their own way, that they do not attain happiness in this world, and that every man in his own place does not possess the peace and quietness which belong to him. It is then with the highest propriety that David passes from the doctrine of the preceding context to this exhortation: for if the meek possess the earth, then every one, as he regards his own happiness and peace, ought also to endeavour to walk uprightly, and to apply himself to works of beneficence. It should also be observed, that he connects these two things, first, that the faithful should strictly do good; and, secondly, that they should restrain themselves from doing evil: and this he does not without good reason: for as we have seen in the thirty-fourth psalm, it often happens that the same person who not only acts kindly towards certain persons, but even with a bountiful hand deals out largely of his own, is yet all the while plundering others, and amassing by extortion the resources by means of which he displays his liberality. Whoever, therefore, is desirous to have his good offices approved by God, let him endeavour to relieve his brethren who have need of his help, but let him not injure one in order to help another, or afflict and grieve one in order to make another glad. Now David, under these two expressions, has briefly comprised the duties of the second table of the law: first, that the godly should keep their hands free from all mischief, and give no occasion of complaint to any man; and, secondly, that they should not live to themselves, and to the promotion merely of their own private interests, but should endeavour to promote the common good of all according to their opportunities, and as far as they are able. But we have already said, that the blessing which is promised to the righteous, that "they shall inherit the earth," is not always realised in an equal degree as to all the people of God; and the reason we assigned for this is, that God cannot find among men an example of such great uprightness, but that even the most perfect procure to themselves much misery by their own fault: and therefore it need not surprise us though God withdraw, at least in some measure, his blessing even from his own. We know too to what excess the lusts of the flesh run riot, unless the Lord lay a restraint upon them. Besides, there is no one who is ready cheerfully to engage in meditation upon the divine life, who is not urged and encouraged to it by various motives. Hence it is that the possession of the earth, which David here assigns to the children of God, does not (as the lawyers would define the term) always consist in having the feet planted within it, and in being securely established in it; for there are many sources of disquietude and affliction here to trouble them. And yet it does not follow that it is a mere fiction or imaginary thing which he promises. For although daily experience shows us that the children of God do not as yet inherit the earth, yet, according to the measure of our faith, we feel how efficacious the blessing of God is, which, like a spring that cannot be drained, flows continually. They are indeed more than blind who do not perceive that the righteous have at present this reward, that God defends and upholds them by his power.

28. *For Jehovah loveth judgment.* This, it ought to be observed, is a confirmation of the doctrine contained in the preceding sentence; and it is here made to rest upon a higher principle, namely, that God takes pleasure in righteousness and truth. The argument indeed appears to be incomplete; but as David takes for granted—what ought to be deeply fixed in the hearts of all the faithful—that the world is directed by the providence of God, his conclusion is admirable. In the first place, then, it must be admitted that the condition of the human race is not under the direction of chance, but of the providence of God, and that the world is conducted and governed by his counsel, so that he

regulates according to his pleasure the issue of all things, and controls them by his power; and, secondly, to this it must be added what David here states, that righteousness and truth are pleasing to God. Hence it follows, that all who lead an upright and blameless life among men shall be happy, because, enjoying the favour of God, every thing at length must in regard to them have a happy and successful result. But let us bear in mind, that the promise which is spoken of in this verse is to be understood in this sense, that while God has undertaken the preservation of the godly, it is not to cherish them continually in retirement and ease, but after he has for a time exercised them under the cross, at length to come to their help : for the language here employed, *Jehovah forsaketh not his meek ones*, is tacitly very emphatic. Those, therefore, who separate the exercise of patience from the favour which God bestows upon the godly in this life, misinterpret this psalm. On the contrary, lest any one should hastily and rashly pronounce judgment, the prophet entreats the faithful to suspend their judgment, until God manifest his displeasure after the death of the wicked, in inflicting punishment upon their posterity: *The seed of the wicked shall be cut off*. This is of the same import as if he had again asserted, that although the judgments of God are not immediately executed upon the wicked and ungodly, yet they are not on that account anything the better of it, since the punishment justly due to them will extend to their children. If then the curse of God is not forthwith inflicted upon them, it need not surprise us if he delay for a time to manifest the favour which he bears towards the faithful.

29. *The righteous shall inherit the earth.* The repetition of the same doctrine here is not superfluous, since it is so very difficult to impress it deeply upon our minds. For while all men seek after happiness, scarcely one in a hundred looks for it from God, but rather all, on the contrary, in making provision for themselves, provoke the vengeance of God, as it were deliberately, and strive to excel each other in doing so, so that some of them stain themselves with fraud and

perjury, some indulge in robbery and extortion, some practise all sorts of cruelty, and others commit violence and outrage even with the sword and poison. Moreover, I have just now, and on several other occasions, stated the sense in which this everlasting habitation upon the earth, which is here promised to the righteous, is to be understood, namely, that although they are surrounded by the troubles and changes which occur in this world, yet God preserves them under his wings; and although there is nothing lasting or stable under heaven, yet he keeps them in safety as if they were sheltered in a secure haven. And, finally, they enjoy in addition to this that inward peace of mind which is better than a hundred lives, and which is therefore justly regarded as a privilege surpassing in value and importance all others.

30. *The mouth of the righteous will speak wisdom, and his tongue will utter judgment.*
31. *The law of his God is in his heart: his steps shall not slide.*
32. *The wicked watcheth the righteous, and seeketh to slay him.*
33. *Jehovah will not leave him in his hand, nor condemn him when he is judged.*

30. *The mouth of the righteous will speak wisdom.* As it is customary with hypocrites confidently to draw to their own advantage whatever the Spirit of God declares concerning the just and upright, David here gives a definition of the righteousness which God requires on the part of his children, and divides it into three principal parts—that their speech should be in sincerity and truth; that the law of God should reign in their heart; and that they should order their conversation aright. Some give a different exposition of the first part from what we have given: they say that the righteous serve as teachers and guides, by instructing others to live well, and leading them in the way; and, therefore, *to speak wisdom*, and *to utter judgment*, is, in their view, of the same import as to instruct others in holy doctrine, and to train them to the fear of God. I do not altogether disapprove of this exposition, but I fear it is too restricted. Wisdom and uprightness are here opposed as much to the profane and filthy language by which the wicked endeavour to blot out the name of God, as

to cunning and fraud, and every species of stratagem and deceit; and also to the threats and terrors by which they endeavour to frighten the simple.[1] The meaning therefore is, first, that the righteous speak honourably and reverently of the righteousness of God, that they may cherish in themselves and others, to a large extent, the knowledge and the fear of God;[2] secondly, that both in their own affairs and those of others, they approve, without disguise or deceit, of what is just and reasonable, and are not given to justify what is wrong under the colour and varnish of sophistry; and, finally, that they never depart from the truth.

To this there is added integrity of heart: *The law of the Lord is in his heart.* This, though it should precede in point of order, is not improperly put in the second place here. For the Scriptures are not particular in observing an exact arrangement in the enumeration of virtues and vices. Besides, the source whence this integrity of heart proceeds is, that the Law of God has its seat in the heart; and it is it alone which prescribes the best rule of life, restrains all the depraved affections and lusts, and imbues the minds of men with the love of righteousness. No man will constantly and steadily devote himself to a life of uprightness, exert himself in behalf of others in preference to his own personal interests, renounce covetousness, subdue pride, and maintain a constant warfare with his own nature, unless he is endued with the fear of God. There next follows the third division, which relates to the external conduct: *His steps shall not slide.* Some, indeed, think that this is a promise; but I have no doubt, that in this clause David still continues the definition of righteousness. The meaning therefore is, that although the children of God are tempted in a variety of ways to commit sin, and many things occur urging them to it, —and although men, for the most part, too, endeavour, as far as in them lies, by their maliciousness to turn them aside from the fear of God,—yet, because the Law of God rules and reigns in their hearts, they *do not slide,* but stand to their purpose with firm and determined resolution, or at least adhere to the right course.

[1] " Par lesquelles ils taschent d'espouvanter les simples."—*Fr.*
[2] " En toutes les parties de la cognoissance et crainte de Dieu."—*Fr.*

32 and 33. *The wicked watcheth the righteous, &c.* David here illustrates more plainly the nature of the possession of the earth, of which he had spoken, namely, that God preserves his own people, though they are beset with enemies round about. And hence we are again taught, that the faithful are not promised in the preceding context a quiet state of life, and one free from all trouble and distress. If so, these two statements would be contradictory: first, that the faithful possessing an inheritance, enjoy repose and pleasure; and, secondly, that yet they are daily delivered as sheep out of the mouth of wolves. These two verses, however, contain this special ground of consolation, that the faithful, though surrounded by such a variety of dangers, shall notwithstanding escape, and be preserved in safety by the help of God. Accordingly, David here teaches them, that when they shall see their enemies lying in wait for them, and seeking by every means in their power to annoy them, they, on the contrary, ought to consider how deeply interested God is in the welfare of his own people, and how carefully he watches over them to preserve them in safety. David indeed confesses that the stratagems to which the wicked have recourse in seeking not only to deprive good men of their property, but even to take away their lives, are terrible in themselves, because they cruelly plot their destruction; but still he teaches us at the same time, that we ought to continue to preserve firm and undaunted courage, because God has promised that he will be our guardian and defender: *Jehovah will not leave him in his hand.* This circumstance, however, ought to be considered, that God does not always grant us deliverance at the first, but often delays it till we seem to be even at the point of death. In the last clause of the verse, we are also admonished, that however carefully good men may guard against giving offence to any, and endeavour to secure the good-will of all, and shun debate and strife, yet they shall not be exempted from false accusations: *Jehovah will not condemn them when they are judged.* David does not say that they shall receive the applause of the world, and that their virtues shall be celebrated in such praises as they deserve; but he exhorts them, when they shall be

haled to judgment, and as it were overwhelmed with slander, so that they already resemble those who are condemned, to rest contented with the protection of God, who will at length manifest their innocence, and maintain it against the unrighteous judgments of men. If any one object, that, on the contrary, many of the children of God, after having been condemned, have suffered a cruel and bitter death, I answer, that their avenger nevertheless is in heaven. Christ was put to death in the most cruel form, and in circumstances of the deepest ignominy, but notwithstanding, as the prophet Isaiah says, chap. liii. 8, " he was taken from that distress and condemnation;" and in the same manner God is still acting daily towards those who are his members. If it may still be objected, that David is here discoursing not of the life to come, but of the state of the godly in the present life, I must again repeat in answer to this, the explanation which I have given before, namely, that earthly blessings are at God's disposal, and are regulated entirely according to his will; and hence it is that he never bestows them in an equal measure upon all, but according to his wisdom, and as he sees meet, sometimes withdrawing them either in whole or in part, and at other times displaying them to the view of all. Accordingly, it may happen, that the holy martyrs, after they have been condemned, may also be put to death, as if God had forsaken them; but this is only because it is better for themselves, and because they desire nothing more than to glorify God by their death. Yet he who permits the ungodly to exercise their cruelty, ceases not to be the assertor of the righteousness of his servants: for he openly shows before his angels, and before his whole Church, that he approves it, and declares that he will make inquisition for it; nay, more, raising them from the darkness in which they have been hid, he makes their ashes yield a sweet and pleasant odour. Finally, after the Lord has suffered them to be overwhelmed by reproach and violence, he will pronounce the judgment by which he will vindicate their righteous cause from wicked calumnies and false accusations.

34. *Wait upon Jehovah, and keep his way, and he shall exalt thee, that thou mayest inherit the earth: when the wicked are cut off, thou shalt see it.*
35. *I have seen the wicked terrible,*[1] *and spreading himself like a green bay tree:*[2]
36. *And he passed away,*[3] *and, lo! he was not: and I sought for his place, and he was not found.*

34. *Wait upon Jehovah, and keep his way.* David again returns to the style of exhortation, in order that the faithful, trusting to God's promises and sustained by them, may not suffer themselves to be drawn hither and thither by any temptations through devious and sinful ways, but may persevere stedfastly in the service of God. In the first place, he exhorts them to hope and patience, as if he wished them, amidst the tumults and troubles of life, to trust in God, and hold their peace till he again show them his countenance, which for a time he had hid from them. Hence arises, in the second place, another exhortation, that they should not turn aside from the way of the Lord; for wherever hope and patience prevail, they will so restrain the minds of men that they will not break out into any thing unlawful and wicked. It will doubtless be found, that the reason why every man

---

[1] Striking terror in all around.
[2] The proper signification of the word אזרח, *azrach,* has been controverted among interpreters, and it has been variously rendered. Most of the Rabbins, and many modern commentators, as Mudge, Waterland, Gesenius, and others, are of opinion, that the preferable reading is, "like an indigenous or native tree;" that is, a tree which flourishes in its native soil, where it grows most vigorously, and acquires its largest and most luxuriant growth. The Septuagint translates it, ὡς τὰς κέδρους τοῦ Λιβάνου, "as the cedars of Lebanon;" being self-growing, spreading, and lofty trees. Some suppose that the translators of this version must have had a different reading in their Hebrew Bibles from what is in our present copies; and others, that, as is common with them, they paraphrase the original words, the more clearly to express their meaning. The translation of the Septuagint is followed by the Vulgate, Arabic, and Æthiopic versions, by Houbigant, Boothroyd, Geddes, and other good authorities. Ainsworth reads, "as a green self-growing laurel." Bythner says he is at a loss for the reason of translating the word *laurel.* "For the reading of *bay tree,*" says the illustrated Commentary upon the Bible, "we are not aware of any authority, except the very feeble one which is offered by some of the older of the modern versions in this country and on the Continent."
[3] The Septuagint, Vulgate, Syriac, and Arabic versions, Jerome, Houbigant, Horsley, and Walford, read the verb in the first person, "But I passed by." The Chaldee adheres to the Hebrew, "And he passed, *or* failed, from the age, *or* world, and, lo! he was not."

endeavours to promote his own advantage by wicked practices is, that no one depends upon God, or else that he thinks, if fortune do not quickly smile upon him, that it is vain for him to persevere in the practice of equity and uprightness. Moreover, we may learn from this place, that if many, even of the good and the upright, are subjected to poverty, and lead a life of protracted affliction and trial, they suffer their punishment justly, because, so far from being firmly persuaded that it belongs to God as his proper office, not only to lift up his servants from the dunghill, but also to bring them forth even from their graves, scarcely one in a hundred of them patiently waits upon God, and continues perseveringly in the right course. Nor is it without good reason that David makes use of the word *exalt*, that we may know that God often stretches forth his hand to the faithful when they appear to be overwhelmed by the weight of their calamities. He then adds, that the *wicked* shall perish before the eyes of the godly. If their end were not very different from that of the righteous, the state in which the reprobate now rejoice for a time would easily allure even the best of men to evil. And, indeed, God would make us daily to behold such sights if we had eyes to behold his judgments. And yet, although the whole world were blinded, God does not cease to render a just reward to the wickedness of men; but by punishing them in a more private manner, he withdraws from us that fruit of which our own dulness deprives us.

35 and 36. *I have seen the wicked terrible, &c.* David here confirms from his own experience what I have just said, namely, that although the wicked are intoxicated with their prosperity, and held in admiration by all on account of it, yet their happiness is transitory and evanescent, and, therefore, nothing else than a mere illusion. In the 35th verse he tells us, that it is no strange or unwonted thing for the ungodly, puffed up with their prosperity, to spread themselves far and wide, and to give occasion of terror to the innocent. Then he adds, that their greatness, which had been regarded with so much wonder, disappears in a moment. As to the meaning of the words, עריץ, *arits*, which we have rendered

terrible, might also be translated *strong,* because the word from which it is derived signifies sometimes *to terrify,* and sometimes *to strengthen.* The word מִתְעָרֶה, *mithareh,* is taken by some for *green,* but it rather means *discovering* or *spreading himself out,* as high and broad trees spread out their branches. David, I have no doubt, here rebukes the insolence of those who vaunt themselves immoderately. *To pass away,* in the 36th verse, is used for *to vanish away;* and thus he admonishes us to sit still for a time, in order that it may appear, after it has passed away, that all that the world admires in the prosperity of the wicked has been only a mist.

37. *Observe the perfect man, and consider the just : for the end of that man is peace.*
38. *But the transgressors shall be destroyed together : the end of the wicked shall be cut off.*
39. *The salvation of the righteous is from Jehovah : he is their strength in the time of trouble.*
40. *Jehovah shall help them, and deliver them : he shall deliver them from the wicked : he shall preserve them, because they trust in him.*

37. *Observe the perfect man.* David exhorts the faithful diligently to consider every instance they may meet with of the grace of God, as well as of his judgment; but he teaches, at the same time, that it is in vain for any to sit in judgment upon the first aspect of things. When men do not wait patiently and quietly the time which God has appointed in his good pleasure, it often happens that faith is extinguished, and trust in the promises of God, at the same time, perishes with it. This is the reason why David exhorts us to observe and consider, for when our minds are preoccupied by the temptation which is once presented to our view, a hasty judgment is then the cause of our being deceived. But if a man extend his view, as if it were from a watch-tower, to a great distance, he will find that it has been said with truth, that *the end* of the reprobate and *the end* of the righteous respectively are at length very different. This clause, with respect to the end of these two classes of men, seems to be added by way of caution, that we may learn to suspend our

judgment, if God should not immediately accomplish what he has spoken. If we should become impatient in our desires, let us moderate our minds by the reflection, that the end is not yet come, and that it behoves us to give God time to restore to order the confused state of things. Some explain the word אחרית, *acharith,* which we have rendered the *end* of the wicked, of their posterity. This, however, is incorrect. David refers only to the difference which subsists between them and the righteous in the end; for God, after he has severely tried his servants, and exercised their patience, in the end converts their adversity into a blessing, while he turns the mirth of the ungodly into mourning.

39. *The salvation of the righteous is from Jehovah.* The sum of the whole is, that whatever may happen, the righteous shall be saved, because they are in the hand of God, and can never be forgotten by him. This ought to be particularly noticed, that those who are greatly afflicted may be sustained by the assurance that the salvation which they expect from God is infallibly certain, because God is eternal, and governs the world by his power; as Christ said, " My Father, who gave them me, is greater than all," (John x. 29.) David still inculcates this principle, that as righteousness is approved of God, it can never happen that he should forsake his faithful servants, and deprive them of his help. He, therefore, exhorts true believers to depend upon God, not only when things prosper according to their desires, but even when they are sorely afflicted. By these words he teaches that it is enough, if God only impart strength to his servants, so that, when severely afflicted and oppressed with anguish, they may not faint under it, or that, when groaning under the weight of severe afflictions, they may not sink under the burden. To the same purpose also is the expression which David uses twice in the last verse, that *God will deliver.* By this he admonishes the children of God to learn patiently to endure afflictions, and that, if God should prolong them, they should often recall this to their remembrance, that after he has tried their patience, he will in the end deliver them.

PSALM XXXVIII.

David, suffering under some severe and dangerous malady, as may be conjectured, acknowledges that he is chastened by the Lord, and entreats him to turn away his anger from him. In order the more effectually to induce God to have mercy upon him, he bewails before him the severity of his afflictions in a variety of particulars. These we shall consider separately, and in order.

¶ A Psalm of David to bring to remembrance.[1]

The title of this psalm refers to its subject. Some suppose that it is the beginning of a common song, because in other psalms the beginning of the song, to the tune of which they were set, is commonly prefixed : but such an interpretation is unnatural, and without foundation. Instead of this, I rather think that the title indicates that David composed this psalm as a memorial for himself, as well as others, lest he should too soon forget the chastisement by which God had afflicted him. He knew how easily and speedily the chastisements with which God visits us, and which ought to serve as a means of instruction to us all our life, pass away from the mind. He was also mindful of his own high calling; for, as he was appointed master and teacher over the whole Church, it was necessary that whatever he had himself learned in particular by divine teaching should be made known, and appropriated to the use of all, that all might profit thereby. Thus we are admonished that it is a very profitable exercise often to recall to remembrance the chastisements with which God has afflicted us for our sins.

[1] This title occurs only here and in the 70th psalm. This psalm is the third of what are called the Penitential Psalms. The two before this are the 6th and the 32d; and the four which follow it are the 51st, the 102d, the 130th, and the 143d. It is a curious fact, that when Galileo was sentenced to be confined in the dungeons of the Inquisition for an indefinite period, for having maintained the Copernican system, he was enjoined to repeat as a penance these seven Penitential Psalms every week for three years; by which it was doubtless intended to extort a sort of confession from him of his guilt, and an acknowledgment of the justice of his sentence.

1. O Jehovah! rebuke me not in thy wrath, and chasten me not in thy anger.
2. For thy arrows go down in me,[1] and thy hand has come down upon me.
3. There is no soundness in my flesh because of thy anger; nor any peace in my bones because of my sin.
4. For my iniquities have passed over my head, and as a weighty burden they have become too heavy for me.
5. My wounds have become putrid, they are corrupt, because of my foolishness.

1. *O Jehovah! rebuke me not in thy wrath.* As I have already expounded this verse in the beginning of the sixth psalm, where it occurs, and that I may not prove tedious to the reader, I shall notice it more briefly here. David does not expressly ask that his afflictions should be removed, but only that God would moderate the severity of his chastisements. Hence we may infer, that David did not give loose reins to the desires of the flesh, but offered up his earnest prayer in a duly chastened spirit of devotion. All men would naturally desire that permission should be granted them to sin with impunity. But David lays a restraint upon his desires, and does not wish the favour and indulgence of God to be extended beyond measure, but is content with a mitigation of his affliction; as if he had said, Lord, I am not unwilling to be chastised by thee, but I entreat thee, meanwhile, not to afflict me beyond what I am able to bear, but to temper the fierceness of thy indignation according to the measure of my infirmity, lest the severity of the affliction should entirely overwhelm me. This prayer, as I have said, was framed according to the rule of godliness; for it contains nothing but what God promises to all his children. It should also be noticed, that David does not secretly indulge a fretful and repining spirit, but spreads his complaint before God; and this he does, not in the way of sinful complaining, but

---

[1] That is, they enter deep into the flesh. The Septuagint reads, "'Ενεπάγησάν μοι;" the Vulgate, "Infixæ sunt mihi;"—"Are fastened in me;" which is a natural consequence of entering deep, and rather expresses the meaning, than conveys the precise idea of the original word. The Syriac and Arabic versions give the same rendering with the Vulgate.

of humble prayer and unfeigned confession, accompanied with the hope of obtaining forgiveness. He has used *anger* and *wrath* as denoting extreme rigour, and has contrasted them with fatherly chastisement.

2. *For thy arrows go down in me.* He shows that he was constrained by dire necessity to ask an alleviation of his misery; for he was crushed under the weight of the burden which he sustained. This rule is always to be observed in our prayers—to keep God's promises present to our view. But God has promised that he will chastise his servants, not according to their deserts, but as they are able to bear. This is the reason why the saints so often speak of their own weakness, when they are severely oppressed with affliction. David very properly describes the malady under which he laboured, by the terms, *the arrows* and *the hand*, or the chastisement *of God*. Had he not been persuaded that it was God who thus afflicted him, he could never have been brought to seek from him deliverance from his affliction. We know that the great majority of men are blinded under the judgments of God, and imagine that they are entirely the events of chance; and scarcely one in a hundred discerns in them the hand of God. But, in his sickness, as in all his other adversities, David views the hand of God lifted up to punish him for his sins. And certainly, the man who estimates his affliction only by the feeling of pain which it produces, and views it in no other light, differs nothing from the beasts of the field. As every chastisement of God should remind us of his judgment, the true wisdom of the saints, as the prophet declares, Isaiah ix. 13, is, "to look to the hand of him who smiteth." The pronoun *thy* is therefore emphatic. David's words are, as if he had said, I have not to do with a mortal man, who can shoot his arrows with a force only in proportion to his own strength, but I have to do with God, who can discharge the arrows that come from his hand with a force altogether overwhelming.

3. *There is no soundness in my flesh because of thy anger.* Others translate, *There is no beauty;* but this does not seem

to be so suitable. In the clause which follows, David ascribes to God the praise of righteousness, without which, the acknowledgment which he formerly made would be of little avail; nay, instead of this, such an acknowledgment sometimes rather exasperates the minds of men, so that they provoke the wrath of God still more, by charging him with cruelty, and pouring forth horrible blasphemies against him. Nothing, therefore, can be more preposterous, than to imagine that there is in God a power so supreme and absolute, (as it is termed,) as to deprive him of his righteousness. David, as soon as he recognised his affliction as coming from God, turns to his own sin as the cause of the Divine displeasure; for he had already been fully satisfied in his own mind, that he is not like a tyrant who exercises cruelty needlessly and at random, but a righteous judge, who never manifests his displeasure by inflicting judgments but when he is grievously offended. If, then, we would render to God the praise which is due to him, let us learn by the example of David to connect our sins with his wrath.

4. *For my iniquities have passed over my head.* Here he complains that he is overwhelmed by his sins as by a heavy burden, so that he utterly faints under their weight; and yet he again confirms the doctrine which we have already stated, that he deservedly suffered the wrath of God, which had been inflicted on him in a manner so severe and dreadful. The word עון, *avon*, which we have translated *iniquities*, no doubt often signifies *punishment*, but this is only in a secondary and metaphorical sense. I am also willing to admit, that David assigns to the effect what is proper to the cause, when he describes by the appellation *iniquities*, the punishment which he had procured by his own sin; and yet his object at the same time is plainly and distinctly to confess, that all the afflictions which he suffered were to be imputed to his sins. He quarrels not with God for the extreme severity of his punishment, as Cain did, who said, " My punishment is greater than I can bear," (Gen. iv. 13.) It is true, indeed, that Moses uses the same word עון, *avon*, in that passage, so

that there is some similarity between the language of David
and Cain. But David's meaning is very different. When
such temptations as these were insinuating themselves into his
mind, Could God afflict thee more severely than he does?
certainly, since he is doing nothing to relieve thee, it is a
sure sign that he wishes thee destroyed and brought to
nought; he not only despises thy sighs and groanings, but
the more he seeth thee cast down and forsaken, he pursueth
thee the more fiercely and with the greater rigour;—to preclude the entrance of such evil thoughts and surmisings, he
defended himself as with a shield by this consideration, that
he was afflicted by the just judgment of God. He has here
attributed to his own sins as the cause the weight of the
wrath of God which he felt; and, as we shall find in the
following verse, he again acknowledges, that what he is now
suffering was procured by his own foolishness. Although,
then, in bewailing his own miseries, he may seem in some
measure to quarrel with God, yet he still cherishes the
humble conviction, (for God afflicteth not beyond measure,)
that there is no rest for him but in imploring the Divine
compassion and forgiveness; whereas the ungodly, although
convicted by their own consciences of guilt, murmur against
God, like the wild beasts, which, in their rage, gnaw the
chains with which they are bound.

5. *My wounds*[1] *have become putrid.* In this verse, he pleads
the long continuance of his disease as an argument for obtaining some alleviation. When the Lord declares in Isaiah xl.
2, concerning his Church, "that her warfare is accomplished,
that her iniquity is pardoned, for she hath received of the
Lord's hand double for all her sins," his meaning is, that
when he has sufficiently chastised his people, he is quickly
pacified towards them; nay, more, that if he continue to
manifest his displeasure for too long a time, he becomes
through his mercy, as it were, weary of it, so that he hastens

---

[1] "The proper meaning of חבר is not a wound, but a bruise or wale made by a severe blow. My wales through my severe chastisement are become putrid and running sores."—*Fry.*

to give deliverance, as he says in another place, (Isa. xlviii. 9, 10,) "For my name's sake will I defer mine anger, and for my praise will I refrain for thee, that I cut thee not off. Behold, I have refined thee, but not with silver; I have chosen thee in the furnace of affliction." The object, therefore, which David has in view, in complaining of the long continuance of his misery is, that when he had endured the punishment which he had merited, he might at length obtain deliverance. It was certainly no slight trial to this servant of God to be thus kept in continual languishing, and, as it were, to putrify and be dissolved into corruption in his miseries. In this his constancy is the more to be admired, for it neither broke down from the long period of delay, nor failed under the immense load of suffering. By using the term *foolishness* instead of *sin*, he does not seek in this way to extenuate his faults, as hypocrites do when they are unable to escape the charge of guilt; for in order to excuse themselves in part, they allege the false pretence of ignorance, pleading, and wishing it to be believed, that they erred through imprudence and inadvertence. But, according to a common mode of expression in the Hebrew language, by the use of the term *foolishness*, he acknowledges that he had been out of his right mind, when he obeyed the lusts of the flesh in opposition to God. The Spirit, by employing this term in so many places to designate crimes the most atrocious, does not certainly mean to extenuate the criminality of men, as if they were guilty merely of some slight offences, but rather charges them with maniacal fury, because, blinded by unhallowed desires, they wilfully fly in the face of their Maker. Accordingly, sin is always conjoined with folly or madness. It is in this sense that David speaks of his own foolishness; as if he had said, that he was void of reason and transported with madness, like the infatuated rage of wild beasts, when he neglected God and followed his own lusts.

6. *I am bent, I am bowed down beyond measure : I go mourning*
   [literally *black*] *all the day long.*
7. *For my reins are filled with burning,* [or, *inflammation:*[1]] *and there is no soundness in my flesh.*
8. *I am very feeble and sore broken: I have roared because of the roaring of my heart.*
9. *O Lord !*[2] *thou knowest all my desire, and my groaning is not hid from thee.*
10. *My heart hath turned round, my strength hath failed me : and as for the light of my eyes, it also is gone from me.*

6. *I am bent.* This description clearly shows that this holy man was oppressed with extreme grief, so much so, that it is marvellous how, under such a vast accumulation of miseries, his faith was sufficiently strong to bear up his mind. When he says *bowed down,* he seems tacitly to contrast his humility and dejection with the pride and stubbornness of many, who refuse to be humbled by the many chastisements with which God afflicts them, but rather harden themselves, daring to resist and oppose him. They must, no doubt, of necessity, feel the pain of their afflictions, but they fall into such a state of insensibility, that they are not affected by it. David then, from this circumstance, draws an argument to induce his heavenly Judge to have compassion on him, showing that he was not one of those who obstinately rebel against him, and refuse to bow in humble submission, even while the hand of God is upon them ; but that he is abased and humbled, even as the Apostle Peter (1 Ep. v. 6) exhorts all the godly to " humble themselves under the mighty hand of God." Let us therefore learn, that there is no other way by which we can obtain consolation under our afflictions, than by laying aside all stubbornness and pride, and humbly submitting to the chastisement of God. The word קודר, *koder,* which I have translated *black,* is rendered by others *clad in black,*[3] and explained as referring to the outward apparel,

---

[1] Berlin reads, " æstu torrente ;" Horsley, " with a parching heat ;" and this is the view taken by Hare, Dathe, Gesenius, and the Chaldee.
[2] Dominus. In the Hebrew Bible it is אדני, *Adonai ;* but several MSS. read יהוה, *Yehovah.*
[3] " קדר is literally 'dressed in mourning ;' hence it may, by an easy figure, denote the melancholy looks of a mourner."—*Horsley.* This is the sense

the black colour of which has always been a token of grief. But the opinion of those who understand it of the blackness of the skin is more correct; for we know that grief renders men's countenances lean, wan, and black. David, therefore, by this token of grief, describes the greatness of his affliction, because the natural colour of his face had faded, and he was like a corpse, already withered and shrunk.

In the next verse, the word כסלים, *kesalaim*, which I have rendered *reins*, is by some translated *the flanks*. But the more generally received opinion is, that it denotes the part under the reins, which extends towards the haunch, or the space between the thighs and flanks, where it is supposed there had been a sore. Commentators also differ in their opinion respecting the word נקלה, *nikleh*, which I have rendered *burning*. In my translation I have followed those who adhere to the original meaning of the word; for the verb קלה, *kalah*, signifies *to burn*, or *to consume with fire*. Others, indeed, explain it not improperly in the sense of *filthiness and corruption*. I am, however, not inclined to limit it to a sore. In my opinion, the sense simply is, that his reins, or flanks, or thighs, were filled with an inflammatory disease, or at least were covered over with putrid sores; for these parts of the body are most subject to inflammation, and most liable to contract putrid humours. Some expound it allegorically, as meaning, that David seemed loathsome in his own eyes, when he thought of his reproach; but this appears too forced. When he adds that he was *weakened* and *sore broken*, he still farther confirms what he had said in the preceding verses: for by these various terms he wished to express the intolerable vehemence of his grief. Now, as a man, who is distinguished by courage, does not cry out and complain, and as we know that David did not shrink in bearing his afflictions, we may gather from this, that his sufferings were severe and painful in the extreme, inasmuch as he not only wept bitterly, but was also forced to cry out and complain. The noun נהמת, *nahamath*, which I have rendered *roaring*, may be derived from another verb than that which David has

---

put upon the expression by the Septuagint, "Ὅλην τὴν ἡμέραν σκυθρωπάζων ἐπορευόμην;"—" I went with a mourning countenance all the day."

here used; but the meaning is obvious, namely, that the incontrollable emotions of his heart forced him to cry out.

9. *O Lord! thou knowest all my desire.* He adds this, not so much in respect of God, as to strengthen himself in the hope of obtaining some alleviation of his trouble, and thus to animate himself to persevering prayer. It may be explained in a twofold sense, either as denoting his confident assurance that his prayers and groanings were heard by the Lord, or a simple declaration that he had poured out before God all his cares and troubles; but the meaning is substantially the same: for as long as men entertain any doubt whether their groanings have come up before God, they are kept in constant disquietude and dread, which so fetters and holds captive their minds, that they cannot elevate their souls to God. On the contrary, a firm persuasion that our groanings do not vanish away in their ascent to God, but that he graciously hears them, and familiarly listens to them, produces promptitude and alacrity in engaging in prayer. It might, therefore, prove no small ground of encouragement to David, that he approached God, not with a doubting and trembling heart, but strengthened and encouraged by the assurance of which we have spoken, and of which he himself speaks in another place, that his tears were laid up in God's bottle, (Ps. lvi. 8.) In order that we may obtain access to God, we must believe that he is "a rewarder of them that diligently seek him," as the apostle states in his Epistle to the Hebrews, (chap. xi. 6.) But I rather approve of the other interpretation, That David here declares that he had disburdened all his sorrows into the bosom of God. The reason why the greater part of men derive no profit from complaining grievously in their sorrow is, that they direct not their prayers and sighs to God. David, then, in order to encourage himself in the assured conviction that God will be his deliverer, says, that he had always been a witness of his sorrows, and was well acquainted with them, because he had neither indulged in a fretful spirit, nor poured out into the air his complaints and howlings as the unbelieving are wont to do, but had spread out before God himself all the desires of his heart.

10. *My heart hath turned round.* The verb which David here uses signifies *to travel* or *wander hither and thither;* but here it is taken for the agitation or disquietude which distress of heart engenders when we know not what to do. According as men are disquieted in mind, so do they turn themselves on all sides, and so their heart may be said to turn round, or to run to and fro. But since faith, when it has once brought us into obedience to God, holds our minds fixed on his word, it might here be asked by way of objection, How it is that the heart of David was so affected by disquietude and trouble? To this I answer, That although he continued to walk in the ways of God, while he was sustained by the promises of God, yet he was not altogether exempted from human infirmity. And, indeed, it will always happen, that as soon as we fall into some danger, our flesh will suggest to us various shifts and devices, and lead us into many errors in search of counsel; so that even the most confident would fail and go astray, unless he laid upon himself the same restraint by which David was preserved and kept in subjection, namely, by keeping all his thoughts shut up within the limits of God's word. Nay, even in the prayers which we offer up when our minds are at ease, we experience too well how easily our minds are carried away, and wander after vain and frivolous thoughts, and how difficult it is to keep them uninterruptedly attentive and fixed with the same degree of intensity upon the object of our desire. If this happen when we are not exercised by any severe trial, what will be the case when we are agitated by violent storms and tempests which threaten a thousand deaths, and when there is no way to escape them? It is, therefore, no great wonder if they carried away the heart of David, so that it was subject to various emotions amidst such tempestuous agitations. He adds, that *his strength had failed him,* as if he had compared himself to a dead man. What he adds concerning *the light of his eyes* some understand as if he had said, that he was so much oppressed with despair on all sides, that no counsel or foresight was left to him. The more simple meaning, however, is, that the light of life was taken away from him, because in it the energy of the soul principally shows itself.

11. *My friends and my companions stand away from my sore;
and my kinsfolk stand afar off.*
12. *They also that sought for my life have laid snares for me;
and they that sought after my hurt have talked of treachery, and imagine deceit daily.*
13. *But I, as a deaf man, hear not; and am as a dumb man
that openeth not his mouth.*
14. *And I was as a man that heareth not, and in whose mouth
are no reproofs.*

11. *My friends and my companions stand away from my sore.* Here David enumerates other circumstances to show the aggravated character of his misery, that he might excite the compassion of God. One of these is, that he finds no help or solace among men. In saying that his *friends stand away from him,* he means, that they cease from performing any of the offices of humanity towards him. This might happen either from pride or fear. If they withdrew from this poor afflicted man because they despised him, they were cruel and proud; and if they refused him their assistance for fear of being brought into odium, it was most unpardonable cowardice. But in the meantime, it augmented not a little the calamity of David, that even his friends and kinsfolk dared not to show any token of compassion towards him. It is, indeed, a very sore trial, when a man, who has had a great number of friends, comes to be abandoned by them all.

12. *They also that sought for my life have laid snares for me, &c.* Here another circumstance is added, that the enemies of David laid snares for him, and talked about his destruction, and framed deceits among themselves.[1] The purport of what is stated is, that while his friends cowardly sit still and will do nothing to aid him, his enemies vigorously bestir themselves, and seek by every means to destroy him. He says that *they seek his life,* for as they were his deadly enemies and blood-thirsty men, they were not content with doing him some common injury, but furiously sought his destruction. He, however, here complains not so much that they assailed

---

[1] " Et machiné des finesses pour le surprendre."—*Fr.* "And devised stratagems for ensnaring him."

him by force of arms and with violence, as he accuses them of guileful conspiracy, which he designates in the first place metaphorically by the term *snares*, and afterwards adds in plain terms, that they *talk about his destruction*, and secretly consult among themselves how they might do him hurt. Now, as it is certain that David borrows not an artificial rhetoric from the bar, (as profane orators[1] do when they plead their cause,) in order to win the favour of God, but rather draws his arguments from the Word of God, the sentences which he here brings together for the confirmation of his faith we ought to appropriate to our own use. If we are altogether destitute of human aid and assistance, if our friends fail us in the time of need, and if others seek our ruin, and breathe out nothing but destruction against us, let us remember that it is not in vain for us to lay these things in prayer before God, whose province it is to succour those who are in misery, to take under his protection those who are perfidiously forsaken and betrayed, to restrain the wicked, and not only to withstand their violence, but also to anticipate their deceitful counsels and to frustrate their designs.

13. *But I, as a deaf man, hear not, &c.* The inspired writer here compares himself to a dumb and deaf man, for two reasons. In the first place, he intimates that he was so overwhelmed with the false and wicked judgments of his enemies, that he was not even permitted to open his mouth in his own defence. In the second place, he alleges before God his own patience, as a plea to induce God the more readily to have pity upon him; for such meekness and gentleness, not only with good reason, secures favour to the afflicted and the innocent, but it is also a sign of true piety. Those who depend upon the world, and have respect only to men, if they cannot avenge the injuries that are done them, plainly show by their loud complaints the burning rage and fury of their hearts. In order, therefore, that a man may quietly and patiently endure the insolence, violence, calumny, and deceit of his enemies, it is necessary that he trust in God. The man who is fully persuaded in his own heart

---

[1] " Comme celles des orateurs profanes."—*Fr.*

that God is his defender, will cherish his hope in silence, and, calling upon him for help, will lay a restraint upon his own passions. Accordingly, Paul, in Rom. xii. 19, very properly says, that we "give place unto wrath" when, oppressed before the world, we nevertheless still repose on God. On the other hand, whoever gives loose reins to his passions, takes away as much as he can from God, to whom alone it belongs, the right of taking vengeance, and deprives himself of his assistance. It is indeed certain, that if David had obtained a hearing, he would have been ready to defend his own innocence; but perceiving that it availed him nothing, nay, that he was shut out and debarred from all defence of his cause, he humbly submitted, waiting patiently for the heavenly Judge. He therefore says that he held his peace, as if he had already been convicted and struck dumb. And it is indeed very difficult, when we are conscious of our own innocence, patiently and silently to bear an unjust condemnation, as if all argument had failed us, and we had no excuse or reply left us.

15. *For on thee, O Jehovah! do I wait: thou wilt answer me, O Lord!*[1] *my God.*
16. *For I said, lest they rejoice over me: when my foot slippeth, they magnify themselves against me.*
17. *Surely I am ready to halt, and my sorrow is continually before me.*
18. *Surely I declare my iniquity; and I am dismayed because of my sin.*
19. *And yet my enemies living are become strong; and they that oppose me wrongfully are become mighty.*
20. *And they that render me evil for good are opposed to me; because I follow that which is good.*

15. *For on thee, O Jehovah! do I wait.* David here shows the source of his patience. It consisted in this, that, trusting

---

[1] Dominus. Heb. אדני, *Adonai*. But instead of אדני, *Adonai*, one hundred and two of Kennicott's and De Rossi's MSS. read יהוה, *Yehovah*, which may be presumed to be the true reading. As the Jews, from the sacredness which they attach to the name *Jehovah*, never pronounce it, and when it occurs in reading the Scriptures, pronounce אדני, *Adonai*, it may readily be supposed that Jewish scribes, in writing out copies of the Scriptures, from their constantly reading *Adonai* for *Jehovah*, would be very apt to fall into the mistake of writing the former word for the latter.

in the grace of God, he overcame all the temptations of the world. And certainly, the mind of man will never be framed to gentleness and meekness, nor will he be able to subdue his passions, until he has learned never to give up hope. The Psalmist, at the same time, adds, that he cherished his hope by constant meditation, lest he should yield to despair. And this is the only means of our perseverance, when, on the ground of his own promises, with which we are furnished, we appeal to him, yea, rather when setting before our view his fidelity and his constancy in fulfilling what he has promised, we are sureties to ourselves for him. Accordingly, Paul, in Rom. v. 4, very properly joins patience to hope and consolation. The repetition of terms in this verse shows, that this holy man was subjected to a severe and arduous conflict. *Thou,* he says, *O Lord! my God, wilt answer me.* His language implies, that if God should delay to come to his help, there was reason to fear that he would faint from weariness, or fall into despair, unless, setting this double defence before him, he persevered valiantly in the conflict.

16. *For I said, lest they rejoice over me.* Here he also confirms his faith and his earnestness in prayer from this consideration, that if he should be forsaken of God, his enemies would triumph. This indignity, on their part, is of no small weight in inducing God to help us; for the wicked, in thus magnifying themselves against us, and indulging in derision, not only make war with our flesh, but also directly assail our faith, and endeavour to destroy whatever there is of religion and the fear of God in our hearts. What is the object of all their mockery, but to persuade us that what God has promised is vain and worthless? The Psalmist immediately adds, that it is not without cause that he is struck with the fear that his enemies would rejoice over him, since he had already had experience of their proud boastings. We are taught from this passage, that in proportion as our enemies increase in insolence and cruelty towards us, or, seeing us already overwhelmed by a heavy load of adversities, in their proud disdain trample us under their feet, we ought to cherish the greater hope that God will come to our help.

17. *Surely I am ready to halt.* This verse has led expositors to suppose that David was afflicted with some sore, from which he was afraid of having brought upon him the infirmity of halting all his days; but I have already shown, in Psalm xxxv. 15, that this supposition is very improbable. We have certainly no greater reason for supposing that David was lame than that Jeremiah was so, when he said, (chap. xx. 10,) "All my familiars watched for my halting." I therefore think that David here employs a metaphorical mode of expression, and that his meaning is, that if God did not soon come to his aid, there was no hope of his ever being restored to his former condition; and that he was so greatly afflicted, that he would walk as if he had been maimed or lame all the days of his life.[1] It next follows by way of exposition, that *his sorrow was continually before him.* The sense is, that he was so grievously afflicted, that he could not forget it for a single moment, so as to obtain some relaxation. In both the clauses of the verse, David confesses that his disease is incurable, unless he obtain some remedy from God, and that he cannot endure it, unless he be raised up and sustained by the hand of God himself. This is the reason why he directs all his thoughts and his requests to God alone; for as soon as he shall turn aside from him, he sees nothing but immediate ruin.

18 and 19. *Surely I declare my iniquity.* By comparison, he amplifies what he had just said concerning the pride and the reproachful conduct of his enemies; for he says, that whilst he is lying in a filthy and wretched condition, like a wicked man, and one abandoned by God, they fly about in mirth and gladness, nay, they carry their heads high, because they are rich and powerful. But first, it is proper to notice in what sense it is that *he declares his sin.* Those, in my judgment, are mistaken, who understand this passage simply in the sense of a confession of his guilt before God, that he might obtain forgiveness. According to their interpretation,

---

[1] "Et que son affliction est telle, qu'il ne sera jour de sa vie qu'il ne s'en sente."—*Fr.* "And that his affliction was such, that there would not be a day of his life but he would feel it."

the Psalmist is supposed to repeat here what we have seen he said in Psalm xxxii. 5, " I acknowledged my sin unto thee, and mine iniquity have I not hid." But in this place he is not speaking so much of his repentance, as he is bewailing his sad and miserable condition; and, therefore, *sin* and *iniquity* are to be understood of the afflictions and chastisements which are the tokens of God's wrath; as if he had said, that the hand of God was against him, and lying so heavily upon him, that from the very sight of the misery to which he was reduced, the world in general might regard him as a condemned and reprobate man. In order to render the meaning more obvious, the 18th and 19th verses must be read together, thus: *I declare my iniquity, and my enemies are living; I am dismayed because of my sin, but they are become strong.* I do not, however, deny that he regards the miseries to which he was subjected as proceeding from his sins. In this respect, the godly differ from the wicked, that, being admonished of their transgression by adversity, they humbly sist themselves before the judgment-seat of God. Accordingly, judging of the cause from the effects, he takes into account these two things: First, That thus overwhelmed and afflicted, he is lying under a heavy load of miseries; and, secondly, That all these evils are justly inflicted as chastisements for sin.

This *living*[1] which he attributes to his enemies, implies as much as to enjoy continued and abundant prosperity in all things; and therefore he adds, that they *are become strong and increase in power.* I interpret the word רבב, *rabbab,* in this place, *increase in power,* because he would speak improperly were he to be understood as saying, *that they were multiplied.* He does not here complain that they increased

---

[1] Ainsworth reads, "*are alive,* or *living;*" " that is," says he, " lively, lusty, cheerful, hale, and sound, or rich, as the word seemeth to mean in Eccl. vi. 8." Dr Lowth, instead of חיים, *chayim, living,* proposes to read here, חנם, *chinam, without cause—without cause have strengthened themselves.* " I think," says he, " חנם, here for חיים, is a remarkable instance of a reading merely conjectural, unsupported by any authority but that of the context, of the truth of which, no possible doubt can be made. Hare and Houbigant, and I suppose every other competent reader, has hit upon it. You see the two hemistichs are parallel and synonymous, word answering to word."—*Dr Lowth in Mr Merrick's Note on this place.*—Street and Dr Adam Clarke agree in this alteration.

in number, but rather exalts their greatness, because the more they acquired of riches, they acquired so much the greater audacity in oppressing the good and the simple. He tells us that he is *assailed by them wrongfully,* and without cause, that he may induce God to be the more favourable and propitious to him. And surely, if we would have the favour of God for our defence, we must always take care not to injure any man, and to do nothing to provoke the hatred of any against us.

This is more fully confirmed in the following verse, in which he declares that they requited him evil for the good which he had done them. More than this, however, is implied in the language of David. It implies that he not only abstained from all hurtful dealing towards his enemies, but that he had done them all the good which was in his power; and on this account the rage of the wicked is the less excusable, which not only moves them to do harm to others without cause, but which likewise cannot be appeased by any marks of kindness exercised towards them. It is indeed true, that there is nothing which wounds those of an ingenuous disposition of mind more than when wicked and ungodly men recompense them in a manner so dishonourable and unjust; but when they reflect upon this consolatory consideration, that God is no less offended with such ingratitude than those to whom the injury is done, they have no reason to be troubled beyond measure. To mitigate their sorrow, let this doctrine be the subject of their frequent meditation, That whenever the wicked, to whom we have endeavoured to do good, shall requite us evil for good, God will certainly be their judge. In the last place, it is added, as the highest degree of their desperate wickedness, that they hated David because he studied to practise uprightness: *They are opposed to me, because I follow that which is good.* It must be admitted, that those are froward and wicked in the extreme, nay, even of a devilish disposition, who hold uprightness in such abhorrence that they deliberately make war upon those who follow after it. It is, indeed, a very sore temptation, that the people of God, the more sincerely they endeavour to serve him, should procure to themselves so much the more trouble and sorrow;

but this consideration ought to prove a sufficient ground of consolation to them, that they are not only supported by the testimony of a good conscience, but that they also know that God is ever ready, and that, too, for this very reason, to manifest his mercy towards them. On the ground of this assurance, they dare to appear in the presence of God, and entreat him, as it is his cause as well as theirs, that he would maintain and defend it. There can be no doubt that David, by his own example, has prescribed this as a common rule to all the faithful, rather to incur the hatred and ill-will of the world, than in the least degree to swerve from the path of duty, and without any hesitation to regard those as their enemies whom they know to be opposed to that which is just and righteous.

21. *Forsake me not, O Jehovah! my God, and be not far from me.*
22. *Make haste to come to my aid, O Lord!*[1] *my salvation.*[2]

In these concluding verses, David briefly states the chief point which he desired, and the sum of his whole prayer; namely, that whereas he was forsaken of men, and grievously afflicted in every way, God would receive him and raise him up again. He uses three forms of expression; first, that *God would not forsake him*, or cease to take care of him; secondly, that *he would not be far from him;* and, thirdly, that *he would make haste to help him.* David was, indeed, persuaded that God is always near to his servants, and that he delays not a single moment longer than is necessary. But, as we have seen in another place, it is not at all wonderful that the saints, when they unburden themselves of their cares and sorrows into the bosom of God, should make their requests in language according to the feeling of the flesh. They are not ashamed to confess their infirmity, nor is it proper to conceal the doubts which arise in their minds. Although, however, waiting was wearisome to David according to the flesh, yet in one word he plainly shows that he did not pray

[1] Dominus. Heb. אדני, Adonai.
[2] "Ou, de mon salut."—*Fr. marg.* "Or, of my salvation."

in uncertainty when he calls God *his salvation,* or the author of his salvation. Some render it *to my salvation,* but this is forced. David rather sets up this as a wall of defence against all the devices by which, as we have seen, his faith was assailed, That whatever might happen, he was, nevertheless, well assured of his salvation in God.

PSALM XXXIX.

In the beginning of the psalm, David intimates that his heart had been seized with extreme bitterness of grief, which forced him to give utterance to complaints with too much vehemence and ardour. He confesses that whilst he was disposed to be silent, and to exercise patience, he was nevertheless compelled, by the vehemence of his sorrow, to break out into an excess which he by no means intended. Then he relates the complaints which he had made mingled with prayers, which indicate great trouble of mind; so that from this it appears that he had wrestled with no ordinary effort in resisting temptation, lest he should fall into despair.

¶ To the chief musician, Jeduthun. A Psalm of David.

It is well known that Jeduthun was one of the chief singers of whom sacred history makes mention.[1] It is, therefore, probable that this psalm was delivered to the chief singer, who was of his household. Some, indeed, understand it as denoting the particular kind of tune, and suppose that it was the beginning of some other song; but this I consider too forced an interpretation. Nor can I agree with others who suppose that David here complains of some disease; for unless some urgent reason require it, it is improper to limit general statements to particular cases. On the contrary, from the extreme character of the sufferings which he here describes, it may be presumed that a variety of afflictions is here included, or, at least, that some one is referred to which was more severe than all the others, and one which had continued for a long time. Besides, it ought to be considered that in this psalm David is not proclaiming his own merit, as if in his affliction he had presented his

[1] See 1 Chron. ix. 16; xvi. 38, 41, 42.

prayers to God in the language, and according to the spirit dictated by true piety: he rather confesses the sin of his infirmity in bursting forth into immoderate sorrow, and in being led by the vehemence of this affection to indulge in sinful complaints.

1. *I said, I will take heed to my ways, that I sin not with my tongue : I will keep my mouth with a muzzle, while the wicked standeth before me.*
2. *I was dumb in silence ; I held my peace from good ; and my sorrow was stirred.*
3. *My heart became hot within me ; in my musing a fire burned : I spake with my tongue.*

1. *I said, I will take heed to my ways.* David explains and illustrates the greatness of his grief by this circumstance, that, contrary to his inclination and resolution, he broke forth into the severest complaints. The meaning substantially is, that although he had subdued his heart to patience, and resolved to keep silence, yet the violence of his grief was such that it forced him to break his resolution, and extorted from him, if we might so speak, expressions which indicate that he had given way to an undue degree of sorrow. The expression, *I said,* it is well known, does not always mean what is expressed in words, but is often used to denote the purpose of the heart, and, therefore, the words *in heart* are sometimes added. David, therefore, means not that he boasted of his fortitude and constancy, and made a display of them before men, but that before God he was, by continued meditation, well fortified and prepared to endure patiently the temptations by which he was now assailed. We ought to mark particularly the carefulness by which he was distinguished. It was not without cause that he was so much intent on exercising watchfulness over himself. He did so because he was conscious of his own weakness, and also well knew the manifold devices of Satan. He, therefore, looked on the right hand and on the left, and kept watch on all sides, lest temptation stealing upon him unawares from any quarter might reach even to his heart. Access to it, then, had been impossible, since it was shut up on every side, if the extreme severity of his grief had not overpowered him,

and broken his resolution. When he says, *I will keep my mouth with a muzzle*,[1] *that I sin not with my tongue*, it is not to be understood as if he could with difficulty restrain and conceal his grief, (for it is mere pretence for a man to show by the countenance and speech the appearance of meekness when the heart still swells with pride;) but as there is nothing more slippery or loose than the tongue, David declares that he had endeavoured so carefully to bridle his affections, that not so much as one word should escape from his lips which might betray the least impatience. And that man must indeed be endued with singular fortitude who unfeignedly and deliberately restrains his tongue, which is so liable to fall into error. As to what follows, *while the wicked standeth before me*, it is generally understood, as if David had concealed his grief, lest he should give occasion of blasphemy to the wicked, who, as soon as they see the children of God fail under the weight of their afflictions, insolently break forth into derision against them, which amounts to a contempt of God himself. But it appears to me that by the term *standeth*, David meant to express something more,—that even while he saw the wicked bearing rule, exercising authority, and exalted to honour, he resolved not to speak a single word, but to bear patiently the poverty and indignity which otherwise grieve and torment not a little even good men. Accordingly, he says not merely that when he was in the presence of the wicked he restrained himself, lest he should be subjected to their scorn, but that even while the worst of men prospered,[2] and, proud of their high rank, despised others, he was fully determined in his own mind not to be troubled at it. By this he very plainly shows that he was so beset with wicked men, ever ready for mischief, that he could not freely heave a sigh which was not made the subject of

---

[1] The Hebrew word מחסום, *machsom*, rendered *bridle* in our English version, properly signifies a *muzzle*, and is so rendered in Deut. xxv. 4. "Our translations," observes Mant, "say 'as with a bridle.' But we do not see how a bridle would preclude the person from speaking; nor is it a correct phrase, which the word muzzle is." It is probable that the bridles of the ancients were made in the form of muzzles.

[2] Dr Geddes renders the last clause of the verse, "While the wicked prosper before me."

ridicule and scorn. Since, then, it was so hard a task for David to restrain his tongue, lest he should sin by giving way to complaints, let us learn from his example, whenever troubles molest us, to strive earnestly to moderate our affections, that no impious expression of dissatisfaction against God may slip from us.

2. *I was dumb in silence.* He now declares that this resolution of which he has spoken had not been a mere passing and momentary thought, but that he had shown by his conduct that it was indeed a resolution deeply fixed in his heart. He says, then, that he held his peace for a time, just as if he had been deaf, which was a singular manifestation of his patience. When he thus determined to be silent, it was not such a resolution as persons of a changeable disposition, who scarcely ever know their own mind, and who can with difficulty be brought to carry their desires into effect, often make: he had long and stedfastly inured himself to the exercise of patience; and this he had done, not only by keeping silence, but by making himself utterly dumb, as if he had been deprived of the power of speech. The expression *from good* is expounded by some in the sense that he not only refrained from uttering sinful and unadvised words, but also that he abstained from speaking on any subject whatever. Others think that he held his peace from good, either because, being overwhelmed with miseries and afflictions, he found no relief to whatever side he turned, or else, because, by reason of the greatness of his sorrow, he was unable to sing the praises of God. But in my opinion the natural sense is, that although he was able adequately to defend himself, and it could not be shown that he wanted just and proper grounds of complaint, yet he refrained from speaking of his own mere will.[1] He might have encountered

---

[1] French and Skinner read, "I held my peace from good and bad." In the Hebrew it is simply "from good;" but they observe, "This expression occurs frequently in Scripture, and it would seem, that owing to the constant use of it, one part only of the sentence has been here expressed. Thus, 'Take heed that thou speak not to Jacob *either good or bad*,' (Gen. xxxi. 24.) Again, 'Absalom spake *neither good nor bad*,' (2 Sam. xiii. 22.")

the ungodly with a good defence of his own innocence, but he rather preferred to forego the prosecution of his righteous cause than indulge in any intemperate sorrow. He adds in the last clause of the verse, that although he thus restrained himself for a time, yet at length the violence of his grief broke through all the barriers which he had set to his tongue. If David, who was so valiant a champion, failed in the midst of his course, how much greater reason have we to be afraid lest we fall in like manner? He says that *his sorrow was stirred*, because, as we shall soon see, the ardour of his affections was inflamed so as to become tumultuous. Some render the phrase in this sense, that *his sorrow was corrupted*, as if his meaning were, that it became worse; just as we know that a wound becomes worse when it happens to putrify or fester: but this sense is forced.

3. *My heart became hot within me.* He now illustrates the greatness of his grief by the introduction of a simile, telling us that his sorrow, being internally suppressed, became so much the more inflamed, until the ardent passion of his soul continued to increase in strength. From this we may learn the very profitable lesson, that the more strenuously any one sets himself to obey God, and employs all his endeavours to attain the exercise of patience, the more vigorously is he assailed by temptation: for Satan, whilst he is not so troublesome to the indifferent and careless, and seldom looks near them, displays all his forces in hostile array against that individual. If, therefore, at any time we feel ardent emotions struggling and raising a commotion in our breasts, we should call to remembrance this conflict of David, that our courage may not fail us, or at least that our infirmity may not drive us headlong to despair. The dry and hot exhalations which the sun causes to arise in summer, if nothing occurred in the atmosphere to obstruct their progress, would ascend into the air without commotion; but when intervening clouds prevent their free ascent, a conflict arises, from which the thunders are produced. It is similar with respect to the godly who desire to lift up their hearts to God. If they would resign themselves to the vain imaginations which arise in their

minds, they might enjoy a sort of unrestrained liberty to indulge in every fancy; but because they endeavour to resist their influence, and seek to devote themselves to God, obstructions which arise from the opposition of the flesh begin to trouble them. Whenever, therefore, the flesh shall put forth its efforts, and shall kindle up a fire in our hearts, let us know that we are exercised with the same kind of temptation which occasioned so much pain and trouble to David. In the end of the verse he acknowledges that the severity of the affliction with which he was visited had at length overcome him, and that he allowed foolish and unadvised words to pass from his lips. In his own person he sets before us a mirror of human infirmity, that, being warned by the danger to which we are exposed, we may learn betimes to seek protection under the shadow of God's wings. When he says that *he spake with his tongue*, it is not a superfluous mode of expression, but a true and fuller confession of his sin, in that he had not only given way to sinful murmuring, but had even uttered loud complaints.

4. *O Jehovah! cause me to know my end, and the number of my days, that I may understand how long I may live.*[1]
5. *Behold, thou hast made my days as a hand-breadth, and mine age as if it were nothing before thee: truly every man, while he standeth, is wholly vanity. Selah.*
6. *Surely man walketh in a shadow; surely he disquieteth himself in vain: they heap together* [*riches,*[2]] *and know not who shall gather them.*

4. *O Jehovah! cause me to know my end.* It appears from this, that David was transported by an improper and sinful excess of passion, seeing he finds fault with God. This will appear still more clearly from the following verses. It is true, indeed, that in what follows he introduces pious and becoming prayers, but here he complains, that, being a mor-

---

[1] Or, as Horsley reads, "how brief I am."
[2] The word *riches* is a supplement; there being no word for it in Calvin's version, nor in the Hebrew text; but the meaning evidently is, "they heap up, accumulate, or amass riches." Horsley reads, "His accumulated riches—he knoweth not who shall gather them."

tal man, whose life is frail and transitory, he is not treated more mildly by God. Of this, and similar complaints, the discourses of Job are almost full. It is, therefore, not without anger and resentment that David speaks in this manner : " O God, since thou art acting with so much severity towards me, at least make me to know how long thou hast appointed me to live. But is it so, that my life is but a moment, why then dost thou act with so great rigour ? and why dost thou accumulate upon my head such a load of miseries, as if I had yet many ages to live ? What does it profit me to have been born, if I must pass the period of my existence, which is so brief, in misery, and oppressed with a continued succession of calamities ?"

Accordingly, this verse should be read in connection with the following one. *Behold, thou hast made my days as a hand-breadth.* A hand-breadth is the measure of four fingers, and is here taken for a very small measure; as if it had been said, the life of man flies swiftly away, and the end of it, as it were, touches the beginning. Hence the Psalmist concludes that all men are only *vanity* before God. As to the meaning of the words, he does not ask that the brevity of human life should be shown to him, as if he knew it not. There is in this language a kind of irony, as if he had said, Let us count the number of the years which still remain to me on earth, and will they be a sufficient recompense for the miseries which I endure ? Some render the word חדל, *chedel, mundane;* and others *temporal,* that is to say, that which endures only for a time. But the latter rendering is not appropriate in this place : for David does not as yet expressly declare the shortness of his life, but continues to speak on that subject ambiguously. If the word *mundane* is adopted, the sense will be, Show me whether thou wilt prolong my life to the end of the world. But in my judgment, the translation which I have followed is much more appropriate ; and, besides, there may have been a transposition of the letters ד, *daleth,* and ל, *lamed,* making the word *chedel* for *cheled.* It may, however, very properly be taken for an age or period of life.[1] When he says that *his age is, as it were, nothing*

---

[1] " Mine age, i. e., the whole extent of my life."—*Cresswell.*

before God, in order to excite God so much the more to pity and compassion, he appeals to him as a witness of his frailty, intimating, that it is not a thing unknown to him how transitory and passing the life of man is. The expression, *wholly* or *altogether vanity*,[1] implies that among the whole human race there is nothing but vanity. He declares this of men, even whilst *they are standing;*[2] that is to say, when, being in the prime and vigour of life, they wish to be held in estimation, and seem to themselves to be men possessed of considerable influence and power. It was the pangs of sorrow which forced David to give utterance to these complaints; but it is to be observed, that it is chiefly when men are sore oppressed by adversity that they are made to feel their nothingness in the sight of God. Prosperity so intoxicates them, that, forgetful of their condition, and sunk in insensibility, they dream of an immortal state on earth. It is very profitable for us to know our own frailty, but we must beware lest, on account of it, we fall into such a state of sorrow as may lead us to murmur and repine. David speaks truly and wisely in declaring, that man, even when he seems to have risen to the highest state of greatness, is only like the bubble which rises upon the water, blown up by the wind; but he is in fault when he takes occasion from this to complain of God. Let us, therefore, so feel the misery of our present condition, as that, however cast down and afflicted, we may, as humble suppliants, lift up our eyes to God, and implore his mercy. This

---

[1] The word הבל. *hebel*, rendered *vanity*, according to some, means *the mirage*, that deceptive appearance of a collection of waters in the distance, which the traveller, through the Arabian deserts, imagines he sees before him, and from which he fondly hopes to quench his thirst; but which, upon his coming up to it, he finds to be only burning sands, to which the reflection of the light of the sun had given the appearance of a lake of water. According to others, vanity means *a vapour*, as the breath of one's mouth, which speedily vanishes; to which the apostle refers in James iv. 14. " I take the word in its proper sense," [vapour,] says Bishop Mant, " as more poetical and energetic than the derivative one of 'vanity.'" See Simonis and Parkhurst on הבל. Abel gave to his second son the name of *Hebel*, *vanity*, and here David declares that כל-אדם, *col-adam*, all adam, every man is *hebel*, vanity.

[2] This word here rendered *standeth* " is well paraphrased by Dathe, ' Dum firmissime constitutus videatur.'"—*Rogers' Psalms in Heb.*, vol. ii. p. 200.

we find David does a little after, having corrected himself; for he does not continue to indulge in rash and inconsiderate lamentations, but lifting up his soul in the exercise of faith, he attains heavenly consolation.

6. *Surely man walketh in a shadow.*[1] He still prosecutes the same subject. By the word *shadow*, he means, that there is nothing substantial in man, but that he is only, as we say, a vain show, and has I know not how much of display and ostentation.[2] Some translate the word *darkness*, and understand the Psalmist's language in this sense, That the life of man vanishes away before it can be known. But in these words David simply declares of every man individually what Paul extends to the whole world, when he says, 1 Cor. vii. 31, " The fashion of this world passeth away." Thus he denies that there is any thing abiding in men, because the appearance of strength which displays itself in them for a time soon passes away. What he adds, that men *disquiet themselves in vain*, shows the very height of their vanity; as if he had said, It seems as if men were born for the very purpose of rendering themselves more and more contemptible: for although they are only as a shadow, yet as if they were fools, or rather insane, they involve themselves needlessly in harassing cares, and vexing themselves to no purpose. He expresses still more plainly how they manifest their folly, when he declares that while they anxiously and carefully heap up riches, they never think that they must soon, and it may be suddenly, leave their present abode. And why is it that they thus fret away their mind and body,

---

[1] In the Hebrew it is literally, " Man walketh in an image;" a phantasm, that which seems to be something real and substantial, but which does not deserve that character, which is an appearance only. Life is a mere show; " the baseless fabric of a vision;" it has the semblance of solidity, but there is no reality in it. The word occurs again in Ps. lxxiii. 20, " Thou shalt despise their image;" their vain show, or phantastic prosperity. Walford reads, " walketh *as* a shadow;" observing, that " the prefix ב is often used for כ as a particle of similitude." He farther observes, that Dathe's translation, " he pursues a shadow," gives a good sense, but does not convey the exact notion of the figure that is conveyed by the Hebrew.

[2] " Et je ne scay quelle parade et ostentation."—*Fr.*

but only because they imagine that they can never have enough? for by their insatiable desire of gain, they eagerly grasp at all the riches of the world, as if they had to live a hundred times the life of man. Moreover, David does not in this passage hold up to scorn the covetousness of man in the same sense in which Solomon does, Eccles. v. 10; for he not only speaks of their heirs, but declares generally, that men disquiet and vex themselves with care, although they know not who shall reap the fruit of their labour in amassing riches.[1] They may indeed wish to make provision for themselves; but what madness and folly is it for them to torment themselves with incessant and unprofitable cares which have no certain object or limit? David here condemns those ardent and unbridled desires, under the influence of which worldly men are carried away, and talk in a strange manner, confounding heaven and earth; for they admit not that they are mortal, much less do they consider that their life is bounded by the narrow limits of a hand-breadth. David spoke under the influence of a distempered and troubled state of mind; but there is included in his language this very profitable lesson, that there is no remedy better fitted for enabling us to rise above all unnecessary cares, than the recollection that the brief period of our life is only, as it were, a hand-breadth.

[1] It is important to mark the difference between the Hebrew word צבר, *tsubar*, here rendered *to heap together*, and the word אסף, *asaph*, rendered *to gather*. "The former," says Hammond, "here appears to contain all the toil of the harvest, in reaping, binding, setting up, and heaping things together, bringing them from the several places where they grow, into a *cumulus*. The latter denotes the stowing or housing, laying it up, removing or carrying it out of the field, where it is heaped or set up, ready for carriage. For so אסף signifies sometimes *to lay up*, sometimes *to take away*. This, then, is the description of the vanity of our human estate, that when a man hath run through all the labours of acquisition, and hath nothing visible to interpose betwixt him and his enjoyments, yet even then he is uncertain, not only whether himself shall possess it at last, but whether his heir shall do it; nay, he knows not whether his enemy may not; he cannot tell 'who shall gather them into the barn,' or enjoy them when they are there."

7. *And now, O Lord!*[1] *what do I wait for? my hope is towards thee.*
8. *Deliver me from all my sins : do not make me the reproach of the foolish.*[2]
9. *I was dumb ; I will not open my mouth, because thou hast done it.*

7. *And now, O Lord! what do I wait for?* David, having acknowledged that his heart had been too much under the influence of ardent and impetuous emotion, from which he had experienced great disquietude, now returns to a calm and settled state of mind; and from this what I have before stated is rendered still more obvious, namely, that this psalm consists partly of appropriate prayers and partly of inconsiderate complaints. I have said that David here begins to pray aright. It is true, that even worldly men sometimes feel in the very same way in which David here acknowledges that he felt; but the knowledge of their own vanity does not lead them so far as to seek substantial support in God. On the contrary, they rather wilfully render themselves insensible, that they may indulge undisturbed in their own vanity. We may learn from this passage, that no man looks to God for the purpose of depending upon him, and resting his hope in him, until he is made to feel his own frailty, yea, and even brought to nought. There is tacitly great force in the adverb *now*, as if David had said, The flattery and vain imaginations by which the minds of men are held fast in the sleep of security no longer deceive me, but I am now fully sensible of my condition. But we must go beyond this elementary stage; for it is not enough, that, being aroused by a sense of our infirmity, we should seek with fear and trembling to know our duty, unless at the same time God manifest himself to us, on whom alone all our expectation should depend. Accordingly, as it serves no end for worldly men to be convinced of their utter vanity, because, although convinced of this, they never improve by it, let us learn to press forward and make

[1] In the original it is אדני ; but in some MSS. it is יהוה, which is probably the true reading.
[2] "Ou, vauneant et desbauché, ou, meschant."—*Fr. marg.* "Or, the idle and debauched, or, wicked."

still further progress, in order that, being as it were dead, we may be quickened by God, whose peculiar office it is to create all things out of nothing; for man then ceases to be vanity, and begins to be truly something, when, aided by the power of God, he aspires to heavenly things.

8. *Deliver me from all my sins.* In this verse the Psalmist still continues his godly and holy prayer. He is now no longer carried away by the violence of his grief to murmur against God, but, humbly acknowledging himself guilty before God, he has recourse to his mercy. In asking to be delivered from his transgressions, he ascribes the praise of righteousness to God, while he charges upon himself the blame of all the misery which he endures; and he blames himself, not only on account of one sin, but acknowledges that he is justly chargeable with manifold transgressions. By this rule we must be guided, if we would wish to obtain an alleviation of our miseries; for, until the very source of them has been dried up, they will never cease to follow one another in rapid succession. David unquestionably wished an alleviation of his miseries, but, as he expected that, as soon as he should be reconciled to God, the chastisement of his sins would also cease, he only here asks that his sins may be forgiven him. We are thus taught by the example of David, not merely to seek deliverance from the miseries which afflict and trouble us, but to trace them to their cause and source, entreating God that he would not lay our sins to our charge, but blot out our guilt. What follows concerning the *reproach* or *scorn of the foolish* may be understood in an active as well as a passive signification, denoting, either that God would not abandon him to the mockery of the wicked, or that he would not involve him in the same disgrace to which the ungodly are given over. As, however, either of these senses will agree very well with the design of the Psalmist, I leave it to the reader to adopt the one which he prefers. Besides, the word נבל, *nabal*, signifies not only a foolish person, but also a contemptible man, one who is utterly worthless and base. It is at least certain, that by this word the reprobate, whom the Scriptures condemn for their folly, are intended; because,

being deprived of their reason and understanding, they break forth into every excess in contemning and reproaching God.

9. *I was dumb.* Here David blames himself, because he had not preserved that silence which, as we have already seen, the violence of his grief forced him to break. When he says then that he was *dumb,* he does not mean this as a commendation of the uniform and persevering restraint which he had exercised over himself. It is rather a correction of his error, as if reproving his own impatience, he had spoken within himself in this way : What doest thou ? thou hadst enjoined upon thyself silence, and now thou murmurest proudly against God; what wilt thou gain by this presumption ? We have here a very profitable and instructive lesson ; for nothing is better fitted to restrain the violent paroxysms of grief, than the recollection that we have to do, not with a mortal man, but with God, who will always maintain his own righteousness in opposition to all that men may say against it in their murmuring complaints, and even in their outrageous accusations. What is the reason why the great majority of men run to such excess in their impatience, but because they forget that, in doing so, they dare to plead a controversy with God? Thus, while some impute all their miseries to fortune, and others to men, and others account for them from a variety of causes which their own fancy suggests, while scarcely one in a hundred recognises in them the hand of God, they allow themselves to indulge in bitter complaints, without ever thinking that in so doing they offend God. David, on the contrary, in order to subdue every unholy desire and sinful excess, returns to God, and resolves to keep silence, because the affliction which he is now suffering proceeded from God. As David, who was thus afflicted with the severest trials, resolved nevertheless to keep silence, let us learn from this, that it is one of the chief exercises of our faith to humble ourselves under the mighty hand of God, and to submit to his judgments without murmuring or complaint. It is to be observed, that men humbly and calmly submit themselves to God only when they are persuaded, not only that he does by his almighty power whatever he pleases, but that he

is also a righteous Judge; for although the wicked feel that the hand of God is upon them, yet as they charge him with cruelty and tyranny, they cease not to pour forth horrible blasphemies against him. In the meantime, David regards the secret judgments of God with such reverence and wonder, that, satisfied with his will alone, he considers it sinful to open his mouth to utter a single word against him.

> 10. *Take away thy stroke from me : I have failed* [or *fainted*] *by the blow of thy hand.*
> 11. *Thou chastisest man with rebukes for his iniquity ; and as a moth, thou makest his excellency to consume away : surely every man is vanity. Selah.*

10. *Take away thy stroke from me.* David here confirms the prayer which he had already presented, namely, that having obtained pardon from God, he might, at the same time, be gently dealt with by him. This prayer, however, does not disturb the silence of which he had just made mention ; for our desires and prayers, if they are framed according to the rule of God's word, are not inconsiderate and noisy so as to provoke the divine displeasure against us, but proceed from the calm stillness which faith and patience produce in our hearts. It is indeed true, that when any one prays earnestly to God, he cannot fail to mix up with it his own feelings, pour forth his complaints, and manifest an extreme ardour. But we see that David, who formerly bewailed his miseries in loud lamentations, now sets himself calmly to consider and weigh what he merited, and prays for pardon. His meaning is, that God would mitigate the punishment which he had inflicted upon him. The reason immediately follows; for *I have fainted by the blow of thy hand.* In thus speaking, David does not allege this as an excuse to extenuate his fault, but desires that he may be borne with in his infirmity.

As he says with respect to himself individually, that he is consumed, because he feels that the hand of God is against him, so he immediately states in the 11th verse the same truth in general terms, telling us, that if God should begin to deal with us according to the strict demands of the law, the consequence would be, that all would perish, and be utterly overwhelmed under his wrath. He plainly shows, first, that he is speaking not of any one man, or even of men generally, for he makes use of a Hebrew word, which denotes a man renowned for his valour, courage, or excellence;[1] and then, secondly, he says, that if God should set himself to chastise such persons, every thing which they esteem precious in themselves would consume away or be dissolved. The sum is, that among men there is no one endued with such power and glory whom the wrath of God, if it burn fiercely against him, will not forthwith bring to nothing. But it will be necessary to examine the words more minutely. David does not simply describe the dreadful character of God's wrath; but at the same time he declares and sets forth his righteousness in all the punishments which he inflicts upon men. The judgments of God sometimes strike fear and dread into the hearts even of heathen men, but their blindness fills them with such rage, that they still continue to fight against God. By the term *rebukes*, David means severe punishments, such as are the tokens of strict justice and signs of divine wrath. We know that God often exercises the rod of his chastisement upon true believers, but he does it in such a manner as that in punishing them he at the same time gives them a taste of his mercy and his love, and not only tempers the chastisements with which he visits them, but also mingles them with comfort, which serves to render them much more tolerable. David, then, is not speaking in this place of fatherly chastisement, but of the punishment which God inflicts upon the reprobate, when, like an inexorable judge in the exercise of his office, he executes against them the judgment which they have merited. He tells us that when God makes this rigour to be felt, there is no man who does not forthwith consume or pine away. At first view the comparison of God to a moth may seem absurd; for what relation is there, it may be said, between a small moth-worm and the infinite majesty of

---

[1] " Car il use d'un mot par lequel les Hebrieux signifient un homme vertueux, courageux, ou excellent."—*Fr.* The Hebrew word is איש, *ish.* See vol. i. p. 40, note.

God? I answer, That David has with much propriety made use of this simile, that we may know that although God does not openly thunder from heaven against the reprobate, yet his secret curse ceases not to consume them away, just as the moth, though unperceived, wastes by its secret gnawing a piece of cloth or wood.[1] At the same time, he alludes to *the excellency*[2] of man, which he says is destroyed as it were by corruption, when God is offended, even as the moth destroys the most precious cloths by wasting them. The Scriptures often very appropriately employ various similitudes in this way, and are wont to apply them sometimes in one view and sometimes in another. When Hezekiah (Isaiah xxxviii. 13) compares God to a lion, he does so in reference to the feelings of his own mind, because he was so prostrated and overwhelmed with fear and terror. But in this place David teaches us, that although the world may not perceive the dreadful vengeance of God, yet it consumes the reprobate by secretly gnawing them. This sentence, *that every man is vanity*, is again very properly repeated; for until we are overcome by the power of God, and as it were humbled in the dust, we never search into our own hearts, that the knowledge of our own vanity may divest us of all presumption. Whence is it that men are so foolishly satisfied with themselves, yea, and even applaud themselves, unless it be that, so long as God bears with them, they are wilfully blind to

---

[1] The meaning according to our English version seems to be, that the beauty of man is consumed as the moth is consumed. "But," says Walford, "this gives no correct or suitable sense. The design is to state, not that the moth is consumed, but that it is a consumer or spoiler of garments." He reads,

"With rebukes thou chastisest man for iniquity,
Then thou destroyest his goodliness as a moth destroyeth a garment."

This is precisely Calvin's interpretation. The moth is called in Hebrew וי, *ash*, from its *corroding* and *destroying* the texture of cloth, &c. See Parkhurst's Lexicon on the word וי. The metaphor here employed is of frequent occurrence in Scripture. For example, in Hosea v. 12, God says, "I will be to Ephraim as a moth," that is, I will consume them; and in Isaiah i. 9, it is said, "The moth shall eat them as a garment."

[2] The original word, which Calvin renders "excellency," is translated by Hammond "precious things;" by which he understands wealth, greatness, health, beauty, strength, and, in short, whatever is most precious to us.

their own infirmities? The only remedy, then, by which men are cured of pride is when, alarmed with a sense of God's wrath, they begin not only to be dissatisfied with themselves, but also to humble themselves even to the dust.

> 12. *Hear my prayer, O Jehovah! and hearken to my cry; and hold not thy peace*[1] *at my tears: for I am a stranger before thee, and a sojourner, as all my fathers were.*
> 13. *Let me alone, that I may recover strength, before I depart, and be no more.*

12. *Hear my prayer, O Jehovah!* David gradually increases his vehemence in prayer. He speaks first of *prayer;* in the second place, of *crying;* and in the third place, of *tears.* This gradation is not a mere figure of rhetoric, which serves only to adorn the style, or to express the same thing in different language. This shows that David bewailed his condition sincerely, and from the bottom of his heart; and in this he has given us, by his own example, a rule for prayer. When he calls himself a *stranger* and a *sojourner,* he again shows how miserable his condition was; and he adds expressly, *before God,* not only because men are absent from God so long as they dwell in this world, but in the same sense in which he formerly said, *My days are before thee as nothing;* that is to say, God, without standing in need of any one to inform him, knows well enough that men have only a short journey to perform in this world, the end of which is soon reached, or that they remain only a short time in it, as those who are lodged in a house for pay.[2] The purport of the Psalmist's discourse is, that God sees from heaven how miserable our condition would be, if he did not sustain us by his mercy.

13. *Let me alone, that I may recover strength.* Literally, it is, *cease from me,* and therefore some explain it, Let there be a wall raised betwixt us, that thy hand may not reach me. Others read, as a supplement, the word *eyes;* but as to the sense, it matters little which of the expositions be adopted,

---

[1] " Ne dissimule point."—*Fr.* " Dissemble not."
[2] " Comme des gens qui sont logez en une maison par emprunt."—*Fr.*

for the meaning is the same, That David entreats God to grant him a little relaxation from his trouble, that he might recover strength, or, at least, enjoy a short respite, before he depart from this world. This concluding verse of the psalm relates to the disquietude and sinful emotions which he had experienced according to the flesh; for he seems in the way of complaining of God, to ask that at least time might be granted him to die, as men are wont to speak who are grievously harassed by their affliction. I admit, that he speaks in a becoming manner, in acknowledging that there is no hope of his being restored to health, until God cease to manifest his displeasure; but he errs in this, that he asks a respite, just that he may have time to die. We might, indeed, regard the prayer as allowable, by understanding it in this sense: Lord, as it will not be possible for me to endure thy stroke any longer, but I must, indeed, miserably perish, if thou continuest to afflict me severely, at least grant me relief for a little season, that in calmness and peace I may commit my soul into thy hands. But we may easily infer, from the language which he employs, that his mind was so affected with the bitterness of his grief that he could not present a prayer pure and well seasoned with the sweetness of faith; for he says, *before I depart, and be no more:* a form of speech which indicates the feeling almost of despair. Not that David could regard death as the entire annihilation of man, or that, renouncing all hope of his salvation, he resigned himself to destruction; but he employs this language, because he had previously been so much depressed by reason of grief, that he could not lift up his heart with so much cheerfulness as it behoved him. This is a mode of expression which is to be found more than once in the complaints of Job. It is obvious, therefore, that, although David endeavoured carefully to restrain the desires of the flesh, yet these occasioned him so much disquietude and trouble, that they forced him to exceed the proper limits in his grief.

PSALM XL.

David, being delivered from some great danger, and it may be, not from one only, but from many, extols very highly the grace of God, and by means of this, his soul is filled with admiration of the providence of God, which extends itself to the whole human race. Then he protests that he will give himself wholly to the service of God, and defines briefly in what manner God is to be served and honoured. Afterwards, he again returns to the exercise of thanksgiving, and celebrates the praises of the Eternal by rehearsing many of his glorious and powerful deeds. Lastly, when he has complained of his enemies, he concludes the psalm with a new prayer.

¶ To the chief musician. A Psalm of David.

1. *In waiting I waited*[1] *for Jehovah, and he inclined unto me, and heard my cry.*
2. *And he drew me out of the roaring pit, out of the miry clay, and set my feet upon a rock, and established my steps.*
3. *And he hath put into my mouth a new song, even praise to our God: many shall see it, and fear, and shall trust in Jehovah.*

1. *In waiting I waited.* The beginning of this psalm is an expression of thanksgiving, in which David relates that he had been delivered, not only from danger, but also from present death. Some are of opinion, but without good reason, that it ought to be understood of sickness. It is rather to be supposed that David here comprehends a multitude of dangers from which he had escaped. He had certainly been more than once exposed to the greatest danger, even of death, so that, with good reason, he might be said to have

---

[1] " C'est, paciemment."—*Fr. marg.* " That is, patiently." Calvin in the text gives the literal rendering of the Hebrew. *In waiting I waited* is a Hebraism which signifies vehement desire, and yet entire resignation of mind. " The doubling of the word," says Ainsworth, " denotes earnestness, constancy, patience."

been swallowed up in the gulf of death, and sunk in the *miry clay.* It, nevertheless, appears that his faith had still continued firm, for he ceased not to trust in God, although the long continuance of the calamity had well nigh exhausted his patience. He tells us, not merely that he had waited, but by the repetition of the same expression, he shows that he had been a long time in anxious suspense. In proportion then as his trial was prolonged, the evidence and proof of his faith in enduring the delay with calmness and equanimity of mind was so much the more apparent. The meaning in short is, that although God delayed his help, yet the heart of David did not faint, or grow weary from delay; but that after he had given, as it were, sufficient proof of his patience, he was at length heard. In his example there is set before us this very useful doctrine, that although God may not forthwith appear for our help, but rather of design keep us in suspense and perplexity, yet we must not lose courage, inasmuch as faith is not thoroughly tried, except by long endurance. The result, too, of which he speaks in terms of praise, ought to inspire us with increased fortitude. God may succour us more slowly than we desire, but, when he seems to take no notice of our condition, or, if we might so speak, when he seems to be inactive or to sleep, this is totally different from deceit: for if we are enabled by the invincible strength and power of faith to endure, the fitting season of our deliverance will at length arrive.

2. *And he drew me out of the roaring pit.* Some translate, *from the pit of desolation,*[1] because the verb שָׁאָה, *shaäh,* from which the noun שָׁאוֹן, *shaon,* is derived, signifies *to destroy* or *to waste,* as well as *to resound* or *echo.* But it is more appro-

---

[1] The Septuagint reads, "'Εκ λάκκου ταλαιπωρίας."—" Out of a pit of misery;" and Ainsworth, "the pit of sounding calamity," or "dungeon of tumultuous desolation," "which," says he, "echoed and resounded with dreadful noises." "The sufferings of the Psalmist," observes Bishop Mant, "are here described under the image of a dark subterraneous cavern from which there was no emerging; and where roaring cataracts of water broke in upon him, overwhelming him on every side, till, as it is expressed in the 18th psalm, 'God sent from above and took him, and drew him out of many waters.'"

priate to consider that there is here an allusion to the deep gulfs, where the waters gush with a tumultuous force.[1] By this similitude he shows that he was placed in as imminent peril of death as if he had been cast into a deep pit, roaring with the impetuous rage of waters. To the same purpose also is the similitude of *the miry clay*, by which he intimates that he had been so nearly overwhelmed by the weight of his calamities, that it was no easy matter to extricate him from them. Next, there follows a sudden and incredible change, by which he makes manifest to all the greatness of the grace which had been bestowed upon him. He declares that *his feet were set upon a rock*, whereas formerly he had been overwhelmed with water; and that his *steps were established* or *upheld*, whereas before they were not only unsteady and slippery, but were also stuck fast in the mire.

3. *And he hath put into my mouth a new song.* In the first clause of the verse he concludes the description of what God had done for him. By God's putting *a new song into his mouth* he denotes the consummation of his deliverance. In whatever way God is pleased to succour us, he asks nothing else from us in return but that we should be thankful for and remember it. As often, therefore, as he bestows benefits upon us, so often does he open our mouths to praise his name. Since God, by acting liberally towards us, encourages us to sing his praises, David with good reason reckons, that having been so wonderfully delivered, the matter of a new song had been furnished to him. He uses the word *new* in the sense of exquisite and not ordinary, even as the manner of his deliverance was singular and worthy of everlasting remembrance. It is true, that there is no benefit of God so small that it ought not to call forth our highest praises; but the more mightily he stretches forth his hand to help us, the more does it become us to stir up ourselves to fervent zeal in this holy exercise, so that our songs may correspond to the greatness of the favour which has been conferred upon us.

Many shall see it. Here the Psalmist extends still farther

---

[1] " Un marveilleux bruit."—*Fr.* " A marvellous noise."

the fruit of the aid which he had experienced, telling us, that it will prove the means of instruction common to all. And certainly it is the will of God that the benefits which he bestows upon any individual of the faithful should be proofs of the goodness which he constantly exercises towards all of them, so that the one, instructed by the example of the other, should not doubt that the same grace will be manifested towards himself. The terms *fear,* and *hope,* or *trust,* do not seem at first view to harmonise; but David has not improperly joined them together; for no man will ever entertain the hope of the favour of God but he whose mind is first imbued with the fear of God. I understand *fear* in general to mean the feeling of piety which is produced in us by the knowledge of the power, equity, and mercy of God. The judgment which God executed against the enemies of David served, it is true, to inspire all men with fear; but, in my opinion, David rather means, that by the deliverance which he had obtained, many would be induced to yield themselves to the service of God, and to submit with all reverence to his authority, because they would know him to be the Judge of the world. Now, whoever submits cordially to the will of God will of necessity join hope with fear; especially when there is presented to his view the evidence of the grace by which God commonly allures all men to himself; for I have already said that God is presented to our view as merciful and kind to others, that we may assure ourselves that he will be the same towards us. As to the word *see,* of which David makes use, we are to understand it as referring not only to the eyes, but chiefly to the perception of the mind. All without distinction saw what had happened, but to many of them it never occurred to recognise the deliverance of David as the work of God. Since, then, so many are blind regarding the works of God, let us learn, that those only are considered to see clearly to whom the Spirit of understanding has been given, that they may not occupy their minds in dwelling upon the mere events which take place, but may discern in them by faith the secret hand of God.

4. *Blessed is the man who hath set Jehovah for his confidence, and hath not regarded the proud, and those who turn aside to lying.*[1]

5. *Many are thy wonderful works which thou hast done, O Jehovah! my God: and it is impossible to reckon up in order to thee*[2] *thy counsels towards us. I will declare and speak of them; they are more than can be told.*

4. *Blessed is the man who hath set Jehovah for his confidence.* David here relates what ground for good hope his deliverance would give to all the faithful; inasmuch as, setting aside all the allurements of the world, they would thereby be encouraged to commit themselves with confidence to the protection of God; persuaded not only that they are happy who trust in him alone, but that all other expectations at variance with this are deceitful and cursed. This assurance is not natural to us, but is derived partly from the word of God, and partly from his works; although, as I have said before, the contemplation alone of the works of God would not kindle this light within us, unless God, illuminating us by his word, should show us his benevolence. After having promised to be gracious to us, in manifesting also his goodness by indubitable proofs, he confirms with his own hand what he had previously uttered with his lips. David, therefore, from the fact of his having been restored to life from the abyss of death, justly declares that the faithful are taught from this proof—what men are naturally so reluctant to believe—that they are happy who trust in God alone.

As the instability of our nature commonly tends to draw us downward, and as all of us, from our proneness to yield to delusions, are tempted by many wicked examples, David immediately adds, that he is blessed *who regardeth not the proud.* Some, indeed, render רהבים, *rehabim, the rich,* or *the great of this world,* but improperly, in my opinion; because *pride,* and *turning aside to lies,* are two things which David here joins together. *To regard the great of the earth,* therefore, does not signify, as they suppose, to rely upon their

---

[1] "A vanité."—*Fr.* "To vanity."
[2] "Devant toy."—*Fr.* "Before thee, or in thy presence."

power and riches, as if a man's welfare depended thereupon, but it rather means to be carried away by their examples, to imitate their conduct. When we are everywhere constantly seeing men puffed up with pride, who despise God, and place their highest felicity in ambition, in fraud, in extortion, in guile, a perverse desire of imitating them steals upon us by degrees; and, especially when every thing turns out according to their wishes, a vain and delusive expectation solicits us to try the same course. David, therefore, wisely, and not without good reason, warns us, that in order to have our mind constantly fixed in simple reliance upon God alone, we must guard against those evil examples which ever seek to allure us on all sides to apostatize from him. Moreover, when he says that the proud *turn aside to lying,* or *vanity,*[1] in this way he describes briefly the foolish confidence of the flesh. What else is the pride of those who put their own fancies in the place of God but a vain illusion? Certainly the man who, puffed up by the breath of fond conceit, arrogates any thing in the least degree to himself, flatters himself to his own destruction. In short, pride and vanity are opposed to the holy confidence which relies upon God alone; for there is nothing more difficult to the flesh than to trust in God alone, and the world is always full of proud and haughty men, who, soothing themselves with vain allurements, would soon corrupt the minds of the godly, if this arrest were not laid upon them, to restrain, as with a bridle, their erroneous and extravagant opinions.

5. *Many are thy wonderful works which thou hast done, O Jehovah!* Interpreters are not entirely agreed as to these words; but it is generally admitted that David here contemplates with admiration the providence of God in the government of mankind. And first of all, he exclaims that the *wonders of God's works are great* or *many;*[2] meaning by this, that God in his inscrutable wisdom so governs human affairs, that his works, which come to be little thought of by men, from their constant familiarity with them, far surpass the

[1] " Ou vanité."—*Fr.*
[2] " Sont grandes ou infinies."—*Fr.* " Are great or innumerable."

comprehension of the human understanding. Thus we find, that from one particular species he ascends to the whole class; as if he had said, God has proved not only by this particular act the paternal care which he exercises towards men, but that, in general, his wonderful providence shines forth in the several parts of creation. Then he adds, that *the counsels of God* concerning us are so high and so hidden, that it is impossible to reckon them up in order distinctly and agreeably to their nature. Some think that the word אלינו, *elenu, towards us,* is employed by way of comparison, in this sense, The counsels of God are far beyond the reach of our understanding, (but David rather commends the care which God vouchsafes to take of us;) and as, in this way, the connection of the words is broken, they are constrained to render the word ערוך, *aroch,* which I have rendered *to count in order,* differently, namely, that none is equal to God, or can be compared with him.[1] But that I may not enter upon any lengthened refutation, the intelligent reader will agree with me in considering that the true meaning is this: That God, by his incomprehensible wisdom, governs the world in such a manner that we cannot reckon up his works in their proper order, seeing our minds, through their very dulness, fail us before we can reach to so great a height. It follows, *to thee,* for although we should in so far reflect how wonderfully the Lord can make provision for our wants, yet this consideration is limited by the imperfection of our understanding: and hence it falls far short of the infinite glory of God. Those who give this explanation, that *the counsels of God* are not referred to him, because the greatest part of men imagine that every thing is subject to chance and fortune, as if David meant in passing to censure the ingratitude of those who defraud God of his praise, are no doubt mistaken as to the

---

[1] "This verb," says Ainsworth, "is sometimes used for matching or comparing." In this sense the word occurs in Ps. lxxxix. 7; and this is the sense in which the Septuagint understands it here: "Καὶ τοῖς διαλογισμοῖς σου οὐκ ἔστι τις ὁμοιωθήσεται σοι;"—" and in thy thoughts there is none who shall be likened to thee." Street reads, "There is none to be compared to thee;" and observes, that "above sixty copies of Dr Kennicott's collection have ערוך, the passive participle here, instead of ערך."

meaning. In stating, as David does, immediately after, that however much he might set himself to rehearse the works of God, he yet would fail ere he could declare the half of them;—in stating this he shows with sufficient plainness that the godly and devout meditation, in which the children of God are often engaged, gives them only, as it were, a slight taste of them and nothing more. We have now arrived then at the Psalmist's meaning. Having spoken before of the deliverance which God had vouchsafed to him, he takes occasion from it to set forth the general providence of God in nourishing and sustaining men. It is also his design in this to exhort the faithful to a consideration of God's providence, that they may not hesitate to cast all their cares upon it. Whilst some are in constant pain by reason of their own anxiety and discontent, or quake at the slightest breeze that blows, and others labour hard to fortify and preserve their life by means of earthly succours,—all this proceeds from ignorance of the doctrine, that God governs the affairs of this world according to his own good pleasure. And as the great majority of men, measuring the providence of God by their own understanding, wickedly obscure or degrade it, David, placing it on its proper footing, wisely removes this impediment. The meaning of the sentence, therefore, amounts to this, that in the works of God men should reverently admire what they cannot comprehend by their reason; and whenever the flesh moves them to contradiction or murmuring, they should raise themselves above the world. If God cease to work, he seems to be asleep, because, binding up his hands to the use of outward means, we do not consider that he works by means which are secret. We may therefore learn from this place, that although the reason of his works may be hidden or unknown to us, he is nevertheless wonderful in his counsels.

This verse is closely connected with the preceding. No man places, as he ought, entire trust in God, but he who, shutting his eyes upon external circumstances, suffers himself to be governed by him according to his good pleasure. Moreover, having spoken hitherto in the third person, David now suddenly addresses his discourse, not, however, unadvisedly, to God, that he might lead us the more effectually to this sobriety and discretion. When, however, he affirms that the works of God cannot be distinctly known by us, it is not for the purpose of deterring us from seeking the knowledge of them, or from the examination of them, but only to lay a restraint upon our rashness, which would otherwise go beyond the proper boundaries in this respect. To this end, the words *to thee,* or *before thee,* are expressly employed, by which we are admonished that however diligently a man may set himself to meditate upon the works of God, he can only attain to the extremities or borders of them. Although then so great a height be far above our reach, we must, notwithstanding, endeavour, as much as in us lies, to approach it more and more by continual advances; as we see also the hand of God stretched forth to disclose to us, so far as it is expedient, those wonders, which we are unable of ourselves to discover. There is nothing so preposterous as to affect, of one's own accord, a gross ignorance of the providence of God, because as yet we cannot comprehend it perfectly, but only discern it in part; even as at this day we find some who employ all their endeavours to bury it in oblivion, for no other pretence than that it surpasses our understanding, as if it were unreasonable to allow to God anything more than what appears right and proper, according to our carnal reason. David acts very differently regarding it. Feeling all his senses absorbed by an inconceivable majesty and brightness, which he could not bear to look upon,[1] he confesses frankly that these are wonderful things of which he could not comprehend the reason; but still he does not abstain wholly and everywhere from making mention of them, but, according to the measure of his capacity, sets himself devoutly to meditate upon them. From this we learn how foolish and vain a thing it is to say, by way of caution, that none should speak of the counsels or purposes of God, because they are high and incomprehensible. David, on the contrary, though he was ready to sink under the weight, ceased not to contemplate them, and abstained not from speaking of them, because he felt unequal to the task

[1] " Sentant tous ses sens engloutis d'une majesté et resplendeur infinie, que sa veuë ne pouvoit porter."—*Fr.*

of rehearsing them, but was content, after having declared his faith on this subject, to finish his discourse in admiration.

> 6. *In sacrifice and oblation thou hast not taken pleasure : thou hast bored my ears : thou hast not required burnt-offering nor sin-offering.*
> 7. *Then I said, Lo ! I come : in the roll of the book it is written of me,*
> 8. *That I may do thy pleasure, O my God ! I have delighted to do it, and thy law is in the midst of my bowels.* (Heb. x. 5.)

6. *In sacrifice and oblation thou hast not taken pleasure.* Here David offers not only the sacrifice of praise, or, as the prophet Hosea calls it, (ch. xiv. 2,) "the calves of the lips," but, in token of his gratitude, offers and consecrates himself entirely to God; as if he had said, I am now wholly devoted to God, because, having been delivered by his wonderful power, I am doubly indebted to him for my life. At the same time, treating of the true worship of God, he shows that it consists not in outward ceremonies, but rather that it is spiritual. Accordingly, the meaning is, that he came into the presence of God not only in the outward pomp or ceremony and figures of the law, but that he brought with him the true devotion of the heart. We know, indeed, that all men have some sense of religion impressed upon their hearts, so that no one dares to withdraw openly and wholly from his service, and yet the greater part of men turn aside into winding and crooked paths; and hence it happens, that in serving God in a perfunctory manner, their worship is scarcely anything else than a mockery of him. We see then the reason why David, on the present occasion, shows in what the true worship of God consists; it is, that he may distinguish between himself and hypocrites, who draw near to God with their lips only, or at least seek to pacify him with cold and unmeaning ceremonies.

We now come to the exposition of the words. I have no doubt that David, under the four different kinds of sacrifices which he here enumerates, comprehends all the sacrifices of the law. His meaning, to express it in a few words, is, that God requires not mere ceremonies of those who serve him, but that he is satisfied only with sincerity of heart, with faith and holiness of life : and that he takes no pleasure merely in the visible sanctuary, the altar, the burning of incense, the killing of beasts, the lights, the costly apparel, and outward washings. From this he concludes, that he ought to be guided by another principle, and to observe another rule in the service of God, than a mere attention to these—that he should yield himself wholly to God.

Thou hast bored my ears. Some think that in using this form of expression, David has a reference to the ordinance under the Law of which we read in Exodus xxi. 6. If any bond-servant, when the time of his being discharged from servitude had arrived, made no account of his freedom, he was brought to the public place of judgment, and having there declared that he wished to continue in servitude, his master pierced his ear with an awl, as a mark of perpetual bondage. But this mode of interpretation appears to be too forced and refined.[1] Others more simply consider that it is of the same meaning as to render fit, or qualify for service, for David mentions not one ear only, but both. Men, we

---

[1] The objections to this interpretation are, 1. That the verb כרה, *carah*, here used, does not mean *to bore*, but that the radical idea of the word is, *to dig, to hollow out;* as to dig a well, Gen. xxvi. 25 ; a pit, Ps. vii. 15 ; to carve or cut out a sepulchre from a rock, 2 Chron. xvi. 14 ; and hence we find it transferred from the grottoes of the sepulchre to the quarry of human nature, Isa. li. 1, 2. Williams, viewing the verb as properly signifying *digged, carved,* or *cut out,* in the sense of *forming,* explains the words as if the Psalmist had said, "Mine ears hast thou made, or *prepared,* for the most exact and complete obedience." Stuart, (Commentary on Heb. x. 5,) and Davidson, (Sacred Hermeneutics, p. 461,) viewing the word as meaning *digged, hollowed out,* simply in the sense of *opening,* read, "Mine ears hast thou opened;" which they explain as meaning, Thou hast made me obedient, or, I am entirely devoted to thy service ; observing, that *to open* or *uncover the ear* was a customary expression among the Hebrews, to signify a revealing something to any one, including the idea of listening to the communication, followed by prompt obedience, Isa. l. 5 ; 1 Sam. xx. 2. There is another verb of the same radical letters, which means to *purchase* or *provide;* and this is the sense in which the LXX. understood כרה, *carah,* as is evident from their rendering it by κατηρτίσω. 2. That the verb used in Exodus is not כרה, as here, but רצע, *ratsang.* 3. That only one ear was pierced, as appears from the passages in the Pentateuch in which the rite is described. But here the dual number is used, denoting both ears. From these considerations, it is concluded that there is here no allusion to the custom of boring the ear of a servant under the Law.

know, are naturally deaf, because they are so dull, that their ears are stopped until God pierce them. By this expression, therefore, is denoted the docility to which we are brought and moulded by the grace of the Holy Spirit. I, however, apply this manner of expression more closely to the scope of the passage before us, and explain it in this sense, That David was not slow and dull of hearing, as men usually are, so that he could discern nothing but what was earthly in the sacrifices, but that his ears had been cleansed, so that he was a better interpreter of the Law, and able to refer all the outward ceremonies to the spiritual service of God. He encloses the sentence, *Thou hast bored my ears,* as it were, in parenthesis, whilst he is treating professedly of sacrifices, so that the sentence might be explained in this way: Lord, thou hast opened my ears, that I may distinctly understand whatever thou hast commanded concerning the sacrifices, namely, that of themselves they afford thee no pleasure: for thou, who art a Spirit, takest no delight in these earthly elements, and hast no need of flesh or blood; and, therefore, thou requirest something of a higher and more excellent nature. If, however, it is objected that sacrifices were offered by the express commandment of God, I have just said that David here distinguishes between the spiritual service of God, and that which consisted in outward types and shadows. And in making this comparison, it is no great wonder to find him saying that the sacrifices are of no value, since they were only helps designed to lead men to true piety, and tended to a far higher end than that which was at first apparent. Seeing, then, God made use of these elements, only to lead his people to the exercises of faith and repentance, we conclude that he had no delight in being worshipped by sacrifices. We must always bear in mind, that whatever is not pleasing to God for its own sake, but only in so far as it leads to some other end, if it be put in the place of his true worship and service is rejected and cast away by him.

7. *Then said I, Lo! I come.* By the adverb *then* he intimates, that he had not been a good scholar, and capable of profiting by instruction, until God had opened his ears; but

as soon as he had been instructed by the secret inspirations of the Spirit, he tells us, that then his heart was ready to yield a willing and cheerful obedience. Here true obedience is very properly distinguished from a constrained and slavish subjection. Whatever service, therefore, men may offer to God, it is vain and offensive in his sight, unless at the same time they offer themselves; and, moreover, this offering of one's self is of no value unless it be done willingly. These words, *Lo! I come,* ought to be observed, and likewise the words, *I have delighted to do thy will;* for the Hebrew word חפצתי, *chaphatsti,* means, I was well pleased, or, I willingly condescended. Here David indicates his readiness to yield obedience, as well as the cordial affection of his heart and persevering resolution. His language implies, that he cordially preferred the service of God to every other desire and care, and had not only yielded a willing subjection, but also embraced the rule of a pious and holy life, with a fixed and steady purpose of adhering to it. This he confirms still further in the third clause of the verse, in which he says, that *the Law of God* was deeply fixed *in the midst of his bowels.*[1] It follows from this, first, that however beautiful and splendid the works of men may appear, yet unless they spring from the living root of the heart, they are nothing better than a mere pretence; and, secondly, that it is to no purpose that the feet, and hands, and eyes, are framed for keeping the Law, unless obedience begin at the heart. Moreover, it appears from other places of Scripture, that it is the peculiar office of the Holy Spirit to engrave the Law of God on our hearts. God, it is true, does not perform his work in us as if we were stones or stocks, drawing us to himself without the feeling or inward moving of our hearts towards him. But as there is in us naturally a will, which, however, is depraved by the corruption of our nature, so that it always inclines us to sin, God changes it for the better, and thus leads us cordially to seek after righteousness, to which our hearts were previously altogether averse. Hence arises that true freedom

---

[1] This is the literal rendering of the Hebrew, and means, As dear to me as life itself; (John vi. 38; Job xxxviii. 36.)

which we obtain when God frames our hearts, which before were in thraldom to sin, unto obedience to himself.

In the roll of the book. As the Septuagint has made use of the word *head* instead of *roll*,[1] some have been inclined to philosophise upon this clause with so much refinement of speculation, that they have exposed themselves to ridicule by their foolish and silly inventions. But the etymology of the word במגלת, *bemegilath,* is the same as the Latin word *volumen,*[2] which we call *a roll.* It is necessary to ascertain in what sense David claims peculiarly to himself what is common or alike to all men. Since the Law prescribes to all men the rule of a holy and upright life, it does not appear, it may be said, that what is here stated pertains to any one man or any set of men. I answer, that although the literal doctrine of the Law belongs to all men in common, yet as of itself it is dead, and only beats the air, God teaches his own people after another manner; and that, as the inward and effectual teaching of the Spirit is a treasure which belongs peculiarly to them, it is written of them only in the secret book of God, that they should fulfil his will. The voice of God, indeed, resounds throughout the whole world, so that all who do not obey it are rendered inexcusable; but it penetrates into the hearts of the godly alone, for whose salvation it is

---

[1] Anciently, books did not consist, like ours, of a number of distinct leaves bound together, but were composed of sheets of parchment joined to each other, and rolled up for preservation upon wooden rollers, as our charts of geography are; and in this form are all the sacred MSS. of the Jewish synagogues to this day. The *roll of the book,* therefore, simply means *the book* itself. With respect to the reading of the Septuagint, "Ἐν κεφαλίδι βιβλίου;"—"In the head of the book;" and which Paul, in Heb. x. 7, quotes instead of the Hebrew: this is an expression which the LXX. employ simply to mean *the book,* as in Ezra vi. 2; Ezekiel ii. 9; and iii. 1-3; and not the *beginning* or *head of the book.* At the extremity of the cylinder on which the Hebrew ספר, βιβλίον, book or manuscript, was rolled, were *heads* or *knobs* for the sake of convenience to those who used the MS. The *knob* or *head,* κεφαλίς, is here taken as a *part* put for the *whole.* Κεφαλίς βιβλίου means therefore βιβλίον, or ספר, with a κεφαλίς, *i. e.,* a manuscript roll.—*Stuart on Heb.* x. 7. Hence it is evident, that we are not to understand this phrase, *the head of the book,* as referring to that prophecy in Gen. iii. 15. As to what book is here referred to, there is some diversity of opinion among interpreters. Some understand it to be the book of the divine decrees, some the Pentateuch, and others all that was written concerning Christ "in the Law of Moses, in the Prophets, and in the Psalms."

[2] Volumen is from *volvo, I roll.*

ordained. As a general, therefore, enrols the names of his soldiers, that he may know their exact number, and as a schoolmaster writes the names of his scholars in a scroll, so has God written the names of his children in the book of life, that he may retain them under the yoke of his own discipline.

There still remains another difficulty connected with this passage. The Apostle, in Heb. x. 5, seems to wrest this place, when he restricts what is spoken of all the elect to Christ alone, and expressly contends that the sacrifices of the Law, which David says are not agreeable to God in comparison of the obedience of the heart, are abrogated; and when quoting rather the words of the Septuagint[1] than those of the prophet, he infers from them more than David intended to teach. As to his restricting this passage to the person of Christ, the solution is easy. David did not speak in his own name only, but has shown in general what belongs to all the children of God. But when bringing into view the whole body of the Church, it was necessary that he should refer us to the head itself. It is no objection that David soon after imputes to his own sins the miseries which

---

[1] The Septuagint here reads, "Σῶμα δὲ κατηρτίσω μοι;"—"But a body hast thou prepared [or fitted] for me." This reading is widely different from that of our Hebrew Bibles; and, to account for it, critics and commentators have had recourse to various conjectures: nor is the subject without considerable difficulty. Some think that the Septuagint has been corrupted, and others the Hebrew. Grotius is of opinion, and he is followed by Houbigant, that the original reading of the Septuagint was ἄκουσμα, *auditum*, which afterwards, in the process of transcription, had been changed into σῶμα; while Drs Owen and Hammond think that the original reading was ὠτία, ears. It is conjectured by Kennicott that the Hebrew text has been changed from אז גוה, *az gevah, then a body*, into אזנים, *aznayim, ears*; a conjecture which meets with the approbation of Dr Lowth, Dr Adam Clarke, and Dr Pye Smith. But it goes far to support the accuracy of the Hebrew text as it now stands, that the Syriac, Chaldee, and Vulgate versions agree with it, and that in all the MSS. collated by Kennicott and De Rossi there is not a single variation. With respect to the Apostle's quoting from the Septuagint instead of the Hebrew, it is sufficient to say, that he did so because the Septuagint was then in common use. And it is worthy of observation, that his argument does not depend on the words σῶμα δὲ κατηρτίσω μοι: his design is to show the insufficiency of the legal sacrifices, and to establish the efficacy of Christ's *obedience* unto death; and his argument would be equally complete had these words been omitted: for it is not made to depend on the *manner* of the obedience.—See Archbishop Secker's able Dissertation on the subject in the Appendix to Merrick's Notes on the Psalms; and Stuart on Heb. x. 5, and Excursus xx.

he endures; for it is by no means an uncommon thing to find our errors, by a mode of expression not strictly correct, transferred to Christ. As to the abrogation of the sacrifices that were under the Law, I answer thus: That their abrogation may be fairly inferred from the language of the prophets; for this is not like many other places in which God condemns and rejects the sacrifices which were offered by hypocrites, and which were deservedly offensive to him on account of their uncleanness: for in these God condemns the outward ceremony, on account of the abuse and corruption of it, which rendered it nothing but a vain mockery; whereas here, when the Prophet speaks of himself as one who worshipped God sincerely, and yet denies that God had pleasure in these sacrifices, it may easily be inferred, that the rudiments which God had enjoined upon his ancient people for a time had some other end in view, and were only like infantile instructions designed to prepare them for some higher state. But if their truth and substance are contained in Christ, it is certain that they have been abolished by his coming. They were indeed still in use in the time of David: and yet he admonishes us that the true service of God, even when performed without sacrifices, was perfect and complete in all its parts, and every where; and that the ceremonies are things which might be regarded as non-essential, and, as we speak, adventitious. This is worthy of being noticed, that we may know that God, even after he has removed the figures which he had commanded for a time, does not cease always to resemble himself; for in these outward services he had respect solely to men. As to this, that the Apostle, following the Septuagint, has made subservient to his own use the word *body*, which is not used here by David, in such an allusion there is no inconsistency; for he does not undertake expressly to unfold and explain in every point the Psalmist's meaning: but as he had said, that by the one sacrifice of Christ all the others had been abolished, he adds at the same time that a body had been prepared for Christ, that by the offering up of it he might fulfil the will of God.

9. *I have proclaimed thy righteousness in the great assembly: behold, I will not refrain my lips: O Jehovah! thou knowest it.*
10. *I have not hidden thy righteousness within my heart; I have declared thy truth and thy salvation: I have not concealed thy goodness nor thy truth in the great assembly.*
11. *O thou Jehovah! withhold not thy tender mercies from me: let thy goodness and thy truth always preserve me.*

9. *I have proclaimed thy righteousness in the great assembly.* Here David again brings forward his own thankfulness, and for no other reason but to induce God to continue his goodness towards him. God, whenever he manifests his liberality towards us, encourages us to render thanks to him; and he continues to act in a similar manner towards us when he sees that we are thankful and mindful of what he has done for us. In the first place, David makes use simply of the word *righteousness;* but it must be understood of the righteousness of God, which he expressly mentions soon after. Nor does he say, that it was only in the secret affection of the heart, or in private, that he offered praise to God, but that he had openly proclaimed it in the solemn assembly, even as the faithful in those days were wont to testify their devotion by presenting peace-offerings to God when they had been delivered from any great danger. *The great assembly* of which he speaks is not to be understood of the concourse of people that assemble at courts of law, or at the public market-places, but it denotes the true and lawfully constituted Church of God, which we know assembled in the place of his sanctuary. Accordingly, he declares that he had not concealed in his heart the righteousness of God, which it becomes us publicly to make known for the edification of one another. Those who keep it hid in their hearts are surely seeking as much as in them lies that the memory of God may be buried in oblivion. He calls upon God as a witness of this, not only to distinguish between himself and hypocrites, who often proclaim loudly, and with all their might, the praises of God, and yet do so without the least spark of affection; but also to make it the more abundantly obvious that he had sincerely and heartily uttered the praises of God, and was careful not to defraud him of any part of them. This affirmation teaches

us that the subject which is here treated of is one of no small importance; for although God stands in no need of our praises, yet it is his will that this exercise for many reasons should prevail amongst us.

10. *I have not hidden thy righteousness within my heart.* Here it is necessary to observe the accumulation of terms which are employed to denote the same thing. To the righteousness of God the Psalmist adds his truth, his salvation, and his mercy. And what is the design of this, but to magnify and set forth the goodness of God by many terms or expressions of praise? We must, however, notice in what respects these terms differ; for in this way we may be able to ascertain in what respects they apply to the deliverance of which David here discourses. If these four things should be taken in their proper order, *mercy* will hold the first place, as it is that by which alone God is induced to vouchsafe to regard us. *His righteousness* is the protection by which he constantly defends his own people, and the goodness by which, as we have already said elsewhere, he preserves them. And, lest any should doubt that it will flow in a constant and uninterrupted course, David adds in the third place *truth;* by which we are taught that God continues always the same, and is never wearied of helping us, nor at any time withdraws his hand. There is, at the same time, implied in this an exhibition of the promises; for no man will ever rightly take hold of the righteousness of God but he who embraces it as it is offered and held forth in the Word. *Salvation* is the effect of righteousness, for God continues to manifest his free favour to his people, daily affording them aid and assistance, until he has completely saved them.

11. *O thou Jehovah! withhold not thy tender mercies from me.* We now see more clearly, what I have just adverted to, that David speaks of his own thankfulness, that he might secure a continuance of God's favour towards him; and that he opened his mouth in the praises of God, that he might continue to acquire new favours, against which our perverse and ungrateful silence very often closes the gate. We ought, therefore, carefully to observe the relation which the clause, in

which David affirms that he closed not his lips, bears to what follows, namely, that God on his part would not contract or stop up the course of his tender mercies; for by this we are taught that God would always be ready to relieve us by his goodness, or rather that it would flow down upon us as from a never-failing fountain, if our own ingratitude did not prevent or cut off its course. *The tender mercies* of God, which he expresses by the word רחמיך, *rachamecha*, and of which he here speaks, differ little from his goodness. It was not, however, without cause that David chose to make this distinction. It could only be, first, because he was unable otherwise to satisfy himself in extolling the grace of God; and, secondly, because it was requisite to show that the source from which the mercy and goodness of God proceed, when he is moved in compassion for our miseries to aid and succour us. Then he places his confidence of salvation in the goodness and faithfulness of God, for we must of necessity begin (as I have said a little before) at the free favour of God, that his bounty may extend even to us. But as we are unable to discern that God is gracious to us until he grant us some assurance of his love, his constancy is, with much propriety, placed in connection with his truth in keeping his promises.

12. *For innumerable evils have compassed me on all sides; my iniquities have laid hold upon me, so that I cannot look up:*[1] *they are more in number than the hairs of my head; and my heart has failed me.*
13. *Be thou pleased, O Jehovah! to deliver me: O Jehovah! make haste to help me.*
14. *Let them be ashamed and confounded together that seek after my life to destroy it; let them be turned backward, and put to shame, that seek after my hurt.*
15. *Let them be destroyed for a reward of their shame who have said to me,*[2] *Aha, aha!*

12. *For innumerable evils have compassed me on all sides.* This phrase, in the original, denotes more than can be ex-

---

[1] "Mes iniquitez m'ont attrappé, *voire en si grand nombre* que ne les ay peu veoir."—*Fr.* "My iniquities have laid hold upon me, *even in such vast numbers* that I cannot see *them.*"

[2] "Ou, dit de moy."—*Fr. marg.* "Or, who have said concerning me."

pressed in an English translation; for he says, עָלַי, *alay, upon me*, meaning by this, that he was not only beset on all sides, but that also an accumulation of evils pressed upon his head. He, however, does not now complain of being punished unjustly, or above his desert, but rather confesses plainly that it is the just recompense of his sins which is rendered to him. For although the word עָוֹן, *avon*, which we have rendered *iniquity*, signifies also *the punishment of iniquity*, (as we have elsewhere seen more than once;) yet we must take into consideration the derivation of the word.[1] Accordingly, since David calls the afflictions which he endures the fruit or effect of his transgressions, there is implied in this a humble confession, from which we may ascertain with what reverence and meekness he submitted to the judgments of God, seeing that, when overwhelmed with an accumulation of miseries, he sets forth his sins in all their magnitude and aggravation, lest he should suspect God of undue severity. When we see David treated so severely, let us also learn, when we are oppressed with extreme afflictions, and are groaning under them, humbly to implore the grace and mercy of our Judge. Nor is it his design to show that he had been stupid or hardened, when he says that *his heart failed* or *forsook him*. His language means, that he was not only broken-hearted, but that he lay as if he had been dead. We must, however, understand this *fainting* or *failing of the heart* as referring to the sense of the flesh; for his perseverance in prayer is a certain proof that his faith was never altogether extinguished. But since he was, in so far as man was concerned, destitute of counsel, and was altogether without strength, it is not without cause that he says that his heart failed him.

13. *Be thou pleased, O Jehovah! to deliver me.* The verb which David here makes use of, signifies to desire a thing from pure kindness and good-will.[2] He desires, therefore, to

---

[1] The word עָוֹן, *avon*, is derived from עָוָה, *avah, he was crooked, oblique;* and hence the noun signifies iniquity, depravity, perverseness; but it is also put for the punishment due to iniquity. See vol. i. p. 507, note.

[2] "רְצֵה, *retse, be pleased.* From רָצָה, *ratsah, he wished well, was pleased, accepted,* excluding any merit as a ground for that acceptance."—*Bythner's Lyra.*

be delivered by the free mercy of God. As to his desire, that God would *make haste*, we have elsewhere spoken of it. Even when God delays to help us, it is our duty to contend against a feeling of weariness; but such is his goodness, that he permits us to use this form of prayer, That he would make haste according to our desires. Then, according to his usual practice, citing his enemies to the judgment-seat of God, he feels confident, that, on account of their cruelty, and unjust and wicked hatred, he shall obtain what he asks. We must maintain it as a fixed principle, that the more unjustly our enemies afflict us, and the more cruelly they wrong us, God is so much the more disposed to give us help. And it is no slight consolation that the mercy of God strives against their wickedness, so that the more fiercely our enemies pursue us to effect our hurt, the more ready is he to bring us help. We have already frequently spoken of the feelings with which David uttered these imprecations, and it is necessary here again to refresh our memories on the subject, lest any man, when giving loose reins to his passions, should allege the example of David in palliation or excuse. This wicked and counterfeit imitation on the part of those who follow the powerful impulse of the flesh, instead of being guided by the zeal of the Spirit, is always to be held up to condemnation.

When the Psalmist prays (verse 15) that his enemies *may be destroyed for a reward of their shame*, the meaning is this: As their sole desire has been to overwhelm me with shame, in order that, while thus dismayed and confounded, they might make me the object of their derision; so let a similar confusion fall upon their own heads. In the second clause of the verse he describes the nature of this confusion by relating the terms of their wicked triumphing, by which they poured contempt upon him while he was so oppressed with misery and affliction. We are here taught that, when our enemies shall have persecuted us to the uttermost, a recompense is also prepared for them; and that God will turn back, and cause to fall upon their own heads, all the evil which they had devised against us; and this doctrine ought to act as a restraint upon us, that we may behave ourselves compassionately and kindly towards our neighbours.

16. *Let all those that seek thee be glad and rejoice in thee : and let those that love thy salvation say continually, Jehovah be magnified!*

17. *But I am poor and needy : Jehovah hath regarded me ; thou art my help and my deliverer : O thou my God! make no delay.*

16. *Let all those that seek thee be glad and rejoice in thee.* David here uses another argument—one which he often adduces elsewhere—in order to obtain deliverance; not that it is necessary to allege reasons to persuade God, but because it is profitable to confirm our faith by such supports. As, then, it is the will of God that he should be known in his gracious character, not only of one or two, but generally of all men, whenever he vouchsafes deliverance to any of his children, it is a common benefit which all the faithful ought to apply to themselves when they see in the person of one man in what manner God, who is never inconsistent with himself, will act towards all his people. David, therefore, shows that he asks nothing for himself individually but what pertains to the whole Church. He prays that God would gladden the hearts of all the saints, or afford them all common cause of rejoicing: so that, assured of his readiness to help them, they may have recourse to him with greater alacrity. Hence we conclude, that, in the case of every individual, God gives a proof of his goodness towards us. What is added, *those that love thy salvation,* is also worthy of being observed by us. We may infer from this, that our faith is only proved to be genuine when we neither expect nor desire preservation otherwise than from God alone. Those who devise various ways and means of preservation for themselves in this world, despise and reject the salvation which God has taught us to expect from him alone. What had been said before, *those who seek thee,* is to the same purpose. If any individual would depend wholly upon God, and desire to be saved by his grace, he must renounce every vain hope, and employ all his thoughts towards the reception of his strength. Here, again, we must observe that two things are contrasted with each other. Formerly David had said

that the wicked *sought* his life ; now he ascribes to the faithful quite a contrary feeling, namely, that they seek God. In like manner he had related the reproaches and derision of the ungodly, while they said, *Aha, aha!* and now he introduces the godly speaking very differently, saying, The Lord be magnified !

17. *But I am poor and needy.* In this concluding clause he mingles prayer with thanksgiving, although it may be that he records a request which he had made when he was placed in extreme danger. The first clause of the verse might be rendered thus : Although I was miserable and poor, God did think upon me. As according to the extent in which any one is afflicted, so is he despised by the world, we imagine that he is disregarded by God, we must, therefore, stedfastly maintain that our miseries in no respect produce on the part of God a feeling of weariness towards us, so that it should become troublesome to him to aid us. In this way, however, let us rather read the clause : When I was miserable and poor, the Lord looked upon my necessity : So that by this circumstance he enhances the grace of God. If God anticipate us with his goodness, and do not wait till adversity presses upon us, then his favour towards us is not so apparent. This comparison, therefore, illustrates very clearly the glory of God in the deliverance of David, inasmuch as he vouchsafed to stretch forth his hand to a man who was despised and rejected of all men, nay, who was destitute of all help and hope. Now, if it was necessary that David should have been reduced to this extremity, it is no wonder if persons in a more private station are often humbled after this manner, that they may feel and acknowledge in good earnest that they have been delivered out of despair by the hand of God. The simple and natural meaning of the prayer is this, Lord, thou art my help and my deliverer, therefore delay not to come to my aid. As it is a foolish thing to approach God with a doubtful and wavering mind, the Psalmist takes courage, as he was wont to do from his own experience, and persuades himself that the help of God, by which he had been hitherto preserved, would not fail him.

PSALM XLI.

David, while he was severely afflicted by the hand of God, perceived that he was unjustly blamed by men who regarded him as one who had already been condemned and devoted to eternal destruction. Under this trial he fortifies himself by the consolation of hope. At the same time, he complains partly of the cruelty, and partly of the treachery, of his enemies. And although he recognises the affliction with which he is visited as a just punishment of his sins, yet he charges his enemies with cruelty and malice, inasmuch as they troubled and afflicted one who had always endeavoured to do them good. Finally, he records an expression of his gratitude and joy, because he had been preserved by the grace of God.

¶ *To the chief musician. A Psalm of David.*

1. *Blessed is he that judgeth wisely of the poor :*[1] *Jehovah will deliver him*[2] *in the day of evil.*
2. *Jehovah will keep him, and preserve him in life : he shall be blessed upon the earth ;*[3] *and thou wilt not abandon him to the will of his enemies.*
3. *Jehovah will support*[4] *him upon the bed of sorrow : thou hast turned all his bed in his sickness.*

1. *Blessed is he that judgeth wisely of the poor.* Interpreters are generally of opinion that the exercise of kindness and compassion manifested in taking care of the miserable, and helping them, is here commended. Those, however, who maintain that the Psalmist here commends the considerate candour of those who judge wisely and charitably of men in adversity, form a better judgment of his meaning. Indeed, the participle מַשְׂכִּיל, *maskil,* cannot be explained in any other way. At the same time, it ought to be observed on what account it is that David declares those to be blessed who form a wise and

---

[1] " C'est, de l'affligé."—*Fr. marg.* " That is, the afflicted."
[2] " Asçavoir, l'affligé."—*Fr. marg.* " Namely, the afflicted."
[3] " Il prosperera en la terre."—*Fr.* " He shall prosper on the earth."
[4] " Confortera."—*Fr. text.* " Soulagera."—*Fr. marg.* " Will comfort."

prudent judgment concerning the afflictions by which God chastises his servants. We have said that he had to contend in his own heart against the perverse judgments of foolish and wicked men, because, when affliction was pressing heavily upon him, many considered that he had fallen into a desperate condition, and was altogether beyond the hope of recovery. Doubtless, it happened to him as it did to the holy patriarch Job, whom his friends reckoned to be one of the most wicked of men, when they saw God treating him with great severity. And certainly it is an error which is by far too common among men, to look upon those who are oppressed with afflictions as condemned and reprobate. As, on the one hand, the most of men, judging of the favour of God from an uncertain and transitory state of prosperity, applaud the rich, and those upon whom, as they say, fortune smiles; so, on the other hand, they act contemptuously towards the wretched and miserable, and foolishly imagine that God hates them, because he does not exercise so much forbearance towards them as he does towards the reprobate. The error of which we speak, namely, that of judging wrongfully and wickedly, is one which has prevailed in all ages of the world. The Scriptures in many places plainly and distinctly declare, that God, for various reasons, tries the faithful by adversities, at one time to train them to patience, at another to subdue the sinful affections of the flesh, at another to cleanse, and, as it were, purify them from the remaining desires of the flesh, which still dwell within them; sometimes to humble them, sometimes to make them an example to others, and at other times to stir them up to the contemplation of the divine life. For the most part, indeed, we often speak rashly and indiscriminately concerning others, and, so to speak, plunge even into the lowest abyss those who labour under affliction. To restrain such a rash and unbridled spirit, David says that they are blessed who do not suffer themselves, by speaking at random, to judge harshly of their neighbours; but, discerning aright the afflictions by which they are visited, mitigate, by the wisdom of the Spirit, the severe and unjust judgments to which we are naturally so prone. I have just adduced as an example the case of Job, whom his friends, when they saw him involved in extreme misery, hesitated not to account an outcast, and one whose case was altogether hopeless.[1] If any one endued with candour, and possessed of a humane disposition, should meet with such a case, he would regard it in the exercise of the same discretion which David here commends. As to ourselves, being admonished by this testimony of the Holy Spirit, let us learn to guard against a too precipitate judgment. We must therefore judge prudently of our brethren who are in affliction; that is to say, we must hope well of their salvation, lest, if we condemn them unmercifully before the time, this unjust severity in the end fall upon our own heads. It ought, however, especially to be observed, what indeed I have already noticed, that the object which David had in view, when he saw himself, as it were, overwhelmed by the malicious and cruel judgments which were expressed concerning him, was to fortify himself by this as a ground of consolation, lest he should sink under the temptation. If, therefore, at any time Satan should endeavour to destroy the foundation of our faith, by the rash and presumptuous judgments of men, let us also learn to have recourse to this device of wisdom, lest unawares we fall into despair. This is the proper use of the doctrine contained in this passage.

The Lord will deliver him in the day of evil. Some connect these words, *in the day of evil,* with the preceding clause; and the reading thus suggested might indeed be admitted; but the distinction which I have followed is better adapted to the sense, and is also supported by the Hebrew accent. Thus at least the doctrine deducible from these words is susceptible of a fuller meaning, namely, that the Lord will deliver the poor in the day of his adversity. Some think that David here prays for a blessing in behalf of the upright and compassionate; as if he had said, May the Lord himself recompense them again for their kindness, if at any time it happen that they are grievously afflicted! Others suppose that David here records the language of such men from which we may come to the knowledge of their wisdom and

---

[1] " Pour un homme reprouvé et forclos d'esperance de salut."—*Fr.*

uprightness. In my opinion, however, both are equally in error in reading this clause in the form of a desire or prayer. Whether, indeed, David speaks in his own name, or in the name of others, he briefly recommends and enjoins the kindness which we ought to exercise towards the afflicted; for although God may for a time manifest his displeasure against them, yet he will, nevertheless, be gracious to them, so that the issue will at length be happier and more joyful than the judgment we might be led to form from the present aspect of things. We now see that the sense in which I have explained this verse is much more copious and fuller of meaning, namely, that we ought to hope for salvation and deliverance from the hand of the Lord, even in the day of adversity; for otherwise, no man who had once fallen into a state of sorrow and sadness would ever be able to rise again. And this I say, because the design of the Holy Spirit in this passage is not only to exhort the faithful to be ready in showing kindness towards their brethren when they see them in affliction, but also to point out the remedy which has been provided for the mitigation of our sorrow, whenever our faith is shaken by adversity.

2. *Jehovah will keep him, and preserve him in life.* Here David follows out the same sentiment expressed in the preceding verse, when he says that the Lord will keep the afflicted, whose destruction cruel and unjust men represent as inevitable. It is likewise necessary always to bear in mind the contrast which is stated between the day of evil and the blessing of deliverance. In this verse the expressions denoting *restoration to life,* and *blessedness on the earth,* are of similar import. By these expressions, David means to show that although he had been to all appearance a dead man, yet the hope of life both for himself and for all the faithful had not been extinguished. There might, it is true, appear some inconsistency in his promising himself a happy life in this world, seeing our condition here would be miserable indeed if we had not the expectation of a better state in the world to come. But the answer to this is, that as many had despaired of his recovery, he expressly declares that he will yet

be restored to his former state, and will continue alive, nay, that in him there will be seen manifest tokens of the favour of God. He does not in the least exclude by these expressions the hope of a better life after death. What follows concerning the *bed of sorrow* has led some to form a conjecture which, in my opinion, is not at all probable. What David says of affliction in general, without determining what kind of affliction, they regard as applicable exclusively to sickness. But it is no uncommon thing for those who are sorrowful and grieved in their minds to throw themselves upon their bed, and to seek repose; for the hearts of men are sometimes more distressed by grief than by sickness. It is, certainly, highly probable that David was at that time afflicted with some very heavy calamity, which might be a token that God was not a little displeased with him. In the second clause of the verse there is some obscurity. Some understand the expression, *turning the bed*, in the same sense as if God, in order to give some alleviation to his servant in the time of trouble, had made his bed and arranged it, as we are wont to do to those who are sick, that they may lay themselves more softly.[1] Others hold, and, in my opinion, more correctly, that when David was restored to health, his bed, which had formerly served him as a sick couch, was *turned*, that is to say, changed.[2] Thus the sense would be, that although he now languish in sorrow, whilst the Lord is chastening him and training him by means of affliction, yet in a little while he will experience relief by the hand of the same God, and thus recover his strength.

[1] Viewed in this sense, the passage is very beautiful and highly consolatory. How refreshing is it in sickness to have the bed turned and made anew! and this is the way in which God refreshes and relieves the merciful man in his sickness. He acts towards him the part of a kind nurse, turning and shaking his whole couch, and thus making it easy and comfortable for him.

[2] " C'est à dire, changé."

4. *I have said, O Jehovah! have mercy upon me : heal my soul, for I have sinned against thee.*
5. *My enemies have spoken evil of me, When shall he die, and his name perish?*
6. *And if he come to see me, he speaketh lies: his heart heapeth up iniquity to himself; when he shall have gone forth he will tell it.*

4. *I have said, O Jehovah! have mercy upon me.* By this verse he shows that in his adversity he did not seek to soothe his mind by flattery, as the greater part of men do, who endeavour to assuage their sorrows by some vain consolation. And, certainly, the man who is guided by the Spirit of God will, when warned of God by the afflictions with which he is visited, frankly acknowledge his sins, and quietly submit to the admonitions of his brethren, nay, he will even anticipate them by a voluntary confession. David here lays down a mark by which he distinguishes himself from the reprobate and wicked, when he tells us that he earnestly entreated that his sin might not be laid to his charge, and that he had sought refuge in the mercy of God. He indeed requests that some alleviation might be granted to him under the affliction which he endured: but he rises to a higher source of relief, when he asks that through the forgiveness of his sins he might obtain reconciliation to God. Those, as we have said elsewhere, invert the natural order of things, who seek a remedy only for the outward miseries under which they labour, but all the while neglect the cause of them; acting as a sick man would do who sought only to quench his thirst, but never thought of the fever under which he labours, and which is the chief cause of his trouble. Before David, therefore, speaks at all of the healing of his soul, that is to say, of his life,[1] he first says, *Have mercy upon me :* and with this we must connect the reason which immediately follows—*for I have sinned against thee.* In saying so, he confesses that God is justly displeased with him, and that he can only be restored again to his favour by his sins being blotted out. I take the particle כי, *ki,* in its proper and natural signification, and not

---

[1] "C'est à dire, de sa vie."—*Fr.*

adversatively, as some would understand it. He asks then that God would have mercy upon him because he had sinned. From that proceeds *the healing of the soul,* which he interposes between his prayer and confession, as being the effect of the compassion and mercy of God; for David expects that as soon as he had obtained forgiveness, he would also obtain relief from his affliction.

5. *My enemies have spoken evil of me.* *To speak* is here used in the sense of *to imprecate.* In thus describing the unbecoming conduct of his enemies, he seeks, as has been elsewhere said, to induce God to have mercy upon him: because the more that God sees his own people cruelly treated, he is so much the more disposed mercifully to succour them. Thus David, by his own example, stirs up and encourages us to greater confidence in God; because the more that our enemies break forth in their cruelty towards us, so much the more does it procure for us favour in the sight of God. The terms in which his enemies uttered this imprecation show how cruel their hatred had been towards him, since it could only be appeased by his destruction, and that, too, accompanied with shame and ignominy; for they wished that with his life the very remembrance of his name should also be blotted out.

6. *And if he come to see me, he speaketh lies.* What is contained in this verse relates to his false and treacherous friends. Those who were his professed enemies made no secret of their enmity against him, but openly persecuted him; and that he has already shown in the preceding verse. In addition to this, he now complains that many came to him with professions of attachment to him, as if they had been his friends, who, nevertheless, afterwards poured forth their malicious ill-will in secret against him. Enemies of this sort, who thus cover and conceal their malice, and insinuate themselves under the mask of a fair appearance, only for the purpose of secretly doing us mischief, are indeed much more to be feared than those who openly declare their wicked intentions. Accordingly, having complained of his open enemies, he proceeds to speak of his pretended friends, of whom he declares

that they come to see him with no other design than *to speak lies*, and yet that they are meanwhile devising some deceitful and malicious purpose against him, nay, that they are even secretly *heaping up iniquity*, and, so to speak, laying it up in store in their hearts; and then he adds, that when *they have gone forth* from his presence, they manifest their hypocrisy and deceitfulness.

7. *All they that hate me whisper together against me : they plot mischief against me.*
8. *An evil deed of Belial cleaveth fast to him : and he that lieth down shall never be able to rise again.*
9. *Even the man of my peace, in whom I trusted, who eats of my bread, has lifted up the heel against me.*

7. *All they that hate me whisper together against me.* Here he seems generally to include both classes of his enemies; those who sought to oppress him in an open manner, and in the character of avowed enemies; and those who, under the pretence of friendship, attempted to do the same thing by deceit and stratagem. Accordingly, he says that all of them took counsel together about his destruction, just as we know that wicked men hold much secret consultation respecting their intended deeds of treachery, and whisper to one another concerning them. Hence he adds the words *to meditate*, or *plot*, which he employs to denote their base conspiracies and sinful consultations.

8. *An evil deed of Belial cleaveth fast to him.* From this verse it appears that they had thus conspired together for his destruction, on the ground that they regarded him as a wicked man, and a person worthy of a thousand deaths. The insolence and arrogance which they manifested towards him proceeded from the false and wicked judgment which they had formed concerning him, and of which he made mention in the beginning of the psalm. They say, therefore, that *an evil deed of Belial* holds him shut up, and, as it were, bound fast. This verb יָצוּק, *yatsuk*, properly signifies; but in translating the verse I have followed the rendering which is

most commonly received, reading *cleaveth fast to him, &c.* This expression is by others rendered *spreadeth upon him,* but this interpretation seems to me to be too constrained. As to the word *Belial,* we have already spoken of it in the eighteenth psalm. But as grammarians maintain that it is compounded of בְּלִי, *beli,* and יָעַל, *yaäl,* which signify *not to rise,* the expression, *thing of Belial,* (for so it is literally in the Hebrew,) I understand in this place as meaning an extraordinary and hateful crime, which, as we commonly say, can never be expiated, and from which there is no possibility of escape; unless, perhaps, some would rather refer it to the affliction itself under which he laboured, as if his enemies had said that he was seized by some incurable malady.[1] But whatever may be as to this, his enemies regarded it as absolutely certain that God was altogether hostile to him, and would never be reconciled towards him, since he was chastising him with so much severity. When they add in the following clause, *he shall never be able to rise again,*[2] this clearly

[1] There seems some difficulty as to what is meant by the words בְּלִיַּעַל דָּבָר, *debar beliyaäl.* They are literally *a word of Belial.* But *word* in Hebrew is often used for *a thing* or *matter,* Exod. xviii. 16; Deut. xvii. 4; 1 Kings xiv. 13. And *Belial* is used by the Hebrews to designate any detestable wickedness. Thus the original words bring out the meaning which Calvin fixes upon them; and in the same sense they are understood by several critics. Dr Geddes reads " a lawless deed;" and he explains the expression as referring to " David's sin in the case of Uriah; which his enemies now assign as the cause of his present calamity; as if they had said, 'This sin hath at length overtaken him,' &c." Horsley reads, " Some cursed thing presseth heavily upon him;" and by " some cursed thing" he understands " the crime which they supposed to be the cause of the divine judgment upon him." Fry reads, " Some hellish crime cleaveth unto him." Cresswell adopts the interpretation of M. Flaminius: " They say, Some load of iniquity presses upon him, (or clings to him,) so that from the place where he lieth he will rise no more." But there is another sense which the words will bear. The Septuagint reads, " λόγος παράνομος;" the Vulgate, " a wicked word;" the Chaldee, " a perverse word;" the Syriac, " a word of iniquity;" and the Arabic, " words contrary to law;" and so the expression may mean a grievous slander or calumny. This is the sense in which it is understood by Hammond. " And this," says he, " is said *to cleave* to him on whom it is fastened; it being the nature of calumnies, when strongly affixed on any, to cleave fast, and leave some evil mark behind them: *Calumniare fortiter, aliquid hærebit.*" In our vulgar version it is "an evil disease." And דָּבָר, *debar,* no doubt sometimes signifies a *plague* or *pestilence.* According to this rendering, the sense will be, he is smitten with an evil disease on account of his crimes, from which he will never recover.

[2] Hammond reads with our English version, *Now that he lieth he shall rise up no more,* and thinks that this is a proverbial phrase which was in

shows that they utterly cut off from him all hope of recovery. And certainly it was a sore temptation to David, who had in himself the testimony of a good conscience, to think that he was regarded by men as one who was pursued by the vengeance of God, nay, that they even cast him headlong into hell. But it pleased God thus to try his servant, that, trusting to the testimony of his own conscience, he should pay no regard to what men might say, or be troubled by the reproaches they might cast upon him. It was also his design to teach us, by his example, that we must seek the reward of our righteousness elsewhere than in this world, since we see with what unequal balances the world often sets itself to estimate the difference between virtue and vice.

9. *Even the man of my peace.* As the very height of all his miseries, David here declares that he had found the same treachery in some one, or, indeed, in many of his greatest friends. For the change of number is very frequent in the Hebrew language, so that he may speak of several individuals as if they were only one person. Thus the meaning would be: Not only the common people, or strangers of whom I had no knowledge or acquaintance, but my greatest friends, nay, even those with whom I was most intimate, and those of my own household, whom I admitted to eat and drink with me at my table, vaunt themselves reproachfully against me. Among the Hebrews, the expression, *men of peace,* denotes their kinsfolk and connections; but it was a much closer alliance, and one which ought to have secured a stricter observance of the laws of friendship, *to eat the bread* of David in company with himself: for it is as if he had employed the appellation, My companion.[1] If, however, any would rather understand it of some particular traitor than of several persons, I have no objection to it. *To lift up the heel* is, in

use among the Hebrews, and which was applied to any sort of ruin, as well as to that which is effected by bodily disease. "The calumniator," he observes, "may destroy and ruin as well as the pestilence; and from him was David's danger most frequently, and not from a pestilential disease."

[1] "Mon compagnon ordinaire, et qui estoit à pot et à feu avec moy, ainsi qu'on dit en commun proverbe."—*Fr.* "My usual companion, and one who, according to the common proverb, had bed and board with me."

my opinion, to be understood metaphorically, and signifies *to rise up disdainfully* against a man who is afflicted and cast down.[1] Others explain the expression by *to lay wait secretly;* but the former interpretation is more appropriate, That the wicked, seeing that David was placed in embarrassed circumstances, or already prostrated in the dust, took occasion from this to assail him indirectly indeed, but, nevertheless, always with insolence; a thing which usually happens among people of a wicked and servile disposition. Christ, in quoting this passage, (John xiii. 18,) applies it to the person of Judas. And certainly we ought to understand that, although David speaks of himself in this psalm, yet he speaks not as a common and private person, but as one who represented the person of Christ, inasmuch as he was, as it were, the example after which the whole Church should be conformed—a point well entitled to our attention, in order that each of us may prepare himself for the same condition. It was necessary that what was begun in David should be fully accomplished in Christ; and, therefore, it must of necessity come to pass, that the same thing should be fulfilled in each of his members, namely, that they should not only suffer from external violence and force, but also from internal foes, ever ready to betray them, even as Paul declares that the Church shall be assailed, not only by "fightings without," but also by "fears within," (2 Cor. vii. 5.)

> 10. *Do thou, O Jehovah! have mercy upon me : raise me up, and I will recompense them.*
> 11. *By this I know that I have been acceptable to thee, because my enemy doth not triumph over me.*
> 12. *And as for me, thou wilt uphold me in my integrity,*[2] *and establish me before thy face for ever.*
> 13. *Blessed be Jehovah, the God of Israel, for ever and ever. Amen and Amen.*

10. *Do thou, O Jehovah! have mercy upon me.* From a

---

[1] "*Hath lifted against me his heel; i. e.* hath spurned me, hath kicked at me, as a vicious beast of burden does, hath insulted me in my misery. Comp. Ps. xxxvi. 11."—*Cresswell.*

[2] Or soundness.

consideration of the wrongful cruelty of his enemies, he again takes encouragement to pray. And there is included in what he says a tacit contrast between God and men; as if he had said, Since there is to be found no aid or help in the world, but as, on the contrary, a strange degree of cruelty, or secret malice, every where prevails, be thou, at least, O Lord! pleased to succour me by thy mercy. This is the course which ought to be pursued by all the afflicted, whom the world unjustly persecutes; that is to say, they ought not only to occupy themselves in bewailing the wrongs which are done them, but they ought also to commend their cause to God: and the more Satan endeavours to overthrow their faith, and to distract their thoughts, the more should they fix their minds attentively on God alone. In using such language, the Psalmist again ascribes his restoration to the mercy of God as its cause. What he says in the concluding clause of the verse of taking vengeance seems harsh and unaccountable. If he confessed truly and from the heart, in the preceding part of the psalm, that God was just in thus afflicting him, why does he not extend forgiveness to others, as he desires that forgiveness should be granted to himself? Surely it were a shameful abuse of the grace of God, if, after having been restored and pardoned by him, we should refuse to follow his example in showing mercy. Besides, it would have been a feeling far removed from that of humility or kindness, for David, even while he was yet in the midst of death, to have desired revenge. But here two things are to be taken into account: First, David was not as one of the common people, but a king appointed by God, and invested with authority; and, secondly, It is not from an impulse of the flesh, but in virtue of the nature of his office, that he is led to denounce against his enemies the punishment which they had merited. If, then, each individual indiscriminately, in taking vengeance upon his enemies, should allege the example of David in his own defence, it is necessary, first, to take into account the difference which subsists between us and David, by reason of the circumstances and position in which he was placed by God;[1] and, secondly, it is neces-

[1] "Pour raison de la condition et estat qu'il avoit de Dieu."—*Fr.*

sary to ascertain whether the same zeal which was in him reigns also in us, or rather, whether we are directed and governed by the same divine Spirit. David, being king, was entitled, in virtue of his royal authority, to execute the vengeance of God against the wicked; but as to us our hands are tied. In the second place, As he represented the person of Christ, so he cherished in his heart pure and holy affections: and hence it is, that, in speaking as he does in this verse, he indulged not his own angry spirit, but fulfilled faithfully the duties of the station to which he had been called of God. In short, in acting thus, he executed the righteous judgment of God, just in the same way as it is lawful for us to pray that the Lord himself would take vengeance upon the ungodly; for, as we are not armed with the power of the sword, it is our duty to have recourse to the heavenly Judge. At the same time, in beseeching him to show himself our guardian and defender, by taking vengeance on our enemies, we must do so in a calm and composed state of mind, and exercise a watchful care lest we should give too loose reins to our desires, by casting off the rule prescribed by the Spirit. As to David, the duties of his station required that he should employ means for subduing the rebellious, and that he should be truly the minister of God in inflicting punishment upon all the wicked.

11. *By this I know that I have been acceptable to thee.* David now proceeds to the exercise of thanksgiving; unless, indeed, by altering the tense of the verb, we would rather with some read this verse in connection with the preceding, in this way: In this I shall know that thou favourest me, if thou suffer not my enemies to triumph over me; but it suits much better to understand it as an expression of joy on account of some deliverance which God had vouchsafed to him. After having offered up his prayers, he now ascribes his deliverance to God, and speaks of it as a manifest and singular benefit he had received from him. It might, however, be asked, whether it is a sufficiently sure method of our coming to the knowledge of God's love towards us, that he does not suffer our enemies to triumph over us? for it will often happen, that a man is

delivered from danger, whom, nevertheless, God does not regard with pleasure; and, besides, the good-will of God towards us is known chiefly from his word, and not simply by experience. The answer to this is easy: David was not destitute of faith, but for the confirmation of it he took advantage of the helps which God had afterwards added to his word. In speaking thus, he seems to refer not only to the favour and good-will which God bears to all the faithful in common, but to the special favour which God had conferred upon him in choosing him to be king; as if he had said, Now, Lord, I am more and more confirmed in the belief that thou hast vouchsafed to adopt me to be the first-born among the kings of the earth. Thus he extends to the whole state of the realm the help of God, by means of which he had been delivered from some particular calamity.

12. *And as for me, thou wilt uphold me in my integrity.* Some expound the clause thus: That, as David followed after uprightness, God had stretched out the hand to him. But this interpretation does not agree very well with a preceding sentence, in which he acknowledged that he had been justly punished by God. The calamity which had befallen him exposed him to the insult and derision of his enemies; but it is not likely that they were the authors of it: and hence, it would have been out of place to have adduced his integrity for this purpose, because the Lord is said to have respect to our integrity, when he defends us against our enemies, and delivers us from the outrage of men. We must therefore seek another meaning. The Hebrew word which we have rendered *integrity* might be referred to the body as well as the mind, thus: I shall continue *sound*, because thou wilt preserve and establish me. He seems, however, to extend the favour of God still farther; as if he had said, that he had been assisted not only once by his hand, but that, during the whole course of the period he had enjoyed prosperity, he had always been upheld in safety by the power of God. If any would rather understand by this term the piety and sincere disposition for which David was distinguished,—and this meaning would be very suitable,—it will not follow from this that David boasts of his past life, but only that he declares

that, when brought to the test, or in the midst of the conflict, even although Satan and wicked men endeavoured to shake his faith, he had not turned aside from the fear of God. By these words, then, he bears testimony to his patience, because, when sorely vexed and tormented, he had not forsaken the path of uprightness. If this meaning should be adopted, it must be observed, that this benefit, namely, that David continued invincible, and boldly sustained these assaults of temptation, is immediately after ascribed to God, and that for the future, David looked for preservation by no other means than by the sustaining power of God. If the language should be understood as referring to his external condition, this will be found to suit equally well the scope of the passage, and the meaning will be this, That God will never cease to manifest his favour, until he has preserved his servants in safety, even to the end. As to the form of expression, *that God establishes them before his face*, this is said of those whom he defends and preserves in such a manner, that he shows by evident tokens the paternal care which he exercises over them; as, on the other hand, when he seems to have forgotten his own people, he is said to hide his face from them.

13. *Blessed be Jehovah, the God of Israel, for ever and ever.*[1] Here the Psalmist confirms and repeats the expression of

---

[1] The Hebrew Psalter is divided into five books. This is the end of the first book. The second ends with the 72d psalm, the third with the 89th, the fourth with the 106th, and the fifth with the 150th. It is worthy of remark, that each of these five books solemnly concludes with a distinct ascription of praise to God; only no distinct doxology appears at the end of the fifth book, probably because the last psalm throughout is a psalm of praise. The Jewish writers affirm that this form of benediction was added by the person who collected and distributed The Psalms into their present state. How ancient this division is, cannot now be clearly ascertained. Jerome, in his Epistle to Marcella, and Epiphanius, speak of The Psalms as having been divided by the Hebrews into five books; but when this division was made, they do not inform us. The forms of ascription of praise, added at the end of each of the five books, are in the Septuagint version, from which we may conclude that this distribution had been made before that version was executed. It was probably made by Ezra, after the return of the Jews from Babylon to their own country, and the establishment of the worship of God in the new temple; and it was perhaps made in imitation of a similar distribution of the books of Moses. In making this division of the Hebrew Psalter, regard appears to have been paid to the subject-matter of the psalms.

thanksgiving contained in a preceding verse. By calling God expressly *the God of Israel*, he testifies that he cherished in his heart a deep and thorough impression of the covenant which God had made with the Fathers; because it was the source from which his deliverance proceeded. The term *amen* is repeated twice, to express the greater vehemence, and that all the godly might be the more effectually stirred up to praise God.

PSALM XLII.

In the first place, David shows that when he was forced to flee by reason of the cruelty of Saul, and was living in a state of exile, what most of all grieved him was, that he was deprived of the opportunity of access to the sanctuary; for he preferred the service of God to every earthly advantage. In the second place, he shows that being tempted with despair, he had in this respect a very difficult contest to sustain. In order to strengthen his hope, he also introduces prayer and meditation on the grace of God. Last of all, he again makes mention of the inward conflict which he had with the sorrow which he experienced.

¶ To the chief musician. A lesson of instruction to the sons of Korah.

The name of David is not expressly mentioned in the inscription of this psalm. Many conjecture that the sons of Korah were the authors of it. This, I think, is not at all probable. As it is composed in the person of David, who, it is well known, was endued above all others with the spirit of prophecy, who will believe that it was written and composed for him by another person? He was the teacher generally of the whole Church, and a distinguished instrument of the Spirit. He had already delivered to the company of the Levites, of whom the sons of Korah formed a part, other psalms to be sung by them. What need, then, had he to borrow their help, or to have recourse to their assistance in a matter which he was much better able of himself to execute than they were? To me, therefore, it seems more probable, that the sons of Korah are here mentioned because this psalm was committed as a precious treasure to be preserved by them, as we know that out of the number of the singers, some were chosen and appointed to be keepers of the psalms. That there is no mention made of David's name does not of itself involve any difficulty, since we see the same omission in other psalms, of which there is, notwithstanding, the strongest grounds for concluding that he was the author. As to the word משכיל, *maskil*, I have already made some remarks upon it in the thirty-second psalm. This word, it is true, is sometimes found in the inscription of other psalms besides those in which David declares that he had been subjected to the chastening rod of God. It is, however, to be observed, that it is properly applied to chastisements, since the design of them is to instruct the children of God, when they do not sufficiently profit from doctrine. As to the particular time of the composition of this psalm, expositors are not altogether agreed. Some suppose that David here complains of his calamity, when he was expelled from the throne by his son Absalom. But I am rather disposed to entertain a different opinion, founded, if I mistake not, upon good reasons. The rebellion of Absalom was very soon suppressed, so that it did not long prevent David from approaching the sanctuary. And yet, the lamentation which he here makes refers expressly to a long state of exile, under which he had languished, and, as it were, pined away with grief. It is not the sorrow merely of a few days which he describes in the third verse; nay, the scope of the entire composition will clearly show that he had languished for a long time in the wretched condition of which he speaks. It has been alleged as an argument against referring this psalm to the reign of Saul, that the ark of the covenant was neglected during his reign, so that it is not very likely that David at that time conducted the stated choral services in the sanctuary; but this argument is not very conclusive: for although Saul only worshipped God as a mere matter of form, yet he was unwilling to be regarded in any other light than as a devout man. And as to David, he has shown in other parts of his writings with what diligence he frequented the holy assemblies, and more especially on festival days. Certainly, these words which we shall meet with in Psalm lv. 14, "We walked unto the house of God in company," relate to the time of Saul.

1. *As the hart crieth*[1] *for the fountains of water, so my soul crieth after thee, O Jehovah!*
2. *My soul hath thirsted for God, even for the living God: when shall I come to appear before the face of God?*
3. *My tears have been my bread day and night, while they say daily to me, Where is thy God?*

1. *As the hart crieth for the fountains of water, &c.* The meaning of these two verses simply is, that David preferred to

---

[1] Horsley also reads, "crieth." In the Hebrew it is "brayeth." In Hebrew there are distinct words to mark the peculiar cries of the hart, the bear, the lion, the zebra, the wolf, the horse, the dog, the cow, and the sheep. The distressing cry of the hart seems to be here expressed. Being naturally of a hot and sanguine constitution, it suffers much from thirst in the Oriental regions. When in want of water, and unable to

all the enjoyments, riches, pleasures, and honours of this world, the opportunity of access to the sanctuary, that in this way he might cherish and strengthen his faith and piety by the exercises prescribed in the Law. When he says that he *cried for the living God,* we are not to understand it merely in the sense of a burning love and desire towards God : but we ought to remember in what manner it is that God allures us to himself, and by what means he raises our minds upwards. He does not enjoin us to ascend forthwith into heaven, but, consulting our weakness, he descends to us. David, then, considering that the way of access was shut against him, cried to God, because he was excluded from the outward service of the sanctuary, which is the sacred bond of intercourse with God. I do not mean to say that the observance of external ceremonies can of itself bring us into favour with God, but they are religious exercises which we cannot bear to want by reason of our infirmity. David, therefore, being excluded from the sanctuary, is no less grieved than if he had been separated from God himself. He did not, it is true, cease in the meantime to direct his prayers towards heaven, and even to the sanctuary itself; but conscious of his own infirmity, he was specially grieved that the way by which the faithful obtained access to God was shut against him. This is an example which may well suffice to put to shame the arrogance of those who without concern can bear to be deprived of those means,[1] or rather, who proudly despise them, as if it were in their power to ascend to heaven in a moment's flight; nay, as if they surpassed David in zeal and alacrity of mind. We must not, however, imagine that the prophet suffered himself to rest in earthly elements,[2] but only

find it, it makes a mournful noise, and eagerly seeks the cooling river ; and especially when pursued over the dry and parched wilderness by the hunter, it seeks the stream of water with intense desire, and braying plunges into it with eagerness, as soon as it has reached its wished-for banks, at once to quench its thirst and escape its deadly pursuers. It is the female hart which is here meant, as " brayeth" is feminine, and as the reading of the LXX. also shows, which is ἡ ἔλαφος.

[1] " Qui ne soucient pas beaucoup d'estre privez de ces moyens."—*Fr.*
[2] " C'est assavoir, és ceremonies externes commandees en la Loy."—*Fr. marg.* "That is to say, in the external ceremonies commanded by the Law."

that he made use of them as a ladder, by which he might ascend to God, finding that he had not wings with which to fly thither. The similitude which he takes from *a hart* is designed to express the extreme ardour of his desire. The sense in which some explain this is, that the waters are eagerly sought by the harts, that they may recover from fatigue; but this, perhaps, is too limited. I admit that if the hunter pursue the stag, and the dogs also follow hard after it, when it comes to a river it gathers new strength by plunging into it. But we know also that at certain seasons of the year, harts, with an almost incredible desire, and more intensely than could proceed from mere thirst, seek after water; and although I would not contend for it, yet I think this is referred to by the prophet here.

The second verse illustrates more clearly what I have already said, that David does not simply speak of the presence of God, but of the presence of God in connection with certain symbols; for he sets before himself the tabernacle, the altar, the sacrifices, and other ceremonies by which God had testified that he would be near his people; and that it behoved the faithful, in seeking to approach God, to begin by those things. Not that they should continue attached to them, but that they should, by the help of these signs and outward means, seek to behold the glory of God, which of itself is hidden from the sight. Accordingly, when we see the marks of the divine presence engraven on the word, or on external symbols, we can say with David that there *is the face of God*, provided we come with pure hearts to seek him in a spiritual manner. But when we imagine God to be present otherwise than he has revealed himself in his word, and the sacred institutions of his worship, or when we form any gross or earthly conception of his heavenly majesty, we are only inventing for ourselves visionary representations, which disfigure the glory of God, and turn his truth into a lie.

3. *My tears have been my bread.* Here the Psalmist mentions another sharp piercing shaft with which the wicked and malevolent grievously wounded his heart. There can be no

doubt that Satan made use of such means as these to fan the flame that consumed him with grief. "What," we may suppose that adversary to say, "wouldst thou have? Seest thou not that God hath cast thee off? For certainly he desires to be worshipped in the tabernacle, to which you have now no opportunity of access, and from which you are as it were banished." These were violent assaults, and enough to have overturned the faith of this holy man, unless, supported by the power of the Spirit in a more than ordinary degree, he had made a strong and vigorous resistance. It is evident that his feelings had been really and strongly affected. We may be often agitated, and yet not to such an extent as to abstain from eating and drinking; but when a man voluntarily abstains from food, and indulges so much in weeping, that he daily neglects his ordinary meals, and is continually overwhelmed in sorrow, it is obvious that he is troubled in no light degree; but that he is wounded severely, and even to the heart.[1] Now, David says, that he did not experience greater relief in any thing whatever than from weeping; and, therefore, he gave himself up to it, just in the same manner as men take pleasure and enjoyment in eating; and this he says had been the case every day, and not only for a short time. Let us, therefore, whenever the ungodly triumph over us in our miseries, and spitefully taunt us that God is against us, never forget that it is Satan who moves them to speak in this manner, in order to overthrow our faith; and that, therefore, it is not time for us to take our ease, or to yield to indifference, when a war so dangerous is waged against us. There is still another reason which ought to inspire us with such feelings, and it is this, that the name of God is held up to scorn by the ungodly; for they cannot scoff at our faith without greatly reproaching him. If, then, we are not altogether insensible, we must in such circumstances be affected with the deepest sorrow.

[1] "Mais qu'il est nauré à bon escient et jusques au bout."—*Fr.*

4. *When I remember these things*,[1] *I pour out my soul within me, because I had gone in company with them,* [literally in number,] *leading them even to the house of God, with the voice of joy and praise, even the multitude dancing for joy.*[2]

5. *O my soul! why art thou cast down? and why art thou disquieted within me? Wait thou upon God: for I shall yet praise him for the helps* [or *salvations*] *of his countenance.*

6. *O my God! my soul is cast down within me, when I remember thee from the land of Jordan and of Hermonim,* [or, *and from the Hermons,*] *from the hill Mizar.*

4. *When I remember these things.* This verse is somewhat obscure, on account of the variation of the tenses in the Hebrew. And yet I have no doubt that the true and natural sense is, that David, when he called to remembrance his former condition, experienced so much the greater sadness by comparing it with his present condition. The remembrance, I say, of the past had no small influence in aggravating his misery, from the thought that he, who had formerly acted the part of a leader and standard-bearer in conducting others to the holy assemblies, should now be debarred from access to the temple. We know that those who have been accustomed to suffering from their childhood become insensible to it, and the very continuance of misery produces in us a certain degree of callousness, so that we cease to think of it, or to regard it as anything unusual. It is different with those who have not been so accustomed to it. And, therefore, it is no wonder if David,

---

[1] "Things" is a supplement. Boothroyd prefers reading "these times."

[2] In this verse, there is evidently a reference to the festive religious solemnities of the Jews, in which singing and dancing were used. These also formed an eminent part of the religious rites of the ancient Greeks and other heathen nations. Among the Greeks at the present day, it is the practice for a lady of distinction to lead the dance, and to be followed by a troop of young females, who imitate her steps, and if she sings, make up the chorus. This serves to throw light on the description given of Miriam, when she "took a timbrel in her hand, and all the women went out after her with timbrels and dances," (Exod. xv. 20.) She led the dance; they followed and imitated her steps. When David "danced before the Lord" at the bringing up of the ark, "with shouting and with the sound of the trumpet," it is probable that he was accompanied by others whom he led in the dance, (2 Sam. vi. 15, 16.) To this practice there is evidently an allusion in this passage; and the allusion greatly enhances its beauty.

who had been not one of the common people, but who had lately occupied a chief place among the princes, and had been leader of the foremost ranks among the faithful, should be more grievously disquieted, when he saw himself utterly cast off, and not admitted to a place even among the lowest. Accordingly, I connect the demonstrative pronoun *these* with the declaration which follows, namely, that he remembered how he had been accustomed to mingle in the company of the godly, and to lead them to the house of God. *To pour out the soul* is taken metaphorically by some for *to give utterance to his grief;* others are of opinion, that it signifies *to rejoice greatly,* or, as we commonly speak, *to be melted or dissolved in joy.* It appears to me that David rather means to say, that his affections were, as it were, melted within him, whether it were from joy or sorrow. As the soul of man sustains him, so long as it keeps its energies collected, so also it sinks within him, and, as it were, vanishes away, when any of the affections, by excessive indulgence, gains the ascendancy.[1] Accordingly, he is said to pour out his soul, who is so excited, that his affections lose their vigour, and begin to flow out. David's language implies, that his soul melted and fainted within him by the greatness of his sorrow, when he thought of the condition from which he had fallen. If any would rather understand it of *joy,* the language will admit of such an illustration as this: Formerly I took such a delight in walking foremost in the ranks of the people, and leading them in procession to the sanctuary, that my heart melted within me for joy, and I was quite transported with it: if, therefore, I should again be restored to the same happy condition, all my feelings would be ravished with the same delight. I have, however, already stated what appeared to me to be the best exposition. We must not suppose that David had been overwhelmed with the sorrow of the world; but, as in his present misery he discerned the wrath of God, he sorrowed after a godly sort, because, by his own fault, he had provoked the displeasure of God against him. And, even

---

[1] " Car ainsi que l'ame de l'homme le soustient tandis qu'elle conserve sa vigueur et la tient comme amasse, aussi elle se fond, et par maniere de dire, s'esvanouit quand quelque affection desmesuree vient à y dominer "—*Fr.*

without touching this reason of his sorrow, we see the source from which it proceeded. Even when afflicted by so many personal privations, he is nevertheless grieved only for the sanctuary, thereby showing that it would have been less distressing to him to have been deprived of life, than to continue in a state of exile from the presence of God. And, indeed, the way in which we ought to regulate all our affections is this, That, on the one hand, our joy may have respect to the paternal love and favour of God towards us, and that, on the other, the only cause of our grief may arise from feeling that he is angry with us. This is the "godly sorrow" of which Paul speaks, 2 Cor. vii. 10. By the term *number*, which in the Hebrew is called סך, *sach*, David, I have no doubt, intended *ranks*, or *companies in procession;* for when they went to the tabernacle on the holy days, they went not in confusion or in crowds, but walked in regular order, (Luke ii. 44.)

5. *O my soul! why art thou cast down?* From this it appears that David contended strongly against his sorrow, lest he should yield to temptation: but what we ought chiefly to observe is, that he had experienced a strong and bitter contest before he obtained the victory over it; or we might rather say, that he was not delivered from it after one alarming assault, but was often called upon to enter into new scenes of conflict. It need not excite our wonder that he was so much disquieted and cast down, since he could not discern any sign of the divine favour towards him. But David here represents himself as if he formed two opposing parties. In so far as in the exercise of faith he relied upon the promises of God, being armed with the Spirit of invincible fortitude, he set himself, in opposition to the affections of his flesh, to restrain and subdue them; and, at the same time, he rebuked his own cowardice and imbecility of heart. Moreover, although he carried on war against the devil and the world, yet he does not enter into open and direct conflict with them, but rather regards himself as the enemy against whom he desires chiefly to contend. And doubtless the best way to overcome Satan is, not to go out of ourselves, but to maintain an in-

ternal conflict against the desires of our own hearts. It ought, however, to be observed, that David confesses that his soul was cast down within him : for when our infirmities rise up in vast array, and, like the waves of the sea, are ready to overwhelm us, our faith seems to us to fail, and, in consequence, we are so overcome by mere fear, that we lack courage, and are afraid to enter into the conflict. Whenever, therefore, such a state of indifference and faint-heartedness shall seize upon us, let us remember, that to govern and subdue the desires of their hearts, and especially to contend against the feelings of distrust which are natural to all, is a conflict to which the godly are not unfrequently called. But here there are two evils specified, which, however apparently different, yet assail our hearts at the same time; the one is *discouragement*, and the other *disquietude*. When we are quite downcast, we are not free of a feeling of disquietude, which leads us to murmur and complain. The remedy to both of them is here added, *hope in God*, which alone inspires our minds, in the first place, with confidence in the midst of the greatest troubles; and, secondly, by the exercise of patience, preserves them in peace. In what follows, David very well expresses the power and nature of hope by these words, *I shall yet praise him;* for it has the effect of elevating our thoughts to the contemplation of the grace of God, when it is hidden from our view. By the term *yet*, he confesses that for the present, and in so far as the praises of God are concerned, his mouth is stopped, seeing he is oppressed and shut up on all sides. This, however, does not prevent him from extending his hope to some future distant period; and, in order to escape from his present sorrow, and, as it were, get beyond its reach, he promises himself what as yet there was no appearance of obtaining. Nor is this an imaginary expectation produced by a fanciful mind; but, relying upon the promises of God, he not only encourages himself to cherish good hope, but also promises himself certain deliverance. We can only be competent witnesses to our brethren of the grace of God when, in the first place, we have borne testimony to it to our own hearts. What follows, *The helps of his countenance,* may be differently expounded. Commentators, for the most part, supply the word *for:* so that, according to this view, David here expresses the matter or cause of thanksgiving—that *yet he would give praise or thanks to God for the help of his countenance.* This interpretation I readily admit. At the same time, the sense will not be inappropriate if we read the terms separately, thus: *helps or salvations* are *from the countenance of God;* for as soon as he is pleased to look upon his people he sets them in safety. *The countenance of God* is taken for the manifestation of his favour. His countenance then appears serene and gracious to us; as, on the contrary, adversity, like the intervening clouds, darkens or obscures its benign aspect.

6. *O my God! my soul is cast down within me.* If we suppose that this verse requires no supplement, then it will consist of two distinct and separate sentences. Literally it may be read thus: *O my God! my soul is cast down within me, therefore will I remember thee, &c.* But the greater number of expositors render the word עַל־כֵּן, *al-ken,* by *forasmuch as,* or *because,* so that it is employed to express the reason of what is contained in the preceding clause. And certainly it would be very appropriate in this sense, That as often as David, from the land of Jordan, in which he now lay hid as an exile, set himself to think of the sanctuary, his sorrow was so much the more increased. If, however, any would rather, as I have already observed, distinguish this verse into two parts, it must be understood as meaning that David thought of God in his exile, not to nourish his grief, but to assuage it. He did not act the part of those who find no relief in their afflictions but in forgetting God; for although wounded by his hand, he, nevertheless, failed not to acknowledge him to be his physician. Accordingly, the import of the whole verse will be this, I am now living in a state of exile, banished from the temple, and seem to be an alien from the household of God; but this will not prevent me from regarding him, and having recourse to him: I am now deprived of the accustomed sacrifices, of which I stand much in need, but he has not taken from me his word. As, however, the first interpretation is the one more generally received, and

this also seems to be added by way of exposition, it is better not to depart from it. David then complains that his soul was oppressed with sorrow, because he saw himself cast out of the Church of God. At the same time, there is in these words a tacit contrast;[1] as if he had said, It is not the desire to be restored to my wife, or my house, or any of my possessions, which grieves me so much as the distressing consideration, that I now find myself prevented from taking part in the service of God. We ought to learn from this, that although we are deprived of the helps which God has appointed for the edification of our faith and piety, it is, nevertheless, our duty to be diligent in stirring up our minds, that we may never suffer ourselves to be forgetful of God. But, above all, this is to be observed, that as in the preceding verse we have seen David contending courageously against his own affections, so now we here see by what means he stedfastly maintained his ground. He did this by having recourse to the help of God, and taking refuge in it as in a holy sanctuary. And, assuredly, if meditation upon the promises of God do not lead us to prayer, it will not have sufficient power to sustain and confirm us. Unless God impart strength to us, how shall we be able to subdue the many evil thoughts which constantly arise in our minds? The soul of man serves the purpose, as it were, of a workshop to Satan in which to forge a thousand methods of despair. And, therefore, it is not without reason that David, after a severe conflict with himself, has recourse to prayer, and calls upon God as the witness of his sorrow. By *the land of Jordan* is to be understood that part of the country which, in respect of Judea, was beyond the river of that name. This appears still more clearly from the word Hermonim or Hermons. Hermon was a mountainous district, which extended to a considerable distance; and because it had several tops, was called in the plural number Hermonim.[2]

---

[1] " C'est à dire, consideration d'autres choses a l'opposite."—*Fr. marg.* " That is to say, the consideration of other things quite opposite."

[2] Just as we say the Alps and the Appenines. The Hermons formed part of the ridge of the high hills called Antilibanus. The sources of the Jordan are in the vicinity. Davidson reads, "*From the land of Jordan,*

Perhaps David also has purposely made use of the plural number on account of the fear by which he was forced frequently to change his place of abode, and wander hither and thither. As to the word *Mizar,* some suppose that it was not the proper name of a mountain, and therefore translate it *little,* supposing that there is here an indirect comparison of the Hermons with the mountain of Sion, as if David meant to say that Sion, which was comparatively a small hill, was greater in his estimation than the lofty Hermons; but it appears to me that this would be a constrained interpretation.

> 7. *Depth calleth unto depth*[1] *at the noise of thy waterspouts* :[2] *all thy waves and thy floods have passed over me.*
> 8. *Jehovah will command his loving-kindness by day : and by night his song shall be with me ; and prayer to the God of my life.*

7. *Depth calleth unto depth.* These words express the grievousness, as well as the number and long continuance, of the miseries which he suffered ; as if he had said, I am oppress-

---

even *of the Hermons;* the two expressions signifying the same district."— *Sacred Hermeneutics,* p. 667.

[1] " Un abysme crie à l'autre abysme."—*Fr.* " One depth crieth to another depth."

[2] A waterspout is a large tube or cylinder formed of clouds, by means of the electric fluid, the base being uppermost, and the point let down perpendicularly from the clouds. It has a particular kind of *circular motion* at the point ; and being hollow within attracts vast quantities of water ; which it frequently pours down in torrents on the earth or the sea. So great is the quantity of water, and so sudden and precipitate the fall, that if it happen to break on a vessel, it shatters it to pieces, and sinks it in an instant. Those waterspouts which Dr Shaw saw in the Mediterranean, he informs us, "seemed to be so many cylinders of water falling down from the clouds ;" and he states, that they " are more frequent near the capes of Latikea, Greego, and Carmel, than in any other part of the Mediterranean."—(*Travels,* p. 333.) " These are all places," as Harmer observes, " on the coast of Syria, and the last of them every body knows in Judea, it being a place rendered famous by the prayers of the prophet Elijah. The Jews then could not be ignorant of what happened on their coasts ; and David must have known of these dangers of the sea, if he had not actually seen some of them."—(*Observations,* vol. iii. p. 222.) In the description of a violent and dangerous storm at sea, by which he here portrays his great distress, he would, therefore, naturally draw his imagery from these awful phenomena, which were of frequent occurrence on the Jewish coasts.

ed not only with one kind of misery, but various kinds of distress return one after another, so that there seems to be neither end nor measure to them. In the first place, by the term *depth,* he shows that the temptations by which he was assailed were such, that they might well be compared to gulfs in the sea; then he complains of their long continuance, which he describes by the very appropriate figure, that his temptations cry out from a distance, and call to one another. In the second part of the verse, he continues the same metaphor, when he says, that *all the waves and floods of God have passed over his head.* By this he means that he had been overwhelmed, and as it were swallowed up by the accumulation of afflictions. It ought, however, to be observed, that he designates the cruelty of Saul, and his other enemies, *floods of God,* that in all our adversities we may always remember to humble ourselves under the mighty hand of God which afflicts us. But it is of importance to go beyond this, and to consider, that if it should please God to rain with violence upon us, as soon as he shall have opened his sluices or *waterspouts,* there will be no termination to our miseries till he is appeased; for he has in his power means marvellous and unknown for executing his vengeance against us. Thus, when once his anger is kindled against us, there will be not only one depth to swallow us up, but depth will call unto depth. And as the insensibility of men is such, that they do not stand in awe of the threatenings of God, to the degree in which they ought, whenever mention is made of his vengeance, let us recall this verse to our recollection.

8. *Jehovah will command his loving-kindness by day.* The verb here used is of the future tense; but I do not deny that, according to the Hebrew idiom, it might be rendered in the past tense, as some do who think that David here enumerates the benefits which he had formerly received from God, in order by contrast to add greater force to the complaint which he makes of his present sad and miserable condition; as if he had said, How comes it to pass that God, who formerly manifested so much kindness towards me, having as it were changed his mind, now deals towards me with

great severity? But as there is no sufficient reason for changing the tense of the verb, and as the other interpretation seems more in accordance with the scope of the text, let us adhere to it. I do not, indeed, positively deny, that for the strengthening of his faith, David calls to memory the benefits which he had already experienced from God; but I think that he here promises himself deliverance in future, though it be as yet hidden from him. I have, therefore, no desire to raise any discussion regarding the verb, whether it should be taken in the future or in the past tense, provided only it be fully admitted that the argument of David is to this effect: Why should I not expect that God will be merciful to me, so that in the day-time his loving-kindness may be manifested towards me, and by night upon my bed a song of joy be with me? He, no doubt, places this ground of comfort in opposition to the sorrow which he might well apprehend from the dreadful tokens of the divine displeasure, which he has enumerated in the preceding verse. The *prayer* of which he speaks in the end of the verse is not to be understood as the prayer of an afflicted or sorrowful man; but it comprehends an expression of the delight which is experienced when God, by manifesting his favour to us, gives us free access into his presence. And, therefore, he also calls him *the God of his life,* because from the knowledge of this arises cheerfulness of heart.

9. *I will say to God my rock, Why hast thou forgotten me? Why go I mourning because of the oppression of the enemy?*
10. *It is as a wound*[1] *in my bones when my enemies reproach me, saying to me daily, Where is thy God?*
11. *O my soul! why art thou cast down? and why art thou disquieted within me? Hope in God; for I shall yet praise him, the helps* [or *salvations*] *of my countenance, and my God.*

9. *I will say to God my rock.* If we read the preceding verse in the past tense, the meaning of this verse will be, Since God has, in this way, heretofore shown himself so kind towards me, I will pray to him now with so much the

---

[1] " Ou, tuerie."—*Fr. marg.* " Or, slaughter."

greater confidence: for the experience which I have had of his goodness will inspire me with courage. But if the preceding verse is rendered in the future tense, David, in this verse, combines the prayer which it contains with the reflections which faith led him to make. And, surely, whoever, from a persuasion of the paternal love of God, anticipates for himself the same favour which David has just described, will also be induced from his example to pray for it with greater confidence. The meaning, then, will be this: Since I expect that God will be favourable to me, inasmuch as by day he manifests his favour towards me, and continues to do this, so that even by night I have occasion to praise him, I will bewail the more frankly my miseries before him, saying, *O Lord! my rock, why hast thou forgotten me?* In making such a complaint, the faithful are not to be understood as meaning that God has utterly rejected them: for if they did not believe that they were under his care and protection, it were in vain for them to call upon him. But they speak in this manner according to the sense of the flesh. This forgetfulness, then, relates both to outward appearance, and to the disquietude by which the faithful are troubled according to the flesh, although, in the meantime, they rest assured by faith that God regards them, and will not be deaf to their request.

10. *It is as a slaughter in my bones.* This verse is somewhat involved in point of expression; but as to the meaning of it there is no obscurity. David here affirms that the grief which he experienced from the reproaches of his enemies, wounded him in no degree less than if they had pierced through his bones. The word ברצח, *beretsach,* signifies *killing;* and, therefore, I have retained this idea in the translation of it. And yet I do not condemn the opinion of those who render it *a slaughtering sword.*[1] There is here a difference as to the

---

[1] The original word רצח, *retsach,* is constantly used in prose for a *homicide,* or *murderer,* being derived from the verb רצח, *ratsach,* which signifies *to slay, to murder;* and although it is not used in any other passage for *a sword,* "it may," as Horsley observes, "very naturally, in poetry, be applied to the instrument of slaughter, the sword." In support of this view, he refers to a passage in one of the tragedies of Sophocles, in which

reading, arising from the great similarity which there is between the two letters ב, *beth*, and כ, *caph*, the mark of similitude. As the letter ב, *beth*, is often superfluous, I would rather be disposed, in a doubtful matter like this, to omit it altogether. But as I have said, the sense is perfectly plain, except that interpreters do not seem to take this sufficiently into their consideration, that by the terms *my bones*, the bitterness of grief is referred to; for we feel much more acutely any injury which is done to the bones, than if a sword should pierce the bowels, or the other parts of the body which are soft and yielding. Nor should the children of God regard this similitude as hyperbolical; and if one should wonder why David took so sorely to heart the derision of his enemies, he only manifests in this his own insensibility. For of all the bitter evils which befall us, there is nothing which can inflict upon us a severer wound than to see the wicked tear in pieces the majesty of God, and endeavour to destroy and overturn our faith. The doctrine taught by Paul, (Gal. iv. 24,) concerning the persecution of Ishmael, is well known. Many consider his childish jesting as of little moment, but as it tended to this effect, that the covenant of God should be esteemed as a thing of no value, it is on that account, according to the judgment of the Holy Spirit, to be accounted a most cruel persecution. David, therefore, with much propriety, compares to a slaughtering sword, which penetrates even within the bones and marrow, the derision of his enemies, by which he saw his own faith and the word of God trampled under foot. And would to God that all who boast themselves of being his children would learn to bear their private wrongs more patiently, and to manifest the same vehement zeal for which David is here distinguished, when their faith is assailed to the dishonour of God, and when the word also which gives them life is included in the same reproach!

11. *O my soul! why art thou cast down?* This repetition

Ajax calls his sword, upon which he is about to fall, Ὁ σφαγεύς; which gives the literal rendering of the Hebrew רצח, *retsach*, *murderer*. Horsley's rendering is, "While the sword is in my bones."

shows us that David had not so completely overcome his temptations in one encounter, or by one extraordinary effort, as to render it unnecessary for him to enter anew into the same conflict. By this example, therefore, we are admonished, that although Satan, by his assaults, often subjects us to a renewal of the same trouble, we ought not to lose our courage, or allow ourselves to be cast down. The latter part of this verse differs from the fifth verse in one word, while in every other respect they agree. In the fifth verse, it is the *helps of* HIS *countenance*, but here we have the relative pronoun of the first person, thus, *The helps* of MY *countenance*. Perhaps in this place, the letter ו, *vau*, which in the Hebrew language denotes the third person, is wanting. Still, as all the other versions agree in the reading which I have adopted,[1] David might, without any absurdity, call God by this designation, *The helps* or *salvations* of MY *countenance*, inasmuch as he looked with confidence for a deliverance, manifest and certain, as if God should appear in a visible manner as his defender, and the protector of his welfare. There can, however, be no doubt, that in this place the term *helps or salvations* is to be viewed as an epithet applied to God; for immediately after it follows, *and my God.*

[1] All the ancient versions, with the exception of the Chaldee, read both in this and the fifth verse, " my countenance." Hammond thinks that as these words are the burden of this and the following psalm, and as the meaning of the other words of the sentence in which they occur is the same in the different verses, it is not improbable that the old reading in both places may have been " my countenance."

PSALM XLIII.

This psalm is very similar to the preceding.[1] David, who probably was the author of it, being chased and driven out of his country by the unjust violence and tyranny of his enemies, calls upon God for vengeance, and encourages himself to hope for restoration.

1. *Judge me, O God! and plead my cause: deliver me from the cruel* [or *unmerciful*] *nation, free me from the deceitful and wicked man.*
2. *For thou art the God of my strength; why art thou estranged from me? why go I sad because of the oppression of the enemy?*
3. *Send forth thy light and thy truth: let them direct me, let them conduct me to thy holy hill, and to thy tabernacles.*
4. *And I will go to the altar of God, to God my exceeding joy,* [literally *the joy of my rejoicing:*] *and I will praise thee upon the harp, O God! my God.*
5. *O my soul! why art thou cast down? and why art thou disquieted within me? for I will yet praise him who is the help of my countenance, and my God.*

1. *Judge me, O God!* David, in the first place, complains of the extreme cruelty of his enemies; but in the verses which immediately follow, he shows that there was nothing which he felt to be more grievous, than to be deprived of the opportunity of access to the sanctuary. We have an evidence of his enjoying the testimony of a good conscience in

---

[1] This and the preceding psalm have been considered by the greater number of critics as having originally formed only one psalm, and they make but one in forty-six MSS. The similarity of the style, sentiment, and metrical structure, and the occurrence of the intercalary verse at verses 5th and 10th of Psalm xlii., and verse 5th of Psalm xliii., confirm this opinion. "The fact, indeed," says Williams, "is self-evident, and easily accounted for. The Jewish choristers having, on some occasion, found the anthem too long, have divided it for their own conveniency, (no uncommon thing among choristers,) and, being once divided, it was ignorantly supposed it ought to be so divided."

this, that he commends the defence of his cause to God. The term *judge*, which he first makes use of, is nothing else than *to undertake the defence of one's cause;* and he expresses his meaning more clearly by adding, *plead my cause.* The substance and object of his prayer, indeed, were, that he might be delivered from the wicked and malicious men by whom he was undeservedly persecuted. But as it is to the miserable and guiltless, who are wrongfully afflicted, that God promises his help, David, in the first place, submits himself to be examined by him, that, having discovered and thoroughly proved the rectitude of his cause, he may at length grant him aid. And as it is a most cheering source of consolation for us to find that God disdains not to take cognizance of our cause, so also, it is vain for us to expect that he will avenge the injuries and wrongs which are done to us, unless our own integrity be so manifest as to induce him to be favourable to us against our adversaries. By *the unmerciful nation* is to be understood the whole company of David's enemies, who were cruel, and destitute of all the feelings of humanity. What follows, concerning *the deceitful and wicked man*, might indeed be applied to Saul; but it seems rather to be a form of speech in which, by enallage, the singular number is used for the plural.

2. *For thou art the God of my strength.* This verse differs very little from the ninth verse of the preceding psalm, and the difference consists more in words than in matter. Setting as a shield against temptation the fact, that he had experienced the power of God to be present with him, he complains that his life is spent in mourning, because he sees himself as it were abandoned to the will of his enemies. He considered it absolutely certain that his enemies had no power to do him harm except in so far as the Lord permitted them; and therefore he asks, as if it were something altogether unaccountable, how it happened that his enemies prevailed against him whilst he was under the assured protection and guardianship of God. From this he gathers courage to pray, that God would be pleased again to manifest his favour, which he seemed to have hid from him for a time. The term *light* is

to be understood as denoting *favour;* for as adversities not only obscure the face of God, but also overcast the heavens, as it were, with clouds and fogs, so also, when we enjoy the divine blessing which makes rich, it is like the cheerful light of a serene day shining around us; or rather the light of life, dispelling all that thick obscurity which overwhelmed us in sorrow. By this word the Psalmist intimates two things; first, that all our miseries arise from no other source than this, that God withdraws from us the tokens of his paternal love; and, secondly, that as soon as he is pleased to manifest towards us his serene and gracious countenance, deliverance and salvation also arise to us. He adds *truth,* because he expected this light only from the promises of God. The unbelieving desire the favour of God, but they do not raise their eyes to his light; for the natural disposition of man always tends towards the earth, unless his mind and all his feelings are raised up on high by the word of God. In order, then, to encourage himself in the hope of obtaining the grace of God, David rests with confidence in this, that God, who is true, and cannot deceive any, has promised to assist his servants. We must therefore explain the sentence thus: Send forth thy light, that it may be a token and testimony of thy truth, or that it may really and effectually prove that thou art faithful and free from all deceit in thy promises. The knowledge of the divine favour, it is true, must be sought for in the Word of God; nor has faith any other foundation on which it can rest with security except his word; but when God stretches out his hand to help us, the experience of this is no small confirmation both of the word and of faith. David declares what was the chief object of his desire, and what end he had in view in seeking deliverance from his calamities, when he says, *Let them direct me, and lead me to thy holy hill.* As the chief cause of his sorrow consisted in his being banished from the congregation of the godly, so he places the height of all his enjoyments in this, that he might be at liberty to take part in the exercises of religion, and to worship God in the sanctuary. Tacitly, indeed, David makes a vow of thanksgiving to God; but there can be no doubt, that by these words he intimates, that the end which he had in view in seeking deliverance from his afflictions was, that as formerly he might be at liberty to return to the sanctuary, from which he was driven by the tyranny of his enemies. And it deserves to be particularly noticed, that although he had been deprived of his wife, spoiled of his goods, his house, and all his other earthly comforts, yet he always felt such an ardent desire to come to the temple, that he forgot almost every thing else. But it is enough for me at present briefly to notice this, as in the preceding psalm I have treated at greater length of this holy desire of David, which ought to be imitated by all the faithful.[1] Still, however, it might be asked, How it is that mention is here made of *Mount Sion*, which was not appointed to the service of God till after the death of Saul? The only solution of this difficulty which I can give is, that David, composing this psalm at an after period of his life, employs, in accordance with the revelation which had subsequently been given to him, language which otherwise he would have used more generally in speaking only of the tabernacle, and without at all specifying the place.[2] In this I see no inconsistency.

4. *And I will go to the altar of God.* Here he promises to God a solemn sacrifice, in commemoration of the deliverance which he should obtain from him; for he speaks not only of the daily or ordinary service, but in making mention of the altar on which it was customary to offer the peace-offerings, he expresses the token of gratitude and thanksgiving of which I have spoken. For this reason, also, he calls God *the God of his joy*, because, being delivered from sorrow, and restored to a state of joy, he resolves to acknowledge openly so great a benefit. And he calls him the *joy of his rejoicing*, that he may the more illustriously set forth the grace of his deliverance. The second word in the genitive is added by way of an epithet, and by it he signifies that his heart had been filled with joy of no common kind, when God restored him, contrary to the expectation of all. As to the fifth verse,

---

[1] "Laquelle tous fideles doyvent ensuyvre."—*Fr.*
[2] "Sans specifier le lieu."—*Fr.*

I have already treated of it sufficiently in the preceding psalm, and therefore deem it superfluous to speak of it here.

PSALM XLIV.

This psalm is divided into three principal parts. In the beginning of it the faithful record the infinite mercy of God towards his people, and the many tokens by which he had testified his fatherly love towards them. Then they complain that they do not now find that God is favourable towards them, as he had formerly been towards their fathers. In the third place, they refer to the covenant which God had made with Abraham, and declare that they have kept it with all faithfulness, notwithstanding the sore afflictions to which they had been subjected. At the same time, they complain that they are cruelly persecuted for no other cause but for having continued stedfastly in the pure worship of God. In the end, a prayer is added, that God would not forget the wrongful oppression of his servants, which especially tends to bring dishonour and reproach upon religion.

¶ To the chief musician of the sons of Korah, giving instruction.

It is uncertain who was the author of this psalm; but it is clearly manifest that it was composed rather by any other person than by David. The complaints and lamentations which it contains may be appropriately referred to that miserable and calamitous period in which the outrageous tyranny of Antiochus destroyed and wasted every thing.[1] Some, indeed, may be disposed to apply it more generally; for after the return of the Jews from the captivity of Babylon, they were scarcely ever free from severe afflictions. Such a view, doubtless, would not be applicable to the time of David, under whose reign the Church enjoyed prosperity. It may be, too, that during the time of their captivity in

---

[1] Dr Geddes supposes with Calvin that this psalm was composed during the persecution of Antiochus Epiphanes; and that Matthias may have been its author. See 1 Mac. ch. i. and ii. Walford refers it to the same period. There is, certainly, no part of the history of the Jews with which we are acquainted, to which the statement made in the 17th verse is so applicable as to the time when they were so cruelly persecuted for their religion by Antiochus Epiphanes, King of Syria, and when, notwithstanding, the great mass of the people displayed an invincible determination to keep themselves from the pollutions of idolatry, and to adhere to the worship of the true God.

Babylon, some one of the prophets composed this complaint in name of all the people. It is, however, at the same time to be observed, that the state of the Church, such as it was to be after the appearance of Christ, is here described. Paul, in Rom. viii. 36, as we shall afterwards see in its proper place, did not understand this psalm as a description of the state of the Church in one age only, but he warns us, that Christians are appointed to the same afflictions, and should not expect that their condition on earth, even to the end of the world, will be different from what God has made known to us, as it were by way of example, in the case of the Jews after their return from captivity. Christ, it is true, afterwards appeared as the Redeemer of the Church. He did not however appear, that the flesh should luxuriate in ease upon the earth, but rather that we should wage war under the banner of the cross, until we are received into the rest of the heavenly kingdom. As to the meaning of the word משכיל, *maskil,* it has been already elsewhere explained. It is sometimes found in the inscription of psalms whose subject is cheerful; but it is more commonly used when the subject treated of is distressing; for it is a singular means of leading us to profit by the instruction of the Lord, when, by subduing the obduracy of our hearts, he brings us under his yoke.

> 1. *O God! we have heard with our ears, our fathers have declared to us, the work which thou hast done in their days, even in the days of old.*
> 2. *Thou hast expelled the heathen* [or *nations*[1]] *with thy hand, and planted them :*[2] *thou hast wasted the peoples,*[3] *and multiplied them,* [or *made them*[4] *to spread.*]
> 3. *For they got not possession of the land by their own sword, and their own arm did not save them : but thy right hand, and thy arm, and the light of thy countenance, because thou hadst a favour for them.*

1. *O God! we have heard with our ears.* The people of God here recount the goodness which he had formerly mani-

---

[1] That is, the Canaanites.
[2] " Asçavoir, nos peres."—*Fr. marg.* " Namely, our fathers." Israel is here compared to a vine planted in the promised land. See Exod. xv. 17; Isa. v. 1-7. See also Ps. lxxx. 8, where this elegant figure is carried out with remarkable force and beauty of language.
[3] The Canaanites.
[4] " Asçavoir, nos peres."—*Fr. marg.* " That is, our fathers." The reading in our English version is, " and cast them out," namely, the heathen. But Calvin's rendering seems to be more suitable to the genius of the Hebrew poetry, and it also agrees with the meaning of the original. " The whole metaphor," says Dr Geddes, " is taken from the vine, or some other

fested towards their fathers, that, by showing the great dissimilarity of their own condition, they may induce God to alleviate their miseries. They begin by declaring that they speak not of things unknown or doubtful, but that they related events, the truth of which was authenticated by unexceptionable witnesses. The expression, *We have heard with our ears*, is not to be considered as a redundant form of speech, but one of great weight. It is designed to point out that the grace of God towards their fathers was so renowned, that no doubt could be entertained respecting it. They add, that their knowledge of these things was handed down from age to age by those who witnessed them. It is not meant that their fathers, who had been brought up out of Egypt, had, a thousand and five hundred years after, declared to their posterity the benefits God had conferred upon them. The import of the language is, that not only the first deliverance, but that also the various other works which God had wrought from time to time in behalf of his people, had come down, as it were, from hand to hand, in an uninterrupted series, even to the latest age. As, therefore, those who, after the lapse of many ages, became witnesses and heralds of the grace which God had exercised towards this people, spake upon the report of the first generation, the faithful are warranted in saying, as they here do, that their fathers have declared to them that which they certainly knew, because the knowledge of it had not been lost by reason of its antiquity, but was continually preserved by the remembrance of it from the fathers to the children. The sum of the whole is, that God had manifested his goodness towards the children of Abraham, not only for ten or twenty years, but that ever since he had received them into his favour, he had never ceased to bestow upon them continued tokens of his grace.

2. *Thou hast expelled the heathen with thy hand.* This is

luxuriant tree. In our common version, 'and cast them out,' the parallelism is lost, and the beauty of the sentence disappears." The Hebrew verb here used is generally applied to the germination of plants, or to the shooting and spreading forth of branches. God caused his chosen people to spread abroad, to cast or shoot forth like the branches of a vine.

an illustration of the preceding verse : for the inspired writer had not yet expressly referred to that work of God, the fame of which had been preserved by their fathers. He therefore now adds, that God *with his own hand expelled the heathen,* in order *to plant* in their room the children of Abraham : and that *he wasted and destroyed them, that he might increase and multiply* the seed of Abraham. He compares the ancient inhabitants of the land of Canaan to trees ; for, from long continued possession of the country, they had, as it were, taken root in it. The sudden change, therefore, which had happened to them, was as if a man plucked up trees by the roots to plant others in their stead. But as it would not have been enough for God's ancient people to have been planted at first in the country, another metaphor is here added, by which the faithful testify that the blessing of God had caused this chosen people to increase and multiply, even as a tree, extending it roots and its branches far and wide, gains still greater strength in the place where it has been planted. Besides, it is necessary to observe for what purpose it is that the faithful here magnify this manifestation of the grace of God. It often happens that our own hearts suggest to us grounds of despair, when we begin to conclude that God has rejected us, because he does not continue to bestow upon us the same benefits which in his goodness he vouchsafed to our fathers. But it were altogether inconsistent, that the faithful here disposing their hearts for prayer, should allow such an obstacle to prevent them from exercising the confidence which is proper in prayer. I freely admit, that the more we think of the benefits which God has bestowed upon others, the greater is the grief which we experience when he does not relieve us in our adversities. But faith directs us to another conclusion, namely, that we should assuredly believe that we shall also in due time experience some relief, since God continues unchangeably the same. There can be no reason to doubt, that the faithful now call to remembrance the things which God had formerly done for the welfare of his Church, with the view of inspiring their minds with stronger hope, as we have seen them acting in a similar manner in the beginning of the twenty-second psalm. They do not simply state the comparison, which would tend to draw a line of separation between those who have in former times been preserved by the power of God, and those who now laboured and groaned under afflictions; but they rather set forth the covenant of God as the bond of holy alliance between them and their fathers, that they might conclude from this, that whatever amount of goodness the Church had at any time experienced in God pertained also to them. At first, indeed, they use the language of complaint, asking why it is that the course of God's fatherly favour towards his people is, as it were, interrupted; but straightway they correct their mistake, and take courage from a new consideration—the consideration that God, who had adopted them as well as their fathers, is faithful and immutable. It is, however, no great wonder if the faithful, even in prayer, have in their hearts divers and conflicting affections. But the Holy Spirit, who dwells in them, by assuaging the violence of their sorrow, pacifies all their complaints, and leads them patiently and cordially to obey. Moreover, when they here say that their fathers have declared to them the deliverances which God had accomplished in behalf of his Church, what the fathers did in this respect corresponds with the precept of the law, by which the fathers were commanded to teach their children. And all the faithful ought to reflect that the same charge is enjoined upon them by God even to this day. He communicates to them the doctrine of salvation, and commits it to their charge for this purpose—that they may transmit it to their posterity, and, as much as in them lies, endeavour to extend its authority, that his worship may be preserved from age to age.

3. *For they got not possession of the land by their own sword.* Here the sacred writer confirms by contrast what he has just said; for if they obtained not possession of the land by their own power and skill, it follows that they were planted in it by the hand of another. The multitude of men who went out of Egypt was very great; but not being trained to the art of war, and accustomed only to servile works, they would soon have been defeated by their enemies, who far excelled

them in numbers and strength. In short, there were not wanting evident signs by which the people were made to know as well their own weakness as the power of God; so that it was their bounden duty to confess that the land was not conquered by their own sword, and also, that it was the hand of God which had preserved them. The Psalmist, not content with mentioning *thy right hand,* adds, *thy arm,* to amplify the matter, and give greater weight to his discourse, that we may know that they were preserved in a wonderful manner, and not by any ordinary means. *The light of thy countenance* is here taken, as in other places, for the manifestation of the divine favour. As, on the one hand, when God is afflicting us severely, he seems to frown upon us, and to overshadow his face with thick clouds; so, on the other, when the Israelites, sustained by his power, overthrew their enemies without any great difficulty, and pursued them in every direction far and near, it is said, that then they beheld the face of God serene and placid, just as if he had manifested himself in a visible manner near them. Here it is necessary to observe the mode of reasoning which the prophet employs, when he argues that it is by the free gift of God that the people obtained the land in heritage, seeing they had not acquired it by their own power. We then truly begin to yield to God what belongs to him, when we consider how worthless our own strength is. And certainly, the reason why men, as it were through disdain, conceal and forget the benefits which God has conferred on them, must be owing to a delusive imagination, which leads them to arrogate somewhat to themselves as properly their own. The best means, therefore, of cherishing in us habitually a spirit of gratitude towards God, is to expel from our minds this foolish opinion of our own ability. There is still in the concluding part of the verse another expression, which contains a more illustrious testimony to the grace of God, when the Psalmist resolves the whole into the good pleasure of God: *Thou hadst a favour for them.* The prophet does not suppose any worthiness in the person of Abraham, nor imagine any desert in his posterity, on account of which God dealt so bountifully with them, but ascribes the whole to the good pleasure of God. His words seem to be taken from the solemn declaration of Moses, "The Lord did not set his love upon you, nor choose you, because ye were more in number than any people; (for ye were the fewest of all people;) but because the Lord loved you," (Deut. vii. 7, 8.) Special mention is here made of the land of Canaan; but the prophet has stated the general principle why it was that God vouchsafed to reckon that people for his flock and peculiar heritage. And certainly, the source and origin of the Church is the free love of God; and whatever benefits he bestows upon his Church, they all proceed from the same source. The reason, therefore, why we are gathered into the Church, and are nourished and defended by the hand of God, is only to be sought in God. Nor does the Psalmist here treat of the general benevolence of God, which extends to the whole human race; but he discourses of the difference which exists between the elect and the rest of the world; and the cause of this difference is here referred to the mere good pleasure of God.

4. *Thou, even thou, art my King,*[1] *O God! command* [or *ordain*] *deliverances for Jacob.*
5. *Through thee we have pushed* [or *smitten*] *with the horn our adversaries: in thy name we have trampled under foot those that rose up against us.*
6. *For I will not trust in my bow, and my sword will not save me.*
7. *Surely thou hast saved us from our enemies, and hast put to shame those that hated us.*
8. *In God we will boast all the day, and confess thy name for ever. Selah.*

4. *Thou, even thou, art my King, O God!* In this verse the faithful express still more plainly what I have already alluded to a little before, namely, that the goodness of God

---

[1] Geddes reads, "Our King." "The Hebrew," says he, "has *my King;* but as the Psalmist speaks in the name of his nation, the plural number is preferable in English, as in numerous other instances." "The speaker throughout the psalm," says Walford, "is the Church, which accounts for the use of both the singular and plural numbers in different parts."

was not only apparent in the deliverance of his people, but also flowed upon them in continued succession from age to age; and therefore it is said, *Thou, even thou, art my King.* In my judgment, the demonstrative pronoun הוּא, *hu,* imports as much as if the prophet had put together a long series of the benefits of God after the first deliverance; so that it might appear, that God, who had once been the deliverer of his people, did not show himself otherwise towards their posterity: unless, perhaps, it might be considered as emphatic, and employed for the purpose of asserting the thing stated the more strongly, namely, that the faithful praise God alone as the guardian of their welfare to the exclusion of all others, and the renunciation of aid from any other quarter. Hence they also present the prayer, that God would ordain and send forth new *deliverances* to his people; for, as he has in his power innumerable means of preservation and deliverance, he is said to appoint and send forth deliverances as his messengers wherever it seems good to him.

5. *Through thee we have pushed,* or *smitten, with the horn our adversaries.*[1] The prophet here declares in what respect God had manifested himself to be the King of this people. He did so by investing them with such strength and power, that all their enemies stood in fear of them. The similitude, taken from bulls, which he here uses, tends to show, that they had been endued with more than human strength, by which they were enabled to assail, overturn, and trample under foot, every thing which opposed them. *In God,* and *in the name of God,* are of the same import, only the latter expression denotes, that the people had been victorious, because they fought under the authority and direction of God. It ought to be observed, that what they had spoken before concerning their fathers, they now apply to themselves, because they still formed a part of the same body of the Church.

---

[1] The allusion is to the pushing, striking, or butting of oxen and other animals with their horns, and means *o vanquish* or *subdue,* (Deut. xxxiii. 17; 1 Kings xxii. 11; Dan. viii. 4.) "Literally," says Dr Adam Clarke, "'We will toss them in the air with our horn;' a metaphor taken from an ox or bull tossing the dogs into the air which attack him."

And they do this expressly to inspire themselves with confidence and courage, for had they separated themselves from their fathers, this distinction would, in a certain sense, have interrupted the course of God's grace, so that it would have ceased to flow down upon them. But now, since they confess that whatever God had conferred upon their fathers he had bestowed upon them, they may boldly desire him to continue his work. At the same time, it ought to be observed again in this place, that, as I have stated a little before, the reason why they ascribe their victories wholly to God is, that they were unable to arrive at such a consummation by *their own sword or their own bow.* When we are led to consider how great is our own weakness, and how worthless we are without God, this contrast much more clearly illustrates the grace of God. They again declare, (verse 7,) that they were saved by the power of God, and that he also had chased away and put to shame their enemies.

8. *In God we will boast* [1] *all the day.* This is the conclusion of the first part of the psalm. To express the meaning in a few words, they acknowledge, that in all ages the goodness of God had been so great towards the children of Abraham, that it furnished them with continual matter of thanksgiving. As if the thing were still present to their view, they acknowledge that, without ceasing, they ought to give praise to God, because they had flourished and triumphed, not merely for one age, or a short period of time, but because they had continued to do so successively from age to age:[2] for whatever prosperity had befallen them, they ascribe it to the grace of God. And, certainly, it is then that men experience from the prosperity which befalls them, a holy and a well-regulated joy, when it bursts forth in the praises of God.[3] Let us then, in the first place, bear in mind that this verse relates to the time of joy and prosperity in which God mani-

[1] Hammond reads, "We have praised God." He considers the preposition ב, *beth,* prefixed to the name of God, as a pleonasm.
[2] "Mais que la chose a continué d'aage en aage."—*Fr.*
[3] "Quand d'icelle ils entrent à rendre louanges à Dieu."—*Fr.* "When from it they are led to give praise to God."

fested his favour towards his people; secondly, that the faithful here manifest that they are not ungrateful, inasmuch as, having laid aside all vain boasting, they confess that all the victories by which they had become great and renowned proceeded from God, and that it was by his power alone that they had hitherto continued to exist, and had been preserved in safety; and, thirdly, that it was not only once or twice that matter of joy had been afforded them, but that this existed for a long time, inasmuch as God had manifested towards them, during a long and uninterrupted period, divers proofs and tokens of his paternal favour, so that the continuance, and, so to speak, the long experience they had had of it, ought to have been the means of confirming their hope.

9. *Nevertheless thou hast abhorred us,*[1] *and put us to shame : and thou goest not forth with our armies.*
10. *Thou hast made us to turn back from the enemy : and they that hate us have made of us a spoil for themselves.*
11. *Thou hast given us as sheep for food : and thou hast scattered us among the heathen.*
12. *Thou hast sold thy people, and not become rich,*[2] *and thou hast not increased the price of them.*
13. *Thou hast made us a reproach to our neighbours, a scorn and derision to them that are round about us.*
14. *Thou hast made us a byword among the heathen, and a nodding of the head among the people.*

9. *Nevertheless thou hast abhorred us.* Here follows a complaint, in which they bewail their present miseries and extreme calamity. There is here described such a change as showed not only that God had ceased to exercise towards them his accustomed favour, but also, that he was openly adverse and hostile to his people. First, they complain that they have been rejected as through hatred, for such is the proper import of the word זָנַחְתָּ, *zanachta*, which, along with others, I have translated *abhorred*. If, however, any

[1] " Ou, mis en oubli."—*Fr. marg.* " Or, hast forgotten us."
[2] " C'est, sans aucun profit pour toy."—*Fr. marg.* " That is, without any profit to thee."

would rather translate it *to forget,* or *to be cast off,* I have no great objection to it. They next add, that they had been *put to shame,* namely, because it must necessarily follow that every thing should go ill with them when deprived of the protection of God. This they declare immediately after, when they say, that God *no longer goes forth with their armies* —goes forth as their leader or standard-bearer, when they go forth to war.

10. *Thou hast made us to turn back from the enemy.* Here the people of God still further complain, that he had made them to flee before their enemies, and had given them up as a prey to be devoured by them. As the saints firmly believe that men are strong and valiant only in so far as God upholds them by his secret power, they also conclude, that when men flee, and are seized with trembling, it is God who strikes them with terror, so that the poor wretched creatures are deprived of reason, and both their skill and courage fail them. The expression here used is taken from the Law, Deut. xxxii. 30, where Moses says, " How should one chase a thousand, and two put ten thousand to flight, except their Rock had sold them, and the Lord had shut them up ?" The faithful, fully persuaded of this truth, do not ascribe to fortune the change which had passed over them, that those who were wont vigorously and fearlessly to assail their enemies, were now terrified by their very appearance ; but they feel assured that it was by the appointment of heaven that they were thus discomfited, and made to flee before their enemies. And as they formerly confessed that the strength which they had hitherto possessed was the gift of God, so, on the other hand, they also acknowledge that the fear by which they are now actuated was inflicted upon them as a punishment by God. And when God thus deprived them of courage, they say that they are exposed to the will of their enemies; for in this sense I interpret the word למו, *lamo,* which I have rendered, *for themselves,* namely, that their enemies destroyed them at their pleasure and without any resistance, as their prey.

To the same purpose is that other comparison, (verse 11,)

in which they say that *they were given as sheep for food.*[1] By
this the prophet intimates, that being already vanquished
previous to the battle, they fell down, as it were, upon the
earth before their enemies, ready to be devoured by them,[2]
and not fit for any thing else than to gratify their insatiable
cruelty. It ought to be observed, that when the faithful
represent God as the author of their calamities, it is not in
the way of murmuring against him, but that they may with
greater confidence seek relief, as it were, from the same
hand which smote and wounded them. It is certainly impossible that those who impute their miseries to fortune can
sincerely have recourse to God, or look for help and salvation from him. If, therefore, we would expect a remedy
from God for our miseries, we must believe that they befall
us not by fortune or mere chance, but that they are inflicted
upon us properly by his hand. Having stated that they were
thus abandoned to the will of their enemies, they add, at the
same time, that they were *scattered among the heathen:* a dispersion which was a hundred times more grievous to them than
death. The whole glory and felicity of that people consisted
in this, that, being united under one God and one King, they
formed one body; and that such being the case, it was a sign
that the curse of God lay heavy upon them to be mingled
among the heathen, and scattered hither and thither like
broken members.

12. *Thou hast sold thy people, and not become rich.* In
saying that they were sold without any gain, it is meant that
they were exposed to sale as slaves that are contemptible, and
of no value. In the second clause, too, *And hast not increased
the price of them,* there seems to be an allusion to the custom
of exposing things to auction, and selling them to the highest
bidder. We know that those slaves who were sold were

[1] "This very strongly and strikingly intimates the extent of the persecution and slaughter to which they were exposed; there being no creature
in the world of which such vast numbers are constantly slaughtered as of
sheep, for the subsistence of man. The constancy of such slaughter is also
mentioned in verse 22, as illustrating the continual oppression to which
the Hebrews were subject."—*Illustrated Commentary upon the Bible.*

[2] "Prests à estre par eux devorez."—*Fr.*

not delivered to the buyers till the price of them had been increased by bidding. Thus the faithful mean, that they were cast out as being altogether worthless, so that their condition had been worse than that of any bond-slave.[1] And as they rather appeal to God than turn to their enemies, of whose pride and cruelty they had just cause to complain, let us learn from this, that there is nothing better, or more advantageous for us in our adversity, than to give ourselves to meditation upon the providence and judgment of God. When men trouble us, it is no doubt the devil who drives them to it, and it is with him we have to do; but we must, notwithstanding, raise our thoughts to God himself, that we may know that we are proved and tried by him, either to chastise us, or to exercise our patience, or to subdue the sinful desires of our flesh, or to humble us and train us to the practice of self-denial. And when we hear that the Fathers who lived under the Law were treated so ignominiously, there is no reason why we should lose courage by any outrage or ill treatment, if God should at any time see meet to subject us to it. It is not here said simply that God sold some people, but that he sold his own people, as if his own inheritance were of no estimation in his sight. Even at this day, we may in our prayers still make the same complaint, provided we, at the same time, make use of this example, for the purpose of supporting and establishing our faith, so that, however much afflicted we may be, our hearts may not fail us. In Isaiah lii. 3, God, using the same form of speech, says that he sold his people without price; but there it is to be understood in a different sense, namely, to show that he will have no difficulty in redeeming them, because he is under no obligation to those that bought them, and had received nothing from them in return.

13. *Thou hast made us a reproach to our neighbours.* Here the Psalmist speaks of their neighbours, who were all actuated either by some secret ill-will, or avowed enmity to the

[1] As if they had said, Thou hast sold us to our enemies at whatever price they would give; like a person who sells things that are useless at any price, not so much for the sake of gain, as to get quit of what he considers of no value and burdensome.

people of God. And certainly it often happens, that neighbourhood, which ought to be the means of preserving mutual friendship, engenders all discord and strife. But there was a special reason in respect of the Jews; for they had taken possession of the country in spite of all men, and their religion being hateful to others, so to speak, served as a trumpet to stir up war, and inflamed their neighbours with rage against them. Many, too, cherished towards them a feeling of jealousy, such as the Idumeans, who were inflated on the ground of their circumcision, and imagined that they also worshipped the God of Abraham as well as the Jews. But what proved the greatest calamity to them was, that they were exposed to the reproach and derision of those who hated them on the ground of their worship of the true God. The faithful illustrate still farther the greatness of their calamity by another circumstance, telling us, in the last clause of the verse, that they were met by reproaches on all sides; for they were beset round about by their enemies, so that they would never have enjoyed one moment of peace unless God had miraculously preserved them. Nay, they add still farther, (verse 14,) that they were a *proverb*, a *byword*, or *jest*, even among the nations that were far off. The word משל, *mashal*, which is translated *proverb*, might be taken in the sense of *a heavy imprecation* or *curse*, as well as of *a byword* or *jest;* but the sense will be substantially the same, namely, that there were no people under heaven held in greater detestation, insomuch that their very name was bandied about every where in proverbial allusions, as a term of reproach. To the same purpose also is *the wagging*, or *shaking, of the head*, which occurs in Psalm xxii., of which we have already spoken. There can be no doubt that the faithful recognised this as inflicted upon them by the vengeance of God, of which mention was made in the Law. In order to arouse themselves to the consideration of the judgments of God, they carefully compared with the threatenings of God all the punishments which he inflicted upon them. But the Law had declared beforehand, in express terms, this derision of the Gentiles, which they now relate as a thing that had come to pass, (Deut. xxviii. 3.) Moreover, when it is said, *among the heathen*, and *among the people*, the repetition is very emphatic and expressive; for it was a thing quite unseemly and intolerable, that the heathen nations should presume to torment with their scoffings the chosen people of God, and revile them by their blasphemies at their pleasure. That the godly complained not of these things without cause is abundantly obvious from a passage in Cicero, in his oration in defence of Flaccus, in which that heathen orator, with his accustomed pride, scoffs no less against God than against the Jews, asserting that it was perfectly clear that they were a nation hated of the gods, inasmuch as they had often, and, as it were, from age to age, been wasted with so many misfortunes, and in the end subjected to a most miserable bondage, and kept, as it were, under the feet of the Romans.[1]

15. *My reproach is daily*[2] *before me, and the shame of my face hath quite covered me,*
16. *Because of the voice of him who reproached me; because of the face of the enemy and the avenger.*
17. *All this has come upon us, and we have not forgotten thee, nor dealt falsely in thy covenant:*
18. *Our heart has not turned back, nor have our steps declined from thy path.*
19. *Although thou hast wasted us in the place of dragons, and covered us with the shadow of death:*
20. *If we have forgotten the name of our God, and have stretched out our hands to a strange god:*
21. *Shall not God search this out? for he knoweth the secrets of the heart.*

15. *My reproach is daily before me.* The Hebrew words כל־היום, *col-hayom,* mean all the day, and denote long continuance: but they may be understood in two ways, either for the whole or entire day, from morning to evening, or for continued succession of days. According to either of these interpretations, the meaning is, that there is no end to their misfortunes. As to the change of the number from the plural to

---

[1] "Et comme tenue sous les pieds des Romains."—*Fr.*
[2] "Ou, tout le jour."—*Fr. marg.* "Or, all the day."

the singular, it is not at all inconsistent that what is spoken in the name of the Church should be uttered, as it were, in the person of one man. The reason is added why they were so overwhelmed with shame, that they dared not to lift up their eyes and their *face,* namely, because they had no respite, but were incessantly subjected to the insolence and reproach of their enemies. Had they been allowed to hide themselves in some corner, they might have endured, as well as they were able, their calamities in secret; but when their enemies openly derided them with the greatest insolence, it served to redouble the wound inflicted upon them. They, therefore, complain that their calamities had accumulated to such an extent, that they were forced unceasingly to hear blasphemies and bitter reproaches. They describe their enemies by the epithet *avengers,* a term which, among the Hebrews, denotes barbarity and cruelty, accompanied with pride, as we have remarked on the 8th Psalm.

17. *All this has come upon us, &c.* As they have already attributed to God all the afflictions which they endured, if they should now say that they were undeservedly afflicted, it would be the same thing as to accuse God of injustice; and thus what is here spoken would no longer be a holy prayer, but rather an impious blasphemy. It is, however, to be observed, that the faithful, although in their adversities they do not perceive any obvious reason for being so dealt with, yet they rest assured of this, and regard it as a fixed principle, that God has some good reasons for treating them so severely. At the same time, it is proper to observe, that the godly do not speak in this place of the time past, but rather allege their patient endurance, which was no small token of their piety, since, in the most humble manner, they thus bowed their neck to the yoke of God. We see how the great majority of men murmur and obstinately fret against God, like refractory horses which rage furiously against their masters, and strike them with their feet. And, therefore, we know that the man who, in affliction, imposes a holy restraint upon himself, that he may not by any impatience be carried away from the path of duty, has made no incon-

siderable attainments in the fear of God. It is an easy matter even for hypocrites to bless God in the time of their prosperity; but as soon as he begins to deal hardly with them, they break forth into a rage against him. Accordingly, the faithful declare that, although so many afflictions as they endured tended to turn them aside from the right path, they did not forget God, but always served him, even when he did not show himself favourable and merciful towards them. They do not, therefore, proclaim their virtues in a former and distant period of their history, but only allege, that even in the midst of afflictions they stedfastly kept *the covenant of God.* It is well known, that long before the persecution of Antiochus, there were many abuses and corruptions which provoked the vengeance of God against them, so that, in respect of that period, they had no ground to boast of such integrity as is here described. True it is that, as we shall very soon see, God spared them, thus showing that they had been afflicted more for his name's sake than for their own sins; but the forbearance which God exercised towards them in this respect was not sufficient to warrant them to plead exemption from guilt. We must, therefore, consider that in this place they do nothing more than allege their own patience, in that, amidst such grievous and hard temptations, they had not turned aside from the service of God. In the first place, they affirm, *We have not forgotten thee:* for, indeed, afflictions are, as it were, like so many clouds which conceal heaven from our view, so that God might then readily slip from our remembrance, as if we were far removed from him. They add, secondly, *We have not dealt falsely in thy covenant:* for, as I have said, the wickedness of men discovers itself more especially when they are tried more severely than they had anticipated. Thirdly, they declare *that their heart had not turned back.* And, lastly, *that their footsteps declined not from the paths of God.* As God is daily inviting us, so our hearts must be always ready to proceed in the paths into which he calls us. Hence follows the direction of our ways; for by our outward works, and by our whole life, we testify that our heart is unfeignedly devoted to God. Instead of the translation, *Nor have our steps declined,* which I have given, some suggest another reading, which is not without some degree of plausibility, namely, *Thou hast made our steps to decline;* for, in the first place, the term תט, *tet,* may be so rendered; and, secondly, according to the arrangement of the words, there is no negative in this clause. As to the meaning, however, I am not at all of their opinion; for they connect this passage with that in Isaiah, (lxiii. 17,) "O Lord, why hast thou made us to err from thy ways?" The complaint which is here made amounts rather to this, That the faithful are like poor wretched creatures wandering in desert places, seeing God had withdrawn his hand from them. The expression, *The paths of God,* does not always refer to doctrine, but sometimes to prosperous and desirable events.

19. *Although thou hast broken us in the place of dragons.* In the Hebrew it is, *For thou hast broken us, &c.;* but the causal particle, כי, *ki,* according to the idiom of the Hebrew language, is often taken in the sense of *although* or *when.*[1] And certainly it must be so rendered in this place, for these three verses are connected, and the sentence is incomplete till the end of the words, *For he knoweth the secrets of the heart.* The faithful repeat more largely what we have already seen, namely, that although plunged into the greatest depth of miseries, yet they continued stedfast in their resolution, and in the right way. If we consider the distressing circumstances in which they were placed, it will not appear to us a hyperbolical mode of speech, when they say that they were *broken* even within the depths of the sea; for by *the place of dragons* I understand not the deserts and solitary places, but the deepest gulfs of the sea. Accordingly, the word תנים, *tannim,* which others translate *dragons,*[2] I would

---

[1] "Il y a en Hebrieu, Car tu nous as, &c. Mais souvent selon la maniere de la langue Hebraique, Car, se prend pour Combien que, ou Quand."—*Fr.*

[2] "Lequel les autres traduisent dragons." This is the sense in which the expression is understood by several eminent critics. Aquila explains it thus: "In a desert place where great serpents are found;" and Bishop Hare thus: "In desert places among wild beasts and serpents." "*The place of dragons,*" observes Bishop Mant, "appears to mean the wilderness; in illustration of which, it may be noticed from Dr

rather render *whales*,[1] as it is also understood in many other places. This interpretation is obviously confirmed by the following clause, in which they complain that *they had been covered with the shadow of death*, which implies that they were swallowed up of death itself. Let us, however, remember, that in these words the Holy Ghost dictates to us a form of prayer; and that, therefore, we are enjoined to cultivate a spirit of invincible fortitude and courage, which may serve to sustain us under the weight of all the calamities we may be called to endure, so that we may be able to testify of a truth, that even when reduced to the extremity of despair, we have never ceased to trust in God; that no temptations, however unexpected, could expel his fear from our hearts; and, in fine, that we were never so overwhelmed by the burden of our afflictions, however great, as not to have our eyes always directed to him. But it is proper for us to notice still more particularly the style of speaking here employed by the faithful. In order to show that they still continued stedfastly in the pure service of God, they affirm that they have not lifted up their hearts or their hands to any but to the God of Israel alone. It would not have been enough for them to have cherished some confused notion of the Deity: it was necessary that they should receive in its purity the true religion. Even those who murmur against God may be constrained to acknowledge some Divinity; but they frame for themselves a god after their own pleasure. And this is an artifice of the devil, who, because he cannot at once eradicate from our hearts all sense of religion, endeavours to over-

---

Shaw, that 'vipers, especially in the wilderness of Sin, which might be called the inheritance of dragons, (see Mal. i. 3,) were very dangerous and troublesome; not only our camels, but the Arabs who attended them, running every moment the risk of being bitten.'" Viewed in this light, we must understand the language either as meaning that the Israelites had been driven from their dwellings and places of abode, and compelled to dwell in some gloomy wilderness infested by serpents; or that the fierce and cruel persecutors into whose hands God had delivered them are compared to serpents, and that the circumstances in which the chosen tribes were now placed resembled those of a people who had fallen into a wilderness, where they heard nothing but the hissing of serpents, and the howlings of beasts of prey.

[1] Williams reads, "*In the place of sea-monsters*, perhaps crocodiles;" and thinks the allusion is to a shipwreck.

throw our faith, by suggesting to our minds these devices—that we must seek another God; or that the God whom we have hitherto served must be appeased after another manner; or else that the assurance of his favour must be sought elsewhere than in the Law and the Gospel. Since, then, it is a much more difficult matter for men, amidst the tossings and waves of adversity, to continue stedfast and tranquil in the true faith, we must carefully observe the protestation which the Holy Fathers here make, that even when reduced to the lowest extremity of distress by calamities of every kind, they nevertheless did not cease to trust in the true God.

This they express still more clearly in the following clause, in which they say, *We have not stretched out our hands*[1] *to a strange god.* By these words they intimate, that, contented with God alone, they did not suffer their hopes to be divided on different objects, nor gazed around them in search of other means of assistance. Hence we learn, that those whose hearts are thus divided and distracted by various expectations are forgetful of the true God, to whom we fail to yield the honour which is due to him, if we do not repose with confidence in him alone. And certainly, in the true and rightful service of God, faith and supplication which proceeds from it hold the first place: for we are guilty of depriving him of the chief part of his glory, when we seek apart from him in the least degree our own welfare. Let us then bear in mind, that it is a true test of our piety, when, being plunged into the lowest depths of disasters, we lift up our eyes, our hopes, and our prayers, to God alone. And it only serves to demonstrate more convincingly and clearly the impiety of Popery, when, after having confessed their faith in the one true God with the mouth, its votaries the next moment degrade his glory by ascribing it to created objects. They indeed excuse themselves by alleging, that in having recourse to Saint Christopher and other saints of their own making, they do not claim for them the rank of Deity, but only employ them as intercessors with God to obtain his favour. It is, however, well known to every one,

[1] That is, in the attitude of worship.

that the form of the prayers which they address to the saints[1] is in no respects different from those prayers which they present to God. Besides, although we should yield this point to them, it will still be a frivolous excuse to pretend that they are seeking advocates or intercessors for themselves. This is as much as to say, that Christ is not sufficient for them, or rather, that his office is wholly lost sight of among them. Moreover, we should carefully observe the scope of this passage. The faithful declare, that they did not stretch forth their hands to other gods, because it is an error too common among men to forsake God, and to seek for other means of relief when they find that their afflictions continue to oppress them. So long as we are gently and affectionately treated of God we resort to him, but as soon as any adversity befalls us we begin to doubt. And if we are pressed still further, or if there be no end to our afflictions, the very continuance of them tempts us to despair; and despair generates various kinds of false confidence. Hence arises a multitude of new gods framed after the fancy of men. Of *the lifting up of the hands* we have spoken elsewhere.

21. *Shall not God search this out?* We have here a solemn and emphatic protestation, in which the people of God dare to appeal to him as the judge of their integrity and uprightness. From this it appears, that they did not plead their cause openly before men, but communed with themselves as if they had been before the judgment-seat of God; and moreover, as a token of still greater confidence, they add, that nothing is hidden from God. Why is it that hypocrites often call God to witness, if it is not because they imagine that, by concealing their wickedness under some specious disguise, they have escaped the judgment of God? and thus they would represent the character of God to be different from what it is, as if by their deceptions they could dazzle his eyes. Whenever, therefore, we come before God, let us at the same time remember, that there is nothing to be gained by any vain pretence in his presence, inasmuch as he knows the heart.

[1] " Que le formulaire des prieres qui ils font aux saincts."—*Fr.*

22. *Surely for thy sake we are killed all the day; we are accounted as sheep for slaughter.*
23. *Arise, O Lord! why sleepest thou? awake, do not forget us for ever.*[1]
24. *Why hidest thou thy face? wilt thou forget our misery and our affliction?*[2]
25. *For our soul is humbled to the dust: our belly cleaveth to the earth.*
26. *Arise for our help, and redeem us, for thy goodness' sake.*

22. *Surely for thy sake we are killed all the day.* Here the faithful urge another reason why God should show mercy to them, namely, that they are subjected to sufferings not on account of crimes committed by themselves, but simply because the ungodly, from hatred to the name of God, are opposed to them. "This," it may be said, " seems at first sight a foolish complaint, for the answer which Socrates gave to his wife was apparently more to the purpose, when, upon her lamenting that he was about to die wrongfully,[3] he reproved her, saying, That it was better for him to die innocently than from any fault of his own. And even the consolation which Christ sets forth in Matth. v. 10, 'Blessed are they which are persecuted for righteousness' sake,' seems to differ widely from the language here expressed by the people of God. It seems also opposed to what Peter says, 1 Epist. iv. 16, 'Yet if any man suffer as a Christian, let him not be ashamed; but let him glorify God on this behalf.'" To this I answer, That although it is the greatest alleviation of our sorrow that the cause for which we suffer is common to us with Christ himself, yet it is neither in vain nor out of place that the faithful here plead with God that they suffer wrongfully for his sake, in order that he may the more vigorously set himself for their defence. It is right that he should have respect to the maintenance of his glory, which the wicked endeavour to overthrow, when they insolently persecute those who serve him. And from this it appears the more clearly that this psalm

---

[1] Fry reads the last clause, "Awake, do not fail for ever;" and observes, "The term is sometimes applied to the failing of a stream through drought."

[2] "*Et oublies nostre affliction et nostre oppression?*"—*Fr.* "And forgettest our affliction and our oppression?"

[3] "*Quand elle se lamentant de ce qu'on le faisoit-mourir à tort.*"—*Fr.*

was composed when the people languished in captivity, or else when Antiochus laid waste the Church, because religion was at that time the cause of suffering. The Babylonians were enraged by the constancy of the people, when they perceived that the whole body of the Jews, vanquished and routed as they were, ceased not on that account to condemn the superstitions of the country; and the rage of Antiochus was wholly bent upon extinguishing entirely the name of God. Moreover, what made the thing appear more strange and difficult to bear was, that God, so far from repressing the insolence and the wrongs inflicted by the wicked, left them, on the contrary, to continue in their cruelty, and gave them, as it were, loose reins. Accordingly, the godly declare that *they are killed all the day long*, and that they are counted of no more value than *sheep for slaughter*. It is, however, proper always to bear in mind, what I have already remarked, that they were not so free from all blame as that God, in afflicting them, might not justly chastise them for their sins. But whilst in his incomparable goodness he fully pardons all our sins, he yet allows us to be exposed to unmerited persecutions, that we may with greater alacrity glory in bearing the cross with Christ, and thereby become partakers with him in his blessed resurrection. We have already said, that there was no other reason why the rage of the enemy was so inflamed against them, but that the people would not revolt from the law, and renounce the worship of the true God. It now remains for us to apply this doctrine to our own circumstances; and, first, let us consider that it becomes us, after the example of the fathers, patiently to submit to the afflictions by which it is necessary to seal the confession of our faith; and, secondly, that even in the deepest afflictions we must continue to call upon the name of God and abide in his fear. Paul, however, in his Epistle to the Romans, chap. viii. 36, proceeds still farther; for he quotes this not only by way of example, but also affirms that the condition of the Church in all ages is here portrayed. Thus, then, we ought to regard it as a settled point, that a state of continual warfare in bearing the cross is enjoined upon us by divine appointment. Sometimes, it is true, a truce or respite may be granted us; for God has compassion upon our infirmity: but although the sword of persecution is not always unsheathed against us, yet, as we are the members of Christ, it behoves us always to be ready to bear the cross with him. Lest, therefore, the severity of the cross should dismay us, let us always have present to our view this condition of the Church, that as we are adopted in Christ, we are appointed to the slaughter. If we neglect to do this, the same thing will befall us which happens to many apostates; for as it is in their judgment too severe and wretched a state, even while they live, to be continually dying, to be exposed to the mockery of others, and not to have one moment free from fear,—to rid themselves of that necessity they shamefully forsake and deny Christ. In order, therefore, that weariness, or dread of the cross, may not root up from our hearts true godliness, let us continually reflect upon this, that it behoves us to drink the cup which God puts into our hands, and that no one can be a Christian who does not dedicate himself to God.

23. *Arise, O Lord! why sleepest thou?* Here the saints desire that God, having pity upon them, would at length send them help and deliverance. Although God allows the saints to plead with him in this babbling manner, when in their prayers they desire him to rise up or awake; yet it is necessary that they should be fully persuaded that he keeps watch for their safety and defence. We must guard against the notion of Epicurus, who framed to himself a god who, having his abode in heaven,[1] delighted only in idleness and pleasure. But as the insensibility of our nature is so great, that we do not at once comprehend the care which God has of us, the godly here request that he would be pleased to give some evidence that he was neither forgetful of them nor slow to help them. We must, indeed, firmly believe that God ceases not to regard us, although he appears not to do so; yet as such an assurance is of faith, and not of the flesh, that is to say, is not natural to us,[2] the faithful familiarly give utterance before God to this contrary sentiment, which they conceive from the state of things as it is presented to their

---

[1] " Lequel estant au ciel."—*Fr.*
[2] " C'est à dire, en nostre sens naturel."—*Fr.*

view; and in doing so, they discharge from their breasts those morbid affections which belong to the corruption of our nature, in consequence of which faith then shines forth in its pure and native character. If it is objected, that prayer, than which nothing is more holy, is defiled, when some froward imagination of the flesh is mingled with it, I confess that this is true; but in using this freedom, which the Lord vouchsafes to us, let us consider that, in his goodness and mercy, by which he sustains us, he wipes away this fault, that our prayers may not be defiled by it.

25. *For our soul is humbled to the dust.* The people of God again deplore the greatness of their calamities, and in order that God may be the more disposed to help them, they declare to him that they are afflicted in no ordinary manner. By the metaphors which they here employ, they mean not only that they are cast down, but also that they are crushed and laid upon the earth, so that they are not able to rise again. Some take the word *soul* for the body, so that there would be in this verse a repetition of the same sentiment; but I would rather take it for the part in which the life of man consists; as if they had said, We are cast down to the earth, and lie prostrate upon our belly, without any hope of getting up again. After this complaint they subjoin a prayer, (verse 26,) that God would *arise for their help.* By the word *redeem* they mean not ordinary kind of help, for there was no other means of securing their preservation but by redeeming them. And yet there can be no doubt, that they were diligently employed in meditating upon the great redemption from which all the deliverances which God is daily effecting in our behalf, when he defends us from dangers by various means, flow as streams from their source. In a previous part of the psalm, they had boasted of the stedfastness of their faith; but to show us that, in using this language, they boasted not in their own merits, they do not claim here some recompense for what they had done and suffered for God. They are contented to ascribe their salvation to the unmerited goodness of God as the alone cause of it.

PSALM XLV.

In this psalm, the grace and beauty of Solomon, his virtues in ruling the kingdom, and also his power and riches, are illustrated and described in terms of high commendation. More especially, as he had taken to wife a stranger out of Egypt, the blessing of God is promised to him in this relationship, provided the newly espoused bride, bidding adieu to her own nation, and renouncing all attachment to it, devote herself wholly to her husband. At the same time, there can be no doubt, that under this figure the majesty, wealth, and extent of Christ's kingdom are described and illustrated by appropriate terms, to teach the faithful that there is no felicity greater or more desirable than to live under the reign of this king, and to be subject to his government.

¶ *To the chief musician upon the lilies; of the sons of Korah; for instruction; a song of loves.*

It is well known that this psalm was composed concerning Solomon; but it is uncertain who was its author. It is, in my opinion, probable, that some one of the prophets or godly teachers (whether after Solomon's death, or while he was yet alive, it is of no importance to inquire) took this as the subject of his discourse, with the design of showing, that whatever excellence had been seen in Solomon had a higher application. This psalm is called *a song of loves*, not, as some suppose, because it illustrates the fatherly love of God, as to the benefits which he had conferred in such a distinguished manner upon Solomon, but because it contains an expression of rejoicing on account of his happy and prosperous marriage. Thus the words, *of loves*, are put for a descriptive epithet, and denote, that it is a love-song. Indeed, Solomon was called ידידיה, *Yedidyah*, which means *beloved of the Lord*, 2 Sam. xii. 25. But the context, in my opinion, requires that this term ידידות, *yedidoth*, that is to say, *loves*, be understood as referring to the mutual love which husband and wife ought to cherish towards each other. But as the word *loves* is sometimes taken in a bad sense, and as even conjugal affection itself, however well regulated, has always some irregularity of the flesh mingled with it; this song is, at the same time, called משכיל, *maskil*, to teach us, that the subject here treated of is not some obscene or unchaste amours, but that, under what is here said of Solomon as a type, the holy and divine union of Christ and his Church is described and set forth. As to the remaining part of the inscription, interpreters explain it in various ways. שושן, *shushan*, properly signifies *a lily*; and the sixtieth psalm has in its inscription the same term in the singular number. Here, and in the eightieth psalm, the plural number is employed. It is therefore probable, that it was either the beginning of a common song, or else some instrument of music. But as this is a matter of no great consequence, I give no opinion, but leave it undecided; for, without any danger to the truth, every one may freely adopt on this point whatever view he chooses.

1. *My heart is boiling over with a good matter : I shall speak of the works which I have made concerning the king : my tongue is as the pen of a swift writer.*
2. *Thou art fairer than the sons of men : grace is poured into thy lips : because God hath blessed thee for ever.*
3. *Gird thy sword upon thy thigh, O mighty one! with glory and majesty.*[1]
4. *And in thy majesty do thou prosper : ride forth upon the word of truth, and meekness, and righteousness ; and thy right hand shall teach thee terrible things.*
5. *Thine arrows are sharp (so that the people fall under thee) in the heart of the enemies of the King.*

1. *My heart is boiling over*[2] *with a good matter.* This preface shows sufficiently that the subject of the psalm is no common one ; for whoever the author of it may have been, he here intimates, at the very outset, that he will treat of great and glorious things. The Holy Spirit is not accustomed to inspire the servants of God to utter great swelling words, and to pour forth empty sounds into the air; and, therefore, we may naturally conclude, that the subject here treated of is not merely a transitory and earthly kingdom, but something more excellent. Were not this the case, what end

---

[1] "(Qui est,) gloire et magnificence."—*Fr.* "(Which is,) glory and majesty."

[2] "רחש, *rachash, boileth,* or *bubbleth up,* denotes the language of the heart, full and ready for utterance."—*Bythner's Lyra.* The Psalmist's heart was so full and warmed with the subject of the psalm, that it could not contain ; and the opening of the poem evinces that it was so, for he abruptly breaks forth into an annunciation of its subject as if impatient of restraint. Ainsworth thinks there is here an allusion to the boiling of the *minchah*, or meat-offering under the law in the frying-pan, (Lev. vii. 9.) It was there boiled in oil, being made of fine flour unleavened, mingled with oil, (Lev. xi. 5 ;) and afterwards was presented to the Lord by the priest, verse 8, &c. "Here," says he, "the matter of this psalm is the *minchah* or oblation, which with the oil, the grace of the Spirit, was boiled and prepared in the prophet's breast, and now presented."

would it serve to announce, as the prophet does in such a magnificent style, that his heart *was boiling over*, from his ardent desire to be employed in rehearsing the praises of the king? Some prefer to translate the word *to utter;* but the other signification of the word appears to me to be more appropriate; and it is confirmed by this, that from this verb is derived the noun מרחשת, *marchesheth,* a word which is found once or twice in Moses, and signifies a frying-pan, in which sweatmeats are baked. It is then of the same import as if the inspired writer had said, My heart is ready to breathe forth something excellent and worthy of being remembered. He afterwards expresses the harmony between the tongue and the heart, when he compares his tongue to *the pen of a swift* and ready *writer.*

2. *Thou art fairer than the sons of men.* The Psalmist commences his subject with the commendation of the beauty of the king, and then he proceeds also to praise his eloquence. Personal excellence is ascribed to the king, not that the beauty of the countenance, which of itself is not reckoned among the number of the virtues, ought to be very highly valued; but because a noble disposition of mind often shines forth in the very countenance of a man. This may have been the case with Solomon, so that from his very countenance it might have appeared that he was endued with superior gifts. Nor is the grace of oratory undeservedly commended in a king, to whom it belongs, by virtue of his office, not only to rule the people by authority, but also to allure them to obedience by argument and eloquence, just as the ancients feigned that Hercules had in his mouth golden chains, by which he captivated the ears of the common people, and drew them after him. How manifestly does this rebuke the mean-spiritedness of kings in our day, by whom it is regarded as derogatory to their dignity to converse with their subjects, and to employ remonstrance in order to secure their submission; nay, who display a spirit of barbarous tyranny in seeking rather to compel than to persuade them, and in choosing rather to abuse them as slaves, than to govern them by laws and with justice as a

tractable and obedient people. But as this excellence was displayed in Solomon, so also did it shine forth more fully afterwards in Christ, to whom his truth serves the part of a sceptre, as we shall have occasion by and by to notice more at large. The term עַל־כֵּן, *al-ken,* which we have translated *because,* is sometimes rendered *wherefore;* but it is not necessary that we should interpret it in this place in the latter sense, as if Solomon had been blessed on account of his beauty and excellence, for both of these are blessings of God. It is rather to be understood as the reason why Solomon was distinguished for these endowments, namely, because God had blessed him. As to the interpretation which others give, *God shall bless thee for thy excellency,* it is both cold and forced.

3. *Gird thy sword upon thy thigh.* Here Solomon is praised as well for his warlike valour, which strikes terror into his enemies, as for his virtues which give him authority among his subjects, and secure him their reverence. On the one hand, no king will be able to preserve and defend his subjects, unless he is formidable to his enemies; and, on the other hand, it will be to little purpose to make war boldly upon foreign realms, if the internal state of his own kingdom is not established and regulated in uprightness and justice. Accordingly, the inspired writer says, that the sword with which he will be girded will be, in the first place, a token of warlike prowess to repel and rout his enemies; and, secondly, of authority also, that he might not be held in contempt among his own subjects. He adds, at the same time, that the glory which he will obtain will not be a merely transient thing, like the pomp and vain-glory of kings, which soon decay, but will be of lasting duration, and will greatly increase.

He then comes to speak of the virtues which flourish most in a time of peace, and which, by an appropriate similitude, he shows to be the true means of adding strength and prosperity to a kingdom. At first sight, indeed, it seems to be a strange and inelegant mode of expression, to speak of *riding upon truth, meekness, and righteousness,* (verse 4;) but, as I have said, he very suitably compares these virtues to chariots, in which the king is conspicuously borne aloft with great majesty. These virtues he opposes not only to the vain pomp and parade in which earthly kings proudly boast; but also to the vices and corruptions by which they endeavour most commonly to acquire authority and renown. Solomon himself says in the Proverbs, chap. xx. 28, "Mercy and truth preserve the king; and his throne is upholden by mercy." But, on the contrary, when worldly kings desire to enlarge their dominions, and to increase their power, ambition, pride, fierceness, cruelty, exactions, rapine, and violence, are the horses and chariots which they employ to accomplish their ends; and, therefore, it is not to be wondered at if God should very often cast them down, when thus elated with pride and vain-glory, from their tottering and decayed thrones. For kings, then, to cultivate faithfulness and justice, and to temper their government with mercy and kindness, is the true and solid foundation of kingdoms. The latter clause of the verse intimates, that every thing which Solomon undertakes shall prosper, provided he combine with warlike courage the qualities of justice and mercy. Kings who are carried headlong with a blind and violent impulse, may for a time spread terror and consternation around them; but they soon fall by the force of their own efforts. Due moderation, therefore, and uniform self-restraint, are the best means for making the hands of the valiant to be feared and dreaded.

5. *Thy arrows are sharp, &c.* Here the Psalmist again refers to warlike power, when he says that the *arrows* of the king shall be sharp, so that they shall pierce the *hearts of his enemies;* by which he intimates that he has weapons in his hand with which to strike, even at a distance, all his enemies, whoever they may be, who resist his authority. In the same sense also he says that *the people shall fall under him;* as if it had been said, Whoever shall engage in the attempt to shake the stability of his kingdom shall miserably perish, for the king has in his hand a sufficiency of power to break the stubbornness of all such persons.

6. *Thy throne, O God! is for ever and ever : the sceptre of thy kingdom is the sceptre of equity.*
7. *Thou lovest righteousness, and hatest wickedness : because God, thy God, hath anointed thee with the oil of gladness above thy fellows.*

6. *Thy throne, O God! is for ever and ever.* In this verse the Psalmist commends other princely virtues in Solomon, namely, the eternal duration of his throne, and then the justice and rectitude of his mode of government. The Jews, indeed, explain this passage as if the discourse were addressed to God, but such an interpretation is frivolous and impertinent. Others of them read the word אלהים, *Elohim,* in the genitive case, and translate it *of God,* thus: *The throne of thy God.* But for this there is no foundation, and it only betrays their presumption in not hesitating to wrest the Scriptures so shamefully, that they may not be constrained to acknowledge the divinity of the Messiah.[1] The simple and natural sense is, that Solomon reigns not tyrannically, as the most of kings do, but by just and equal laws, and that, therefore, his throne shall be established for ever. Although he is called *God,* because God has imprinted some mark of his glory in the person of kings, yet this title cannot well be applied to a mortal man; for we nowhere read in Scripture that man or angel has been distinguished by this title without some qualification. It is true, indeed, that angels as well as judges are called collectively אלהים, *Elohim, gods;* but not individually, and no one man is called by this name without some word added by way of restriction, as when Moses was appointed to be a god to Pharaoh, (Exod. vii. 1.) From this we may naturally infer, that this psalm relates, as we shall soon see, to a higher than any earthly kingdom.

In the next verse there is set before us a fuller statement of the righteousness for which this monarch is distinguished; for we are told that he is no less strict in the punishment of iniquity than in maintaining justice. We know how many and great evils are engendered by impunity and license in doing evil, when kings are negligent and slack

[1] See Appendix.

in punishing crimes. Hence the old proverb, That it is better to live under a prince who gives no allowance, than under one who imposes no restraint. To the same purpose also is the well-known sentiment of Solomon, (Prov. xvii. 15,) " He that justifieth the wicked, and he that condemneth the just, even they both are abomination to the Lord." Just and rightful government, therefore, consists of these two parts: first, That they who rule should carefully restrain wickedness; and, secondly, That they should vigorously maintain righteousness; even as Plato has well and wisely said, that civil government consists of two parts—rewards and punishments. When the Psalmist adds, that the king was *anointed above his fellows*, this is not to be understood as the effect or fruit of his righteousness, but rather as the cause of it: for the love of uprightness and equity by which Solomon was actuated arose from the fact, that he was divinely appointed to the kingdom. In ordaining him to the honour of authority and empire, Jehovah, at the same time, furnished him with the necessary endowments. The particle עַל־כֵּן, *al-ken*, therefore, as in the former instance, is to be understood here in the sense of *because;* as if it had been said, It is no wonder that Solomon is so illustrious for his love of justice, since, from the number of all his brethren, he was chosen to be consecrated king by holy anointing. Even before he was born, he was solemnly named by a divine oracle, as successor to the kingdom, and when he was elevated to the throne, he was also adorned with princely virtues. From this it follows, that anointing in respect of order preceded righteousness, and that, therefore, righteousness cannot be accounted the cause of the anointing. The royal dignity is called *the oil of gladness,* because of the effect of it; for the felicity and welfare of the Church depended upon the kingdom promised to the house of David.[1]

Hitherto, I have explained the text in the literal sense. But it is necessary that I should now proceed to illustrate somewhat more largely the comparison of Solomon with Christ, which I have only cursorily noticed. It would be quite suf-

---

[1] " Promis à la maison de David."—*Fr.*

ficient for the pious and humble simply to state what is obvious, from the usual tenor of Scripture, that the posterity of David typically represented Christ to the ancient people of God; but as the Jews and other ungodly men refuse to submit cordially to the force of truth, it is of importance to show briefly from the context itself, the principal reasons from which it appears that some of the things here spoken are not applicable fully and perfectly to Solomon. As I intimated at the outset, the design of the prophet who composed this psalm was to confirm the hearts of the faithful, and to guard them against the terror and alarm with which the melancholy change that happened soon after might fill their minds. An everlasting duration, it might be said, had been promised to this kingdom, and it fell into decay after the death of one man. To this objection, therefore, the prophet replies, that although Rehoboam, who was the first successor of that glorious and powerful king, had his sovereignty reduced within narrow limits, so that a great part of the people were cut off and placed beyond the bounds of his dominion, yet that was no reason why the faith of the Church should fail; for in the kingdom of Solomon God had exhibited a type or figure of that everlasting kingdom which was still to be looked for and expected. In the first place, the name of king is ascribed to Solomon, simply by way of eminence, to teach us, that what is here said is not spoken of any common or ordinary king, but of that illustrious sovereign, whose throne God had promised should endure as long as the sun and moon continued to shine in the heavens, (Ps. lxxii. 5.) David certainly was king, and so were those who succeeded Solomon. It is necessary then to observe, that there is in this term some special significance, as if the Holy Spirit had selected this one man from all others, to distinguish him by the highest mark of sovereignty. Besides, how inconsistent would it be to commend very highly warlike valour in Solomon, who was a man of a meek and quiet disposition, and who having ascended the throne when the kingdom enjoyed tranquillity and peace, devoted himself only to the cultivation of those things that are suitable to a time of peace, and never distinguished himself by any action in battle? But, above all, no clearer testimony could be adduced of the application of this psalm to Christ, than what is here said of the eternal duration of the kingdom. There can be no doubt, that allusion is here made to the holy oracle of which I have already made mention, That as long as the sun and moon shall endure in the heavens the throne of David shall endure. Even the Jews themselves are constrained to refer this to the Messiah. Accordingly, although the prophet commenced his discourse concerning the son of David, there can be no doubt, that, guided by the Holy Spirit to a higher strain, he comprehended the kingdom of the true and everlasting Messiah. Besides, there is the name אלהים, *Elohim*, which it is proper to notice. It is no doubt also applied both to angels and men, but it cannot be applied to a mere man without qualification. And, therefore, the divine majesty of Christ, beyond all question, is expressly denoted here.[1]

I now proceed to notice the several parts, which however I shall only refer to briefly in passing. We have said that while this song is called a *love song*, or *wedding song*, still

[1] It is somewhat strange, after making the above observations, that Calvin should consider this beautiful psalm as referring primarily to Solomon, and to his marriage with the daughter of Pharaoh. That this is an epithalamium or nuptial song, is readily admitted; but that it refers to the nuptials of Solomon with Pharaoh's daughter, there seems no just ground for concluding. If Solomon could not be described as " fairer than the children of men," as " a mighty warrior," as " a victorious conqueror," as " a prince, whose throne is for ever and ever ;"—if the name " God" could not be applied to him ;—if it could not be said that his " children," in the room of their father, were " made princes in all the earth," (verse 16;) that "his name" " would be remembered in all generations," and that " the people would praise him for ever and ever," (verse 17 ;)—if these things could not be spoken of him without much incongruity, it may well be doubted whether the primary application of this psalm is to him. Besides, although Solomon was a type of Christ, he was not so in all things, and there is nothing in this poem, nor in any other part of Scripture, which can lead us to regard the marriage of this prince with the daughter of Pharaoh as an image or type of the mystical marriage of Jesus Christ to the Church. We therefore agree with Rosenmüller, that " the notion of Rudinger and Grotius," and other critics, " that this song is an epithalamium—a song in celebration of the marriage of Solomon, and his chief wife, the daughter of Pharaoh, (1 Kings iii. 5,) is altogether to be abandoned ;" and that it applies exclusively to the Messiah, and to the mystical union between him and his Church ; set forth in an allegory borrowed from the manners of an Eastern court, and under the image of conjugal love, he being represented as the bridegroom, and the Church as his bride.—See Appendix.

divine instruction is made to hold the most prominent place in it, lest our imaginations should lead us to regard it as referring to some lascivious and carnal amours. We know also, that in the same sense Christ is called " the perfection of beauty;" not that there was any striking display of it in his countenance, as some men grossly imagine, but because he was distinguished by the possession of singular gifts and graces, in which he far excelled all others. Nor is it an unusual style of speaking, that what is spiritual in Christ should be described under the form of earthly figures. The kingdom of Christ, it is said, shall be opulent; and in addition to this it is said, that it shall attain to a state of great glory, such as we see where there is great prosperity and vast power. In this description there is included also abundance of pleasures. Now, there is nothing of all this that applies literally to the kingdom of Christ, which is separated from the pomps of this world. But as it was the design of the prophets to adapt their instruction to the capacity of God's ancient people, so in describing the kingdom of Christ, and the worship of God which ought to be observed in it, they employ figures taken from the ceremonies of the Law. If we bear in mind this mode of statement, in accordance with which such descriptions are made, there will no longer be any obscurity in this passage. It is also deserving of our notice, that, after the Psalmist has commended this heavenly king for his eloquence, he also describes him as armed with *his sword*. As, on the one hand, he governs by the influence of persuasion, those who willingly submit to his authority, and manifest docility of disposition; so, on the other hand, as there have been in all ages, and will continue to be, many who are rebellious and disobedient, it is necessary that the unbelieving should be made to feel in their own destruction that Christ has not come unarmed. While, therefore, he is alluring us with meekness and kindness to himself, let us promptly and submissively yield to his authority, lest he should fall upon us, armed as he is with his sword and with deadly arrows. It is said, indeed, with much propriety, that *grace is poured into his lips;* for the Gospel, in its very nature, breathes the odour of life: but if we are stubborn and rebellious, this grace will become a ground of terror, and Christ himself will convert the very doctrine of his salvation into a sword and arrows against us. From this also there arises no small consolation to us, that the multitude and insolence of the adversaries of Christ may not discourage us. We know well with what arrogance the Papists reject Jesus Christ, whom, nevertheless, they boast to be their King; we know also with what profane contempt the greater part of the world deride him, and how frowardly the Turks and Jews reproach him. In the midst of such disorder, let us remember this prophecy, That Christ has no want of a sword and arrows to overthrow and destroy his enemies. Here I will again briefly repeat what I have noticed above, namely, that however much the Jews endeavour by their cavillings to pervert the sense of this verse, *Thy throne, O God! is for ever and ever*, yet it is sufficient of itself to establish the eternal divinity of Christ: for when the name אלהים *Elohim* is ascribed either to angels or men, some other mark is at the same time usually added, to distinguish between them and the only true God; but here it is applied to Christ, simply and without any qualification. It is of importance, however, to notice, that Christ is here spoken of as he is " God manifested in the flesh," (1 Tim. iii. 16.) He is also called God, as he is the Word, begotten of the Father before all worlds'; but he is here set forth in the character of Mediator, and on this account also mention is made of him a little after, as being subject to God. And, indeed, if you limit to his divine nature what is here said of the everlasting duration of his kingdom, we shall be deprived of the inestimable benefit which redounds to us from this doctrine, when we learn that, as he is the head of the Church, the author and protector of our welfare, he reigns not merely for a time, but possesses an endless sovereignty; for from this we derive our greatest confidence both in life and in death. From the following verse also it clearly appears, that Christ is here exhibited to us in the character of Mediator; for he is said *to have been anointed of God*, yea, even *above his fellows*, (Isa. xlii. 1; Heb. ii. 17.) This, however, cannot apply to the eternal Word of God, but to Christ in the flesh, and in this character he is both the servant of God and our brother.

8. *All thy garments smell of myrrh, and aloes, and cassia, out of the ivory palaces, whence they have made thee glad.*
9. *The daughters of kings were among thy honourable women:*[1] *thy consort stood on thy right hand*[2] *in gold of Ophir.*[3]
10. *Hearken, O daughter! and consider, and incline thy ear: and forget thy own people and thy father's house.*
11. *And the King shall greatly desire thy beauty: for he is thy Lord, and thou shalt worship him.*[4]
12. *And the daughter of Tyre with a gift: the rich among the people shall entreat thy face.*

8. *All thy garments smell of myrrh.* As to the signification of the words I am not disposed to contend much, for I find that even the Jews are not agreed among themselves as to the meaning of the third word, except that from the similarity of pronunciation it may be conjectured to denote cassia. It is sufficient that we understand the prophet as meaning that the garments of the king are perfumed with precious and sweet-smelling odours. He describes Solomon coming forth from his ivory palace amidst shoutings of universal applause and joy. I explain not the word מִנִּי, *minni*, *Out of me*, because no tolerable meaning can be drawn from this. I translate it *whence*,[5] and refer it to the *ivory palaces.* Superfluity and excess in

---

[1] "Ou, dames d'honneur."—*Fr. marg.* "Maids of honour."
[2] The right hand was the place of dignity and honour.
[3] "אוּפִיר, *Ophir;* in gold *of Ophir, in a golden garment.* Ophir, a country in India abounding in precious gold, 1 Kings ix. 28, whose gold was obryzum, or ophrizum, *i.e.*, most excellent."—*Bythner's Lyra.*
[4] "C'est, luy porteras reverence."—*Fr. marg.* "That is, thou shalt do him reverence."
[5] Calvin here seems to take the word מִנִּי, *minni*, which has somewhat perplexed commentators, to be the particle מִן, *min*, *out of*, with י, *yod*, paragogic, as it is in Psalm xliv. 19, and many other places; and to suppose that the relative אשר, *asher, which,* a pronoun frequently omitted, is to be understood,—" *out of which* palaces *they have made thee glad.*" This is the view taken by many interpreters. Others understand the word מִנִּי, *minni,* to be a noun; (and from Jer. li. 27, it appears that מִנִּי, *minni,* was the proper name of a territory, which Bochart shows was a district of Armenia;) and they translate the words thus, " From the ivory palaces of Armenia they make thee glad," make thee glad with presents. Others suppose that מִנִּי, *minni,* is here the name of a region, *Minnaea* in Arabia Felix, which abounded in myrrh and frankincense; and according to this view, the clause may be rendered, "The Minnaeitas from their ivory palaces make thee glad;" that is, coming to thee from their ivory palaces they gladden thee with presents. Rosenmüller thinks with Schmidt, De Wette, and Gesenius, that a more elegant sense will be brought out if we

pleasures cannot be justified, not only in the common people, but not even in kings; yet, on the other hand, it is necessary to guard against too much austerity, that we may not condemn the moderate display of grandeur which is suitable to their dignity, even as, a little after, the prophet describes the queen sumptuously and royally apparelled.[1] We must, however, at the same time, consider that all that is here commended in Solomon was not approved of by God. Not to speak of other things, it is well known that from the very first the sin of polygamy was a thing displeasing to God, and yet concubines are here spoken of as included among the blessings of God, for there is no reason to doubt that by *the honourable women*, or *maids of honour*,[2] the prophet means Solomon's wives, of whom mention is made in another place. The daughter of the king of Egypt, whom Solomon had married, was his principal wife, and the first in rank;[3] but it appears that the others, whom sacred history describes as occupying an inferior rank, were provided for in a liberal and honourable manner. These the prophet calls *the daughters of kings*, because some of them were descended of the royal blood. In what sense, then, it might be asked, does the prophet account it among the praises of Solomon that he had many wives,— a thing which God condemns in all private persons, but expressly in kings? (Deut. xvii. 17.) Doubtless it may easily be inferred that in commending, according to a common practice, the wealth and glory of the king, as the prophet here does, he did not mean to approve of the abuse of them. It was not his design to set forth the example of a man in

---

understand מִנִּי, *minni*, as a plural noun in a form somewhat unusual, but of which there are several other examples in the Old Testament, such as ששי, 2 Sam. xxiii. 8; כרי, 2 Kings ix. 4, 19; עמי, 2 Sam. xxii. 44; Psalm cxliv. 2. "The word," says he, "according to these examples, stands for מנים, and signifies, as in the Syriac, Psalm cl. 4, *chords, stringed* instruments of music. The sense of the clause will thus be, 'From the palaces of ivory, musical instruments—players on musical instruments—make thee glad.'" —*Rosenmüller on the Messianic Psalms*, pp. 213-215.—*Biblical Cabinet*, vol. xxxii.

[1] "Comme un peu apres le prophete descrit la Royne ornee somptueusement et magnifiquement."—*Fr.*

[2] "Ou, dames d'honneur."—*Fr.*

[3] "Car combien que la fille du Roy d'Egypte que Salomon avoit espousee, fust sa principale femme, et teinst le premier lieu."—*Fr.*

opposition to the law of God. It is true, indeed, that the power, dignity, and glory, which Solomon enjoyed, were granted to him as singular blessings from God; but as generally happens, he defiled them greatly by not exercising self-control, and in abusing the great abundance with which he was blessed, by the excessive indulgence of the flesh. In short, it is here recorded what great liberality God manifested towards Solomon in giving him every thing in abundance. As to the fact that he took to him so many wives, and did not exercise a due moderation in his pomp, this is not to be included in the liberality of God, but is a thing as it were accidental.

10. *Hearken, O daughter! and consider.* I have no doubt, that what is here said is spoken of the Egyptian woman, whom the prophet has described as standing at the right hand of the king. It was not, indeed, lawful for Solomon to marry a strange woman; but this of itself is to be accounted among the gifts of God, that a king so powerful as the king of Egypt was,[1] sought his alliance. At the same time, as by the appointment of the Law, it was required that the Jews, previous to entering into the marriage relation, should endeavour to instruct their wives in the pure worship of God, and emancipate them from superstition; in the present instance, in which the wife spoken of was descended from a heathen nation, and who, by her present marriage, was included in the body of the Church, the prophet, in order to withdraw her from her evil training, exhorts her to forget her own country and her father's house, and to assume a new character and other manners. If she did not do this, there was reason to fear, not only that she would continue to observe in private the superstitions and false modes of worshipping God to which she had been habituated, but that also, by her public example, she would draw away many into a similar evil course; and, indeed, this actually came to pass soon after. Such is the reason of the exhortation which the prophet here gives her, in which, in order to render his discourse of more weight, he addresses her by the appellation

---

[1] "Comme estoit la Roy d'Egypte."—*Fr.*

of *daughter*, a term which it would have been unsuitable for any private man to have used. The more clearly to show how much it behoved the new bride to become altogether a new woman, he employs several terms thereby to secure her attention, *Hearken, consider, and incline thy ear.* It is certainly a case in which much vehemence and urgent persuasion are needed, when it is intended to lead us to a complete renunciation of those things in which we take delight, either by nature or by custom. He then shows that there is no reason why the daughter of Pharaoh should feel any regret in forsaking *her father*, her kinsfolk, and the land of Egypt, because she would receive a glorious recompense, which ought to allay the grief she might experience in being separated from them. To reconcile her to the thought of leaving her own country, he encourages her by the consideration that she is married to so illustrious a king.

Let us now return to Christ. And, in the first place, let us remember that what is spiritual is here described to us figuratively; even as the prophets, on account of the dulness of men, were under the necessity of borrowing similitudes from earthly things. When we bear in mind this style of speaking, which is quite common in the Scriptures, we will not think it strange that the sacred writer here makes mention of *ivory palaces, gold, precious stones,* and *spices;* for by these he means to intimate that the kingdom of Christ will be replenished with a rich abundance, and furnished with all good things. The glory and excellence of the spiritual gifts, with which God enriches his Church, are indeed held in no estimation among men; but in the sight of God they are of more value than all the riches of the world. At the same time, it is not necessary that we should apply curiously to Christ every particular here enumerated;[1] as for instance,

---

[1] This is certainly a most important rule in interpreting the allegorical compositions of Scripture. It is not to be imagined that there are distinct analogies between every part of an allegorical representation, and the spiritual subjects which it is designed to illustrate. The interpreter who allows his ingenuity to press too closely all the points of the allegory to the spiritual subjects couched under it, seeking points of comparison in the complementary parts, which are introduced merely for the purpose of giving more animation and beauty to the discourse, is in danger by his fanciful analogies of degrading the composition, and falling into absurdities.

what is here said of the many wives which Solomon had. If it should be imagined from this that there may be several churches, the unity of Christ's body will be rent in pieces. I admit, that as every individual believer is called "the temple of God," (1 Cor. iii. 17, and vi. 19,) so also might each be named " the spouse of Christ ;" but properly speaking, there is only one spouse of Christ, which consists of the whole body of the faithful. She is said *to sit by the side of the king*, not that she exercises any dominion peculiar to herself, but because Christ rules in her; and it is in this sense that she is called "the mother of us all," (Gal. iv. 26.)

This passage contains a remarkable prophecy in reference to the future calling of the Gentiles, by which the Son of God formed an alliance with strangers and those who were his enemies. There was between God and the uncircumcised nations a deadly quarrel, a wall of separation which divided them from the seed of Abraham, the chosen people, (Eph. ii. 14;) for the covenant which God had made with Abraham shut out the Gentiles from the kingdom of heaven till the coming of Christ. Christ, therefore, of his free grace, desires to enter into a holy alliance of marriage with the whole world, in the same way as if a Jew in ancient times had taken to himself a wife from a foreign and heathen land. But in order to conduct into Christ's presence his bride chaste and undefiled, the prophet exhorts the Church gathered from the Gentiles to forget her former manner of living, and to devote herself wholly to her husband. As this change, by which the children of Adam begin to be the children of God, and are transformed into new men, is a thing so difficult, the prophet enforces the necessity of it the more earnestly. In enforcing his exhortation in this way by different terms, *hearken, consider, incline thy ear*, he intimates, that the faithful do not deny themselves, and lay aside their former habits, without intense and painful effort ; for such an exhortation would be superfluous, were men naturally and voluntarily disposed to it. And, indeed, experience shows how dull and slow we are to follow God. By the word *consider*, or *understand*, our stupidity is tacitly rebuked, and not without good reason; for whence arise that self-love which is so blind, that false opinion which we have of our own wisdom and strength, the deception arising from the fascinations of the world, and, in fine, the arrogance and pride which are natural to us, but because we do not consider how precious a treasure God is presenting to us in his only begotten Son? Did not this ingratitude prevent us, we would without regret, after the example of Paul, (Phil. iii. 8,) reckon as nothing, or as "dung," those things which we admire most, that Christ might replenish us with his riches. By the word *daughter*, the prophet gently and sweetly soothes the new Church; and he also sets before her the promise of a bountiful reward,[1] to induce her, for the sake of Christ, willingly to despise and forsake whatever she made account of heretofore. It is certainly no small consolation to know that the Son of God will delight in us, when we shall have put off our earthly nature. In the meantime, let us learn, that to deny ourselves is the beginning of that sacred union which ought to exist between us and Christ. By her *father's house* and *her people* is doubtless meant all the corruptions which we carry with us from our mother's womb, or derive from evil custom; nay, under this mode of expression there is comprehended whatever men have belonging to themselves; for there is no part of our nature sound or free from corruption.

It is necessary, also, to notice the reason which is added, namely, that if the Church refuses to devote herself wholly to Christ, she casts off his due and lawful authority. By the word *worship* we must understand not only the outward ceremony, but also, according to the figure synecdoche, a holy desire to yield reverence and obedience. Would to God that this admonition, as it ought, had been thoroughly weighed! for the Church of Christ had then been more obedient to his authority, and we should not in these days have had so great a contest to maintain in reference to her authority against the Papists, who imagine that the Church is not sufficiently exalted and honoured, unless with unbridled license she may insolently triumph over her own husband. They, no doubt, in words ascribe supreme authority to Christ, saying, that every knee should

[1] "En luy proposant bonne recompense."—*Fr.*

bow before him; but when they maintain that the Church has an unlimited power of making laws, what else is this but to give her loose reins, and to exempt her from the authority of Christ, that she may break forth into any excess according to her desire? I stay not to notice how wickedly they arrogate to themselves the title and designation of the Church. But it is intolerable sacrilege to rob Christ and then adorn the Church with his spoils. It is no small dignity which the Church enjoys, in being seated at the right hand of the King, and it is no small honour to be called "the Mother" of all the godly, for to her it belongs to nourish and keep them under her discipline. But at the same time it is easy to gather from innumerable passages of Scripture, that Christ does not so elevate his own Church that he may diminish or impair in the least his own authority.

12. *And the daughter of Tyre with a gift.* This also is a part of the recompense which the prophet promises to the queen in order to mitigate, or rather to extinguish entirely, the longing desire she might still feel after her former condition. He says, that the Tyrians will come humbly to pay her reverence, bringing presents with them. Tyre, we know, was formerly a city of great renown, and, therefore, he accounts it a very high honour that men will come from a city so distinguished and opulent to greet her and to testify their submission to her. It is not necessary for us to examine every word minutely, in order to apply to the Church every thing here said concerning the wife of Solomon; but in our own day we realise some happy fruits of this prophecy when God has so ordered it, that some of the great men of this world, although they themselves refuse to submit to the authority of Christ, act with kindness towards the Church, maintaining and defending her.

13. *The daughter of the King is all glorious within: her clothing is of garments embroidered with gold.*
14. *She shall be brought to the King in raiment of needle-work: the virgins after her, her companions, shall be brought to thee.*
15. *They shall be brought with joy and gladness: they shall enter into the palace of the King.*
16. *Instead of thy fathers shall be thy children: thou shalt make them princes in all the earth.*
17. *I will make thy name to be remembered throughout all generations: therefore the people shall praise thee for ever and ever.*

13. *The daughter of the King is all glorious within.*[1] This verse may be understood in a twofold sense; either as meaning that the queen, not only when she appears in public before all the people, but also when sitting in private in her own chamber, is always sumptuously apparelled; or, that the splendour and gorgeous appearance of her attire is not merely a thing of display, designed to dazzle the eyes of the simple, but consists of expensive and really substantial material. The prophet accordingly enhances the happy and lofty condition of the queen by the circumstance, that she has not only sumptuous apparel in which she may appear on particular occasions, but also for her ordinary and daily attire. Others expound it in this sense, That all her glory consists in the king inviting her familiarly into his presence; and this opinion they rest on the ground that immediately after there is a description given of her as passing into the chamber of the king accompanied with a great and glorious train of followers. This

---

[1] Dathe and Berlin refer *within* to the interior of the queen's palace, which seems to agree best with the context. The original word rendered *within* denotes *the interior of a house* in Lev. x. 18, and 1 Kings vi. 18. Fry explains the words thus: "*Most splendid is the royal daughter within* the awning of her covered vehicle;" and refers to the picture of a bridal procession in Mr Lane's Egypt. Dr Geddes reads:—

"All glorious is the queen in her apartment,
Her robe is bespangled with gold;
To the king she shall be brought in brocade,
Attended by her virgin companions."

"This," says he, namely, verse 13th, "and the two next verses, contain a fine description of Oriental manners. The queen, before she be led to the king's apartment, is gorgeously dressed in her own; and thence proceeds with her female train to the royal palace."

display of pomp exceeds the bounds of due moderation; but, in the meantime, we are taught by it, that while the Church is thus richly apparelled, it is not designed to attract the notice of men, but only for the pleasure of the King. If in our day the Church is not so richly adorned with that spiritual beauty in which the glory of Christ shines forth, the fault ought to be imputed to the ingratitude of men, who either through their own indifference despise the goodness of God, or else, after having been enriched by him, again fall into a state of poverty and want.

16. *Instead of thy fathers shall be thy children.* This also serves to show the glory and transcendent excellence of this kingdom, namely, that the children will not be inferior in dignity to their fathers, and that the nobility of the race will not be diminished after the death of Solomon; for the children which shall be born to him will equal those who had preceded them in the most excellent virtues. Then it is added, that they shall be *princes in all the earth,* because the empire shall enjoy such an extent of dominion on every side, that it might easily be divided into many kingdoms. It is easy to gather, that this prophecy is spoken expressly concerning Christ; for so far were the sons of Solomon from having a kingdom of such an extent, as to divide it into provinces among them, that his first successor retained only a small portion of his kingdom. There were none of his true and lawful successors who attained the same power which he had enjoyed, but being princes only over one tribe and a half of the people, they were, on this account, shut up within narrow limits, and, as we say, had their wings clipped.[1] But at the coming of Christ, who appeared at the close of the ancient Church, and the beginning of the new dispensation, it is an undoubted truth, that children were begotten by him, who were inferior in no respect to their fathers, either in number or in excellence, and whom he set as rulers over the whole world. In the estimation of the world, the ignominy of the cross obscures the glory of the Church; but when

---

[1] " Et (comme on dit) ont eu les ailes rongnees."—*Fr.*

we consider how wonderfully it has increased, and how much it has been distinguished by spiritual gifts, we must confess that it is not without cause that her glory is in this passage celebrated in such sublime language. It ought, however, to be observed, that the sovereignty, of which mention is here made, consists not in the persons of men, but refers to the head. According to a frequent mode of expression in the Word of God, the dominion and power which belong properly to the head, and are applicable peculiarly to Christ alone, are in many places ascribed to his members. We know that those who occupy eminent stations in the Church, and who rule in the name of Christ, do not exercise a lordly dominion, but rather act as servants. As, however, Christ has committed to them his Gospel, which is the sceptre of his kingdom, and intrusted it as it were to their keeping, they exercise, in some sort, his power. And, indeed, Christ, by his ministers, has subdued to his dominion the whole world, and has erected as many principalities under his authority as there have been churches gathered to him in divers nations by their preaching.

17. *I will make thy name to be remembered, &c.* This also is equally inapplicable to Solomon, who, by his shameful and impious rebellion, stained the memory of his name with disgrace. In polluting by superstitious abominations the land which was consecrated to God, did he not bring upon himself indelible ignominy and shame? For this deed alone his name deserves to be buried in everlasting oblivion. Nor was his son Rehoboam in any degree more deserving of praise; for through his own foolish presumption he lost the better part of his kingdom. To find, therefore, the true accomplishment of what is here said, we must come to Christ, the memory of whose name continues to prosper and prevail. It is no doubt despised by the world, nay, wicked men, in the pride of their hearts, even reproach his sacred name, and outrageously trample it under their feet; but still it survives in its undiminished majesty. It is also true, that his enemies rise up on all sides in vast numbers to overthrow his kingdom; but notwithstanding, men are already beginning to bow

the knee before him, which they will continue to do, until the period arrive when he shall tread down all the powers that are opposed to him. The furious efforts of Satan and the whole world have not been able to extinguish the name of Christ, which, being transmitted from one generation to another, still retains its glory in every age, even as at this day we see it celebrated in every language. And although the greater part of the world tear it in pieces by their impious blasphemies, yet it is enough that God stirs up his servants every where to proclaim with fidelity and with unfeigned zeal the praises of Christ. In the meantime, it is our duty diligently to use our endeavours, that the memory of Christ, which ought to prosper and prevail throughout all ages, to the eternal salvation of men, may never at any time lose any of its renown.

PSALM XLVI.

This psalm seems to be an expression of thanksgiving rather for some particular deliverance, than for the constant aid by which God has always protected and preserved his Church. It may be inferred from it that the city of Jerusalem, when stricken with great terror, and placed in extreme danger, was preserved, contrary to all expectation, by the unlooked for and miraculous power of God. The prophet, therefore, whoever composed the psalm, commending a deliverance so singularly vouchsafed by God, exhorts the faithful to commit themselves confidently to his protection, and not to doubt that, relying fearlessly upon him as their guardian and the protector of their welfare, they shall be continually preserved in safety from all the assaults of their enemies, because it is his peculiar office to quell all commotions.

¶ To the chief musician of the sons of Korah, a song upon Alamoth.

Interpreters are not agreed as to the meaning of the word עלמות, *alamoth;* but without noticing all the different opinions, I shall mention only two of them, namely, that it was either an instrument of music, or else the commencement of some common and well known song. The latter conjecture appears to me the most probable. As to the time when this psalm was written it is also uncertain, unless, perhaps, we might suppose that it was written when the siege of the city was suddenly raised by the terrible and sore destruction which God brought upon the army of Sennacherib,[1] (2 Kings xix. 35.) This opinion I readily admit, because it accords most with the whole scope of the psalm. It is abundantly manifest that some favour of God, worthy of being held in remembrance, such as that was, is here commended.

1. *God is our refuge and strength: he is found an exceeding* [or *superlative*] *help in tribulations.*
2. *Therefore we will not fear, though the earth be moved, and the mountains fall into the midst of the sea.*

1. *God is our refuge and strength.* Here the Psalmist begins with a general expression or sentiment, before he comes to speak of the more particular deliverance. He begins by premising that God is sufficiently able to protect his own people, and that he gives them sufficient ground to expect it; for this the word מחסה, *machaseh,* properly signifies. In the second clause of the verse the verb *he is found,* which we translate in the present, is in the past tense, *he has been found;* and, indeed, there would be no impropriety in limiting the language to some particular deliverance which had already been experienced, just as others also have rendered it in the past tense. But as the prophet adds the term *tribulations* in the plural number, I prefer explaining it of a continued act, That God comes seasonably to our aid, and is never wanting in the time of need, as often as any afflictions press upon his people. If the prophet were speaking of the experience of God's favour, it would answer much better to render the verb in the past tense. It is, however, obvious that his design is to extol the power of God and his goodness towards his people, and to show how ready God is to afford them assist-

---

[1] Others refer it, as Rosenmüller, to the victory of Jehoshaphat, which was celebrated with great rejoicing, 2 Chron. xx. 26-30. It is, however, difficult or impossible to ascertain with certainty the occasion on which it was composed. It seems rather the language of faith under threatened difficulties, than of triumph over vanquished foes. Thus, in the midst of threatened danger, it may be employed by Christians to support their faith, hope, and peace. This was Luther's favourite psalm. He composed a famous version of it on his journey to the Diet at Worms, where he went boldly to defend the Reformation at the risk of his life; and he was wont to say when threatened with any fresh trouble, "Come, let us sing the 46th Psalm."

ance, that they may not in the time of their adversities gaze around them on every side, but rest satisfied with his protection alone. He therefore says expressly that God acts in such a manner towards them, to let the Church know that he exercises a special care in preserving and defending her. There can be no doubt that by this expression he means to draw a distinction between the chosen people of God and other heathen nations, and in this way to commend the privilege of adoption which God of his goodness had vouchsafed to the posterity of Abraham. Accordingly, when I said before that it was a general expression, my intention was not to extend it to all manner of persons, but only to all times; for the object of the prophet is to teach us after what manner God is wont to act towards those who are his people. He next concludes, by way of inference, that the faithful nave no reason to be afraid, since God is always ready to deliver them, nay, is also armed with invincible power. He shows in this that the true and proper proof of our hope consists in this, that, when things are so confused, that the heavens seem as it were to fall with great violence, the earth to remove out of its place, and the mountains to be torn up from their very foundations, we nevertheless continue to preserve and maintain calmness and tranquillity of heart. It is an easy matter to manifest the appearance of great confidence, so long as we are not placed in imminent danger: but if, in the midst of a general crash of the whole world, our minds continue undisturbed and free of trouble, this is an evident proof that we attribute to the power of God the honour which belongs to him. When, however, the sacred poet says, *We will not fear*, he is not to be understood as meaning that the minds of the godly are exempt from all solicitude or fear, as if they were destitute of feeling, for there is a great difference between insensibility and the confidence of faith. He only shows that whatever may happen they are never overwhelmed with terror, but rather gather strength and courage sufficient to allay all fear. *Though the earth be moved, and the mountains fall into the midst of the sea*, are hyperbolical modes of expression, but they nevertheless denote a revolution, and turning upside down of the whole world. Some have explained the expression, *the midst of the sea,* as referring to the earth. I do not, however, approve of it. But in order more fully to understand the doctrine of the psalm, let us proceed to consider what follows.

> 3. *Though the waters thereof roar and rage*[1] *tempestuously: though the mountains be shaken with the swelling thereof. Selah.*
> 4. *The streams of her river shall make glad the city of God, the sanctuary of the tabernacles of the Most High.*
> 5. *God is in the midst of her; she shall not be moved: God will help her at the dawn of the morning.*

3. *Though the waters thereof roar, &c.* This verse ought to be read in connection with the verse which follows, because it is necessary to complete the sense, as if it had been said: Though the waters of the sea roar and swell, and by their fierce impetuosity shake the very mountains—even in the midst of these dreadful tumults, the holy city of God will continue to enjoy comfort and peace, satisfied with her small streams. The relative pronoun *her,* according to the common usage of the Hebrew language, is superfluous in this place. The prophet intended simply to say, that the small streams of a river would afford to the holy city abundant cause of rejoicing, though the whole world should be moved and destroyed. I have already mentioned shortly before how profitable is the doctrine taught us in this place, that our faith is really and truly tested only when we are brought into very severe conflicts, and when even hell itself seems opened to swallow us up. In like manner, we have portrayed to us the victory of faith over the whole world, when, in the midst of the utmost confusion, it unfolds itself, and begins to raise its head in such a manner as that although the whole creation seem to be banded together, and to have conspired for the destruction of the faithful, it nevertheless triumphs over all fear. Not that the children of God, when placed in peril, indulge in jesting or make a sport of death, but the help which God has promised them more than overbalances, in their estimation, all the evils which inspire them with fear.

---

[1] " Ou, s'enfleront."—*Fr. marg.* " Or, swell."

The sentiment of Horace is very beautiful, when, speaking of the righteous man and the man who feels conscious of no guilt, he says, (Car., Lib. iii., Od. 3,)

> " Dux inquieti turbidus Adriæ,
> Nec fulminantis magna Jovis manus,
> Si fractus illabitur orbis,
> Impavidum ferient ruinæ."

> " Let the wild winds that rule the seas,
> Tempestuous, all their horrors raise;
> Let Jove's dread arm with thunders rend the spheres;
> Beneath the crush of worlds undaunted he appears."[1]

But as no such person as he imagines could ever be found, he only trifles in speaking as he does. Their fortitude, therefore, has its foundation in the assurance of the divine protection alone, so that they who rely upon God, and put their trust in him, may truly boast, not only that they shall be undismayed, but also that they shall be preserved in security and safety amidst the ruins of a falling world.

The prophet says expressly, that *the city of God shall be glad*, although it had no raging sea, but only a gently flowing stream, to set for its defence against those waves of which he has made mention. By this mode of expression he alludes to the stream which flowed from Shiloah, and passed through the city of Jerusalem. Further, the prophet, I have no doubt, here indirectly rebukes the vain confidence of those who, fortified by earthly assistance, imagine that they are well protected, and beyond the reach of all danger. Those who anxiously seek to strengthen themselves on all sides with the invincible helps of the world, seem, indeed, to imagine that they are able to prevent their enemies from approaching them, just as if they were environed on all sides with the sea; but it often happens that the very defences which they had reared turn to their own destruction, even as when a tempest lays waste and destroys an island by overflowing it. But they who commit themselves to the protection of God, although in the estimation of the world they are exposed to

---

[1] Francis' Translation of Horace.

every kind of injury, and are not sufficiently able to repel the assaults made upon them, nevertheless repose in security. On this account, Isaiah (chap. viii. 6) reproves the Jews because they despised the gently flowing waters of Shiloah, and longed for deep and rapid rivers.

In that passage, there is an elegant antithesis between the little brook Shiloah on the one hand, and the Nile and Euphrates on the other; as if he had said, They defraud God of his honour by the unworthy reflection, that when he made choice of the city of Jerusalem, he had not made the necessary provision in respect of strength and fortifications for its defence and preservation. And certainly, if this psalm was written after the slaughter and flight of the army of Sennacherib, it is probable that the inspired writer purposely made use of the same metaphor, to teach the faithful in all ages, that the grace of God alone would be to them a sufficient protection, independent of the assistance of the world. In like manner, the Holy Spirit still exhorts and encourages us to cherish the same confidence, that, despising all the resources of those who proudly magnify themselves against us, we may preserve our tranquillity in the midst of disquietude and trouble, and not be grieved or ashamed on account of our defenceless condition, so long as the hand of God is stretched out to save us. Thus, although the help of God comes to our aid in a secret and gentle manner, like the still flowing streams, yet it imparts to us more tranquillity of mind than if the whole power of the world were gathered together for our help. In speaking of Jerusalem as *the sanctuary of the tabernacles of the Most High*, the prophet makes a beautiful allusion to the circumstances or condition of that time: for although God exercised authority over all the tribes of the people, yet he made choice of that city as the seat of royalty, from which he might govern the whole nation of Israel. The tabernacles of the Most High were scattered throughout all Judea, but still it was necessary that they should be gathered together and united in one sanctuary, that they might be under the dominion of God.

5. *God is in the midst of her; she shall not be moved.* The Psalmist now shows that the great security of the Church

consists in this, that God dwells in the midst of her; for the verb which we translate, *shall be moved*, is of the feminine gender, nor can it be referred to God, as if it were designed to teach that God is immoveable. The sentence must be explained in this way, The holy city shall not be moved or shaken, because God dwells there, and is always ready to help her. The expression, *the dawn of the morning*,[1] denotes *daily*, as soon as the sun rises upon the earth. The sum of the whole is, If we desire to be protected by the hand of God, we must be concerned above all things that he may dwell amongst us; for all hope of safety depends upon his presence alone. And he dwells amongst us for no other purpose than to preserve us uninjured. Moreover, although God does not always hasten immediately to our aid, according to the importunity of our desires, yet he will always come to us seasonably, so as to make apparent the truth of what is elsewhere said, "Behold, he that keepeth Israel shall neither slumber nor sleep," (Ps. cxxi. 4.)

> 6. *The peoples raged, the kingdoms were moved : he uttered his voice,[2] the earth melted.*
> 7. *Jehovah of armies is with us : the God of Jacob is our fortress. Selah.*
> 8. *Come ye, consider the works of Jehovah, what desolations[3] he hath made in the earth.*
> 9. *He maketh battles to cease even to the end of the earth; he breaketh the bow, he cutteth in pieces the spear; he burneth the chariots with fire.[4]*

[1] " *At the looking forth of the morning;* that is, as the Greek explaineth it, ' very early ;' when the morning peereth or showeth the face."—*Ainsworth.* " *As soon as the morning appears* [or *shows*] *its face; i. e.,* God will come very early to her succour, before any enemy is awakened to annoy her."—*Mudge.* " *Before the dawn of the morning; i. e.,* with the utmost readiness and alacrity. The expression is borrowed from the conduct of a person who, in his anxiety to accomplish a favourite object, engages in it earlier than men ordinarily would. Jer. vii. 13 ; and vii. 25."—*French and Skinner.*

[2] " C'est, fait resonner."—*Fr. marg.* " That is, made to resound."

[3] " Ou, quels deserts."—*Fr. marg.* " Or, what deserts."

[4] There is probably here an allusion to the ancient custom of collecting the arms and armour of the vanquished into a heap, and setting it on fire. The image is employed to express complete victory, and a perfect establishment of peace. This custom prevailed among the Jews, and the first instance of it which we meet with is in Joshua xi. 6. It is also

10. *Be still,*[1] *and know that I am God : I will be exalted among the heathen, I will be exalted in the earth.*[2]

11. *Jehovah of armies is with us : the God of Jacob is our fortress. Selah.*

6. *The peoples raged.* Since the Church of God is never without enemies, and these very powerful, and such as consequently fight against her with cruel and unbridled fury, the prophet now confirms from experience the doctrine which he had advanced concerning the impregnable character of the divine protection. He then deduces from it this general ground of consolation, That it belongs continually to God to restrain and quell all commotions, and that his arm is strong enough to break all the efforts of the enemy. This passage, I admit, might be understood in a more general sense, as meaning that the city of God is liable to be assailed by many storms and tempests; but that by the favour of God she is, nevertheless, always preserved in safety. It is, however, more probable, as I have already said at the beginning, that the Psalmist is here speaking of some notable deliverance, in which God had given a striking proof of the power and favour which he exercises in the constant preservation of the Church. Accordingly, he relates what had taken place, namely, that the enemies of the Church came with a dreadful host to waste and destroy it; but that immediately, by *the voice of God,* they, as it were, *melted* and vanished away. From this we derive an invaluable ground of consolation, when it is said, That although the whole world rise up against us, and confound all things by their increased madness, they can be brought to nought in a moment, as soon as God shows himself favourable towards us. The *voice of God,* no doubt, signifies his will or command; but the prophet, by this

---

referred to in the description of the judgments of God upon Gog, Ezek. xxxix. 8-10. This was also a Roman custom. Virgil alludes to it in Æneid, lib. viii. l. 560. A medal struck by Vespasian the Roman emperor to commemorate the termination of his wars both in Italy and through all parts of the world, represents the Goddess of Peace holding an olive-branch with one hand, and in the other a lighted torch, with which she sets fire to a heap of armour.

[1] " Ou, arrestez, demeurez coy."—*Fr. marg.* " Or, stop, be quiet."
[2] " Par toute la terre."—*Fr.* " Through all the earth."

expression, seems to have an eye to the promises of God, by which he has declared, that he will be the guardian and defender of the Church. At the same time, let us observe the contrast which is here stated between the voice of God and the turbulent commotions of the kingdoms of this world.

7. *Jehovah of armies is with us.* In this verse we are taught how we shall be able to apply to our own use the things which the Scriptures everywhere record concerning the infinite power of God. We shall be able to do this when we believe ourselves to be of the number of those whom God has embraced with his fatherly love, and whom he will cherish. The Psalmist again alludes, in terms of commendation, to the adoption by which Israel was separated from the common condition of all the other nations of the earth. And, indeed, apart from this, the description of the power of God would only inspire us with dread. Confident boasting, then, arises from this, that God has chosen us for his peculiar people, to show forth his power in preserving and defending us. On this account, the prophet, after having celebrated the power of God by calling him *the God of armies,* immediately adds another epithet, *the God of Jacob,* by which he confirms the covenant made of old time with Abraham, that his posterity, to whom the inheritance of the promised grace belongs, should not doubt that God was favourable to them also. That our faith may rest truly and firmly in God, we must take into consideration at the same time these two parts of his character —his immeasurable power, by which he is able to subdue the whole world under him; and his fatherly love which he has manifested in his word. When these two things are joined together, there is nothing which can hinder our faith from defying all the enemies which may rise up against us, nor must we doubt that God will succour us, since he has promised to do it; and as to power, he is sufficiently able also to fulfil his promise, for he is the God of armies. From this we learn, that those persons err egregiously in the interpretation of Scripture, who leave in entire suspense the application of all that is said concerning the power of God, and do not rest assured that he will be a Father to them, inasmuch as they are of his flock, and partakers of the adoption.

8. *Come ye, consider the works of Jehovah.* The Psalmist seems still to continue in this verse the history of a deliverance by which God had given abundant evidence that he is the most efficient and faithful protector of his Church, that the godly might derive from it both courage and strength to enable them to overcome whatever temptations might afterwards arise. The manifestations which God has given of his favour towards us in preserving us, ought to be kept continually before our eyes as a means of establishing in our hearts a persuasion of the stability of his promises. By this exhortation we have tacitly rebuked the indifference and stupidity of those who do not make so great account of the power of God as they ought to do; or rather, the whole world is charged with ingratitude, because there is scarcely one in a hundred who acknowledges that he has abundant help and security in God, so that they are all blinded to the works of God, or rather wilfully shut their eyes at that which would, nevertheless, prove the best means of strengthening their faith. We see how many ascribe to fortune that which ought to be traced to the providence of God. Others imagine that they obtain, by their own industry, whatever God has bestowed upon them, or ascribe to second causes what proceeds from him alone; while others are utterly lost to all sense. The Psalmist, therefore, justly calls upon all men, and exhorts them to consider the works of God; as if he had said, The reason why men repose not the hope of their welfare in God is, that they are indifferent to the consideration of his works, or so ungrateful, that they make not half the account of them which they ought to do. As he addresses himself in general to all men, we learn, that even the godly themselves are drowsy and unconcerned in this respect until they are awakened. He extols very highly the power of God in preserving his chosen people, which is commonly despised or not estimated as it ought to be, when it is exercised after an ordinary manner. He therefore sets before them the desolations of countries, and marvellous devastations, and other miraculous things, which more powerfully move the minds of men. If any one would prefer to understand what follows—*He maketh battles to cease*—of some special help vouchsafed by God, yet still it must be considered as intended to lead the faithful to expect as

much help from him in future as they had already experienced. The prophet, it appears, from one particular instance, designs to show in general how mightily God is wont to defend his Church. At the same time, it happened more than once, that God quelled throughout the land of Judea all the dangerous tumults by which it was distracted, and drove away wars far from it, by depriving the enemies of their courage, breaking their bows, and burning their chariots; and it is very probable that the prophet, from a particular instance, here takes occasion to remind the Jews how often God had disappointed the greatest efforts of their enemies. One thing, however, is quite certain, that God is here set forth as adorned with these titles, that we should look for peace from him, even when the whole world is in uproar, and agitated in a dreadful manner.

10. *Be still, and know that I am God.* The Psalmist seems now to turn his discourse to the enemies of the people of God, who indulge their lust of mischief and revenge upon them: for in doing injury to the saints they do not consider that they are making war against God. Imagining that they have only to do with men, they presumptuously assail them, and therefore the prophet here represses their insolence; and that his address may have the more weight, he introduces God himself as speaking to them. In the first place, he bids them *be still, that they may know that he is God;* for we see that when men are carried away without consideration, they go beyond all bounds and measure. Accordingly, the prophet justly requires the enemies of the Church to be still and hold their peace, so that when their anger is appeased they may perceive that they are fighting against God. We have in the fourth Psalm, at the fourth verse, a sentiment somewhat similar, " Stand in awe, and sin not : commune with your own heart upon your bed, and be still." In short, the Psalmist exhorts the world to subdue and restrain their turbulent affections, and to yield to the God of Israel the glory which he deserves; and he warns them, that if they proceed to act like madmen, his power is not enclosed within the narrow limits of Judea, and that it will be no difficult matter for him to stretch forth his arm afar to the Gentiles and heathen

nations, that he may glorify himself in every land. In conclusion, he repeats what he had already said, that God has more than enough, both of weapons and of strength, to preserve and defend his Church which he has adopted.

PSALM XLVII.

Some think that this psalm was composed at the time when the temple was dedicated, and the ark of the covenant placed in the sanctuary. But as this is a conjecture which has little to support it, it is better, if I am not mistaken, instead of detaining ourselves with this, to consider the subject-matter of the psalm, and the use to which it ought especially to be applied. It was no doubt appointed for the stated holy assemblies, as may be easily gathered from the whole tenor of the poem; and perhaps it was composed by David, and delivered by him to the Levites, to be sung by them before the temple was built, and when the ark as yet abode in the tabernacle. But whoever was its author, he exhorts not only the Israelites, but also all nations, to worship the only true God. It chiefly magnifies the favour which, according to the state of things at that time, God had graciously vouchsafed to the offspring of Abraham; and salvation to the whole world was to proceed from this source. It however contains, at the same time, a prophecy of the future kingdom of Christ. It teaches that the glory which then shone under the figure of the material sanctuary will diffuse its splendour far and wide; when God himself will cause the beams of his grace to shine into distant lands, that kings and nations may be united into fellowship with the children of Abraham.

¶ To the chief musician of the sons of Korah: A Psalm.

1. *Clap your hands, all ye peoples: shout unto God with the voice of triumph.*
2. *For Jehovah is high, terrible, and a great King over all the earth.*
3. *He hath put in order[1] the people under us, and the nations under our feet.*
4. *He hath chosen our inheritance for us, the glory of Jacob, whom he loved. Selah.*

1. *Clap your hands, all ye peoples.* As the Psalmist requires

[1] " Ou, rangé."—*Fr. marg.* " Or, subdued."

the nations, in token of their joy and of their thanksgiving to God, to clap their hands, or rather exhorts them to a more than ordinary joy, the vehemence of which breaks forth and manifests itself by external expressions, it is certain that he is here speaking of the deliverance which God had wrought for them. Had God erected among the Gentiles some formidable kingdom, this would rather have deprived all of their courage, and overwhelmed them with despair, than given them matter to sing and leap for joy. Besides, the inspired writer does not here treat of some common or ordinary blessings of God; but of such blessings as will fill the whole world with incredible joy, and stir up the minds of all men to celebrate the praises of God. What he adds a little after, that all nations were brought into subjection to Israel, must, therefore, necessarily be understood not of slavish subjection, but of a subjection which is more excellent, and more to be desired, than all the kingdoms of the world. It would be unnatural for those who are subdued and brought to submit by force and fear to leap for joy. Many nations were tributary to David, and to his son Solomon; but while they were so, they ceased not, at the same time, to murmur, and bore impatiently the yoke which was imposed upon them, so far were they from giving thanks to God with joyful and cheerful hearts.

Since, then, no servitude is happy and desirable but that by which God subdues and brings under the standard and authority of Christ his Son those who before were rebels, it follows that this language is applicable only to the kingdom of Christ, who is called *a high and terrible King*, (verse 2;) not that he makes the wretched beings over whom he reigns to tremble by the tyranny and violence of his sway, but because his majesty, which before had been held in contempt, will suffice to quell the rebellion of the whole world. It is to be observed, that the design of the Holy Spirit is here to teach, that as the Jews had been long contumeliously treated, oppressed with wrongs, and afflicted from time to time with divers calamities, the goodness and liberality of God towards them was now so much the more illustrious, when the kingdom of David had subdued the neighbouring nations on every side, and had attained to such a height of glory. We may, however, easily gather from the connection of the words the truth of what I have suggested, that when God is called *a terrible and great King over all the earth*, this prophecy applies to the kingdom of Christ. There is, therefore, no doubt, that the grace of God was celebrated by these titles, to strengthen the hearts of the godly during the period that intervened till the advent of Christ, in which not only the triumphant state of the people of Israel had fallen into decay, but in which also the people, being oppressed with the bitterest contumely, could have no taste of the favour of God, and no consolation from it, but by relying on the promises of God alone. We know that there was a long interruption of the splendour of the kingdom of God's ancient people, which continued from the death of Solomon to the coming of Christ. This interval formed, as it were, a gulf or chasm, which would have swallowed up the minds of the godly, had they not been supported and upheld by the Word of God. As, therefore, God exhibited in the person of David a type of the kingdom of Christ, which is here extolled, although there followed shortly after a sad and almost shameful diminution of the glory of David's kingdom, then the most grievous calamities, and, finally, the captivity and a most miserable dispersion, which differed little from a total destruction, the Holy Spirit has exhorted the faithful to continue clapping their hands for joy, until the advent of the promised Redeemer.

3. *He hath set in order the people under us.* Some translate the verb *he hath subjected;* and this agrees with the translation which I have given. Others translate it *he hath led*, which is somewhat more remote from the meaning. But to understand the verb ידבר, *yadebber*, as meaning *to destroy*, as is done by others, is altogether at variance with the mind of the prophet; for it is doubtless an advantageous, joyful, and desirable subjection which is here meant. In the Hebrew, the verb is in the future tense, *he will set in order;* and if any are disposed to prefer retaining it in this tense, I have no great objection to

it. As, however, it is certain that under the figure of the kingdom of David there is here celebrated the grace of God to come, I have readily adopted that rendering which has been preferred by other interpreters. Besides, although in this verse the prophet especially exhorts his own countrymen to gratitude to God, because, through his favour, they ruled over all people; yet it is certain that he means, that those also who were subdued are associated with the Jews in this joy. The body does not differ more from the shadow than the feigned expressions of joy with which the heathen nations honoured David in old time, differ from those with which the faithful through the whole world[1] receive Christ; for the latter flow from the willing obedience of the heart. And assuredly, if after the ark was brought to the temple, there had not appeared hidden under this figure something far higher, which formed the substance of it, it would have been as it were a childish joy to assign to God his dwelling there, and to shut him up within such narrow limits. But when the majesty of God which had dwelt in the tabernacle was manifested to the whole world, and when all nations were brought in subjection to his authority, this prerogative of the offspring of Abraham was then illustriously manifested. The prophet, then, when he declares that the Gentiles will be subdued, so that they will not refuse to obey the chosen people, is describing that kingdom of which he had previously spoken. We are not to suppose that he here treats of that secret providence by which God governs the whole world, but of the special power which he exercises by means of his word; and, therefore, in order that he may be properly called a King, his own people must necessarily acknowledge him as such. It may, however, be asked, " Since Christ has brought the Church under his own authority and celestial power, in what sense can it be said that the nations are subject to the Jews, seeing we know that the order of the Church cannot be settled aright, and as it ought to be, unless Christ the only head stand forth prominently above all, and

---

[1] " Par tout le monde."—*Fr.*

all the faithful, from the greatest to the least, keep themselves in the humble rank of members? Nay, more, when Christ erected his dominion through the whole world, the adoption, which had before been the peculiar privilege of one people, began to be the common privilege of all nations; and by this means liberty was granted to all together, that being united to one another by the ties of true brotherhood, they should aspire to the celestial inheritance." The answer to this is easy: When the yoke of the law[1] was imposed upon the Gentiles, the Jews then obtained the sovereignty over them; even as by the word the pastors of the Church exercise the jurisdiction of the Holy Spirit. For this very reason the Church is called a Queen, and the Mother of all the godly, (Gal. iv. 26,) because divine truth, which is like a sceptre to subdue us all, has been committed to her keeping. Although then the Jews, when the kingdom of Christ emerged into light, were in a state of wretched and ignominious servitude to heathen nations, and had been, as it were, their slaves; yet the sovereignty is truly and justly attributed to them, because God " sent the rod of his strength out of Zion," (Ps. cx. 2;) and as they were intrusted with the keeping of the law, their office was to restrain and subdue the Gentiles by its authority. The only way by which the rest of the world has been brought into subjection to God is, that men, being renewed by the Spirit of God, have willingly yielded themselves docile and tractable to the Jews, and suffered themselves to be under their dominion; as it is said in another passage, " In those days it shall come to pass, that ten men shall take hold out of all languages of the nations, even shall take hold of the skirt of him that is a Jew, saying, We will go with you; for we have heard that God is with you," (Zech. viii. 23.)

4. *He hath chosen our inheritance for us.* The inspired poet here celebrates more distinctly the special grace which God, in his goodness, had bestowed upon the chosen and holy seed

---

[1] " C'est à dire, la reformation selon la vraye religion de Dieu."—*Fr. marg.* " That is to say, the reformation according to the true religion of God."

of Abraham. As he passed by all the rest of the world, and adopted to himself a people who were few in number and contemptible; so it was proper that such a signal pledge of his fatherly love should be distinguished from his common beneficence, which is extended to all mankind without distinction. The word *chosen* is therefore peculiarly emphatic, implying that God had not dealt with the children of Abraham as he had been accustomed indiscriminately to deal with other nations; but that he had bestowed upon them, as it were by hereditary right, a peculiar dignity by which they excelled all others. The same thing is expressed immediately after by the word *glory*. Thus then the prophet enjoins the duty of thanksgiving to God, for having exalted, in the person of Jacob, his chosen people to the highest degree of honour, so that they might boast that their condition was distinguished from that of all other nations. He shows, at the same time, that this was entirely owing to the free and unmerited favour of God. The relative pronoun *whom* is put instead of the causal particle *for* or *because*, as if the Psalmist had attributed the cause of this prerogative by which they were distinguished to God himself. Whenever the favour of God towards the Jews is commended, in consequence of his having loved their fathers, this principle should always be kept in mind, that hereby all merits in man are annihilated. If all the excellence or glory of the holy patriarch depended purely and simply upon the good pleasure of God, who can dare to arrogate any thing to himself as peculiarly his own? If God then has given us any thing above others, and as it were by special privilege, let us learn to ascribe the whole to the fatherly love which he bears towards us, seeing he has chosen us to be his flock. We also gather from this passage that the grace which God displays towards his chosen is not extended to all men in common, but is a privilege by which he distinguishes a few from the great mass of mankind.

5. *God is gone up with triumph, Jehovah with the sound of a trumpet.*
6. *Sing praises to God, sing praises: sing praises to our King, sing praises.*
7. *For God is King of all the earth: sing praises every one who understandeth.*
8. *He hath obtained the kingdom over the heathen: God sitteth upon the throne of his holiness.*
9. *The princes of the peoples* [or *nations*] *are assembled together to the people of the God of Abraham: for the shields of the earth are God's: he is greatly exalted.*

5. *God is gone up with triumph.* There is here an allusion to the ancient ceremony which was observed under the Law. As the sound of trumpets was wont to be used in solemnizing the holy assemblies, the prophet says that God *goes up,* when the trumpets encourage and stir up the people to magnify and extol his power. When this ceremony was performed in old time, it was just as if a king, making his entrance among his subjects, presented himself to them in magnificent attire and great splendour, by which he gained their admiration and reverence. At the same time, the sacred writer, under that shadowy ceremony, doubtless intended to lead us to consider another kind of going up more triumphant—that of Christ when he " ascended up far above all heavens," (Eph. iv. 10,) and obtained the empire of the whole world, and armed with his celestial power, subdued all pride and loftiness. You must remember what I have adverted to before, that the name *Jehovah* is here applied to the ark; for although the essence or majesty of God was not shut up in it, nor his power and operation fixed to it, yet it was not a vain and idle symbol of his presence. God had promised that he would dwell in the midst of the people so long as the Jews worshipped him according to the rule which he had prescribed in the Law; and he actually showed that he was truly present with them, and that it was not in vain that he was called upon among them. What is here stated, however, applies more properly to the manifestation of the glory which at length shone forth in the person of Christ. In short, the import of the Psalmist's language is, When the

trumpets sounded among the Jews, according to the appointment of the Law, that was not a mere empty sound which vanished away in the air; for God, who intended the ark of the covenant to be a pledge and token of his presence, truly presided in that assembly. From this the prophet draws an argument for enforcing on the faithful the duty of *singing praises to God.* He argues, that by engaging in this exercise they will not be acting blindly or at random, as the superstitious, who, having no certainty in their false systems of religion, lament and howl in vain before their idols. He shows that the faithful have just ground for celebrating with their mouths and with a cheerful heart the praises of God;[1] since they certainly know that he is as present with them, as if he had visibly established his royal throne among them.

7. *For God is King of all the earth.* The Psalmist, having called God in the close of the preceding verse *King* of the chosen people, now calls him *King of all the earth;* and thus, while he claims to the Jews the right and honour of primogeniture, he at the same time joins to them the Gentiles as associates and partakers with them of the same blessing. By these words he intimates that the kingdom of God would be much more magnificent and glorious at the coming of the Messiah, than it was under the shadowy dispensation of the Law, inasmuch as it would be extended to the utmost boundaries of the earth. To show the greater earnestness in his exhortation, he repeats the words, *Sing praises to God,* five times. The word משכיל, *maskil,*[2] is put in the singular number instead of the plural; for he invites to this exercise all who are skilful in singing. He, no doubt, speaks of knowledge in the art of music ; but he requires, at the same time,

---

[1] " De faire retentir en leurs bouches et d'un cœur alaigre les louanges de Dieu."—*Fr.*

[2] Calvin renders this word in the Latin version by "intelligens;" and in the French by "entendu;" and in the margin of the French version there is the note, " C'est, O vous chacun entendu !"—" That is, O every one of you who understandeth !" Dr Adam Clarke reads, "Sing an instructive song ;" and observes, " Let *sense* and *sound* go together. Let your *hearts* and *heads* go with your *voices.*"

the worshippers of God to sing the praises of God intelligently, that there may not be the mere sound of tongues, as we know to be the case among the Papists. Knowledge of what is sung is required in order to engage in a proper manner in the singing of psalms, that the name of God may not be profaned, as it would certainly be, were there nothing more but the voice which melts away or is dissolved in the air.[1]

8. *He hath obtained the kingdom over the heathen.* Literally it is, *He hath reigned;* but as the verb מלך, *malach,* is in the past tense, which in Hebrew denotes a continued act, we have translated it, *He hath obtained the kingdom.* The prophet repeatedly informs us that God reigns over the Gentiles; and from this it is easy to gather that he here treats of a new and a previously unheard of manner of reigning. There is an implied contrast between the time of the Law, when God confined his empire, or kingdom, within the boundaries of Judea, and the coming of Christ, when he extended it far and wide, so as to occupy the whole world from one end to the other. The majesty of God sent forth some sparks of its brightness among the heathen nations, when David made them tributary; but the prophet could not, on that account, have properly said that God reigned among them, since they both contemned his worship and the true religion, and also wished to see the Church completely extinguished. To find the fulfilment of this prophecy, we must, therefore, necessarily come to Christ. What is added in the second clause of the verse, *God sitteth upon the throne of his holiness,* may be taken in a twofold sense. By this form of expression is often to be understood *the tabernacle,* or *the temple;* but it also sometimes signifies *heaven.* If any are inclined to explain it of *the temple,* the meaning will be, That while God reigned over the whole world, and comprehended all nations under his dominion, he had established his chief seat at Jerusalem; and it was from thence that the doctrine of the gospel, by which he has

---

[1] "Comme de faict il seroit s'il n'y avoit seulement que la voix qui s'escoule en l'air."—*Fr.*

brought under his dominion all people, flowed. We may, however, very properly take this expression as spoken of *heaven;* and thus the sense will be, That God, in stretching forth his hand to subdue men, and bring them to submit to his authority, evidently shows that, from his heavenly throne, he reigns over men. Unless he show men his power and working by signs manifest and near at hand, he is not acknowledged as Governor of the world.

9. *The princes of the peoples are gathered together.* The Psalmist enriches and amplifies by various expressions the preceding sentence. He again declares that the way in which God obtained dominion over the Gentiles was, that those who before were aliens united in the adoption of the same faith with the Jews; and thus different nations, from a state of miserable dispersion, were gathered together into one body. When the doctrine of the Gospel was manifested and shone forth, it did not remove the Jews from the covenant which God had long before made with them. On the contrary, it has rather joined us to them. As then the calling of the Gentiles was nothing else than the means by which they were grafted and incorporated into the family of Abraham, the prophet justly states, that strangers or aliens from every direction *were gathered together* to the chosen people, that by such an increase the kingdom of God might be extended through all quarters of the globe. On this account Paul says, (Eph. iii. 6,) that the Gentiles were made one body with the Jews, that they might be partakers of the everlasting inheritance. By the abolition of the ceremonies of the Mosaic economy, " the middle wall of partition," which made a separation between the Jews and the Gentiles, is now removed, (Eph. ii. 14;) but it nevertheless remains true, that we are not accounted among the children of God unless we have been grafted into the stock of Abraham. The prophet does not merely speak of the common people: he also tells us that princes themselves will regard it as the height of their felicity to be gathered together with the Jews; as we shall see in another psalm, (lxxxvii. 5,) "And of Zion it shall be said, This and that man was born in her." Farther, it is said that

this gathering together will be *to the people of the God of Abraham*, to teach us that it is not here meant to attribute to the Jews any superiority which they naturally possess above others, but that all their excellence depends upon this, that the pure worship of God flourishes among them, and that they hold heavenly doctrine in high estimation. This, therefore, is not spoken of the bastard or cast-off Jews, whom their own unbelief has cut off from the Church. But as, according to the statement of the Apostle Paul, (Rom. xi. 16,) the root being holy, the branches are also holy, it follows that the falling away of the greater part does not prevent this honour from continuing to belong to the rest. Accordingly, the "consumption," which, as is stated in the prophecy of Isaiah, overflowed the whole earth, is called the people of the God of Abraham, (chap. x. 22, 23.) This passage contains two very important and instructive truths. In the first place, we learn from it, that all who would be reckoned among the children of God ought to seek to have a place in the Church, and to join themselves to it, that they may maintain fraternal unity with all the godly; and, secondly, that when the unity of the Church is spoken of, it is to be considered as consisting in nothing else but an unfeigned agreement to yield obedience to the word of God, that there may be one sheepfold and one Shepherd. Moreover, those who are exalted in the world in respect of honours and riches, are here admonished to divest themselves of all pride, and willingly and submissively to bear the yoke in common with others, that they may show themselves the obedient children of the Church.

What follows immediately after, *The shields of the earth are God's*, is understood by many as spoken of princes.[1] I admit that this metaphor is of frequent occurrence in Scripture, nor does this sense seem to be unsuitable to the scope of the passage. It is as if the prophet had said, It is in the power of God to ingraft into his Church the great ones of the world whenever he pleases; for he reigns over them also. Yet the sense will be more simple if we explain the words thus: That, as it is God alone who defends and preserves the world,

[1] Magistrates and governors are called *shields* in Hosea iv. 18; Ps. lxxxix. 19. In this sense the word is here understood by the Septuagint.

the high and supreme majesty, which is sufficient for so exalted and difficult a work as the preservation of the world, is justly looked upon with admiration. The sacred writer expressly uses the word *shields* in the plural number, for, considering the various and almost innumerable dangers which unceasingly threaten every part of the world, the providence of God must necessarily interpose in many ways, and make use, as it were, of many bucklers.

PSALM XLVIII.

In this psalm there is celebrated some notable deliverance of the city of Jerusalem at a time when many kings had conspired to destroy it. The prophet, (whoever was the author of the psalm,) after having given thanks to God for this deliverance, takes occasion from thence to extol in magnificent terms the happy state of that city, seeing it had God for its continual guardian and protector. It would not have been enough for the people of God to have felt and acknowledged that they were once preserved and defended by the power of God, had they not at the same time been assured of being also preserved and protected by the same God in the time to come, because he had adopted them for his peculiar people. The prophet, therefore, chiefly insists upon this point, that it was not in vain that the sanctuary of God was erected upon mount Zion, but that his name was there called upon in order that his power might be conspicuously manifested for the salvation of his people. It is easy to gather from the subject-matter of the psalm that it was composed after the death of David. I indeed admit that among David's enemies there were some foreign kings, and that it was not for want of will on their part that the city of Jerusalem was not utterly destroyed; but we do not read that they ever proceeded the length of besieging it, and reducing it to such extremity as to render it necessary that their efforts should be repressed by a wonderful manifestation of the power of God. It is more probable that the psalm is to be referred to the time of king Ahaz, when the city was besieged and the inhabitants brought to the point of utter despair, and when, nevertheless, the siege was suddenly raised, (2 Kings xvi. 5;) or else to the time of Jehoshaphat and Asa, (2 Chron. xiv. 9; and xx. 2;) for we know that under their reigns Jerusalem was preserved from utter destruction only by miraculous aid from heaven. This we are to regard as certain, that the Psalmist here exhibited to true believers an example of the favour of God towards them, from which they had reason to acknowledge that their condition was happy, seeing God had chosen for himself a dwelling-place upon mount Zion, that from thence he might preside over them for their good and safety.

¶ A song of praise of the sons of Korah.

1. *Great is Jehovah, and greatly to be praised in the city of our God, in the mountain of his holiness.*
2. *Beautiful for situation, the joy of the whole earth, is mount Zion, on the sides of the north, the city of the great King.*
3. *God in her palaces is known for a defence,* [or *fortress.*]

1. *Great is Jehovah, and greatly to be praised.* The prophet, before proceeding to make mention of that special example of the favour of God towards them, to which I have adverted, teaches in general that the city of Jerusalem was happy and prosperous, because God had been graciously pleased to take upon him the charge of defending and preserving it. In this way he separates and distinguishes the Church of God from all the rest of the world; and when God selects from amongst the whole human race a small number whom he embraces with his fatherly love, this is an invaluable blessing which he bestows upon them. His wonderful goodness and righteousness shine forth in the government of the whole world, so that there is no part of it void of his praise, but we are everywhere furnished with abundant matter for praising him. Here, however, the inspired poet celebrates the glory of God which is manifested in the protection of the Church. He states, that *Jehovah is great, and greatly to be praised* IN THE HOLY CITY. But is he not so also in the whole world? Undoubtedly he is. As I have said, there is not a corner so hidden, into which his wisdom, righteousness, and goodness, do not penetrate; but it being his will that they should be manifested chiefly and in a particular manner in his Church, the prophet very properly sets before our eyes this mirror, in which God gives a more clear and vivid representation of his character. By calling Jerusalem *the holy mountain,* he teaches us in one word, by what right

and means it came to be in a peculiar manner the city of God. It was so because the ark of the covenant had been placed there by divine appointment. The import of the expression is this : If Jerusalem is, as it were, a beautiful and magnificent theatre on which God would have the greatness of his majesty to be beheld, it is not owing to any merits of its own, but because the ark of the covenant was established there by the commandment of God as a token or symbol of his peculiar favour.

2. *Beautiful for situation, the joy of the whole earth, is mount Zion.* For the confirmation of the statement made in the preceding sentence, the prophet celebrates the excellencies for which mount Zion was at that time renowned; and in them was to be seen the glory of God, of which I have just now spoken. The beauty of its situation, which he mentions in the first place, was indeed natural; but by it he gives us to understand, that from the very commencement the agreeable appearance of the city had engraven upon it marks of the favour of God, so that the sight of it alone showed that God had in a special manner adorned and enriched that place, with the view of its being, at some future period, consecrated to sacred purposes. I do not, however, think that the situation is called beautiful and pleasant, merely because it was unequalled in the country of Judea; for there were other cities, as is well known, which were in no respect inferior to Jerusalem, either as to fertility or pleasantness of situation, and other advantages. In my opinion, along with the situation of the city, the Psalmist comprehends the glory which it derived from another source—from the circumstance that the temple of God was built there. When, therefore, we hear the beauty of the city here celebrated, let us call to our remembrance that spiritual beauty which was added to the natural beauty of the place, after the prophecy was given forth that the ark would there abide for ever. With respect to the word נוֹף, *noph*, which I have translated *situation*, commentators are not agreed. Some understand it as meaning *height* or *elevation*, as if it had been said that Jerusalem was situated on high and elevated ground. Others render it

climate;[1] because the Jews metaphorically call climates *branches,*[2] on account of the extent to which they are spread out. In a matter like this, which is of no great consequence, I am not disposed to be so very critical. Only I have selected that translation which seemed to me the most probable, namely, that the country in its appearance was pre-eminently pleasant and delightful. When the Psalmist speaks of mount Zion being *on the sides of the north,* it is doubtful whether he lays it down as a commendation of mount Zion, that it lay or looked towards the north; or whether we should explain the sentence thus: Although mount Zion looks towards the north, that does not in any degree diminish its beauty. The former interpretation, however, seems to me to give the more natural meaning. We find the prophet Isaiah, with the view also of touching upon the excellence of this mountain, applying to it the very expression which is here employed. In the 14th chapter of his Prophecies, at the 13th verse, he represents Sennacherib as speaking thus: "I will ascend into heaven, I will exalt my throne above the stars of God: I will sit also upon the mount of the congregation, in the sides of the north."

The Psalmist, in the next place, calls mount Zion *the joy of the whole earth.* And he thus describes it, not only because, as the Jews foolishly talk, that country was healthy on account of the mildness of the climate; or because it produced sweet and excellent fruits, which might gratify and yield delight to foreign nations—for this also is a cold and unsatisfactory speculation;—but because from thence salvation was to issue forth to the whole world, even as all nations have borrowed from thence the light of life, and the testimony

---

[1] *Beautiful in climate,* that is, mount Zion is situated in a fair and lovely climate. This is the view taken by Montanus and Ainsworth. Bate and Parkhurst read, "*Beautiful in extension, i. e.,* in the prospect which it extends to the eye."

[2] Some ancient copies of the Septuagint have for the original words יפה נוף, *yepheh noph,* which Calvin renders *beautiful for situation,* εὐρύνων, which Augustine and Ambrose translate by *dilatans, spreading.* "This," says Hammond, "may not improbably have respect to a notion of נוף, usual in the *Misneh* for the *boughs* or *top branches of a tree;* which some of the Jews also would have take place here, as comparing *Zion* to *a beautiful well-spreading* tree."

of heavenly grace. If the joy which men experience and cherish is without God, the issue of their joy at length will be destruction, and their laughter will be turned into gnashing of teeth. But Christ appeared with his Gospel out of Zion, to fill the world with true joy and everlasting felicity. In the time of the prophet, the knowledge of the Gospel, it is true, had not yet reached foreign nations; but he makes use of this manner of expression with the highest propriety, to teach the Jews that true blessedness was to be sought for only from the gracious covenant of God, which was deposited in that holy place. At the same time also, he has foretold that which was at length fulfilled in the last time by the coming of Christ. From this we may learn, that to cause the hearts of the godly to rejoice, the favour of God alone abundantly suffices; as, on the contrary, when it is withdrawn, all men must inevitably be thrown into a state of wretchedness and sorrow. What is added immediately after, concerning *the city of the great King,* is intended to show, that mount Zion was not only holy itself, but that this high prerogative had been conferred upon it to render sacred the whole city, where God had chosen his seat, that he might rule over all people.

3. *God in her palaces is known for a defence.* Here the sacred poet again brings forward, for the purpose of setting forth the dignity of the city of Jerusalem, the protection which God afforded it; as we have seen in Psalm xlvi. 5, " God is in the midst of her: she shall not be moved: God shall help her, and that right early." He expressly makes mention of *palaces* for the sake of contrast—to teach the Jews, that although the holy city was fortified by strong towers, and had within it magnificent houses, and such as resembled fortresses, yet its continued safety was owing to the power and aid of God alone. By these words, the people of God are taught, that although they dwell in strongholds and palaces, they must, nevertheless, be carefully on their guard, that this magnificence or loftiness may not shroud or conceal from their view the power of God; and that they be not like worldly men, who, resting satisfied with riches and

earthly means of help, set no value whatever upon having God for their guardian and protector. Worldly wealth, from our natural perverseness, tends to dazzle our eyes, and to make us forget God, and, therefore, we ought to meditate with special attention upon this doctrine, That whatever we possess, which seems worthy of being prized, must not be permitted to obscure the knowledge of the power and grace of God; but that, on the contrary, the glory of God ought always clearly to shine forth in all the gifts with which he may be pleased to bless and adorn us; so that we may account ourselves rich and happy in him, and no where else.

4. *For, behold! the kings assembled, they passed away together.*
5. *They saw, so they marvelled; they were frightened, they fled precipitately.*
6. *Fear*[1] *seized upon them there, and pain as of a woman in travail.*
7. *By the east wind thou breakest in pieces the ships of Tarshish.*

4. *For, behold! the kings assembled.* Here that special deliverance of which I have spoken is touched upon. The prophet relates how, when the kings were assembled together to destroy Jerusalem, their efforts passed away without producing any effect, even as clouds in the atmosphere vanish away; yea, he tells us, that by a simple look at the city, they were defeated and undone, and that not after an ordinary manner, but like a woman who, when the hour of child-birth has come upon her, finds herself suddenly afflicted with pain and sorrow. We cannot affirm with certainty what particular part of Jewish history the prophet here speaks of; but the statements made suit very well both the time of Ahaz, and that of Hezekiah or Asa. It was indeed a wonderful work of God, when two very powerful kings—the king of Syria and the king of Israel, accompanied with an immense army—had smitten the city with such terror, that the king and his people were brought to the brink of despair, to see

---

[1] " Tremblement."—*Fr.* " Trembling."

this formidable host suddenly routed and disappointed of the certain expectation which they entertained of making themselves masters of the city. Hence the prophet Isaiah (ch. vii. 4) ironically calls them "smoking firebrands," because they were, so to speak, burning torches to kindle and consume by fire the whole country of Judea. Nor was the destruction of the countless host of Sennacherib in one night by an angel, without the intervention of man's agency, a less stupendous miracle, (2 Kings xix. 35; Isa. xxxvii. 36.) In like manner, when the king of Ethiopia gathered together an army of ten hundred thousand men, and came to besiege Jerusalem, the overthrow of so great a host was a memorable instance of the power of God, (2 Chron. xiv. 9.) But whatever was the occasion on which this psalm was composed, the sacred writer informs us that the Jews found from manifest experience that God was the guardian and protector of the holy city, when he opposed himself to the invincible power of their enemies. He first declares that *the kings assembled.* By these words he intimates that they had confederated and conspired together to destroy the Church. The expression, *passed away together*, may be explained in two ways; either as meaning that the armies when they had gathered themselves together were reduced to nothing, or that they undertook together, and with one consent, the expedition, as it were marshalled in battle array.

This second sense seems to me the most suitable to the scope of the passage; for it follows immediately after in the fifth verse, that they stood stricken with astonishment whenever they saw the city; and yet there will be no impropriety in understanding this verse as added by way of amplification. But as it affects very little the substance of the passage which of these two interpretations is adopted, I leave the reader to choose that which he considers the most appropriate. When the Psalmist says that upon beholding the city *they marvelled—were frightened—fled precipitately*—and *were seized with sorrow like the pangs of a woman in travail*—he heaps together as many and varied expressions as possible, in order to set forth the greatness of the miracle which God had wrought in the overthrow of such a vast and formidable host. The language should be resolved thus: As soon as they saw the city they marvelled. It is related of Cæsar in ancient times, that when speaking of the ease with which he subdued Egypt, he made use of the laconic saying, "I came, I saw, I conquered;" but the prophet here states, on the contrary, that the ungodly were struck with amazement at the mere sight of the city, as if God had dazzled their eyes with the splendour of his glory. The particle כֵּן, *ken, so,* is put as it were to show the thing by pointing to it with the finger. In the verse which immediately follows, the adverb שָׁם, *sham, there,* is used in the same sense. The comparison of *a woman in travail* is intended to express the sudden change which came upon the enemies of Israel. It afforded a more bright and illustrious manifestation of the grace of God, that they were seized with a fear which they had not anticipated, lost their courage all at once, and from the height of secure and presumptuous pride, instantly fell into such a state of terror, and were so confounded, that they precipitately betook themselves to flight.[1] From this passage we are taught that it is no uncommon thing, if in our day the Church is assailed by powerful adversaries, and has to sustain dreadful assaults; for it has been God's usual way from the beginning thus to humble his own people, in order to give more irrefragable and striking proofs of his wonderful power. At the same time, let us remember that a nod alone on the part of God is sufficient to deliver us; and that, although our enemies may be ready to fall upon us on every side to overwhelm us, it is in his power, whenever he pleases, to strike them with amazement of spirit, and thus to make their hearts fail in a moment in the very midst of their efforts against us. Let this reflection serve as a bridle to keep our minds from being drawn away, to look in all directions for human aid.

7. *By the east wind*[2] *thou breakest in pieces the ships of Tar-*

---

[1] "Et d'une fierté pleine d'asseurance et outrecuidance sont incontinent tombez en espouvantement et ont tellement este estourdis, qu'ils s'en sont fuis grand erre."—*Fr.*

[2] The east wind in Judea and in the Mediterranean is very tempestuous and destructive. It is also very dry and parching, as well as sudden and terrible in its action. Gen. xli. 6; Exod. xiv. 21; Ezek. xix. 12; and xxvii. 26; Job xxvii. 21; Isa. xxvii. 8; Jer. xviii. 17; Jonah iv. 8.

shish. Commentators are divided in their view of this passage.[1] But let us rest contented with the natural sense, which is simply this, that the enemies of the Church were overthrown and plunged into destruction, just as God by suddenly raising storms sinks the ships of Cilicia to the bottom of the sea. The Psalmist celebrates the power which God is accustomed to display in great and violent storms; and his language implies that it is not to be wondered at if God, who breaks by the violence of the winds the strongest ships, had also overthrown his enemies, who were inflated with the presumptuous confidence which they reposed in their own strength. By the *sea of Tarshish* the Hebrews mean the Mediterranean Sea, because of the country of Cilicia, which in ancient times was called Tarshish, as Josephus informs us, although in process of time this name came to be restricted to one city of the country. But as the chief part of the naval traffic of the Jews was with Cilicia, there is here attributed to that country by synecdoche what was common to other countries which were at a greater distance and less known.

Hence the LXX. translate the original words, "Ἐν πνεύματι βιαίῳ," " With a violent wind ;" and the Chaldee reads, " A strong east wind as a fire from before the Lord." " Such a wind," says Bishop Mant, " is well known to the modern mariner by the name of *Levanter*, and is of the same kind as that spoken of in the twenty-seventh chapter of the Acts of the Apostles, under the name of Euroclydon."

[1] It is supposed by some that there is in it an implied similitude ; the particle of similitude used in the preceding verse being understood. Thus French and Skinner translate the 6th and 7th verses—

> " Then did trembling seize upon them—
> Pangs as of a woman in travail—
> As when with a stormy wind,
> Thou breakest in pieces the ships of Tarshish."

According to this translation, " the ships of Tarshish" do not refer to an invading army, nor " the breaking in pieces of them" to an actual storm which had this effect ; but the sacred writer employs another figure, the more vividly to describe the terror which seized upon these confederate powers. He had in the preceding verse compared it with the pangs of a woman in travail ; and here he compares it to the trembling which seized upon mariners when the fury of the east wind, which shattered in pieces the largest and strongest vessels, as the ships of Tarshish probably then were, was let loose upon them.

8. *As we have heard, so have we seen in the city of Jehovah of hosts,* [or *armies,*] *in the city of our God: God will establish it for ever. Selah.*
9. *O God! we have waited for thy mercy in the midst of thy temple.*
10. *As is thy name, O God! so is thy praise unto the ends of the earth: thy right hand is full of righteousness.*

8. *As we have heard, so have we seen.* There are two senses in which this passage may be understood, either of which is suitable. The first is, that the sacred writer, speaking in the name of true believers, declares that the same power which God in the days of old had displayed in delivering their fathers, he now exercised towards their posterity. They had heard from the mouth of their fathers, and had learned from sacred history, how God in his great mercy and fatherly goodness had succoured his Church; but now they affirm that they can bear testimony to this not only from their having heard it spoken about, but also from having seen it,[1] inasmuch as they had actually experienced the same mercy exercised by God towards themselves. The amount of what is stated then is, that the faithful not only had a record of the goodness and power of God in histories, but that they also felt by actual experience, yea, even saw with their eyes, what they knew before by hearsay, and the report of their fathers; and that therefore God continues unchangeably the same, confirming as he does, age after age, the examples of his grace exhibited in ancient times, by renewed and ever-recurring experiences. The other sense is somewhat more refined; and yet it is very suitable, namely, That God actually performed what he had promised to his people; as if the faithful had said, that what they had before only heard of was now exhibited before their eyes. As long as we have only the bare promises of God, his grace and salvation are as yet hidden in hope; but when these promises are actually performed, his grace and salvation are clearly manifested. If this interpretation is admitted, it contains the rich doctrine,

---

[1] "Mais maintenant ils disent qu'ils en sont testmoins non pas par avoir ouy dere seulement, mais par avoir veu."—*Fr.*

that God does not disappoint the hope which he produces in our minds by means of his word, and that it is not His way to be more liberal in promising than faithful in performing what he has promised. When it is said, *in the city*, the letter ב, *beth*, is taken for מ, *mem*, or ל, *lamed;* that is to say, for *of*, or *as to*, or *with respect to the city*. The prophet does not mean to say that in Jerusalem the faithful were informed that God would succour his servants, although this was no doubt true, but that God from the beginning had been the gracious and faithful guardian of his own city, and would continue always to be so. Mention is expressly made of *the city of God*, because he has not promised to extend the same protecting care to all indiscriminately, but only to his chosen and peculiar people. The name *Jehovah of armies* is employed to express the power of God; but immediately after the faithful add, that he is *their God*, for the purpose of pointing to their adoption, that thus they may be emboldened to trust in him, and thus to betake themselves freely and familiarly to him. In the second Council of Nice, the good fathers who sat there wrested this passage to prove that it is not enough to teach divine truth in churches, unless there are at the same time pictures and images for confirming it. This was a piece of silliness very shameful, and unworthy of being mentioned, were it not that it is profitable for us to understand that those who purposed to infect the Church of God with such a corruption, were horribly stricken with a spirit of giddiness and stupidity.

The concluding clause of the verse distinguishes Jerusalem from all the other cities of the world, which are subject to vicissitudes, and flourish only for a time. As Jerusalem was founded by God, it continued stedfast and unmoved amidst the varied commotions and revolutions which took place in the world; and it is not to be wondered at, if he continued through successive ages to maintain the city of which he made choice, and in which it was his will that his name should be called upon for ever. It may, however, be objected, that this city was once destroyed, and the people carried into captivity. But this does not militate against the statement here made; for, before that event happened, the restoration of the city was foretold by Jeremiah, (chap. xxvii. 22;) and, therefore, when it took place, God truly, and in a special manner, showed how stedfast his work was. And now, since Christ by his coming has renewed the world, whatever was spoken of that city in old time belongs to the spiritual Jerusalem, which is dispersed through all the countries of the world. Whenever, therefore, our minds are agitated and perplexed, we should call to remembrance the truth, that, whatever dangers and apprehensions may threaten us, the safety of the Church which God has established, although it may be sorely shaken, can never, however powerfully assaulted, be so weakened as to fall and be involved in ruin. The verb, which is in the future tense, *will establish*, may be resolved into the past tense, *has established;* but this will make no difference as to the sense.

9. *O God! we have waited for thy mercy.* This verse teaches us that the faithful were preserved by the power of God; for, when all things were in a state of the greatest confusion, they continued tranquil and patient until God at length, having pity upon them, brought them help. The Hebrew word דמם, *damam*, which we have rendered *to wait*, properly signifies *to be silent*, and is here used to denote tranquillity of mind. From this we conclude, that the people of God were so harassed with dangers, that, had they listened to the judgment of carnal sense and reason, they would have been overwhelmed with terror; even as we know that men are in a state of continual uneasiness, and are driven hither and thither by contrary waves, until faith tranquillise their minds, and settle them in true patience. The amount of what the Psalmist says is, that the faithful, although severely afflicted, were not driven from their purpose, and prevented from relying upon the aid of God; but that, on the contrary, by their patience and hope, they opened the gate of his grace. It served to magnify and illustrate the greatness of the grace of God, that their expectations of assistance from him were not disappointed. From this we may also deduce the profitable warning, that if the aid of God is withdrawn from us, it is because we distrust

his promises, and, by our impatience, prevent his grace, which is laid up for those who wait in patience, from flowing upon us. But what is meant by the expression, *In the midst of the temple?* Is it that the people of God maintained their faith only in that place, and that each of them ceased to hope as soon as he returned to his own dwelling? No; on the contrary, it is certain that they carried home with them the hope which they had entertained in the temple, that they might continue stedfastly to abide by it. But God having promised that this place, in which he would be called upon, would be the seat and dwelling-place of his power and grace, his people here affirm, that, relying upon this heavenly promise, they were persuaded beyond all doubt that God would show himself merciful and gracious towards them, since they had a real and sure pledge of his presence. We must not conceive, merely because our own fancy suggests it, that God will be our deliverer. We are to believe that he will be so only in so far as he freely and willingly offers himself to us in this character. Now, if this symbol or pledge of the presence of God, which was only a shadow, ought to have had such influence upon the minds of true believers under the former dispensation, as to make them hope for life in the midst of death, surely when Christ has now descended amongst us, to unite us much more closely to his Father, we have sufficient ground for continuing in a state of undisturbed tranquillity, although the world should be embroiled in confusion and turned upside down. Only it must be our endeavour that the service of God may flourish pure and entire amongst us, and that thus the glory of his temple may shine forth in the midst of us.

10. *As is thy name, O God! so is thy praise.* Some connect this verse with the preceding sentence, as if it had been said, Lord, it is not in vain that thou hast enjoined upon us the duty of celebrating thy name; for thou furnishest at the same time matter of praise. Thus the sense will be, that the name of God is magnified and extolled with effect, or that along with his promises his power is at the same time manifested. Others give this exposition, which is somewhat more refined, That

the works of God correspond with his name; for in Hebrew he is called אֵל, *El*,[1] from his power, and he shows in very deed that this name is not applied to him in vain, but that the praise which is ascribed to him by it is right and what is due to him. The former exposition, as it is less forced, so it comes nearer to the words and mind of the sacred writer, namely, that God bore testimony by his works that it was not in vain that he was acknowledged and worshipped by the Jews as the true and only God. Yet when I come to consider the words which follow immediately after, *Unto the ends of the earth*, I think that the prophet meant something else,—that he intended to show, that wherever the fame of the name of God may be spread, men will know that he is worthy of the highest praise. The words contain a tacit contrast. At that time, the names of idols, it is well known, were very common, and had sway through the whole world; and yet, whatever fame these counterfeit gods had acquired, we know that praise in no respect belonged to them, since no sign of divinity whatever could be discovered about them. But here the prophet, on the contrary, declares, Lord, in whatever part of the world thy name is heard, it will always be accompanied with solid and rightful praise, or it will ever carry along with it matter of praise, since the whole world will understand how thou hast dealt with thy chosen people. What is added immediately after is to the same purpose, *Thy right hand is full of righteousness*, teaching us, that God, in succouring his own people, clearly manifests his righteousness, as if he stretched forth his arm to us that we might touch his righteousness with the finger; and that he shows not only one specimen or two of his righteousness, but in every thing and every where exhibits to us a complete proof of it. We ought to bear in mind what we have stated elsewhere, that *the righteousness of God* is to be understood of his faithfulness which he observes in maintaining and defending his own people. From this there accrues to us the inestimable comfort, that the work in which God especially desires to be acknowledged as righteous consists in providing what belongs

[1] "C'est à dire, Fort."—*Fr. marg.* "That is to say, Strong."

to our welfare and to our maintenance in safety.¹ We now see that the meaning of the inspired poet is, That the names of false gods prevailed, and were renowned among men, although they had done nothing to furnish matter of true praise ; but that it was altogether different with respect to the God of Israel : for wherever the report of him was carried, all would understand that he was the deliverer of his people, and that he did not disappoint their hope and desires, nor forsake them in danger.

11. *Mount Zion shall rejoice, the daughters² of Judah shall be glad, because of thy judgments.*
12. *Encompass Zion, and go round about her, number her towers.*
13. *Set your heart³ to her walls, exalt her towers,⁴ that ye may make report to the generation to come.*
14. *For this God is our God for ever and ever : he will be our guide even unto death.*

11. *Mount Zion shall rejoice.* The Psalmist now concludes his exhortation to rejoicing, telling us that Jerusalem and the other cities of Judea shall have cause to commend the righteousness of God,⁶ because they had found from undoubted experience that he was the protector of their welfare. He here makes use of the word *judgment*, because God, who undertook the cause of his Church, openly showed that he was the enemy of her oppressors, and that he would repress their presumption and audacity.

12 and 13. *Encompass Zion, &c.* Here the prophet again commends the situation and beauty of Jerusalem, intimating that the city was strongly fortified and impregnable; and he does this, because in these external things the blessing of God in some respect shone forth. We must always bear in

---

¹ "Que l'œuvre en laquelle Dieu veut singulierement estre recognu juste, c'est in procurant les choses qui appartienent à nostre salut, et à nous maintenir en sauvete."—*Fr.*
² "C'est, villes."—*Fr. marg.* "That is, cities."
³ "C'est, prenez bien garde."—*Fr. marg.* "That is, take good heed."
⁴ "Palais."—*Fr.* "Palaces."
⁵ "Ou, dés l'enfance."—*Fr. marg.* "Or, from infancy."
⁶ "Auront matiere de liesse."—*Fr.* "Shall have matter of gladness."

mind what he stated in a preceding verse, that "God in her palaces is known for a fortress." In making mention here of her *towers* and *walls,* we are not to suppose that he would have the minds of the faithful to rest in these things. He rather sets them before us as a mirror in which the character of God may be seen. He therefore says, *Encompass Zion,* that is, look upon it carefully and attentively on every side;—*number her towers, and apply your mind to consider her walls;* that is, estimate her palaces as they deserve, and thus it will be manifest beyond all doubt that this is a city chosen of God, seeing it far surpasses all other cities. In insisting upon these points, his whole drift is to make manifest the character with which the Lord had invested Jerusalem in making it a sacred place, in which he himself might take up his abode, and in erecting it as a dwelling-place for his people. It seems, moreover, that the prophet, in stating that the object of his exhortation was, that the beauty and magnificence of the holy city *might be reported* to the succeeding generation, tacitly gives us to understand, that the time would at length come when that city would be no longer seen. What need would there be for making this report if it could be seen and were always before the eyes of the world? Although, then, he has said a little before that Jerusalem is established for ever, yet he now teaches us, by way of correction, what kind of perpetuity it will be—that it will endure only till the time of the renovation of the Church. We belong to that generation to come, to whom it is said these things will be reported; for we are sharers in all the benefits which God, in the days of old, bestowed upon his ancient people. The outward splendour for which Jerusalem was admired does not, indeed, stand forth conspicuous amongst us at the present day; but since the coming of Christ into our world, the Church has been no less richly and magnificently adorned with spiritual gifts than Jerusalem, under the shadows of the Law, was in old time surrounded and fortified with strong walls and towers. I have translated the word פסגו, *pasgu, exalt,* referring it to the value which ought to be put upon the towers of the city because of their excellence. To explain it, as is done by some, *fortify* or *strengthen,* seems to be less suitable. If any are inclined rather to follow the interpretation of those who render it *look upon* or *behold,* I have no great objection to it.

14. *For this God is our God for ever and ever.* From these words it appears still more clearly, that when the prophet spake of the palaces of Jerusalem, it was not that the godly should keep their eyes fixed upon them, but that by the aid of these outward things they should elevate their minds to the contemplation of the glory of God. God would have them to behold, as it were, the marks of his grace engraven wherever they turned themselves, or rather, to recognise him as present in these marks. From this we conclude, that whatever dignity or excellence shines forth in the Church, we are not to consider it otherwise than as the means of presenting God to our view, that we may magnify and praise him in his gifts. The demonstrative pronoun זה, *zeh, this,* is not superfluous; it is put to distinguish the only true God, of whose existence and character the faithful were fully persuaded, from all the false gods which men have set themselves to invent. The unbelieving may boldly speak of the name of God, and prate about religion; but however much they may do this, when they are more closely questioned, it will be found that they have nothing certain or settled on the subject. Yea, the vain imaginations and inventions of those who are not grounded in the true faith must necessarily come to nothing. It is, then, the property of faith to set before us not a confused but a distinct knowledge of God, and such as may not leave us wavering, as superstition leaves its votaries, which, we know, is always introducing some new counterfeit deities and in countless numbers. We ought, therefore, so much the more to mark the emphatic demonstrative pronoun *this,* which is here used. We meet with an almost similar passage in the prophecies of Isaiah, (xxv. 9,) "Lo, this is our God; we have waited for him, and he will save us: this is the Lord; we have waited for him, we will be glad and rejoice in his salvation:" as if the faithful had protested and declared, We have not an uncertain God, or a God of whom we have only a confused and an indistinct apprehension, but one of whom we have a true and solid knowledge. When the faithful here declare that God will continue unchangeably stedfast to his

purpose in maintaining his Church, their object is to encourage and strengthen themselves to persevere in a continued course of faith. What follows immediately after, *He will be our guide even unto death*, seems to be added by way of exposition. In making this statement, the people of God assure themselves that he will be their guide and keeper for ever. They are not to be understood as meaning that they will be safe under the government and conduct of God in this life only, and that he will abandon them in the midst of death; but they express generally, and according to the common people's way of speaking,[1] what I have stated, that God will take care of all who rely upon him even to the end. What we translate, *Even unto death*, consists of two words in the Hebrew text, אַל מוּת, *al muth;* but some read in one word, אַלמוּת, *almuth*, and take it for *age* or *eternity*.[2] The sense, however, will be the same whether we read the one way or the other. Others translate it *childhood*,[3] in this sense, As God has from the beginning carefully preserved and maintained his Church, even as a father brings up his children from their infancy, so he will continue to act in the same manner. The first sense, however, in my opinion, is the more appropriate. Others translate it *in secret* or *hidden*,[4] which seems equally remote from the meaning of the prophet; unless, perhaps, we should understand him as intending expressly to say, that God's way of exercising his government is hidden, that we may not measure or judge of it by carnal reason, but by faith.

[1] "Et selon la façon de parler du commun peuple."—*Fr.*
[2] This is the view taken by the Septuagint, which renders it by "'Εις τους αιωνας," "To all eternity." "A very large number of copies," says Street, "both of De Rossi's and Dr Kennicott's collation, have עלמות in one word. Symmachus renders this expression by το διηνεκες, *perpetuum*."
[3] As if the word were derived from עלם, *elem, a young man*. Thus the Chaldee reads, "In the days of our youth." See מה, in Buxtorf's Lexicon.
[4] This is the sense in which Houbigant understands אלמה, *almuth;* for he reads it as one word; and he is of opinion that it belongs to the title of the following psalm, to which, he says, אלמה, *hidden*, agrees very well, as an enigma is set forth in that psalm. Others, who read אל מות, *al muth*, in two words, *upon death*, consider them also as belonging to the inscription of the following psalm, observing that there can be no propriety in saying —*ever and ever*—*unto death*. Merrick, however, remarks, "The words *for ever and ever*, and *unto death*, seem to me very consistent, as they relate to different propositions: This God will be our God to all eternity, and (by that power which he has already thus exerted in our protection) will conduct us through life with safety."

PSALM XLIX.

The wicked and the votaries of worldly pleasure often enjoy prosperity, while such as fear the Lord are exposed to affliction, and disposed to faint under the pressure of it. To moderate that pride which the one class is apt to feel in the midst of their success, and administer a check to the despondency of the other, the Psalmist shows what little reason we have to envy the supposed happiness of the ungodly, which, even when at its height, is vain and evanescent; and he teaches us that good men, however great their trials may be, are objects of the divine regard, and will be eventually delivered from their enemies.

¶ To the chief musician, a psalm of the sons of Korah.[1]

1. *Hear this, all ye people; give ear, all ye inhabitants of the world:*
2. *Both ye sons of Adam,[2] and ye sons of men,[3] rich and poor, together.*
3. *My mouth shall speak of wisdom; and the meditation of my heart shall be of understanding.*
4. *I will incline my ear to a parable:[4] I will open my enigma[5] upon the harp.*

1. *Hear this, all ye people.* Whoever may have been the penman of this psalm, it discusses one of the most important principles in divine philosophy, and there is a propriety in the elevated terms designed to awaken and secure attention, with which the Psalmist announces his purpose to discourse of

---

[1] Ten psalms bear the inscription, "Of or for the sons of Korah." As the prefixed preposition ל may be translated either *of* or *for*, it has been doubted whether this and other psalms, with a similar inscription, were written by or for the sons of Korah. Some, as Calmet, think it most probable that they were composed by them, from certain peculiarities of style in which they agree with each other, and differ from the psalms which bear the name of David. Others ascribe these psalms to David, and suppose that they were committed by him to the chief musician, to be sung by the posterity of Korah.

[2] "C'est, ceux de bas estat."—*Fr. marg.* "That is, those of low estate."

[3] "C'est, les nobles."—*Fr. marg.* "That is, the noble."

[4] "A *mon* proverbe."—*Fr.* "To *my* proverb." "Ou, sentence grave."—*Fr. marg.* "Or, grave sentence."

[5] "Ou, dire obscur."—*Fr. marg.* "Or, obscure saying."

things of a deep and momentous nature. To a superficial view, indeed, the subject might seem trite and common-place, treating, as he does, of the shortness of human life, and the vanity of those objects in which worldly men confide. But the real scope of the psalm is, to comfort the people of God under the sufferings to which they are exposed, by teaching them to expect a happy change in their condition, when God, in his own time, shall interpose to rectify the disorders of the present system. There is a higher lesson still inculcated by the Psalmist—that, as God's providence of the world is not presently apparent, we must exercise patience, and rise superior to the suggestions of carnal sense in anticipating the favourable issue. That it is our duty to maintain a resolute struggle with our afflictions, however severe these may be, and that it were foolish to place happiness in the enjoyment of such fleeting possessions as the riches, honours, or pleasures of this world, may be precepts which even the heathen philosophers have enforced, but they have uniformly failed in setting before us the true source of consolation. However admirably they discourse of a happy life, they confine themselves entirely to commendations upon virtue, and do not bring prominently forward to our view that God, who governs the world, and to whom alone we can repair with confidence in the most desperate circumstances. But slender comfort can be derived upon this subject from the teaching of philosophy. If, therefore, the Holy Ghost in this psalm introduces to our notice truths which are sufficiently familiar to experience, it is that he may raise our minds from them to the higher truth of the divine government of the world, assuring us of the fact, that God sits supreme, even when the wicked are triumphing most in their success, or when the righteous are trampled under the foot of contumely, and that a day is coming when he will dash the cup of pleasure out of the hands of his enemies, and rejoice the hearts of his friends, by delivering them out of their severest distresses. This is the only consideration which can impart solid comfort under our afflictions. Formidable and terrible in themselves, they would overwhelm our souls, did not the Lord lift upon us the light of his countenance. Were we not assured that he watches over our safety, we could find no remedy from our evils, and no quarter to which we might resort under them.

The remarks which have been made may explain the manner in which the inspired writer introduces the psalm, soliciting our attention, as about to discourse on a theme unusually high and important. Two things are implied in this verse, that the subject upon which he proposes to enter is of universal application, and that we require to be admonished and aroused ere we are brought to a due measure of consideration. The words which I have translated, *inhabitants of the world*, are translated by others, *inhabitants of time;* but this is a harsh mode of expression, however much it may agree with the scope of the psalm. He calls upon all men indiscriminately, because all were equally concerned in the truths which he intended to announce. By *sons of Adam*, we may understand the meaner or lower class of mankind; and by *sons of men*,[1] the high, the noble, or such as sustain any pre-eminence in life. Thus, in the outset, he states it to be his purpose to instruct high and low without exception; his subject being one in which the whole human family was interested, and in which every individual belonging to it required to be instructed.

---

[1] The original words for the first of these expressions are, בני אדם, *bene adam;* and those for the second, בני איש, *bene ish.* אדם, *adam*, from אדמה, *adamah, earth*, means an earthly, frail, mortal, mean man. The term איש, *ish*, on the other hand, is often used to describe a man who is great and eminent, distinguished for his extraction, strength, valour, and dignity. Thus, in 1 Sam. xxv. 15, we read, "Art thou not איש, *ish*, a man?" which is explained by what follows, "And who is like thee in Israel?" denoting there the military valour and reputation of Abner. When the two expressions, בני אדם, *bene adam*, and בני איש, *bene ish*, are used together as in this place, in Ps. lxii. 9, Isa. ii. 9, and v. 15, the Jewish Rabbins and modern Christian interpreters have understood a difference of rank to be stated; the former expression, denoting persons of obscure birth, of low rank, the common people: and the latter, meaning men of illustrious descent, the great or nobler sorts of men. See Archbishop Secker's Dissertation on the words אנוש, איש, אדם, in Appendix to Merrick's Annotations on the Psalms, No. 5. The Septuagint translates the former phrase by "Οἱ γηγενεῖς," "the earth-born." The Chaldee expresses the former by *the sons of old Adam*, and the latter by *the sons of Jacob;* thus intending to comprehend Jews and Gentiles, all men in the world. "But," says Hammond, "it is more likely that the phrases denote only the several conditions of men, men of the *lower* and *higher* rank, for so the *consequents* interpret it, *rich* and *poor*."

3. *My mouth shall speak of wisdom.* The prophet was warranted in applying these commendatory terms to the doctrine which he was about to communicate. It is, no doubt, by plain appeals to observation that we find him reproving human folly; but the general principle upon which his instruction proceeds is one by no means obvious to the common sense of mankind, not to say that his design in using such terms is less to assert the dignity of his subject than simply to awaken attention. This he does all the more effectually by speaking as one who would apply his own mind to instruction rather than assume the office of exhortation. He puts himself forward as an humble scholar, one who, in acting the part of teacher, has an eye at the same time to his own improvement. It were desirable that all the ministers of God should be actuated by a similar spirit, disposing them to regard God as at once their own teacher and that of the common people, and to embrace in the first place themselves that divine word which they preach to others.[1] The Psalmist had another object in view. He would secure the greater weight and deference to his doctrine by announcing that he had no intention to vend fancies of his own, but to advance what he had learned in the school of God. This is the true method of instruction to be followed in the Church. The man who holds the office of teacher must apply himself to the reception of truth before he attempt to communicate it, and in this manner become the means of conveying to the hands of others that which God has committed to his own. Wisdom is not the growth of human genius. It must be sought from above, and it is impossible that any should speak with the propriety and knowledge necessary for the edification of the Church, who has not, in the first place, been taught at the feet of the Lord. To condescend upon the words, some read in the third verse, *And the meditation of my heart shall speak of understanding.* But as it were a harsh and improper

---

[1] "Aussi certes il est bien requis que tous les Prophetes de Dieu ayent un tel vouloir et affection, asçavoir qu'ils souffrent volontiers que Dieu soit leur maistre aussi bien que de tout le peuple, et qu'ils reçoyvent tous les premiers sa parolle, laquelle ils portent de leur bouche aux autres."—*Fr.*

expression to say that *the meditation of the heart speaks,* I have adopted the simpler reading.

4. *I will incline my ear*[1] *to a parable.* The Hebrew word מָשָׁל, *mashal,*[2] which I have translated *parable,* properly denotes a *similitude;* but it is often applied to any deep or weighty sayings, because these are generally embellished with figures and metaphors. The noun which follows, חִידָה, *chidoth,*[3] and which I have rendered *an enigma,* or *riddle,* is to be understood in nearly the same sense. In Ezekiel

---

[1] Bythner and Fry are of opinion, that " the inclining of the ear" is a metaphor taken from the position of the minstrel, who, in accommodating his words to the tune, brings his ear close to the harp, that he may catch the sounds. Thus the Psalmist expresses the sense he himself had of the importance of his subject, and his purpose of giving to it the most serious attention.

[2] This word is of great latitude in its signification. It signifies primarily any similitude by which another thing is expressed. Thence it comes to denote a figurative discourse, either in the form of fiction and fable, such as riddles or significant apologues, as that of Jotham, Judges ix. 7, or in which application is made of some true example or similitude, as when the sluggard is bidden " go to the ant," and the impenitent sinner to consider the " swallow and crane," which return at their certain seasons, and so are fitted to give a lesson to sinners to repent. And, finally, it belongs to all moral doctrine, either darkly or sententiously delivered; wise men, in ancient times, having been in the habit of delivering their lessons in short concise sentences, sometimes in schemes and figures, and sometimes without them, as we see in the Proverbs of Solomon, many of which are plain moral sayings without any figure or comparison. Of this sort is that which is here introduced to our attention; it is a moral theme not much veiled with figures, nor so concise as proverbs usually are, but which contains the most instructive lessons on the vanity of the prosperity of all wicked men. See Hammond *in loco.*

[3] This word is derived from an Arabic root which signifies *to bend a thing aside, to tie knots, &c.;* and thus it means *an intricate species of composition, a riddle.* It is used for *a riddle* in the story of Samson, Judges xiv. 14, 15; and for *difficult questions,* as those put by the Queen of Sheba to Solomon, 1 Kings x. 1. See Lowth's Lectures on Sacred Poetry, vol. i. p. 78. Accordingly, it is here rendered by the Septuagint, " τὸ πρόβλημά μου," " my problem or difficult question," which is not only asked in the fifth verse, but also answered in the subsequent verses. The word, however, is also applied to poetical compositions of a highly adorned and finished style, in which nothing enigmatical appears, but which contain weighty and important matter set forth in the parabolic style to secure the reader's or the hearer's attention, Ps. lxxviii. 2. See Gesenius' Lexicon. In the subject-matter of this psalm there does not appear to be any thing peculiarly intricate. It treats of the vanity of riches, and the folly of those who trust in them; their insufficiency to save from the power of death; and the final triumph of all the suffering people of God over their rich and haughty persecutors. This is indeed a dark theme to the worldly-minded man; but it contains nothing occult or mysterious to those who are taught of God.

xvii. 2, we have both the nouns with their corresponding verbs joined together, חוּד חִידָה וּמְשֹׁל מָשָׁל, *chud chedah umshol mashal*, the literal translation being, "Enigmatize an enigma, and parabolize a parable." I am aware that the reference in this place is to an allegorical discourse, but I have already adverted to the reason why, in Hebrew, the name of enigmas or similitudes is given to any remarkable or important sayings. The Psalmist, when he adds that he will *open* his dark saying, shows that nothing was farther from his intention than to wrap the subject of his discourse in perplexing and intricate obscurity. The truths of revelation are so high as to exceed our comprehension; but, at the same time, the Holy Spirit has accommodated them so far to our capacity, as to render all Scripture profitable for instruction. None can plead ignorance: for the deepest and most difficult doctrines are made plain to the most simple and unlettered of mankind. I see little force in the idea suggested by several interpreters, of the Psalmist having employed his *harp*, that he might render a subject in itself harsh and disagreeable more engaging by the charms of music. He would merely follow the usual practice of accompanying the psalm with the harp.

5. *Wherefore should I fear in the days of evil? the iniquity of my heel shall compass me about.*
6. *They trust in their wealth, and boast themselves in the multitude of their riches.*
7. *The brother shall not be able to redeem,* [literally, *shall not redeem by redeeming;*] *none shall give to God the price of his redemption.*
8. *And the redemption of their soul shall be precious, and their continuance for ever.*
9. *That he should still live for ever, and not see the grave.*

5. *Wherefore should I fear in the days of evil?* The Psalmist now enters upon the point on which he proposed to discourse, That the people of God must not yield to despondency even in the most distressing circumstances, when their enemies may seem to have enclosed them on every side, but must rest assured that God, although he connives for a time, is awake

to their condition, and only watches the best opportunity of executing his judgments. This manner of introducing the subject by interrogation is much more emphatic than if he had simply asserted his resolution to preserve his mind undisturbed in the midst of adversity. In the second clause of the verse he particularizes the heaviest and most bitter of all afflictions, those which are experienced by the righteous when their enemies triumph in the unrestrained indulgence of their wickedness. *When,* the adverb of time, must therefore be understood—*When the iniquity of my heel shall compass me about.* There is a different meaning which some interpreters have attached to the words, namely, If I should fear in the days of evil, and be guilty of the excessive anxieties of the unbeliever,—in that case, when the hour of my death came, my iniquity would compass me about. *The heel* they take to be the end of life. But this interpretation is to be dismissed at once as most unnatural. Nor do I see what reason others have for referring this word to *the thoughts,* for I believe that in no other part of Scripture can such a metaphor or similitude be found. Others, with more plausibility, have rendered the original word *liers in wait,*[1] because the Hebrew verb עָקַב, *akab,* signifies *to deceive;* and they consider the Psalmist as intimating, that he would not fear though crafty and treacherous men laid snares for him. In my opinion, there is no figure intended; and he means to say, that he would have no fear when his enemies surrounded him, and in pursuing him, trode, as it were, upon his heel. The French have a similar expression, " Poursuyvre jusques aux talons."[2] I agree with them, that he speaks of enemies, but it is of their wicked persecution as they press upon him in the height of their power, and with design to destroy him, keep themselves near him, and tread, so to speak, upon his very heel.

---

[1] Lowth reads, "The wickedness of those who *lie in wait for me,* or endeavour to *supplant me;*" and Horsley, "When the iniquity of *those who plot against me* environs me." The original word is עקבי, *akabey,* which Dr Adam Clarke thinks is to be considered as the contracted plural of עקבים, *akabim, supplanters,* from עקב, *akab, to supplant, to defraud.* It is literally, "My Jacobs;" that is, those who would act towards me as Jacob acted towards Esau. See Gen. xxvii. 36, and Jer. ix. 4–17, 9. The Syriac and Arabic versions read it, "My enemies."

[2] *i. e.* "To pursue even to the heels."

6. *They trust in their wealth.* We are now furnished with the reason why the suffering children of God should dismiss their apprehensions, and keep themselves from despondency, even when reduced to extremity by the violence and treachery of their enemies. Any boasted power which they possess is fleeting and evanescent. The Psalmist would convince us that the fear of man is unwarrantable; that it argues ignorance of what man is even at his best; and that it were as reasonable to startle at a shadow or a spectre. *They boast themselves,* he adds, *in the multitude of their riches,* and this is an error into which we are disposed to fall, forgetting that the condition of man in this world is fluctuating and transitory. It is not merely from the intrinsic insufficiency of wealth, honours, or pleasures, to confer true happiness, that the Psalmist proves the misery of worldly men, but from their manifest and total incapacity of forming a correct judgment of such possessions. Happiness is connected with the state of mind of that man who enjoys it, and none would call those happy who are sunk in stupidity and security, and are destitute of understanding. The Psalmist satisfactorily proves the infatuation of the wicked from the confidence which they place in their power and wealth, and their disposition to boast of them. It is a convincing sign of folly when one cannot discern what is before his eyes. Not a day passes without forcing the plain fact upon their notice, that none can redeem the life of another; so that their conduct is nothing less than insanity. Some read, *A man shall not be able to redeem his brother;* which amounts to the same meaning, and the text admits of this translation. The Hebrew word אח, *ach,* which I have rendered *brother,* is by others translated *one;* but I do not approve, although I would not absolutely reject, this reading. The Psalmist adds, that *none can give a price to God for the ransom of another,* where he adverts to the truth that men's lives are absolutely at the disposal of God, and that they never can be extended by any human arrangement one moment beyond the period which God has fixed.

He enforces the same lesson in the verse which follows,

where he states that *the redemption of their soul is precious,* an expression not to be understood as implying merely that it is an event of rare occurrence, but that it never can take place, as 1 Samuel iii. 1, where the word of the Lord is said to have been precious under the priesthood of Eli, when it is evidently meant that it had ceased altogether. The Psalmist would assert that no man can hope to purchase an immortality either for himself or others in this world. I have rendered the close of verse 8, *And their continuance for ever;* but others, who construe the Hebrew word חדל, *chadal,* as a verb, meaning *to cease,* read, *And ceaseth for ever,* as if the Psalmist meant that no price was sufficiently great to answer the purpose, and that it must therefore cease for ever, as what could never obtain the end desired. I consider that which I have given to be the real meaning of the word, having had occasion already to observe upon Psalm xxxix. 5, that it signifies the fixed term of human life. The words in verse 9, *That he should still live for ever,* more fully express the truth, that it is not merely impossible to redeem the life of men when they are dead, but impossible, while they are yet living, to extend the term of their existence. A definite limit has been assigned to every man's life. This he cannot pass over, and the Psalmist would impress the fact upon us as one which stamps folly upon the conduct of the wicked, who will cherish their unfounded confidence even at the moment when they are upon the brink of the grave. In all this, it may strike the reader that he has not announced any thing which merits being called a *dark saying,* and has rather been treating a popular subject in a very plain style of language; but if he consider that David here condemns, as by a voice issuing from the awful judgment-seat of God, the stupidity of such as forget that they are men, he will not be disposed to reckon the expression inapplicable. Again, we have seen that he *has opened* his dark saying, it being the divine will that instruction should be delivered in a form adapted to the meanest capacity.

10. *For he shall see that wise men die, the fool and the brutish person shall perish together, and shall leave their wealth to strangers.*
11. *Their inward thought is their houses for ever,*[1] *and their dwelling-places to all generations; they have called out their names upon the earth.*
12. *And man shall not abide in honour; he has become like the beasts: they perish.*

10. *For he shall see that wise men die.* I consider the ninth and tenth verses to be connected, and that it is the intention of the Psalmist to censure the folly of those who dream of spending an eternity in this world, and set themselves seriously to establish a permanent settlement in it, though they cannot but see their fellow-creatures cut down daily before their eyes by the stroke of death. It is a common proverb, that experience teaches fools, and they may be looked upon as something worse who will not lay to heart their mortality, when surrounded by so many convincing illustrations of it. This seems obviously to be the connection. These infatuated enemies of God, as if he had said, cannot fail to perceive that death is the universal lot of mankind, that the wise are equally liable to it with the foolish; and yet they persist in the imagination that they will remain here always, and will live as if they were never to quit with this world! They see what happens to others, that all, without exception or discrimination, are involved in the common mortality; and they must observe how often it happens that wealth passes *into the hands of strangers.* The word אחרים, *acherim,* I translate *strangers,* rather than *others;* for although it may be extended to successors of any kind, yet I think that the Psalmist here supposes the case of wealth passing into the hands of those who are not our natural and lawful heirs, and cannot be considered in any sense as representing us. Many not only die, but die childless, and their name becomes extinct, which is an additional in-

---

[1] "C'est, ils ne pensent à autre chose si non comment ils pourront faire durer leurs maisons."—*Fr. marg.* "That is, they think of nothing else but how they shall be able to make their houses continue for ever."

gredient of bitterness in the cup of the worldling. And yet all these affecting lessons of experience are entirely lost upon them, and they still in their secret thoughts fondly cherish the idea of living here for ever. The Hebrew word קרב, *hereb,* means *the middle* of anything; but it is taken metaphorically to signify *the heart,* or inward parts of the man. Here it denotes that their *secret thoughts* are occupied with an imaginary eternity which they hope to enjoy upon earth. Another and more ingenious interpretation has been suggested by some, that as the word occasionally means *a tomb,* the Psalmist may here be satirising those who think to perpetuate their memory after death by rearing expensive mausoleums.[1] This view of the words is strained and unnatural; and what immediately follows proves that the other is the most correct, when it is added, that worldly men *call out their names upon the earth;* that is, make every exertion in their power to win reputation amongst their fellow-creatures. Their desire should be to have their names written in the book of life, and to be blessed before God and his holy angels; but their ambition is of another kind—to be renowned and extolled upon earth. By the expression, *calling out,* it is insinuated that the fame of ungodly men is but an empty sound. Some interpreters prefer reading, *They have called their lands by their own names,*[2] that they might leave some monument of themselves to posterity. But what the Psalmist seems chiefly to insist upon is, that they are wholly bent upon earthly renown.

12. *And man shall not abide in honour.* Having exposed the vain and delusory nature of the fancies entertained by the ungodly, he next shows that however fondly they may

[1] The reading of the Septuagint is, "Καὶ οἱ τάφοι αὐτῶν οἰκίαι αὐτῶν εἰς τὸν αἰῶνα." "And their sepulchres are their houses for ever." The Vulgate, Syriac, and Chaldee, also read "sepulchres." Kennicott supposes that the authors of these versions must have read קברם, *kaberam, their graves,* instead of קרבם, *kirbam, their inward part.* The text as it stands admits of a good sense. Some eminent critics, however, are disposed to think that the reading of the ancient versions is the true one.

[2] Some also read the verse thus, "Their grave is their house for ever, their dwelling-place through all generations, though their names are celebrated over countries."

cherish them, they must experience the same fate with the beasts of the field. It is true that there is a great difference, so far as the soul is concerned, between man and the brute creation; but the Psalmist speaks of things as they appear in this world, and in this respect he was warranted to say of the ungodly that they die as the beasts. His subject does not lead him to speak of the world to come. He is reasoning with the children of this world, who have no respect to another, and no idea of a farther happiness than that which they enjoy here. He accordingly ridicules their folly in conceiving of themselves as privileged with exemption from the ordinary lot of humanity, and warns them that death will soon be near to humble their presumptuous thoughts, and put them on a level with the meanest of the lower creatures. This I prefer to the more ingenious interpretation which some would put upon the words, that they reduced themselves to the level of beasts by not recognising the true dignity of their nature, which consists in the possession of a never-dying soul. The Psalmist's great aim is to show the vanity of the boasting of the wicked, from the nearness of death, which must join them in one common fate with the beasts of the field. The last word in the verse gives the reason why the ungodly may be compared to the beasts— *they perish.* It matters little whether or not we consider the relative אשר, *asher,* as understood, and read, *that perish.*

> 13. *This their way is foolishness in them,*[1] *and their posterity will acquiesce in their sayings,* [literally, *in their mouth.*] *Selah.*
> 14. *Like sheep they are laid in the grave; death shall feed them; and the upright shall have dominion over them in the morning, and their strength*[2] *shall wax old; the grave shall receive them*[3] *from their dwelling.*

[1] " C'est, est cognue n'estre que folie en eux."—*Fr. marg.* " That is, is known to be only folly in them."
[2] " Ou, figure."—*Fr. marg.* " Or, form."
[3] The words, *shall receive them,* are a supplement, there being nothing for them in the Latin version nor in the Hebrew text. They stand for *le prendra* in the French version.

15. *But God shall redeem my soul from the hand[1] of the grave; for he hath taken me up. Selah.*

13. *This their way is foolishness.* As this verse has been variously rendered, I shall briefly, before giving my own sense of it, state the views which have been taken by others. As the Hebrew word כסל, *kesel*, which I have translated *foolishness*, occasionally means *the kidneys*, some refine upon the term, and consider it to be here taken for *fat;* as if this imagination of theirs were, so to speak, fat which stupified and rendered their senses obtuse. But this reading is too forced to bear examination. Others read, *This their way is their folly;*[2] that is, the reason why they pursue such a line of conduct is, that they are destitute of sound judgment; for, were they not utterly devoid of it, and did they possess one spark of intelligence, would they not reflect upon the end for which they were created, and direct their minds to higher objects? I rather conceive the Psalmist simply to mean, that the event proves them to be wholly destitute of wisdom, in placing their happiness upon earthly objects, and brands them, notwithstanding all the pretensions they make to foresight and shrewdness, with ridicule and contempt. And this he states, to show in a more aggravated light the madness of their posterity, who will not be instructed by the fate of their predecessors. The last clause of the verse has also been variously rendered, and I may state the views which have been taken of it by others. The Hebrew verb רצה, *ratsah*, which I have translated *to acquiesce*, they render, *to walk*, and the noun פי, *phi*, translated *mouth* or *sayings*, they take to mean *a measure*, thus understanding the Psalmist to say, that the children walked by the same rule with their fathers; and they change the letter ב, *beth*, into כ, *caph*, the mark of similitude which is sufficiently

---

[1] " C'est, puissance et domination de la mort."—*Fr. marg.* " That is, the power and dominion of death."
[2] " כסל למו is literally, *folly to them; i. e.,* though this their way (the worldling's trust in his wealth) seem to them a piece of special wisdom, yet in the event it proves otherwise; it becomes perfect folly to them when they come to discern their frustrations."—*Hammond.*

common in the Hebrew language. This view of the passage comes near to the proper meaning of it. Some conceive that there is an allusion to the beasts of the field; but this is improbable. It seems best to understand with others that the word mouth denotes *principles* or *sayings;* and the verb רצה, *ratsah,* may be taken in its more ordinary and most generally received sense, which implies consent or complacency. I have therefore translated it *to acquiesce.* The boasted confidence of the ungodly proving vain in the issue, and exposing them justly to ridicule, it argues a monstrous infatuation in their posterity, with this example before their eyes, to set their affections upon the same trifles, and to feel and express themselves exactly in the same manner as those who went before them. If men reflect at all upon the judgments which God executes in the world, we might expect that they would particularly consider his dealings with their immediate predecessors, and when, wholly insensible to the lessons which should be learned from their fate, they precipitate themselves into the same courses, this convincingly demonstrates their brutish folly.

14. *Like sheep they are laid in the grave; death shall feed them.*[1] The figure is striking. They go down into the grave as sheep are gathered into the fold by the shepherd.

[1] This is also the reading of the Septuagint, "Θάνατος ποιμανεῖ αὐτούς," "Death shall feed them as a shepherd," and of Jerome, "Mors pascet eos;" and this is the view taken by Dr Kennicott, Dr Hammond, and Bishop Horsley. Hammond's explanation of this clause is as follows. He observes, that the Hebrew word רעה, *raäh,* means to give the sheep pasture, or to look to them when they are feeding, Gen. xxix. 7, and xxx. 32; and that this feeding of sheep is very different from feeding on them. He farther observes, that the word is frequently used for *ruling* or *governing.* "In this place," says he, "the metaphor of sheep must needs rule the signification of it. As sheep are put into a pasture, there to continue together in a common place, so men are put into שאול, ᾅδης, the state of the dead, mentioned in the former words, and to that regularly follows—Death ירעם, [shall feed them,]—is as the shepherd that conducts or leads them into this pasture, those Elysian fields:—an excellent piece of divine poesy, to signify, how men like sheep, like beasts, go by flocks and herds out of this life, or more plainly, that men die as ordinarily and regularly as sheep are led to their pasture." Some, however, read, "Death feedeth upon them." "רעה signifies not only *to feed,* but *to feed upon* and lay waste; and thus we render it in Micah v. 6, 'They shall waste Assyria with the sword.'

The entire world might not seem vast enough for men of a haughty spirit. They are so swollen with their vain imaginations, that they would engross universal nature to themselves. But the Psalmist, finding the wicked spread as it were far and wide, in the boundless pride of their hearts, collects them together into the grave, and hands them over to death as their shepherd. He intimates, that whatever superiority they might affect over their fellow-creatures, they would feel, when too late, that their boasting was vain, and be forced to yield themselves up to the irresistible and humiliating stroke of death. In the second part of the verse, the Psalmist points out the very different fate which awaits the children of God, and thus anticipates an obvious objection. It might be said, " Thou tellest us that those who place their confidence in this world must die. But this is no new doctrine. And why convert into matter of reproach what must be considered as a law of nature, attaching to all mankind? Who gave thee a privilege to insult the children of mortality? Art thou not one of them thyself?" This objection he meets effectually, by granting that on the supposition of death being the destruction of the whole man, he would have advanced no new or important doctrine, but arguing that infidel worldlings reject a better life to come, and thus lay themselves justly open to this species of reprehension. For surely it is the height of folly in any man for a mere momentary happiness—a very dream—to abdicate the crown of heaven, and renounce his hopes for eternity. Here

---

See also Psalm lxxx. 14."—Appendix to the Notes in Merrick's version, No. 4, p. 304. This verb also signifies *to feed upon* in Isa. xliv. 20, and Hosea xii. 2. Fry's translation is,

> " They are set apart like sheep for Hades ;
> Death feedeth upon them, and they go down to them ;"

and he thinks that the idea here is, that Death and Hades are the two monsters for whose consumption the flock is destined. This is a personification which we frequently meet with in the Latin poets. Cerberus is often represented by them as feasting on the bodies of men in the grave. Thus, notwithstanding the strong desires which worldly men have for immortality in this world, they shall become the victims of the grave, and the prey of death.

it must be apparent, as I already took occasion to observe, that the doctrine of this psalm is very different from that taught by the philosophers. I grant that they may have ridiculed worldly ambition with elegance and eloquence, exposed the other vices, and insisted upon the topics of our frailty and mortality; but they uniformly omitted to state the most important truth of all, that God governs the world by his providence, and that we may expect a happy issue out of our calamities, by coming to that everlasting inheritance which awaits us in heaven. It may be asked, what that dominion is which the upright shall eventually obtain? I would reply, that as the wicked must all be prostrated before the Lord Jesus Christ, and made his footstool, His members will share in the victory of their Head. It is indeed said, that he "will deliver up the kingdom to God, even the Father," but he will not do this that he may put an end to his Church, but "that God may be all in all," (1 Cor. xv. 24.) It is stated that this will be *in the morning* [1]—a beautiful and striking metaphor. Surrounded as we are by darkness, our life is here compared to the night, or to a sleep, an image which is specially applicable to the ungodly, who lie as it were in a deep slumber, but not inapplicable to the people of God, such being the dark mist which rests upon all things in this world, that even their minds (except in so far as they are illuminated from above) are partially enveloped in it. Here " we see only as through a glass darkly," and the coming of the Lord will resemble the morning, when both the elect and reprobate will awake. The former will then cast aside their lethargy and sloth, and being freed from the darkness which rested upon them, will behold Christ the Sun of Righteousness face to face, and the full effulgence of life which resides in him. The others, who lie at present in a state of total darkness, will be aroused from their stupidity, and begin to discover a new life, of which they had previously no apprehension. We need to be reminded of this event, not only

---

[1] *In the morning*, that is, says Dathe, *in the time of judgment*. He thinks there is here an allusion to the usual time of holding courts of justice, which was in the morning. See Psalm lxxiii. 14, and ci. 8; and Jer. xxi. 12.

because corruption presses us downwards and obscures our faith, but because there are men who profanely argue against another life, from the continued course of things in the world, scoffing, as Peter foretold, (2 Eph. iii. 4,) at the promise of a resurrection, and pointing, in derision, to the unvarying regularity of nature throughout the lapse of ages. We may arm ourselves against their arguments by what the Psalmist here declares, that, sunk as the world is in darkness, there will dawn ere long a new morning, which will introduce us to a better and an eternal existence. It follows, that *their strength*, or *their form*,[1] (for the Hebrew word צוּרָה, *tsurah*, is susceptible of either meaning,) *shall wax old.* If we read *strength*, the words intimate, that though at present they are in possession of wealth and power, they shall speedily decline and fall; but I see no objection to the other meaning, which has more commonly been adopted. Paul tells us, (1 Cor. vii. 31,) that " the *fashion* of this world passes away," a term expressive of the evanescent nature of our earthly condition; and the Psalmist may be considered as comparing their vain and unsubstantial glory to a shadow. The words at the close of the verse are obscure. Some read, *The grave is their dwelling;* and then they make מ, *mem*, the formative letter of a noun. But the other interpretation agrees better both with the words and scope of the psalm, that *the grave awaits them from his dwelling,* which is put for *their dwelling;* such a change of number being common in the Hebrew language. They reside at present in splendid mansions, where they rest in apparent security, but we are reminded that they must soon come out of them, and be received into the tomb. There may be a covert allusion to their goings abroad to places of public resort with gaiety and pomp. These, the Psalmist

---

[1] The LXX. read, 'Η βοήθεια αὐτῶν, *their help*, conceiving the word צוּרָם, *tsuram*, to be derived from צור, *tsur*, *a rock*, and metaphorically, *confidence, aid.* Ainsworth reads, "their form," *their figure, shape,* or *image*, *with all their beauty and proportion;* or " their rock," that is, *their strength.* "The Hebrew *tsur*," says he, "is usually *a rock;* here it seemeth to be all one with *tsurah*, *a form* or *figure;* and this is confirmed by the writing, for though by the vowels and reading it is *tsur*, yet, by the letters, it is *tsir*, which is an *image*, Isa. xlv. 16."

intimates, must give place to the sad procession by which they must be carried down to the grave.

15. *But God will redeem my soul.* The Hebrew particle, אך, *ach*, may be also translated, *surely*, or *certainly*. The Psalmist had made a general assertion of the great truth, that the righteous shall have dominion in the morning, and now he applies it to himself for the confirmation of his own faith. This verse may, therefore, be regarded as a kind of appendix to the former; in it he makes a personal application of what had been said of all the righteous. By the word, *the hand*, is to be understood *the dominion* and *power*, and not *the stroke*, of the grave, as some have rendered it. The prophet does not deny his liability to death; but he looks to God as He who would defend and redeem him from it. We have here a convincing proof of that faith in which the saints under the Law lived and died. It is evident that their views were directed to another and a higher life, to which the present was only preparatory. Had the prophet merely intended to intimate that he expected deliverance from some ordinary emergency, this would have been no more than what is frequently done by the children of the world, whom God often delivers from great dangers. But here it is evident that he hoped for a life beyond the grave, that he extended his glance beyond this sublunary sphere, and anticipated the morning which will introduce eternity. From this we may conclude, that the promises of the Law were spiritual, and that our fathers who embraced them were willing to confess themselves pilgrims upon earth, and sought an inheritance in heaven. It evinced gross stupidity in the Sadducees, educated as they were under the Law, to conceive of the soul as mortal. The man must be blind indeed who can find no mention of a future life in this passage. To what other interpretation can we wrest the preceding verse, when it speaks of a morning altogether new and peculiar? We are sufficiently accustomed to see the return of morning, but it points us to a day of an extraordinary kind, when God himself shall rise upon us as the sun, and surprise us with the discovery of his glory. When the Psalmist adds, *Assuredly God will redeem*

my soul[1] *from the power of the grave*, does he not contemplate a special privilege, such as could not be shared by all other men? If deliverance from death, then, be a privilege peculiar to the children of God, it is evident that they are expectants of a better life. We must not overlook, (what I have already noticed,) that the sure method of profiting by the divine promises is, to apply to ourselves what God has offered generally to all without exception. This is done by the prophet, for how could he have arrived at an assured promise of the redemption of his soul, except by the general fact known to him of the future glory awaiting the children of God, and by concluding himself to be amongst their number? The last clause of the verse runs in the Hebrew literally, *for he will take me up*. Some, however, resolve the causal particle כִּי, *ki*, which we render *for*, into the adverb of time *when*, and the verb לָקַח, *lakach*, which we translate *to receive* or *to take up*, they translate *to cut off*, or *take away from this world*, giving to the passage this sense, When God shall have called my soul out of this world to himself, he will rescue it from the power of the grave. I am afraid that this is rather too strained an interpretation. Those seem to take a juster view of the words who consider that the future tense has been substituted for the perfect, and who retain the proper signification of the causal particle, reading, *for he has taken me up*. The prophet did not consider that the ground of his hope for a better resurrection was to be found in himself, but in the gratuitous adoption of God who had taken him into his favour. There is no need, however, why we should suppose a change of tense, and not understand the Psalmist as meaning that God would redeem his soul from death, by undertaking the guardianship of it when he came to die. The despairing fears which so many entertain when descending to the grave spring from the fact of their not commending their spirit to the preserving care of God. They do not consider it in the light of a precious

---

[1] *Soul* is not here to be understood of the intellectual immaterial spirit. The Hebrew word נַפְשִׁי, *naphshi*, *my soul*, is often put in the Old Testament Scriptures for the personal pronoun; and thus it means *my person, myself, me.*—See Appendix, Note on Psalm xvi. 10.

deposit which will be safe in his protecting hands. Let our faith be established in the great truth, that our soul, though it appears to evanish upon its separation from the body, is in reality only gathered to the bosom of God, there to be kept until the day of the resurrection.

> 16. *Be not thou afraid when one shall be made rich, when the glory of his house shall be increased;*
> 17. *For when he dieth he shall not carry all away: his glory shall not descend after him:*
> 18. *For he will bless his soul in his lifetime, and they shall praise thee when thou doest well to thyself.*[1]
> 19. *He shall come but to the age of his fathers, and will not see the light even for ever.*
> 20. *Man is in honour, and will not understand: he is like the beasts: they shall perish.*

16. *Be not thou afraid.* The Psalmist repeats, in the form of an exhortation, the same sentiment which he had formerly expressed, that the children of God have no reason to dread the wealth and power of their enemies, or to envy their evanescent prosperity; and as the best preservative against despondency, he would have them to direct their eyes habitually to the end of life. The effect of such a contemplation will be at once to check any impatience we might be apt to feel under our short-lived miseries, and to raise our minds in holy contempt above the boasted but delusory grandeur of the wicked. That this may not impose upon our minds, the prophet recalls us to the consideration of the subject of death—that event which is immediately at hand, and which no sooner arrives than it strips them of their false glory, and consigns them to the tomb. So much is implied in the words, *He shall not carry away all these things when he dieth.*[2] Be their lives ever so illustrious in the eyes of their fellow-creatures, this glory is necessarily bounded by the present

---

[1] French and Skinner read, " Yea, though men praise thee when thou indulgest thyself;" and they explain *men* to mean " parasites and flatterers," and " indulgest thyself" as meaning, "indulgest thyself in unrestrained luxury."

[2] " Heb. ' take of all;' that is, ought of all that he hath. ' For we brought nothing into the world, and it is certain that we can carry nothing out.'"—*Ainsworth.*

world. The same truth is further asserted in the succeeding clause of the verse, *His glory shall not descend after him.* Infatuated men may strain every nerve, as if in defiance of the very laws of nature, to perpetuate their glory after death, but they never can escape the corruption and nakedness of the tomb; for, in the language of the poet Juvenal,—

" Mors sola fatetur
Quantula sint hominum corpuscula,"—

" It is death which forces us to confess how worthless the bodies of men are."

18. *For he will bless his soul in his lifetime.* Various meanings have been attached to this verse. Some read, *He ought to have blessed his soul during his life.* Others apply the first clause of the verse to the wicked, while they refer the second to believers, who are in the habit of praising God for all his benefits. Others understand the whole verse as descriptive of believers, but without sufficient ground. There can be little doubt that the reference is to the children of the world. In the first part of the verse it is said that *they bless their own soul*[1] so long as they live on earth, by which is meant, that they indulge and pamper themselves with earthly pleasures, giving way to the excesses of brutish intemperance, like the rich man, of whom Christ spoke in the parable, who said, " Soul, thou hast much goods laid up for many years, take thine ease, eat, drink, and be merry," (Luke xii. 19;) or that they seek their happiness entirely from this world, without cherishing a desire for the life that is to come. Some translate the Hebrew verb, *he will do good,* and read thus, *He will do good to his own soul in his lifetime.* But I conceive the phrase to be synonymous in its import with that which is employed by Moses, (Deut. xxix. 19,) " And it come to pass, that he bless himself in his heart;" that is, flatter himself as if he might despise God with impunity. The inspired penman here represents the stupidity of such as please themselves with a fallacious dream of happiness. In the latter part of the verse the person is changed, and the votary of pleasure is apostro-

[1] That is, themselves.—See note, p. 252.

phized;[1] the prophet insinuating, by the words he uses, that the preposterous pride with which the wicked are inflamed is in part the consequence of the delusive applause of the world, which pronounces them to be happy, and echoes their praises even when they gratify their most unlicensed passions.

19. *He shall come to the age of his fathers.* He proceeds to show how false are the flatteries by which the wicked deceive themselves, and are deceived by others. Be they ever so intoxicated with the praises of the world, or with their own vain imaginations, yet they cannot live beyond the age of their fathers; and, granting their life to be extended to the longest term, it can never stretch into eternity. Others understand the expression as synonymous with *their being gathered to the tomb along with their fathers* who have gone before them; as in Scripture death is usually called "The way of all the earth." The Psalmist, a little above, had spoken of their being gathered together in the grave as sheep in a fold. According to this view, the meaning of the passage is, that having never aspired after heaven, but having been sunk in the low grovelling pursuits of this world, they would come at last to the same fate with their fathers. When it is added, *They shall not see the light even for ever*, we are to understand their consignment to everlasting darkness.[2] In my opinion, both clauses of the verse combine to express the same truth, That however they may flatter and deceive themselves, they cannot prolong their life beyond the common term of mortality. As either interpretation, however, agrees with the general scope of the psalm, the reader may choose for himself.

[1] "There is here a change," says Walford, "from the oblique to the direct form of speech, by which the writer turns himself to the rich man, who prospers in the world, and says to him, Though you now count yourself happy, and meet with applause from persons of a character resembling your own, yet you shall go to the abode of your fathers, who will never behold the light." He reads the 19th verse, "Thou shalt go to the abode of thy fathers, who will never behold the light."

[2] Horsley reads, "To all eternity they shall not see light;" "that light," says he, "which emphatically deserves the name—that light, of which created light is but a faint image; the light of God's glory. He shall have no share in the beatific vision."

Should the latter be adopted, the words in the close of the verse are to be considered as asserting that the ungodly can only enjoy the light of life for a short period, as they have no hope of another existence beyond the grave. We are taught by the Psalmist, in the words which have been under our consideration, to beware of flattering ourselves in the possessions of this world, and to be principally anxious for the attainment of that happiness which is reserved for us in heaven. We are also warned not to allow ourselves to be carried away by the erring influence of worldly applause. Even heathen authors have taught us the same lesson. Thus the poet Persius says,—

> " Non si quid turbida Roma
> Elevet, accedas, examenve improbum in illa
> Castiges trutina : nec te quæsiveris extra,"—

"If Rome, a city full of commotions, exalt or despise any thing, beware of being satisfied with its weight or balance; that is to say, of stopping at its judgment; and do not look to what others say of you, but enter into thyself, and examine what thou art."[1] But the disposition to be deceived by flattery is one so strongly marked in our nature, as to require that we should attend to the weightier admonition of one who was inspired.

20. *Man is in honour, and will not understand.*[2] Here the prophet, that he may not be understood as having represented the present life, which in itself is a singular blessing of God, as wholly contemptible, corrects himself as it were, or qualifies his former statements by a single word, importing that those whom he reprehends have reduced themselves to the level of

---

[1] This is the translation which is given of these lines in the French version.
[2] This verse is precisely the same as the 12th, with the exception of one word. Instead of בל־ילין, *bal-yalin, will not lodge*, in the 12th verse, we have here ולא יבין, *velo yabin, and will not understand*. But the Septuagint and Syriac versions read in the 12th verse as here, " understands not." Houbigant thinks that this is the true reading of the 12th verse. "The very repetition," says he, " proves that it is to be so read. Besides, as the Psalmist immediately subjoins, *They are like brute creatures*, it is sufficiently evident that the reason why men are said to be like the beasts is, because they do not *understand*, and not because *they do not continue in honour*, since *honour* does not belong to the brute creation."

the beasts that perish, by senselessly devouring the blessings which God has bestowed, and thus divesting themselves of that honour which God had put upon them. It is against the abuse of this world that the prophet has been directing his censures. They are aimed at those who riot in the bounties of God without any recognition of God himself, and who devote themselves in an infatuated manner to the passing glory of this world, instead of rising from it to the contemplation of the things which are above.

PSALM L.

There have always been hypocrites in the Church, men who have placed religion in a mere observance of outward ceremonies, and among the Jews there were many who turned their attention entirely to the figures of the Law, without regarding the truth which was represented under them. They conceived that nothing more was demanded of them but their sacrifices and other rites. The following psalm is occupied with the reprehension of this gross error, and the prophet exposes in severe terms the dishonour which is cast upon the name of God by confounding ceremony with religion, showing that the worship of God is spiritual, and consists of two parts, prayer and thanksgiving.

¶ *A Song of Asaph.*[1]

The prophet holds up the ingratitude of such persons to our reprobation, as proving themselves unworthy of the honour which has been

---

[1] The preposition ל, *lamed*, prefixed to the name of Asaph, which Calvin renders *of*, may also be rendered *for*, as we have before observed, and it is, therefore, somewhat doubtful whether he was the author of the psalms in whose inscriptions his name appears, or whether they were merely delivered to him by David to be sung in the temple worship. We, however, know from 2 Chron. xxix. 30, that a seer of the name of Asaph, the son of Berechia, and who, along with his sons, were appointed singers in the sacred services of the temple, (1 Chron. vi. 31, 39; xv. 19; xxv. 1, 2; Neh. xii. 46,) was the inspired writer of several psalms. It is therefore probable that he was the author of the psalms which bear his name. These are twelve, the 50th, and from the 73d to the 83d, both inclusive. It has been thought by some that these psalms differ very remarkably, both in style and subject, from those of David, the composition being more stiff and obscure than the polished, flowing, and graceful odes of the sweet singer of Israel, and the subject-matter being of a melancholy character, and full of reprehension.

placed upon them, and debasing themselves by a degenerate use of this world. From this let us learn, that if we are miserable here, it must be by our own fault; for could we discern and properly improve the many mercies which God has bestowed upon us, we would not want, even on earth, a foretaste of eternal blessedness. Of this, however, we fall short through our corruption. The wicked, even while on earth, have a pre-eminency over the beasts of the field in reason and intelligence, which form a part of the image of God; but in reference to the end which awaits them the prophet puts both upon a level, and declares, that being divested of all their vain-glory, they will eventually perish like the beasts. Their souls will indeed survive, but it is not the less true that death will consign them to everlasting disgrace.

1. *The God of gods, even Jehovah, hath spoken, and called the earth*[1] *from the rising of the sun unto the going down thereof.*
2. *Out of Zion, the perfection of beauty, God hath shined.*
3. *Our God shall come, and shall not keep silence; a fire shall devour before him, and it shall be very tempestuous round about him.*
4. *He shall call to the heavens from above, and to the earth, to judge his people.*
5. *Gather my meek ones (will he say*[2]*) together unto me, those who strike a covenant with me over sacrifices.*

1. *The God of gods, even Jehovah,*[3] *hath spoken.* The inscription of this psalm bears the name of Asaph; but whether he was the author of it, or merely received it as chief singer from the hand of David, cannot be known. This, however,

---

[1] That is, the inhabitants of the earth.
[2] ("Dira-il.")—*Fr.*
[3] The original words here rendered "The God of gods, even Jehovah," are אל אלהים יהוה, *El Elohim Yehovah.* Each of these words is a name of the Divine Being. The first has reference to the power of the Deity; so that it might be translated, "The Mighty One." If we read אל אלהים, *El Elohim,* together, and translate "The God of gods," this is a Hebrewism for "Most mighty God;" the word אלהים, *Elohim,* being placed after the name of any thing to express its excellency, greatness, or might. See p. 7, note 1, of this volume. Comp. Deut. x. 17; Joshua xxii. 22; and Daniel xi. 36. Horsley reads, "The omnipotent God Jehovah hath spoken." The reading of the Chaldee is, "The mighty One, the God Jehovah." The prophet has here joined together these three names of God, to give to the Israelites a more impressive idea of the greatness of Him who, now seated on his throne, and surrounded with awful majesty, was about to plead his controversy with them.

is a matter of little consequence. The opinion has been very generally entertained, that the psalm points to the period of the Church's renovation, and that the design of the prophet is to apprise the Jews of the coming abrogation of their figurative worship under the Law. That the Jews were subjected to the rudiments of the world, which continued till the Church's majority, and the arrival of what the apostle calls "the fulness of times," (Gal. iv. 4,) admits of no doubt; the only question is, whether the prophet must here be considered as addressing the men of his own age, and simply condemning the abuse and corruption of the legal worship, or as predicting the future kingdom of Christ? From the scope of the psalm, it is sufficiently apparent that the prophet does in fact interpret the Law to his contemporaries, with a view of showing them that the ceremonies, while they existed, were of no importance whatever by themselves, or otherwise than connected with a higher meaning. Is it objected, that God never called the whole world except upon the promulgation of the Gospel, and that the doctrine of the Law was addressed only to one peculiar people? the answer is obvious, that the prophet in this place describes the whole world as convened not for the purpose of receiving one common system of faith, but of hearing God plead his cause with the Jews in its presence. The appeal is of a parallel nature with others which we find in Scripture: "Give ear, O ye heavens! and I will speak; and hear, O earth! the words of my mouth," (Deut. xxxii. 1;) or as in another place, "I call heaven and earth to record this day against you, that I have set before you life and death," (Deut. xxx. 19;) and again Isaiah, "Hear, O heaven! and give ear, O earth! for the Lord hath spoken," (Isa. i. 2.)[1]

---

[1] "The Targum, Kimchi, and R. Obediah Gaon, interpret this psalm of the day of judgment, and Jarchi takes it to be a prophecy of the redemption by their future Messiah."—*Dr Gill.* Dr Adam Clarke explains it in the first of these senses; observing, that "to any minor consideration or fact it seems impossible with any propriety to restrain it." It appears, however, as Calvin holds, to be rather the aim and intention of the poem to teach the utter uselessness of all outward ceremonies in the absence of inward piety; and it is constructed on the plan of a dramatic performance, the sole actor being Jehovah seated on his throne in Zion, and the audi-

This vehement mode of address was required in speaking to hypocrites, that they might be roused from their complacent security, and their serious attention engaged to the message of God. The Jews had special need to be awakened upon the point to which reference is here made. Men are naturally disposed to outward show in religion, and, measuring God by themselves, imagine that an attention to ceremonies constitutes the sum of their duty. There was a strong disposition among the Jews to rest in an observance of the figures of the Law, and it is well known with what severity the prophets all along reprehended this superstition, by which the worst and most abandoned characters were led to arrogate a claim to piety, and hide their abominations under the specious garb of godliness. The prophet, therefore, required to do more than simply expose the defective nature of that worship which withdraws the attention of men from faith and holiness of heart to outward ceremonies; it was necessary that, in order to check false confidence and banish insensibility, he should adopt the style of severe reproof. God is here represented as citing all the nations of the earth to his tribunal, not with the view of prescribing the rule of piety to an assembled world, or collecting a church for his service, but with the design of alarming the hypocrite, and terrifying him out of his self-complacency. It would serve as a spur to conviction, thus to be made aware that the whole world was summoned as a witness to their dissimulation, and that they would be stripped of that pretended piety of which they were disposed to boast. It is with a similar object that he addresses Jehovah as *the God of gods*,

---

ence being the whole world, who are summoned to be witnesses of the judgment which he is to execute upon his people. This is the view taken by Bishop Lowth in his Lectures on Sacred Poetry, vol. ii. p. 235. Walford gives the same interpretation. "To interpret this passage," says he, " of the promulgation of the Gospel, as is done by Bishop Horne and other expositors of this book, is for the sake of a favourite theory to confound things that are distinct, and to throw obscurity over the whole, by which its specific design is darkened, and the poem deprived of its consistency and unity. The great purpose of the psalm is to deliver the judgment of God respecting the Jewish people ; and heaven and earth are summoned, as in Isaiah i. 2, to behold the righteousness of Jehovah, and bear their testimony to it."

to possess their minds with a salutary terror, and dissuade them from their vain attempts to elude his knowledge. That this is his design will be made still more apparent from the remaining context, where we are presented with a formidable description of the majesty of God, intended to convince the hypocrite of the vanity of those childish trifles with which he would evade the scrutiny of so great and so strict a judge.

To obviate an objection which might be raised against his doctrine in this psalm, that it was subversive of the worship prescribed by Moses, the prophet intimates that this judgment which he announced would be in harmony with the Law. When God speaks *out of Zion* he necessarily sanctions the authority of the Law; and the Prophets, when at any time they make use of this form of speech, declare themselves to be interpreters of the Law. That holy mountain was not chosen of man's caprice, and therefore stands identified with the Law. The prophet thus cuts off any pretext which the Jews might allege to evade his doctrine, by announcing that such as concealed their wickedness, under the specious covert of ceremonies, would not be condemned of God by any new code of religion, but by that which was ministered originally by Moses. He gives Zion the honourable name of *the perfection of beauty*, because God had chosen it for his sanctuary, the place where his name should be invoked, and where his glory should be manifested in the doctrine of the Law.

3. *Our God shall come, and shall not keep silence.*[1] He repeats that God would come, in order to confirm his doctrine, and more effectually arouse them. He would come, and should not always keep silence, lest they should be encouraged to presume upon his forbearance. Two reasons may be assigned why the prophet calls God *our God*. He may be considered as setting himself, and the comparatively small number of the true fearers of the Lord, in opposition to the hypocrites whom he abhors, claiming God to be his

[1] This negative form of expression is employed to give greater emphasis.

God, and not theirs, as they were disposed to boast; or rather, he speaks as one of the people, and declares that the God who was coming to avenge the corruptions of his worship was the same God whom all the children of Abraham professed to serve. He who shall come, as if he had said, is our God, the same in whom we glory, who established his covenant with Abraham, and gave us his Law by the hand of Moses. He adds, that God would come with *fire* and *tempest*, in order to awaken a salutary fear in the secure hearts of the Jews, that they might learn to tremble at the judgments of God, which they had hitherto regarded with indifference and despised, and in allusion to the awful manifestation which God made of himself from Sinai, (Exod. xix. 16; see also Heb. xii. 18.) The air upon that occasion resounded with thunders and the noise of trumpets, the heavens were illuminated with lightnings, and the mountain was in flames, it being the design of God to procure a reverential submission to the Law which he announced. And it is here intimated, that God would make a similarly terrific display of his power, in coming to avenge the gross abuses of his holy religion.

4. *He shall call to the heavens from above.* It is plain from this verse for what purpose God, as he had already announced, would call upon the earth. This was to witness the settlement of his controversy with his own people the Jews, against whom judgment was to be pronounced, not in the ordinary manner as by his prophets, but with great solemnity before the whole world. The prophet warns the hypocritical that they must prepare to be driven from their hiding-place, that their cause would be decided in the presence of men and angels, and that they would be dragged without excuse before that dreadful assembly. It may be asked, why the prophet represents the true fearers of the Lord as cited to his bar, when it is evident that the remonstrance which follows in the psalm is addressed to the hypocritical and degenerate portion of the Jews? To this I answer, that God here speaks of the whole Church, for though a great part of the race of Abra-

ham had declined from the piety of their ancestors, yet he has a respect to the Jewish Church, as being his own institution. He speaks of them as *his meek ones,* to remind them of what they ought to be in consistency with their calling, and not as if they were all without exception patterns of godliness. The form of the address conveys a rebuke to those amongst them whose real character was far from corresponding with their profession. Others have suggested a more refined interpretation, as if the meaning were, Separate the small number of my sincere worshippers from the promiscuous multitude by whom my name is profaned, lest they too should afterwards be seduced to a vain religion of outward form. I do not deny that this agrees with the scope of the prophet. But I see no reason why a church, however universally corrupted, provided it contain a few godly members, should not be denominated, in honour of this remnant, the holy people of God. Interpreters have differed upon the last clause of the verse: *Those who strike a covenant with me over sacrifices.* Some think *over* is put for *besides,* or *beyond,* and that God commends his true servants for this, that they acknowledged something more to be required in his covenant than an observance of outward ceremonies, and were not chargeable with resting in the carnal figures of the Law.[1] Others think that the spiritual and true worship of God is here directly opposed to sacrifices; as if it had been said, Those who, instead of sacrifices, keep my covenant in the right and appointed manner, by yielding to me the sincere homage of their heart. But in my opinion, the prophet is here to be viewed as pointing out with commendation the true and genuine use of the legal worship; for it was of the utmost consequence that it should be known what was the real end for which God appointed sacrifices under the Law. The prophet here declares that sacrifices were of no value whatever except as seals of God's covenant, an interpretative

---

[1] In Luther's German translation of the Bible this verse is rendered,

" Gather me mine holy ones,
That regard the covenant more than offering."

handwriting of submission to it, or in general as means employed for ratifying it. There is an allusion to the custom then universally prevalent of interposing sacrifices, that covenants might be made more solemn, and be more religiously observed.[1] In like manner, the design with which sacrifices were instituted by God was to bind his people more closely to himself, and to ratify and confirm his covenant. The passage is well worthy of our particular notice, as defining those who are to be considered the true members of the Church. They are such, on the one hand, as are characterised by the spirit of meekness, practising righteousness in their intercourse with the world; and such, on the other, as close in the exercise of a genuine faith with the covenant of adoption which God has proposed to them. This forms the true worship of God, as he has himself delivered it to us from heaven; and those who decline from it, whatever pretensions they may make to be considered a church of God, are excommunicated from it by the Holy Spirit. As to sacrifices or other ceremonies, they are of no value, except in so far as they seal to us the pure truth of God. All such rites, consequently, as have no foundation in the word of God, are unauthorised, and that worship which has not a distinct reference to the word is but a corruption of things sacred.

[1] The manner in which covenants were anciently ratified by sacrifices was this: The victim was cut into two parts, and each half was placed upon an altar. The contracting parties then passed between the pieces, which was a kind of imprecation upon the party who should violate the covenant, being as much as to say, May he or they be cut asunder like that dissected victim. In this manner, the covenant which God made with Abraham and his family was ratified, Gen. xv. 9, 17, 18. This awful ceremony was also observed by God's ancient people at the renovation of the covenant, as appears from Jer. xxxiv. 18. See also a covenant between God and his people with sacrifices in Exod. xxiv. 4-8. This explains the phrase here used, which is literally, "Those who *have cut* a covenant with me by sacrifice," the verb being from כרת, *carath, he cut.* The same mode of ratifying covenants prevailed among some of the heathen nations, as appears from the allusions made to it by Homer and Virgil, Iliad, lib. xix. 1. 260; Æneid, lib. xii. l. 292.

6. *And the heavens shall declare his righteousness : for God is judge himself. Selah.*
7. *Hear, O my people! and I will speak ; O Israel! and I will announce to thee : I am God, even thy God.*
8. *I will not reprove thee for thy sacrifices, and thy burnt-offerings are continually before me.*
9. *I will take no calf out of thy house, nor he-goats out of thy folds.*
10. *For every beast of the forest is mine, and the cattle upon a thousand hills.*
11. *I know all the fowls of the mountains ; and the wild beasts of the field are at my command.*
12. *If I am hungry, I will not tell thee : for the world is mine, and the fulness thereof.*
13. *Will I eat the flesh of bulls,*[1] *and drink the blood of goats?*

6. *And the heavens shall declare his righteousness.* The Jews were vain enough to imagine that their idle and fantastic service was the perfection of righteousness; but they are here warned by the prophet, that God, who had seemed to connive at their folly, was about to reveal his own righteousness from heaven, and expose their miserable devices. " Think you," as if he had said, " that God can take delight in the mockery of your deluded services? Though you send up the smoke of them to heaven, God will make known his righteousness in due time from above, and vindicate it from the dishonours done to it by your wicked inventions. The heavens themselves will attest your perfidy in despising true holiness, and corrupting the pure worship of God. He will no longer suffer your gratuitous aspersions of his character, as if he took no notice of the enmity which lurks under your pretended friendship." There is thus a cogency in the prophet's manner of treating his subject. Men are disposed to admit that God is judge, but, at the same time, to fabri-

---

[1] In explanation of this, Martin observes, " Le feu descendu du ciel," &c.; *i.e.,* " The fire which descended from heaven upon the sacrifices was considered mystically as the mouth of God which devoured the flesh of the victims ; and it was on that account that God had expressly forbidden to consume them by fire brought elsewhere, because this *strange fire*, not being that which descended from heaven, could not be regarded mystically as the mouth of God."

cate excuses for evading his judgment, and it was therefore necessary that the sentence which God was about to pronounce should be vindicated from the vain cavils which might be brought against it.

7. *Hear, O my people! and I will speak.* Hitherto the prophet has spoken as the herald of God, throwing out several expressions designed to alarm the minds of those whom he addressed. But from this to the end of the psalm God himself is introduced as the speaker; and to show the importance of the subject, he uses additional terms to awaken attention, calling them his own people, that he might challenge the higher authority to his words, and intimating, that the following address is not of a mere ordinary description, but an expostulation with them for the infraction of his covenant. Some read, *I will testify against thee.* But the reference, as we may gather from the common usage of Scripture, seems rather to be to a discussion of mutual claims. God would remind them of his covenant, and solemnly exact from them, as his chosen people, what was due according to the terms of it. He announces himself to be the God of Israel, that he may recal them to allegiance and subjection, and the repetition of his name is emphatical: as if he had said, When you would have me to submit to your inventions, how far is this audacity from that honour and reverence which belong to me? I am God, and therefore my majesty ought to repress presumption, and make all flesh keep silence when I speak; and among you, to whom I have made myself known as your God, I have still stronger claims to homage.

8. *I will not reprove thee for thy sacrifices, &c.* God now proceeds to state the charge which he adduced against them. He declares, that he attached no value whatsoever to sacrifices in themselves considered. Not that he asserts this rite of the Jews to have been vain and useless, for in that case it never would have been instituted by God; but there is this difference betwixt religious exercises and others, that they can only meet the approbation of God when performed

in their true spirit and meaning. On any other supposition they are deservedly rejected. Similar language we will find employed again and again by the prophets, as I have remarked in other places, and particularly in connection with the fortieth psalm. Mere outward ceremonies being therefore possessed of no value, God repudiates the idea that he had ever insisted upon them as the main thing in religion, or designed that they should be viewed in any other light than as helps to spiritual worship. Thus in Jer. vii. 22, he denies that he had issued any commandment regarding sacrifices; and the prophet Micah says, (chap. vi. 7,) "Will the Lord be pleased with thousands of rams, or with ten thousands of rivers of oil? and what doth the Lord require of thee, but to do justly, and to love mercy?" "I desire mercy," he says in another place, (Hosea vi. 6,) "and not sacrifice." The same doctrine is every where declared by the prophets. I might refer especially to the prophecies of Isaiah, chap. i. 12; lviii. 1, 2; lxvi. 3. The sacrifices of the ungodly are not only represented as worthless and rejected by the Lord, but as peculiarly calculated to provoke his anger. Where a right use has been made of the institution, and they have been observed merely as ceremonies for the confirmation and increase of faith, then they are described as being essentially connected with true religion; but when offered without faith, or, what is still worse, under the impression of their meriting the favour of God for such as continue in their sins, they are reprobated as a mere profanation of divine worship. It is evident, then, what God means when he says, *I will not reprove thee for thy sacrifices;* he looked to something beyond these. The last clause of the verse may be understood as asserting that their burnt-offerings were before the eyes of the Lord to the producing even of satiety and disgust, as we find him saying, (Isa. i. 13,) that they were "an abomination unto him." There are some, however, who consider the negative in the beginning of the verse as applying to both clauses, and that God here declares that he did not design to reckon with them for any want of regularity in the observance of their sacrifices. It has been well suggested by some, that the relative may be understood, *Thy burnt-offerings* WHICH *are continually before me;* as if he had said, According to the Law these are imperative; but I will bring no accusation against you at this time for omitting your sacrifices.[1]

9. *I will take no calf out of thy house.* Two reasons are given in this and the succeeding verses to prove that he cannot set any value upon sacrifices. The first is, that supposing him to depend upon these, he needs not to be indebted for them to man, having all the fulness of the earth at his command; and the second, that he requires neither food nor drink as we do for the support of our infirm natures. Upon the first of these he insists in the ninth and three following verses, where he adverts to his own boundless possessions, that he may show his absolute independence of human offerings. He then points at the wide distinction betwixt himself and man, the latter being dependent for a frail subsistence upon meat and drink, while he is the self-existent One, and communicates life to all beside. There may be nothing new in the truths here laid down by the Psalmist; but, considering the strong propensity we have by nature to form our estimate of God from ourselves, and to degenerate into a carnal worship, they convey a lesson by no means unnecessary, and which contains profound wisdom, that man can never benefit God by any of his services, as we have seen in Ps. xvi. 2, " My goodness extendeth not unto thee." In the second place, God says that he does not require any thing for his own use, but that, as he is sufficient in his own perfection, he has consulted the good of man in all that he has enjoined. We have a passage in Isaiah to a similar effect, (lxvi. 1, 2,) " The heaven is my throne, and the earth is my footstool: where is the house that ye build unto me, and where is the place of my rest? For all these things hath mine hand made." In these words

---

[1] " I do not well see how it (verse 8th) can be translated otherwise than Leusden has done it."—*Dr Lowth.* Leusden translates it thus:—" Non super sacrificia tua arguam te, et holocausta tua coram me *sunt* semper." —*Merrick's Annotations.* Dr Adam Clarke explains the verse as follows: —" I do not mean to find fault with you for not offering sacrifices; you have offered them; they *have been continually before me;* but you have not offered them in the proper way."

God asserts his absolute independence; for while the world had a beginning, he himself was from eternity. From this it follows, that as he subsisted when there was nothing without him which could contribute to his fulness, he must have in himself a glorious all-sufficiency.

> 14. *Sacrifice unto God praise,*[1] *and pay thy vows*[2] *unto the Most High.*
> 15. *And call upon me in the day of trouble; I will deliver thee, and thou shalt glorify me.*

These verses cast light upon the preceding context. Had it been stated in unqualified terms that sacrifices were of no value, we might have been perplexed to know why in that case they were instituted by God; but the difficulty disappears when we perceive that they are spoken of only in comparison with the true worship of God. From this we infer, that when properly observed, they were far from incurring divine condemnation. There is in all men by nature a strong and ineffaceable conviction that they ought to worship God. Indisposed to worship him in a pure and spiritual manner, it becomes necessary that they should invent some specious appearance as a substitute; and however clearly they may be persuaded of the vanity of such conduct, they persist in it to the last, because they shrink from a total renunciation of the service of God. Men have always, accordingly, been found addicted to ceremonies until they have been brought to the knowledge of that which constitutes true and acceptable religion. *Praise* and *prayer* are here to be considered as representing the whole of the worship of God, according to the figure synecdoche. The Psalmist specifies only one part of divine worship, when he enjoins us to acknowledge God as the Author of all our mercies, and to

---

[1] Dr Adam Clarke reads, "Sacrifice unto God the thank-offering;" and observes, that "תודה, *todah*, *the thank-offering*, was the same as the *sin-offering*, viz., 'a bullock or a ram without blemish;' only there was in addition, 'unleavened cakes mingled with oil, and unleavened wafers anointed with oil, and cakes of fine flour mingled with oil and fried,'" (Lev. vii. 12.)

[2] The same author translates נדריך, *nedareyca*, "*thy vow-offerings.* The *nedar*, or *vow-offering*, was a male without blemish taken from among the beeves, the sheep, or the goats. Comp. Lev. xxii. 19, with verse 22."

ascribe to him the praise which is justly due unto his name: and adds, that we should betake ourselves to his goodness, cast all our cares into his bosom, and seek by prayer that deliverance which he alone can give, and thanks for which must afterwards be rendered to him. Faith, self-denial, a holy life, and patient endurance of the cross, are all sacrifices which please God. But as *prayer* is the offspring of faith, and uniformly accompanied with patience and mortification of sin, while *praise*, where it is genuine, indicates holiness of heart, we need not wonder that these two points of worship should here be employed to represent the whole. Praise and prayer are set in opposition to ceremonies and mere external observances of religion, to teach us, that the worship of God is spiritual. Praise is first mentioned, and this might seem an inversion of natural order. But in reality it may be ranked first without any violation of propriety. An ascription to God of the honour due unto his name lies at the foundation of all prayer, and application to him as the fountain of goodness is the most elementary exercise of faith. Testimonies of his goodness await us ere yet we are born into the world, and we may therefore be said to owe the debt of gratitude before we are called to the necessity of supplication. Could we suppose men to come into the world in the full exercise of reason and judgment, their first act of spiritual sacrifice should be that of thanksgiving. There is no necessity, however, for exercising our ingenuity in defence of the order here adopted by the Psalmist, it being quite sufficient to hold that he here, in a general and popular manner, describes the spiritual worship of God as consisting in praise, prayer, and thanksgiving. In the injunction here given, to *pay our vows*, there is an allusion to what was in use under the ancient dispensation, as Ps. cxvi. 12, 13, "What shall I render unto the Lord for all his benefits towards me? I will take the cup of salvation, and call upon the name of the Lord." What the words inculcate upon the Lord's people is, in short, gratitude, which they were then in the habit of testifying by solemn sacrifices. But we shall now direct our attention more particularly to the important point of the doctrine which is set before us in this passage. And the first thing deserving our notice is, that the Jews, as well as ourselves, were enjoined to yield a spiritual worship to God. Our Lord, when he taught that this was the only acceptable species of worship, rested his proof upon the one argument, that "God is a spirit," (John iv. 24.) He was no less a spirit, however, under the period of the legal ceremonies than after they were abolished; and must, therefore, have demanded then the same mode of worship which he now enjoins. It is true that he subjected the Jews to the ceremonial yoke, but in this he had a respect to the age of the Church; as afterwards, in the abrogation of it, he had an eye to our advantage. In every essential respect the worship was the same. The distinction was one entirely of outward form, God accommodating himself to their weaker and unripe apprehensions by the rudiments of ceremony, while he has extended a simple form of worship to us who have attained a maturer age since the coming of Christ. In himself there is no alteration. The idea entertained by the Manicheans, that the change of dispensation necessarily inferred a change in God himself, was as absurd as it would be to arrive at a similar conclusion from the periodical alterations of the seasons. These outward rites are, therefore, in themselves of no importance, and acquire it only in so far as they are useful in confirming our faith, so that we may call upon the name of the Lord with a pure heart. The Psalmist, therefore, justly denounces the hypocrites who gloried in their ostentatious services, and declares that they observed them in vain. It may occur to some, that as sacrifices sustained a necessary place under the Law, they could not be warrantably neglected by the Jewish worshipper; but by attending to the scope of the Psalmist, we may easily discover that he does not propose to abrogate them so far as they were helps to piety, but to correct that erroneous view of them, which was fraught with the deepest injury to religion.

In the fifteenth verse we have first an injunction to prayer, then a promise of its being answered, and afterwards a call to thanksgiving. We are enjoined to pray *in the day of trouble*, but not with the understanding that we are to pray only then, for prayer is a duty incumbent upon us every day, and every moment of our lives. Be our situation ever so comfortable and exempt from disquietude, we must never cease to engage in the exercise of supplication, remembering that, if God should withdraw his favour for a moment, we would be undone. In affliction, however, our faith is more severely tried, and there is a propriety in specifying it as the season of prayer; the prophet pointing us to God as the only resort and means of safety in the day of our urgent necessity. A promise is subjoined to animate us in the duty, disposed as we are to be overwhelmed by a sense of the majesty of God, or of our own unworthiness. Gratitude is next enjoined, in consideration of God's answer to our prayers. Invocation of the name of God being represented in this passage as constituting a principal part of divine worship, all who make pretensions to piety will feel how necessary it is to preserve the pure and uncorrupted form of it. We are forcibly taught the detestable nature of the error upon this point entertained by the Papists, who transfer to angels and to men an honour which belongs exclusively to God. They may pretend to view these in no other light than as patrons, who pray for them to God. But it is evident that these patrons are impiously substituted by them in the room of Christ, whose mediation they reject. It is apparent, besides, from the form of their prayers, that they recognise no distinction between God and the very least of their saints. They ask the same things from Saint Claudius which they ask from the Almighty, and offer the prayer of our Lord to the image of Catherine. I am aware that the Papists justify their invocation of the dead, by denying that their prayers to them amount to divine worship. They talk so much about the kind of worship which they call *latria*, that is, the worship which they give to God alone, as to make it appear, that in the invocation of angels and saints they give none of it to them.[1] But it is impossible

[1] The Papists have different words by which they express different degrees of worship. The term λατρεια, or *latria*, they say, denotes the divine worship which exclusively belongs to God, and which they yield to him alone; while δουλεια, or *dulia*, signifies that inferior sort of worship which is due to angels and departed saints, and which alone they yield to them. They have also a third degree, which they call ὑπερδουλεια,

to read the words of the Psalmist, now under our consideration, without perceiving that all true religion is gone unless God alone is called upon. Were the Papists asked whether it were lawful to offer sacrifices to the dead, they would immediately reply in the negative. They grant to this day that sacrifice could not lawfully be offered to Peter or to Paul, for the common sense of mankind would dictate the profanity of such an act. And when we here see God preferring the invocation of his name to all sacrifices, is it not plain to demonstration, that those who call upon the dead are chargeable with the grossest impiety? From this it follows, that the Papists, let them abound as they may in their genuflections before God, rob him of the chief part of his glory when they direct their supplications to the saints.[1] The express mention which is made in these verses of affliction is fitted to comfort the weak and the fearful believer. When God has withdrawn the outward marks of his favour, a doubt is apt to steal into our minds whether he really cares for our salvation. So far is this from being well founded, that adversity is sent to us by God, just to stir us up to seek him and to call upon his name. Nor should we overlook the fact, that our prayers are only acceptable when we offer them in compliance with the commandment of God, and are animated to them by a consideration of the promise which he has extended. The argument which the Papists have drawn from the passage, in support of their multiplied vows,

---

or *hyperdulia*, that superior kind of inferior worship which they yield to the Virgin Mary. These distinctions are had recourse to, merely to evade the charge of idolatry. But if the Papists yield to angels and glorified saints the honour due only to God, it is of little consequence by what name it is called. Besides, the words λατρεια and δουλεια are used indifferently by classic Greek authors, by the Greek fathers, by the Septuagint, and in the New Testament, to express divine worship. In the New Testament, δουλεια frequently denotes divine worship. Thus we read, in 1 Thess. i. 9, " Ye turned to God from idols, δουλευειν τῳ Θεῳ ζῶντι, *to serve* the living God;" and in Gal. iv. 8, it is said of the Galatians in their heathen state, that " ἐδουλευσαν, *they did service* unto them which, by nature, are no gods."—See *Calvin's Institutes*, Book I. chap. xii. sections 2 and 3; *Turretine's Works*, vol. iv., *De Necessaria Secessione Nostra ab Ecclesia Romana*, pp. 50–53; and *M'Gavin's Protestant*, vol. i. No. 42, p. 334.

[1] The subject of the invocation of departed saints is discussed at length in Calvin's Institutes, Book III. chap. xx. sections 21-27.

is idle and unwarrantable. The Psalmist, as we have already hinted, when he enjoins the payment of their vows, refers only to solemn thanksgiving, whereas they trust in their vows as meriting salvation. They contract vows, beside, which have no divine warrant, but, on the contrary, are explicitly condemned by the word of God.

> 16. *But unto the wicked God hath said, What hast thou to do to declare my statutes, or that thou shouldest take my covenant into thy lips?*
> 17. *Also thou hatest correction, and castest my words behind thee.*
> 18. *If thou seest a thief, thou wilt run with him, and thou hast been partaker with adulterers.*
> 19. *Thou puttest forth thy mouth to evil, and thy tongue frameth deceit.*
> 20. *Thou sittest and speakest against thy brother; thou slanderest thine own mother's sons.*

16. *But unto the wicked, &c.* He now proceeds to direct his censures more openly against those whose whole religion lies in an observance of ceremonies, with which they attempt to blind the eyes of God. An exposure is made of the vanity of seeking to shelter impurity of heart and life under a veil of outward services, a lesson which ought to have been received by all with true consent, but which was peculiarly ungrateful to Jewish ears. It has been universally confessed, that the worship of God is pure and acceptable only when it proceeds from a sincere heart. The acknowledgment has been extorted from the poets of the heathen, and it is known that the profligate were wont to be excluded from their temples and from participation in their sacrifices. And yet such is the influence of hypocrisy in choking and obliterating even a sentiment so universally felt as this, that men of the most abandoned character will obtrude themselves into the presence of God, in the confidence of deceiving him with their vain inventions. This may explain the frequency of the warnings which we find in the prophets upon this subject, declaring to the ungodly again and again, that they only aggravate their guilt by assuming the semblance of piety.

Loudly as the Spirit of God has asserted, that a form of godliness, unaccompanied by the grace of faith and repentance, is but a sacrilegious abuse of the name of God; it is yet impossible to drive the Papists out of the devilish delusion, that their idlest services are sanctified by what they call their *final intention.* They grant that none but such as are in a state of grace can possess the *meritum de condigno;*[1] but they maintain that the mere outward acts of devotion, without any accompanying sentiments of the heart, may prepare a person at least for the reception of grace. And thus, if a monk rise from the bed of his adultery to chant a few psalms without one spark of godliness in his breast, or if a whoremonger, a thief, or any foresworn villain, seeks to make reparation for his crimes by mass or pilgrimage, they would be loath to consider this lost labour. By God, on the other hand, such a disjunction of the form from the inward sentiment of devotion is branded as sacrilege. In the passage before us, the Psalmist sets aside and refutes a very common objection which might be urged. Must not, it might be said, those sacrifices be in some respect acceptable to God which are offered up in his honour? He shows that, on the contrary, they entail guilt upon the parties who present them, inasmuch as they lie to God, and profane his holy name. He checks their presumption with the words, *What hast thou to do to declare my statutes?* that is, to pretend that you are one of my people, and that you have a part in my covenant. Now, if God in this manner rejects the whole of that profession of godliness, which is unaccompanied by purity of heart, how shall we expect him to treat the observance of mere ceremonies, which hold quite an inferior place to the declaration of the statutes of God?

[1] " The Schoolmen in that Church, ' the Church of Rome,' spoke of *meritum de congruo,* and *meritum de condigno.* By *meritum de congruo,* ' to which Calvin refers in the concluding part of the sentence,' they meant the value of good works and good dispositions previous to justification, which it was fit or congruous for God to reward by infusing his grace. By *meritum de condigno* they meant the value of good works performed after justification, in consequence of the grace then infused."—*Dr Hill's Lectures in Divinity,* vol. ii. p. 348; see also *Turretine's Theology,* vol. ii. p. 778.

17. *Also thou hatest correction.* Here hypocrites are challenged with treacherous duplicity in denying, by their life and their works, that godliness which they have professed with the lip. Their contempt of God he proves from their want of reverential deference to his Word; subjection to the Word of God, and cordial submission to his precepts and instructions, being the surest test of religious principle. One way in which hypocrisy usually displays itself is, by the ingenious excuses it invents for evading the duty of obedience. The Psalmist points to this as the mainspring of their ungodliness, that they had cast the Word of God behind their back, while he insinuates that the principle from which all true worship flows is the obedience of faith. He adverts also to the cause of their perversity, which lies in the unwillingness of their corrupt heart to suffer the yoke of God. They have no hesitation in granting that whatever proceeds from the mouth of God is both true and right; this honour they are willing to concede to his Word; but in so far as it proposes to regulate their conduct, and restrain their sinful affections, they dislike and detest it. Our corruption, indisposing us to receive correction, exasperates us against the Word of God; nor is it possible that we can ever listen to it with true docility and meekness of mind, till we have been brought to give ourselves up to be ruled and disciplined by its precepts. The Psalmist next proceeds to specify some of those works of ungodliness, informing us that hypocrites, who were addicted to theft and adultery, mixed up and polluted the holy name of God with their wickedness. By adverting only to some species of vices, he would intimate, in general, that those who have despised correction, and hardened themselves against instruction, are prepared to launch into every excess which corrupt desire or evil example may suggest. He makes mention, first, of thefts; then of adulteries; and, thirdly, of calumnies or false reproaches. Most interpreters render תָּרִיץ, *tirets, to run,* although others derive it from רָצָה, *ratsah,* rendering it *to consent.* Either translation agrees sufficiently with the scope of the Psalmist, and the preference may be left to the reader's own choice. The charge here brought against hypocrites, that they *put forth their mouth to evil,* may

include not merely slander, but all the different kinds of speaking which injure their neighbours, for it immediately follows, *thy tongue frameth deceit.* It is well known in what a variety of ways the lying and deceitful tongue may inflict injury and pain. When it is added, *Thou sittest, &c.*, the allusion may be to one who sits for the passing of a formal judgment; as if it had been said, Thou defamest thy brethren under pretext of issuing a just sentence.¹ Or there may be a reference to petty calumny; such as men maliciously indulge in, and in which they pass their time as they sit at ease in their houses.² It seems more probable, however, that he refers to the higher crime of accusing the innocent and righteous in open court, and bringing false charges against them. *Brethren*, and *the children of their mother*,³ are mentioned, the more emphatically to express the cruelty of their calumnies, when they are represented as violating the ties of nature, and not even sparing the nearest relations.

21. *These things hast thou done, and I kept silence; thou thoughtest that I would be like thyself:*⁴ *I will reprove thee, and set them in order before thine eyes.*

---

¹ "תשב. Gejerus and others suppose that this word alludes to the mode of sitting in judgment. See Ps. cxix. 23."—*Dimock's Notes on the Book of Psalms.*
² " When you are sitting still, and have nothing else to do, you are ever injuring your neighbour with your slanderous speech. Your table-talk is abuse of your nearest friends."—*Horsley.* The meaning, according to others, is, Thou sittest in the most public places of resort, which were usually the gates of the city, and spendest thy time in calumniating thy brother. See Ps. lxix. 12; and cxix. 23.
³ " *Thine own mother's son.* To understand the force of this expression, it is necessary to bear in mind that polygamy was allowed amongst the Israelites. Those who were born to the same father were all brethren, but a yet more intimate relationship subsisted between those who had the same mother as well as the same father."—*French and Skinner.* Compare Gen. xx. 12. It was a high aggravation of the wickedness and malignity of the persons here spoken of, that they indulged in abusing with their tongues those to whom they were most nearly related, their brother, yea, the son of their mother.
⁴ Horsley translates these two clauses as follows:—

" These things thou hast done, and I was still;
Thou hast thought that I AM is such an one as thyself."

He thinks that the words חיות אֶהְיֶה, *heyoth ehyeh*, which Calvin renders, " I

22. *Now consider this, ye that forget God: lest I seize upon you, and there be none to deliver.*
23. *Whoso offereth praise will glorify me: and to him that ordereth his way aright will I show the salvation of God.*

21. *These things hast thou done.* Hypocrites, until they feel the hand of God against them, are ever ready to surrender themselves to a state of security, and nothing is more difficult than to awaken their apprehensions. By this alarming language the Psalmist aims at convincing them of the certainty of destruction should they longer presume upon the forbearance of God, and thus provoke his anger the more, by imagining that he can favour the practice of sin. The greatest dishonour which any can cast upon his name is that of impeaching his justice. This hypocrites may not venture to do in an open manner, but in their secret and corrupt imagination they figure God to be different from what he is, that they may take occasion from his conceived forbearance to indulge a false peace of mind, and escape the disquietude which they could not fail to feel were they seriously persuaded that God was the avenger of sin. We have a sufficient proof in the supine security which hypocrites display, that they must have formed such false conceptions of God. They not only exclude from their thoughts his judicial character, but think of him as the patron and approver of their sins. The Psalmist reprehends them for abusing the goodness and clemency of God, in the way of cherishing a vain hope that they may transgress with impunity. He warns them, that ere long they will be dragged into the light, and that those

would be," have been misunderstood by all interpreters, and maintains that they should be rendered, " I AM is." " All interpreters," says he, " seem to have forgotten that אהיה, *ehyeh*, is the name which God takes to himself in the third chapter of Exodus; and he observes, that it is with particular propriety, that God, in expostulating with his people for their breach of covenant, " calls himself by the name by which he was pleased to describe himself to that same people, when he first called them by his servant Moses." The LXX. render היות, *heyoth*, as a noun substantive, and אהיה, *ehyeh*, as the first person future of the substantive verb. " ' Ὑπέλαβες ἀνομίαν, ὅτι ἔσομαί σοι ὅμοιος :" " Thou thoughtest wickedly that I should be like thee."

sins which they would have hidden from the eyes of God would be set in all their enormity before their view. He will set the whole list of their sins in distinct order, for so I understand the expression, *to set in order*, before their view, and force them upon their observation.

22. *Now consider this, ye that forget God.* Here we have more of that severe expostulation which is absolutely necessary in dealing with hardened hypocrites, who otherwise will only deride all instruction. While, however, the Psalmist threatens and intends to alarm them, he would, at the same time, hold out to them the hope of pardon, upon their hastening to avail themselves of it. But to prevent them from giving way to delay, he warns them of the severity, as well as the suddenness, of the divine judgments. He also charges them with base ingratitude, in having forgotten God. And here what a remarkable proof have we of the grace of God in extending the hope of mercy to those corrupt men, who had so impiously profaned his worship, who had so audaciously and sacrilegiously mocked at his forbearance, and who had abandoned themselves to such scandalous crimes! In calling them to repentance, without all doubt he extends to them the hope of God being reconciled to them, that they may venture to appear in the presence of his majesty. And can we conceive of greater clemency than this, thus to invite to himself, and into the bosom of the Church, such perfidious apostates and violators of his covenant, who had departed from the doctrine of godliness in which they had been brought up? Great as it is, we would do well to reflect that it is no greater than what we have ourselves experienced. We, too, had apostatized from the Lord, and in his singular mercy has he brought us again into his fold. It should not escape our notice, that the Psalmist urges them to hasten their return, as the door of mercy will not always stand open for their admission—a needful lesson to us all! lest we allow the day of our merciful visitation to pass by, and be left, like Esau, to indulge in unavailing lamentations, (Gen. xxvii. 34.) So much is implied when it

is said, *God shall seize upon you, and there shall be none to deliver.*[1]

23. *Whoso offereth praise will glorify me.* This is the third time that the Psalmist has inculcated the truth, that the most acceptable sacrifice in God's sight is praise, by which we express to him the gratitude of our hearts for his blessings. The repetition is not a needless one, and that on two accounts. In the first place, there is nothing with which we are more frequently chargeable than forgetfulness of the benefits of the Lord. Scarcely one out of a thousand attracts our notice; and if it does, it is only slightly, and, as it were, in passing. And, secondly, we do not assign that importance to the duty of praise which it deserves. We are apt to neglect it as something trivial, and altogether commonplace; whereas it constitutes the chief exercise of godliness, in which God would have us to be engaged during the whole of our life. In the words before us, the sacrifice of praise is asserted to form the true and proper worship of God. The words, *will glorify me,* imply that God is then truly and properly worshipped, and the glory which he requires yielded to him, when his goodness is celebrated with a sincere and grateful heart; but that all the other sacrifices to which hypocrites attach such importance are worthless in his estimation, and no part whatsoever of his worship. Under the word *praise,* however, is comprehended, as I have already noticed, both faith and prayer. There must be an experience of the goodness of the Lord before our mouths can be opened to praise him for it, and this goodness can only be experienced

---

[1] The language here is metaphorical. The Almighty, provoked by the wickedness of these hypocrites, compares himself to a lion, who, with irresistible fury, seizes on his prey, and tears it in pieces, none being able to rescue it from his jaws. We meet with a similar form of expression in Hosea v. 14: "For I will be as a lion unto Ephraim, and as a young lion to the house of Judah: I, even I, will tear and go away; I will take away, and none shall rescue him." We must not, however, suppose that the rage and fury of this relentless destroyer can have place in the bosom of the Deity. Such phraseology is adopted in accommodation to the feebleness of our conceptions, and our contracted modes of thinking, to impress the hearts and consciences of sinners with a conviction of the tremendous character of the judgments of God, and the fearful condition of those who fall under his penal wrath.

by faith. Hence it follows, that the whole of spiritual worship is comprehended under what is either presupposed in the exercise of praise, or flows from it. Accordingly, in the words which immediately follow, the Psalmist calls upon those who desired that their services should be approved of God, *to order their way aright.* By the expression here used of *ordering one's way,* some understand repentance or confession of sin to be meant; others, the taking out of the way such things as may prove grounds of offence, or obstacles in the way of others. It seems more probable that the Psalmist enjoins them to walk in the right way as opposed to that in which hypocrites are found, and intimates that God is only to be approached by those who seek him with a sincere heart and in an upright manner. By *the salvation of God,* I do not, with some, understand a great or signal salvation. God speaks of himself in the third person, the more clearly to satisfy them of the fact, that he would eventually prove to all his genuine worshippers how truly he sustained the character of their Saviour.

PSALM LI.

We learn the cause which led to the composition of this psalm from the title appended to it, and which will immediately come under our consideration. For a long period after his melancholy fall, David would seem to have sunk into a spiritual lethargy; but when roused from it by the expostulation of Nathan, he was filled with self-loathing and humiliation in the sight of God, and was anxious both to testify his repentance to all around him, and leave some lasting proof of it to posterity. In the commencement of the psalm, having his eyes directed to the heinousness of his guilt, he encourages himself to hope for pardon by considering the infinite mercy of God. This he extols in high terms, and with a variety of expressions, as one who felt that he deserved multiplied condemnation. In the after part of the psalm, he prays for restoration to the favour of God, being conscious that he deserved to have been cast off for ever, and deprived of all the gifts of the Holy Spirit. He promises, should forgiveness be bestowed upon him, to retain a deep and grateful sense of it. Towards the conclusion, he declares it to be for the good of the Church that God should grant his request; and, indeed, when the peculiar manner in which God had deposited his covenant of grace with David is considered, it could not but be felt that the common hope of the salvation of all must have been shaken on the supposition of his final rejection.

¶ To the chief musician. A Psalm of David, when Nathan the prophet came to him, after he had gone in to Bathsheba.

When Nathan the prophet came to him. Express mention is made of the prophet having come before the psalm was written, proving, as it does, the deep lethargy into which David must have fallen. It was a wonderful circumstance that so great a man, and one so eminently gifted with the Spirit, should have continued in this dangerous state for upwards of a year. Nothing but satanic influence can account for that stupor of conscience which could lead him to despise or slight the divine judgment, which he had incurred. It serves additionally to mark the supineness into which he had fallen, that he seems to have had no compunction for his sin till the prophet came to him. We have here a striking illustration, at the same time, of the mercy of God in sending the prophet to reclaim him when he had wandered. In this view, there is an antithesis in the repetition of the word *came*. It was when David came in to Bathsheba that Nathan came to him. By that sinful step he had placed himself at a distance from God; and the Divine goodness was signally displayed in contemplating his restoration. We do not imagine that David, during this interval, was so wholly deprived of the sense of religion as no longer to acknowledge the supremacy of the Divine Being. In all probability he continued to pray daily, engaged in the acts of Divine worship, and aimed at conforming his life to the law of God. There is no reason to think that grace was wholly extinct in his heart; but only that he was possessed by a spirit of infatuation upon one particular point, and laboured under a fatal insensibility as to his present exposure to Divine wrath. Grace, whatever sparks it might emit in other directions, was smothered, so to speak, in this. Well may we tremble to contemplate the fact, that so holy a prophet, and so excellent a king, should have sunk into such a condition! That the sense of religion was not altogether extinguished in his mind, is proved by the manner in which he was affected immediately upon receiving the prophet's reproof. Had such been the case, he could not have cried out as he did, "I have sinned against the Lord," (2 Sam. xii. 13;) nor would he have so readily submitted himself, in the spirit of meekness, to admonition and correction. In this respect, he has set an example to all such as may have sinned against God, teaching them the duty of humbly complying with the calls to repentance, which may be addressed to them by his servants, instead of remaining under sin till they be surprised by the final vengeance of Heaven.

1. *Have mercy upon me, O God! according to thy loving-kindness; according to the multitude of thy compassions, blot out my transgressions.*
2. *Multiply to wash me from mine iniquity, and cleanse me from my sin.*

1. *Have mercy upon me.* David begins, as I have already remarked, by praying for pardon; and his sin having been of an aggravated description, he prays with unwonted earnestness. He does not satisfy himself with one petition. Having mentioned the *loving-kindness* of the Lord, he adds *the multitude of his compassions*, to intimate that mercy of an ordinary kind would not suffice for so great a sinner. Had he prayed God to be favourable, simply according to his clemency or goodness, even that would have amounted to a confession that his case was a bad one; but when he speaks of his sin as remissible, only through the countless multitude of the compassions of God, he represents it as peculiarly atrocious. There is an implied antithesis between the greatness of the mercies sought for, and the greatness of the transgression which required them. Still more emphatical is the expression which follows, *multiply to wash me.* Some take הרבה,[1] *herebeh*, for a noun, but this is too great a departure from the idiom of the language. The sense, on that supposition, would indeed remain the same, That God would wash him abundantly, and with multiplied washing; but I prefer that form of expression which agrees best with the Hebrew idiom. This, at least, is certain from the expression which he employs, that he felt the stain of his sin to be deep, and to require multiplied washings. Not as if God could experience any difficulty in cleansing the worst sinner, but the more aggravated a man's sin is, the more earnest naturally are his desires to be delivered from the terrors of conscience.

[1] There are here two verbs, הרבה, *herebeh*, and כבסני, *kabbeseni*, the first signifying *to multiply*, and the second *to wash*. Many expositors think that the verb הרב, *herebeh*, is used in the sense of an adverb, and they read, *Multum lava me.* "When two verbs of the same tense are joined together, whether a copula goes between them or not, the first is often expressed in Latin by an adverb."—Glass. Lib. i. Tract. iii. De Verbo Can. xxix. tom. i. p. 272. See Gen. xxv. 1; Ps. vi. 11; xlv. 5; lxxviii. 41; and cii. 3.

The figure itself, as all are aware, is one of frequent occurrence in Scripture. Sin resembles filth or uncleanness, as it pollutes us, and makes us loathsome in the sight of God, and the remission of it is therefore aptly compared to *washing*. This is a truth which should both commend the grace of God to us, and fill us with detestation of sin. Insensible, indeed, must that heart be which is not affected by it!

3. *For I know my transgressions, and my sin is continually before me.*
4. *Against thee, thee only, have I sinned, and done evil in thy sight; that thou mayest be justified when thou speakest, and be clear when thou judgest.*
5. *Behold, I was born in iniquity, and in sin did my mother conceive me.*
6. *Behold, thou hast desired truth in the inward parts, and hast shown me wisdom in secret.*

3. *For I know my sins.*[1] He now discovers his reason for imploring pardon with so much vehemency, and this was the painful disquietude which his sins caused him, and which could only be relieved by his obtaining reconciliation with God. This proves that his prayer did not proceed from dissimulation, as many will be found commending the grace of God in high terms, although, in reality, they care little about it, having never felt the bitterness of being exposed to his displeasure. David, on the contrary, declares that he is subjected by his sin to constant anguish of mind, and that it is this which imparts such an earnestness to his supplications. From his example we may learn who they are that can alone be said to seek reconciliation with God in a proper manner. They are such as have had their consciences wounded with a sense of sin, and who can find no rest until they have obtained assurance of his mercy. We will never seriously apply to God for pardon, until we have obtained such a view

---

[1] As if he had said, "I confess and acknowledge that I have sinned, nor do I say as Cain did, 'I know not,' (Gen. iv. 9.) What I formerly shamefully and foolishly excused and extenuated, I now acknowledge before thee and thy prophet, and the whole Church, in this penitential psalm." The verb is in the future, *I will know* or *acknowledge*, to intimate that he would continue to retain an humble sense of his guilt.

of our sins as inspires us with fear. The more easily satisfied we are under our sins, the more do we provoke God to punish them with severity, and if we really desire absolution from his hand, we must do more than confess our guilt in words; we must institute a rigid and formidable scrutiny into the character of our transgressions. David does not simply say that he will confess his sins to man, but declares that he has a deep inward feeling of them, such a feeling of them as filled him with the keenest anguish. His was a very different spirit from that of the hypocrite, who displays a complete indifference upon this subject, or when it intrudes upon him, endeavours to bury the recollection of it. He speaks of his *sins* in the plural number. His transgression, although it sprung from one root, was complicated, including, besides adultery, treachery and cruelty; nor was it one man only whom he had betrayed, but the whole army which had been summoned to the field in defence of the Church of God. He accordingly recognises many particular sins as wrapt up in it.

4. *Against thee, thee only, have I sinned.*[1] It is the opinion of some that he here adverts to the circumstance of his sin, although it was committed against man, being concealed from every eye but that of God. None was aware of the double wrong which he had inflicted upon Uriah, nor of the wanton manner in which he had exposed his army to danger; and his crime being thus unknown to men, might be said to have been committed exclusively against God. According to others, David here intimates, that however deeply he was conscious of having injured men, he was chiefly distressed for having violated the law of God. But I conceive his meaning

---

[1] From the confession which David makes in this verse, "Against thee, thee *only*, have I sinned," Horsley is of opinion that the title of the psalm is not authentic, and that it could not have been composed on the occasion to which the title refers. "It ill suits the case of David," says he, "who laid a successful plot against Uriah after he had defiled his bed." But there seems to be no force in this objection. The prefix ל, *lamed*, translated *against*, sometimes means *before, in the presence of*, and is so rendered in Gen. xxiii. 11, and xlv. 1. The Hebrew words לְמִדְּךָ, לְךָ, *lecha, lebaddecha*, may, therefore, be rendered, "before thee, before thee only." If this reading is adopted, then, David alludes to the clandestine manner in which he committed the sin, intimating that it was a secret sin witnessed

to be, that though all the world should pardon him, he felt that God was the Judge with whom he had to do, that conscience hailed him to his bar, and that the voice of man could administer no relief to him, however much he might be disposed to forgive, or to excuse, or to flatter. His eyes and his whole soul were directed to God, regardless of what man might think or say concerning him. To one who is thus overwhelmed with a sense of the dreadfulness of being obnoxious to the sentence of God, there needs no other accuser. God is to him instead of a thousand. There is every reason to believe that David, in order to prevent his mind from being soothed into a false peace by the flatteries of his court, realized the judgment of God upon his offence, and felt that this was in itself an intolerable burden, even supposing that he should escape all trouble from the hands of his fellow-creatures. This will be the exercise of every true penitent. It matters little to obtain our acquittal at the bar of human judgment, or to escape punishment through the connivance of others, provided we suffer from an accusing conscience and an offended God. And there is, perhaps, no better remedy against deception in the matter of our sins than to turn our thoughts inward upon ourselves, to concentrate them upon God, and lose every self-complacent imagination in a sharp sense of his displeasure. By a violent process of interpretation, some would have us read the second clause of this verse, *That thou mayest be justified when thou speakest,* in connection with the first verse of the psalm, and consider that it cannot be referred to the sen-

---

by God only, and known in the first instance only to him. God says of it, "For thou didst it secretly," (2 Sam. xii. 12.) There is, however, no need to alter the translation to meet the objection of Horsley. By these words, "Against thee, thee *only*," David does not mean to say that he had not wronged Uriah, whose wife he had dishonoured, whom he had caused to be made drunk, and afterwards to be slain; for he acknowledges in the 14th verse that "blood-guiltiness" lay heavy upon him, and he prays for deliverance from it. They are an emphatic declaration of the heinousness of his guilt—that he had sinned chiefly against God—more against him than against man. "My offence," as if he had said, "against Uriah, and against society at large, great as it has been, is nothing compared to that which I have committed against thee."

tence immediately preceding.[1] But not to say that this breaks in upon the order of the verses, what sense could any attach to the prayer as it would then run, *Have mercy upon me, that thou mayest be clear when thou judgest?* &c. Any doubt upon the meaning of the words, however, is completely removed by the connection in which they are cited in Paul's Epistle to the Romans, iii. 3, 4, "For what if some did not believe? Shall God be unjust? God forbid: yea, let God be true, but every man a liar; as it is written, That thou mayest be justified in thy sayings, and mightest overcome when thou art judged." Here the words before us are quoted in proof of the doctrine that God's righteousness is apparent even in the sins of men, and his truth in their falsehood. To have a clear apprehension of their meaning, it is necessary that we reflect upon the covenant which God had made with David. The salvation of the whole world having been in a certain sense deposited with him by this covenant, the enemies of religion might take occasion to exclaim upon his fall, " Here is the pillar of the Church gone, and what is now to become of the miserable remnant whose hopes rested upon his holiness? Once nothing could be more conspicuous than the glory by which he was distinguished, but mark the depth of disgrace to which he has been reduced! Who, after so gross a fall, would look for salvation from his seed?" Aware that such attempts might be made to impugn the righteousness of God, David takes this opportunity of justifying it, and charging himself with the whole guilt of the transaction. He declares that God

---

[1] This is the opinion of R. Abraham and other Jewish commentators. They say that these words are not to be joined to the immediately preceding part of this verse, but either to the prayer in the first verse, or to what is stated in the third verse, "I acknowledge my transgressions;" and they put the beginning of the fourth verse, "Against thee, thee only, have I sinned, and done evil in thy sight," within a parenthesis. But there is no just ground for such an interpretation. Green reads the last clause of the verse, "So that thou art just in passing sentence *upon me*, and clear in condemning *me*." And it is not uncommon for לְמַעַן, *le-maän*, to be used in the sense of *so that*, as in Ps. xxx. 12; Isa. xxviii. 13; and Jer. l. 34. According to this reading, the words are a part of David's confession;—he not only confesses his sin in the first part of the verse, but also here acknowledges the divine righteousness should God condemn him. This is the sense in which Calvin understands the passage.

was justified *when he spoke*—not when he spoke the promises of the covenant, although some have so understood the words, but justified should he have spoken the sentence of condemnation against him for his sin, as he might have done but for his gratuitous mercy. Two forms of expression are here employed which have the same meaning, *that thou mayest be justified when thou speakest,* and *be clear when thou judgest.* As Paul, in the quotation already referred to, has altered the latter clause, and may even seem to have given a new turn to the sentiment contained in the verse, I shall briefly show how the words were applicable to the purpose for which they were cited by him. He adduces them to prove that God's faithfulness remained unaffected by the fact that the Jews had broken his covenant, and fallen from the grace which he had promised. Now, at first sight it may not appear how they contain the proof alleged. But their appositeness will at once be seen if we reflect upon the circumstance to which I have already adverted. Upon the fall of one who was so great a pillar in the Church, so illustrious both as a prophet and a king, as David, we cannot but believe that many were shaken and staggered in the faith of the promises. Many must have been disposed to conclude, considering the close connection into which God had adopted David, that he was implicated in some measure in his fall. David, however, repels an insinuation so injurious to the divine honour, and declares, that although God should cast him headlong into everlasting destruction, his mouth would be shut, or opened only to acknowledge his unimpeachable justice. The sole departure which the apostle has made from the passage in his quotation consists in his using the verb *to judge* in a passive sense, and reading, *that thou mightest overcome,* instead of, *that thou mightest be clear.* In this he follows the Septuagint,[1] and it is well known that the apostles

---

[1] There does not appear to be any substantial difference between the reading of the Septuagint, which the apostle follows, and that of the Hebrew text. Calvin says that Paul uses the verb *to judge* in a passive sense, whereas it is here used actively. But this is a mistake. Street, after giving the words of the Septuagint, which are, Νικησης ἐν τῷ κρινεσθαι σε, says, "The verb κρινεσθαι is in the middle, not in the passive voice, and the phrase, ἐν τῷ κρινεσθαι σε, signifies *cum tu judicas,*" [*i.e.* when thou

do not study verbal exactness in their quotations from the Old Testament. It is enough for us to be satisfied, that the passage answers the purpose for which it was adduced by the apostle. The general doctrine which we are taught from the passage is, that whatever sins men may commit are chargeable entirely upon themselves, and never can implicate the righteousness of God. Men are ever ready to arraign his administration, when it does not correspond with the judgment of sense and human reason. But should God at any time raise persons from the depth of obscurity to the highest distinction, or, on the other hand, allow persons who occupied a most conspicuous station to be suddenly precipitated from it, we should learn from the example which is here set before us to judge of the divine procedure with sobriety, modesty, and reverence, and to rest satisfied that it is holy, and that the works of God, as well as his words, are characterized by unerring rectitude. The conjunction in the verse, *that—that thou mayest be justified*, denotes not so much cause as consequence. It was not the fall of David, properly speaking, which caused the glory of God's righteousness to appear. And yet, although men when they sin seem to obscure his righteousness, it emerges from the foul attempt only more bright than ever, it being the peculiar work of God to bring light out of darkness.

judgest.] "I take notice of this the rather, because the passage being cited by Paul, Rom. iii. 4, (and the Septuagint version of it having been inserted instead of the Hebrew, which the apostle quoted,) our translators seem to have mistaken the sense of it; for they render it, 'That thou mightest be justified in thy sayings, and mightest overcome *when thou art judged*.' But who shall judge the Almighty?" In the other instance which Calvin mentions, the difference between the apostle's reading and that of the Hebrew text is more in appearance than in reality. "The word זכה," says Hammond, "is ordinarily rendered *mundus fuit, clean,* or *clear,* or *pure.* But this, as the context evinces, must be understood in a forensic sense, as *pure* is all one with *free from guilt;* and so there is a second notion of the word for *overcoming,* meaning that sort of victory which belongs to him that carries the cause in judicature." After stating that this is the rendering of the Septuagint, he observes, "That is very reconcileable with the notion of *mundus fuit;* for he that doth overcome in the suit is fitly said to be *cleared* or quitted by the law." Thus Hammond, with Chrysostom, supposes the meaning to be, that should God proceed against David, should he indite and arraign him at the bar of justice for his sins, demanding vengeance to be inflicted upon him, God would be justified and cleared, and would overcome in the suit.

5. *Behold, I was born in iniquity, &c.* He now proceeds further than the mere acknowledgment of one or of many sins, confessing that he brought nothing but sin with him into the world, and that his nature was entirely depraved. He is thus led by the consideration of one offence of peculiar atrocity to the conclusion that he was born in iniquity, and was absolutely destitute of all spiritual good. Indeed, every sin should convince us of the general truth of the corruption of our nature. The Hebrew word יְחֶמְתְנִי, *yechemathni*, signifies literally, *hath warmed herself of me*, from יָחַם, *yacham*, or חָמַם, *chamam, to warm;* but interpreters have very properly rendered it *hath conceived me.* The expression intimates that we are cherished in sin from the first moment that we are in the womb. David, then, is here brought, by reflecting on one particular transgression, to cast a retrospective glance upon his whole past life, and to discover nothing but sin in it. And let us not imagine that he speaks of the corruption of his nature, merely as hypocrites will occasionally do, to excuse their faults, saying, " I have sinned it may be, but what could I do? We are men, and prone by nature to everything which is evil." David has recourse to no such stratagems for evading the sentence of God, and refers to original sin with the view of aggravating his guilt, acknowledging that he had not contracted this or that sin for the first time lately, but had been born into the world with the seed of every iniquity.

The passage affords a striking testimony in proof of original sin entailed by Adam upon the whole human family. It not only teaches the doctrine, but may assist us in forming a correct idea of it. The Pelagians, to avoid what they considered the absurdity of holding that all were ruined through one man's transgression, maintained of old, that sin descended from Adam only through force of imitation. But the Bible, both in this and other places, clearly asserts that we are born in sin, and that it exists within us as a disease fixed in our nature. David does not charge it upon his parents, nor trace his crime to them, but sists himself before the Divine tribunal, confesses that he was formed in sin, and that he was a transgressor ere he saw the light of this world. It was therefore a gross error in Pelagius to deny that sin was hereditary, descending in the human family by contagion. The Papists, in our own day, grant that the nature of man has become depraved, but they extenuate original sin as much as possible, and represent it as consisting merely in an inclination to that which is evil. They restrict its seat besides to the inferior part of the soul and the gross appetites; and while nothing is more evident from experience than that corruption adheres to men through life, they deny that it remains in them subsequently to baptism. We have no adequate idea of the dominion of sin, unless we conceive of it as extending to every part of the soul, and acknowledge that both the mind and heart of man have become utterly corrupt. The language of David sounds very differently from that of the Papists, *I was formed in iniquity, and in sin did my mother conceive me.* He says nothing of his grosser appetites, but asserts that sin cleaved by nature to every part of him without exception.

Here the question has been started, How sin is transmitted from the parents to the children? And this question has led to another regarding the transmission of the soul, many denying that corruption can be derived from the parent to the child, except on the supposition of one soul being begotten of the substance of another. Without entering upon such mysterious discussions, it is enough that we hold, that Adam, upon his fall, was despoiled of his original righteousness, his reason darkened, his will perverted, and that, being reduced to this state of corruption, he brought children into the world resembling himself in character. Should any object that generation is confined to bodies, and that souls can never derive anything in common from one another, I would reply, that Adam, when he was endued at his creation with the gifts of the Spirit, did not sustain a private character, but represented all mankind, who may be considered as having been endued with these gifts in his person; and from this view it necessarily follows that when he fell, we all forfeited along with him our original integrity.[1]

[1] Our Author's views on the doctrine of original sin are more fully stated in his Institutes, Book II. chap. 1.

6. *Behold, thou hast desired truth, &c.* This verse confirms the remark which we already made, that David was far from seeking to invent an apology for his sin, when he traced it back to the period of his conception, and rather intended by this to acknowledge that from his very infancy he was an heir of eternal death. He thus represents his whole life to have been obnoxious to condemnation. So far is he from imitating those who arraign God as the author of sin, and impiously suggest that he might have given man a better nature, that in the verse now before us he opposes God's judgment to our corruption, insinuating, that every time we appear before him, we are certain of being condemned, inasmuch as we are born in sin, while he delights in holiness and uprightness. He goes further, and asserts, that in order to meet the approval of God, it is not enough that our lives be conformed to the letter of his law, unless our heart be clean and purified from all guile. He tells us that God desires truth in *the inward parts*,[1] intimating to us, that secret as well as outward and gross sins excite his displeasure. In the second clause of the verse, he aggravates his offence by confessing that he could not plead the excuse of ignorance. He had been sufficiently instructed by God in his duty. Some interpret בסתום, *besathum*, as if he here declared that God had discovered secret mysteries to him, or things hidden from the human understanding. He seems rather to mean that wisdom had been discovered to his mind in

---

[1] The word טחות, *tuchoth*, which is rendered *inward parts*, and which is derived from the verb טוח, *tuach, to spread over*, means *the reins*, which are so called, because they are *overspread* with fat. "Once more it is used in Scripture, Job xxxviii. 36, where, as here, our English Bible renders it *inward parts*, somewhat too generally. The Chaldee expresses it more particularly by *reins*, and these, in the Scripture style, are frequently taken for the seat of the affections, the purity whereof is most contrary to the natural corruption or inbred pollution spoken of in the preceding verse. The word אמת, *emeth, truth*, ordinarily signifies sincerity, uprightness, and integrity; and so *truth in the reins* is equivalent to a hearty sincere obedience, not only of the actions, but of the very thoughts and affections to God; and so, in things of this nature, wherein this psalm is principally concerned, denotes the purity of the heart, the not admitting any unclean desire or thought, the very first degree of indulgence to any lust. And this God is said *to will*, or *desire*, or *delight in*, and so to command and require of us."—*Hammond.*

a secret and intimate manner.[1] The one member of the verse responds to the other. He acknowledges that it was not a mere superficial acquaintance with divine truth which he had enjoyed, but that it had been closely brought home to his heart. This rendered his offence the more inexcusable. Though privileged so highly with the saving knowledge of the truth, he had plunged into the commission of brutish sin, and by various acts of iniquity had almost ruined his soul.

We have thus set before us the exercise of the Psalmist at this time. First, we have seen that he is brought to a confession of the greatness of his offence: this leads him to a sense of the complete depravity of his nature: to deepen his convictions, he then directs his thoughts to the strict judgment of God, who looks not to the outward appearance but the heart; and, lastly, he adverts to the peculiarity of his case, as one who had enjoyed no ordinary measure of the gifts of the Spirit, and deserved on that account the severer punishment. The exercise is such as we should all strive to imitate. Are we conscious of having committed any one sin, let it be the means of recalling others to our recollection, until we are brought to prostrate ourselves before God in deep self-abasement. And if it has been our privilege to enjoy the special teaching of the Spirit of God, we ought to feel that our guilt is additionally heavy, having sinned in this case against light, and having trampled under foot the precious gifts with which we were intrusted.

> 7. *Thou shalt purge me with hyssop, and I shall be clean; thou shalt wash me, and I shall be whiter than the snow.*
> 8. *Make me to hear joy and gladness; and the bones which thou hast broken shall rejoice.*
> 9. *Hide thy face from my sins, and blot out all mine iniquities.*

7. *Thou shalt purge me with hyssop.* He still follows out

---

[1] The word is explained in the first of these senses in the Septuagint: "Τὰ ἄδηλα καὶ τὰ κρύφια τῆς σοφίας ἐδήλωσάς μοι;"—"Thou hast manifested to me the secret and hidden things of thy wisdom." Viewed in this light as well as in the other, the language expresses the aggravated nature of David's sin. He had sinned, although God had revealed to him high and secret mysteries.

the same strain of supplication; and the repetition of his requests for pardon proves how earnestly he desired it. He speaks of *hyssop*,[1] in allusion to the ceremonies of the law; and though he was far from putting his trust in the mere outward symbol of purification, he knew that, like every other legal rite, it was instituted for an important end. The sacrifices were seals of the grace of God. In them, therefore, he was anxious to find assurance of his reconciliation; and it is highly proper that, when our faith is disposed at any time to waver, we should confirm it by improving such means of divine support. All which David here prays for is, that God would effectually accomplish, in his experience, what he had signified to his Church and people by these outward rites; and in this he has set us a good example for our imitation. It is no doubt to the blood of Christ alone that we must look for the atonement of our sins; but we are creatures of sense, who must see with our eyes, and handle with our hands; and it is only by improving the outward symbols of propitiation that we can arrive at a full and assured persuasion of it. What we have said of the *hyssop* applies also to the *washings*[2] referred to in this verse, and

---

[1] Hyssop was much used by the Hebrews in their sacred purifications and sprinklings. The allusion here probably is to the ceremony of sprinkling such as had been infected with leprosy. Two birds were to be taken, cedar wood, scarlet, and hyssop; one of the birds was to be killed, and the priest having dipped the living bird, the cedar wood, scarlet, and hyssop, in the blood of the bird that was killed, sprinkled the leper, (Lev. xiv.) This ceremony, it is to be observed, was not to be performed until the person was cured; and it was intended as a declaration to the people, that, God having healed him of a disease which no human means could remove, he might with safety be restored to society, and to the privileges of which he had been deprived. David, polluted with the crimes of adultery and murder, regarded himself as a man affected with the dreadful disease of leprosy, and he prays that God would sprinkle him with hyssop, as the leper was sprinkled, using this figurative language to express his ardent desires to obtain forgiveness and cleansing by the application of the blood of Christ, and that God would show to the people that he had pardoned his sin, restored him to favour, and purified his soul.

[2] David felt that he was stained, as it were, by the blood of Uriah, and therefore he prays, "Wash me." The word כבסני, *cabbeseni, wash me*, is from כבס, *cabas, to tread, to trample with the feet;* and hence it signifies *to wash, to cleanse,* for example, garments, by treading them in a trough, &c. It differs from רחץ, *rachats, to lave or wash the body,* as the Greek word πλύνειν, *to cleanse soiled garments,* differs from λούειν, *to wash the body.* See Gesenius Lexicon. These two words, כבס, *cabas,* and רחץ, *rachats,* which thus ex-

which were commonly practised under the Law. They figuratively represented our being purged from all iniquity, in order to our reception into the divine favour. I need not say that it is the peculiar work of the Holy Spirit to sprinkle our consciences inwardly with the blood of Christ, and, by removing the sense of guilt, to secure our access into the presence of God.

In the two verses which follow, the Psalmist prays that God would be pacified towards him. Those put too confined a meaning upon the words who have suggested that, in praying *to hear the voice of joy and gladness,* he requests some prophet to be sent, who might assure him of pardon. He prays, in general, for testimonies of the divine favour. When he speaks of his *bones* as having been *broken,* he alludes to the extreme grief and overwhelming distress to which he had been reduced. The joy of the Lord would reanimate his soul; and this joy he describes as to be obtained by *hearing;* for it is the word of God alone which can first and effectually cheer the heart of any sinner. There is no true or solid peace to be enjoyed in the world except in the way of reposing upon the promises of God. Those who do not resort to them may succeed for a time in hushing or evading the terrors of conscience, but they must ever be strangers to true inward comfort. And, granting that they may attain to the peace of insensibility, this is not a state which could satisfy any man who has seriously felt the fear of the Lord. The joy which he desires is that which flows from hearing the word of God, in which he promises to pardon our guilt, and readmit us into his favour. It is this alone which sup-

press different kinds of washing, observes Bishop Mant, "are always used in the Hebrew language with the strictest propriety: the one to signify that kind of washing which *pervades the substance* of the thing washed, and cleanses it thoroughly; and the other to express that kind of washing which only *cleanses the surface* of a substance, which the water cannot penetrate. The former is applied to the washing of clothes; the latter is used for washing some part of the body. By a beautiful and strong metaphor, David uses the former word in this and the second verse: ' *Wash* me thoroughly from mine iniquity, and cleanse me from my sin.' '*Wash* me, and I shall be whiter than snow.' So in Jer. iv. 14, the same word is applied to the heart. There is a similar distinction in the Greek language, which the LXX. constantly observe in their rendering of the Hebrew words above alluded to."

ports the believer amidst all the fears, dangers, and distresses of his earthly pilgrimage; for the joy of the Spirit is inseparable from faith. When God is said, in the 9th verse, to *hide his face* from our sins, this signifies his pardoning them, as is explained in the clause immediately annexed—*Blot out all my sins.* This represents our justification as consisting in a voluntary act of God, by which he condescends to forget all our iniquities; and it represents our cleansing to consist in the reception of a gratuitous pardon. We repeat the remark which has been already made, that David, in thus reiterating his one request for the mercy of God, evinces the depth of that anxiety which he felt for a favour which his conduct had rendered difficult of attainment. The man who prays for pardon in a mere formal manner, is proved to be a stranger to the dreadful desert of sin. "Happy is the man," said Solomon, "that feareth alway," (Prov. xxviii. 14.)

But here it may be asked why David needed to pray so earnestly for the joy of remission, when he had already received assurance from the lips of Nathan that his sin was pardoned? (2 Sam. xii. 13.) Why did he not embrace this absolution? and was he not chargeable with dishonouring God by disbelieving the word of his prophet? We cannot expect that God will send us angels in order to announce the pardon which we require. Was it not said by Christ, that whatever his disciples remitted on earth would be remitted in heaven? (John xx. 23.) And does not the apostle declare that ministers of the gospel are ambassadors to reconcile men to God? (2 Cor. v. 20.) From this it might appear to have argued unbelief in David, that, notwithstanding the announcement of Nathan, he should evince a remaining perplexity or uncertainty regarding his forgiveness. There is a twofold explanation which may be given of the difficulty. We may hold that Nathan did not immediately make him aware of the fact that God was willing to be reconciled to him. In Scripture, it is well known, things are not always stated according to the strict order of time in which they occurred. It is quite conceivable that, having thrown him into this situation of distress, God might keep him in it for a considerable interval, for his deeper humiliation; and that David expresses in these verses the dreadful anguish which he endured when challenged with his crime, and not yet informed of the divine determination to pardon it. Let us take the other supposition, however, and it by no means follows that a person may not be assured of the favour of God, and yet show great earnestness and importunity in praying for pardon. David might be much relieved by the announcement of the prophet, and yet be visited occasionally with fresh convictions, influencing him to have recourse to the throne of grace. However rich and liberal the offers of mercy may be which God extends to us, it is highly proper on our part that we should reflect upon the grievous dishonour which we have done to his name, and be filled with due sorrow on account of it. Then our faith is weak, and we cannot at once apprehend the full extent of the divine mercy; so that there is no reason to be surprised that David should have once and again renewed his prayers for pardon, the more to confirm his belief in it. The truth is, that we cannot properly pray for the pardon of sin until we have come to a persuasion that God will be reconciled to us. Who can venture to open his mouth in God's presence unless he be assured of his fatherly favour? And pardon being the first thing we should pray for, it is plain that there is no inconsistency in having a persuasion of the grace of God, and yet proceeding to supplicate his forgiveness. In proof of this, I might refer to the Lord's Prayer, in which we are taught to begin by addressing God as our Father, and yet afterwards to pray for the remission of our sins. God's pardon is full and complete; but our faith cannot take in his overflowing goodness, and it is necessary that it should distil to us drop by drop. It is owing to this infirmity of our faith, that we are often found repeating and repeating again the same petition, not with the view surely of gradually softening the heart of God to compassion, but because we advance by slow and difficult steps to the requisite fulness of assurance. The mention which is here made of *purging with hyssop*, and of *washing* or *sprinkling*, teaches us, in all our prayers for the pardon of sin, to have our thoughts directed to the great sacrifice by which Christ has reconciled us to God. "Without shedding of blood," says Paul, "is no remission," (Heb.

ix. 22 ;) and this, which was intimated by God to the ancient Church under figures, has been fully made known by the coming of Christ. The sinner, if he would find mercy, must look to the sacrifice of Christ, which expiated the sins of the world, glancing, at the same time, for the confirmation of his faith, to Baptism and the Lord's Supper; for it were vain to imagine that God, the Judge of the world, would receive us again into his favour in any other way than through a satisfaction made to his justice.

10. *Create in me a clean heart, O God! and renew a right spirit*[1] *in my inward parts.*
11. *Cast me not away from thy presence, and take not the Spirit of thy holiness from me.*
12. *Restore unto me the joy of thy salvation, and uphold me with a free spirit.*

10. *Create in me a clean heart, O God!* In the previous part of the psalm David has been praying for pardon. He now requests that the grace of the Spirit, which he had forfeited, or deserved to have forfeited, might be restored to him. The two requests are quite distinct, though sometimes confounded together, even by men of learning. He passes from the subject of the gratuitous remission of sin to that of sanctification. And to this he was naturally led with earnest anxiety, by the consciousness of his having merited the loss of all the gifts of the Spirit, and of his having actually, in a great measure, lost them. By employing the term *create*, he expresses his persuasion that nothing less than a miracle could effect his reformation, and emphatically declares that repentance is the gift of God. The Sophists grant the necessity of the aids of the Spirit, and allow that assisting grace must both go before and come after; but by assigning a middle place to the free will of man, they rob God of a great part of his glory. David, by the word which he here uses, describes the work of God in renewing the heart in a manner

---

[1] French and Skinner read, "*a stedfast spirit; i. e.,* a mind steady in following the path of duty."

suitable to its extraordinary nature, representing it as the formation of a new creature.

As he had already been endued with the Spirit, he prays in the latter part of the verse that *God would renew a right spirit within him.* But by the term *create,* which he had previously employed, he acknowledges that we are indebted entirely to the grace of God, both for our first regeneration, and, in the event of our falling, for subsequent restoration. He does not merely assert that his heart and spirit were weak, requiring divine assistance, but that they must remain destitute of all purity and rectitude till these be communicated from above. By this it appears that our nature is entirely corrupt: for were it possessed of any rectitude or purity, David would not, as in this verse, have called the one *a gift of the Spirit,* and the other *a creation.*

In the verse which follows, he presents the same petition, in language which implies the connection of pardon with the enjoyment of the leading of the Holy Spirit. If God reconcile us gratuitously to himself, it follows that he will guide us by the Spirit of adoption. It is only such as he loves, and has numbered among his own children, that he blesses with a share of his Spirit; and David shows that he was sensible of this when he prays for the continuance of the grace of adoption as indispensable to the continued possession of the Spirit. The words of this verse imply that the Spirit had not altogether been taken away from him, however much his gifts had been temporarily obscured. Indeed, it is evident that he could not be altogether divested of his former excellencies, for he seems to have discharged his duties as a king with credit, to have conscientiously observed the ordinances of religion, and to have regulated his conduct by the divine law. Upon one point he had fallen into a deadly lethargy, but he was not "given over to a reprobate mind;" and it is scarcely conceivable that the rebuke of Nathan the prophet should have operated so easily and so suddenly in arousing him, had there been no latent spark of godliness still remaining in his soul. He prays, it is true, that his spirit may be *renewed,* but this must be understood with a limitation. The truth on which we are now insisting is an important one, as many learned men have been inconsiderately drawn into the opinion that the elect, by falling into mortal sin, may lose the Spirit altogether, and be alienated from God. The contrary is clearly declared by Peter, who tells us that the word by which we are born again is an incorruptible seed, (1 Pet. i. 23;) and John is equally explicit in informing us that the elect are preserved from falling away altogether, (1 John iii. 9.) However much they may appear for a time to have been cast off by God, it is afterwards seen that grace must have been alive in their breast, even during that interval when it seemed to be extinct. Nor is there any force in the objection that David speaks as if he feared that he might be deprived of the Spirit. It is natural that the saints, when they have fallen into sin, and have thus done what they could to expel the grace of God, should feel an anxiety upon this point; but it is their duty to hold fast the truth that grace is the incorruptible seed of God, which never can perish in any heart where it has been deposited. This is the spirit displayed by David. Reflecting upon his offence, he is agitated with fears, and yet rests in the persuasion that, being a child of God, he would not be deprived of what indeed he had justly forfeited.

12. *Restore unto me the joy of thy salvation.* He cannot dismiss his grief of mind until he have obtained peace with God. This he declares once and again, for David had no sympathy with those who can indulge themselves in ease when they are lying under the divine displeasure. In the latter clause of the verse, he prays as in the verses preceding, that the Holy Spirit might not be taken away from him. There is a slight ambiguity in the words. Some take תסמכני, *thismecheni,* to be the third person of the verb, because רוח, *ruach,* is feminine, and translate, *let the Spirit uphold me.* The difference is immaterial, and does not affect the meaning of the passage. There is more difficulty in fixing the sense of the epithet נדיבה, *nedibah,* which I have translated *free.* As the verb נדב, *nadab,* signifies *to deal liberally,* princes are in the Hebrew called, by way of eminence, נדיבים, *nedibim,* which has led several learned men to think that David speaks

here of a *princely* or *royal* spirit; and the translators of the Septuagint rendered it accordingly ἡγεμονικὸν. The prayer, in this sense, would no doubt be a suitable one for David, who was a king, and required a heroical courage for the execution of his office. But it seems better to adopt the more extensive meaning, and to suppose that David, under a painful consciousness of the bondage to which he had been reduced by a sense of guilt, prays for a free and cheerful spirit.[1] This invaluable attainment, he was sensible, could only be recovered through divine grace.

13. *I will teach transgressors thy ways, and sinners shall be converted unto thee.*
14. *Deliver me from bloods, O God! thou God of my salvation, and my tongue shall sing aloud with joy of thy righteousness.*
15. *O Lord! open thou my lips, and my mouth shall show forth thy praise.*

13. *I will teach transgressors thy ways.* Here he speaks of the gratitude which he would feel should God answer his

---

[1] Some commentators refer the clause, upon which Calvin is here commenting, to the Holy Spirit, and others to the qualities of mind with which David desired to be endued. The translators of our English Bible understand the expression in the first sense, reading, "thy free Spirit." The word *thy* is a supplement, but it does not appear to be liable to any material objection. Fry, who adopts the same view, reads, "bountiful or spontaneously flowing Spirit;" and observes, that the word נדיבה, *nedibah*, "is more still than *spontaneously flowing*: it signifies to flow both spontaneously and plentifully: 'præ uberitate succi sponte fluens.' This epithet of the indwelling Spirit will be best explained from our Lord's own words, John iv. 14, and vii. 38." Others refer the expression to the mind of the Psalmist. Mudge reads, "And let a plentiful effusion of spirit support me." Dimock, "Let a free spirit sustain me;" "that is," says he, "let me not be enslaved, as I have been, by my sinful passions." Green, "And support with a cheerful spirit." French and Skinner, "And may a willing spirit uphold me;" by which they understand, "a spirit devoted to the service of God." Walford, following the Septuagint, reads, "And with a princely spirit sustain me." "David," says this critic, "was so overwhelmed by the consciousness of his extreme iniquity, so broken in spirit, courage, and fortitude, as to feel altogether incompetent to the discharge of his office, as the King of Israel. He therefore addresses this petition to God, in the hope that he would grant to him a renewal of that powerful energy by which he had at first been fitted for an employment so every way unsuitable to his lowly descent, and his employment as a shepherd."

prayer, and engages to show it by exerting himself in effecting the conversion of others by his example. Those who have been mercifully recovered from their falls will feel inflamed by the common law of charity to extend a helping hand to their brethren; and in general, such as are partakers of the grace of God are constrained by religious principle, and regard for the divine glory, to desire that others should be brought into the participation of it. The sanguine manner in which he expresses his expectation of converting others is not unworthy of our notice. We are too apt to conclude that our attempts at reclaiming the ungodly are vain and ineffectual, and forget that God is able to crown them with success.

14. *Deliver me from bloods.* His recurring so often to petitions for pardon, proves how far David was from flattering himself with unfounded hopes, and what a severe struggle he sustained with inward terrors. According to some, he prays in this verse to be delivered from the guilt of the blood of Uriah, and, in general, of the whole army.[1] But the term *bloods* in Hebrew may denote any capital crime, and, in my opinion, he is here to be considered as alluding to the sentence of death, to which he felt himself to be obnoxious, and from which he requests deliverance. By *the righteousness of God*, which he engages to celebrate, we are to understand his

---

[1] This opinion, although disapproved of by our Author, is very generally held by commentators. When *blood* is used in the plural number as here, it usually denotes murder or manslaughter, and the guilt following thereupon: as in Gen. iv. 11, "The voice of thy brother's bloods crieth unto me from the ground;" 1 Chron. xxii. 8, "Thou hast shed bloods abundantly;" and Psalm ix. 13, "When he maketh inquisition for bloods." See also Ps. cvi. 38. "A man of bloods" is a bloody man, a man who is guilty of bloodshed, Ps. v. 6; xxvi. 9; lix. 2; and lv. 23. David's conduct towards Uriah, forming as it did a dark and an atrocious deed of treachery and cruelty which has few parallels in the history of mankind, must, on his recovery to a sense of its real character, have inflicted on his soul an agony which cannot be told. He escaped being tried before an earthly tribunal; but his conscience told him that he stood at the bar of Heaven, laden with the guilt of murder; and he was convinced that the mercy of God alone could pardon him and purify his conscience. No wonder then that he cries out with such emphasis and earnestness, *O God! thou God of my salvation! deliver me!* The Chaldee reads, "Deliver me from the judgment of murder."

goodness; for this attribute, as usually ascribed to God in the Scriptures, does not so much denote the strictness with which he exacts vengeance, as his faithfulness in fulfilling the promises and extending help to all who seek him in the hour of need. There is much emphasis and vehemency in the mode of his address, *O God! the God of my salvation,* intimating at once how tremblingly he was alive to the danger of his situation, and how strongly his faith terminated upon God as the ground of his hope. Similar is the strain of the verse which follows. He prays that *his lips may be opened ;* in other words, that God would afford him matter of praise. The meaning usually attached to the expression is, that God would so direct his tongue by the Spirit as to fit him for singing his praises. But though it is true that God must supply us with words, and that if he do not, we cannot fail to be silent in his praise, David seems rather to intimate that his mouth must be shut until God called him to the exercise of thanksgiving by extending pardon. In another place we find him declaring that a new song had been put in his mouth, (Ps. xl. 3,) and it seems to be in this sense that he here desires his lips to be opened. He again signifies the gratitude which he would feel, and which he would express, intimating, that he sought the mercy of God with no other view than that he might become the herald of it to others. *My mouth,* he says emphatically, *shall show forth thy praise.*

16. *For thou wilt not accept a sacrifice; though I should give*[1] *a burnt-offering, it would not please thee.*
17. *The sacrifices of God are a broken spirit: a broken and a contrite heart, O God! thou wilt not despise.*

[1] The original word אתנה, *ve-etenah,* which Calvin renders, *Though I should give,* is considered by some as a noun. "The common interpretation, *Else would I give it thee,*" says Rogers, "is harsh. Gesenius attributes to the word אתנה, with a slight difference in the punctuation, the sense of a *gift, reward.* It is used only in Hos. ii. 14. If this sense might be given to the word in this passage, the verse might be translated,

'For thou desirest no sacrifice or gift,
[In] a burnt-offering thou hast no delight.' "

Book of Psalms in Hebrew, vol. ii. p. 208.

18. *Do good in thy good pleasure unto Zion; build thou the walls of Jerusalem.*
19. *Thou shalt then accept the sacrifices of righteousness, even the burnt-offering and whole oblation; then shall calves come upon thine altar.*

16. *For thou wilt not accept a sacrifice.* By this language he expresses his confidence of obtaining pardon, although he brought nothing to God in the shape of compensation, but relied entirely upon the riches of Divine mercy. He confesses that he comes to God both poor and needy; but is persuaded that this will not prevent the success of his suit, because God attaches no importance to sacrifices. In this he indirectly reproves the Jews for an error which prevailed amongst them in all ages. In proclaiming that the sacrifices made expiation for sin, the Law had designed to withdraw them from all trust in their own works to the one satisfaction of Christ; but they presumed to bring their sacrifices to the altar as a price by which they hoped to procure their own redemption. In opposition to this proud and preposterous notion, David declares that God had no delight in sacrifices,[1] and that he had nothing to present which could purchase his favour. God had enjoined the observance of sacrifice, and David was far from neglecting it. He is not to be understood as asserting that the rite might warrantably be omitted, or that God would absolutely reject the sacrifices of his own institution, which, along with the other ceremonies of the Law, proved important helps, as we have already observed, both to David and the whole Church of God. He speaks of them as observed by the proud and the ignorant, under an impression of meriting the divine favour. Diligent as he was, therefore,

---

[1] There may be another reason why David here affirms that God would not accept of a sacrifice, nor be pleased with a burnt-offering. No particular sacrifices were appointed by the Law of Moses to expiate the guilt of murder and adultery. The person who had perpetrated these crimes was, according to the Divine law, to be punished with death. David therefore may be understood as declaring, that it was utterly vain for him to think of resorting to sacrifices and burnt-offerings with a view to the expiation of his guilt; that his criminality was of such a character, that the ceremonial law made no provision for his deliverance from the doom which his deeds of horror deserved; and that the only sacrifices which would avail were those mentioned in the succeeding verse, "The sacrifices of a broken heart."

in the practice of sacrifice, resting his whole dependence upon the satisfaction of Christ, who atoned for the sins of the world, he could yet honestly declare that he brought nothing to God in the shape of compensation, and that he trusted entirely to a gratuitous reconciliation. The Jews, when they presented their sacrifices, could not be said to bring anything of their own to the Lord, but must rather be viewed as borrowing from Christ the necessary purchase-money of redemption. They were passive, not active, in this divine service.

17. *The sacrifices of God are a broken spirit.* He had shown that sacrifices have no such efficacy in procuring the Divine favour as the Jews imagined; and now he declares that he needed to bring nothing whatever to God but a contrite and humbled heart. Nothing more is necessary, on the part of the sinner, than to prostrate himself in supplication for Divine mercy. The plural number is used in the verse to express more forcibly the truth, that the sacrifice of repentance is enough in itself without any other. Had he said no more than that this kind of sacrifice was peculiarly acceptable to God, the Jews might easily have evaded his argument by alleging that this might be true, and yet other sacrifices be equally agreeable in his sight; just as the Papists in our own day mix up the grace of God with their own works, rather than submit to receive a gratuitous pardon for their sins. In order to exclude every idea of a pretended satisfaction, David represents contrition of heart as comprehending in itself the whole sum of acceptable sacrifices. And in using the term *sacrifices of God*, he conveys a tacit reproof to the proud hypocrite, who sets a high value upon such sacrifices as are of his own unauthorised fancy, when he imagines that by means of them he can propitiate God. But here a difficulty may be started. " If the contrite heart," it may be said, "hold a higher place in the estimation of God than all sacrifices, does it not follow that we acquire pardon by our penitence, and that thus it ceases to be gratuitous ?" In reply to this, I might observe, that David is not speaking at this time of the meritorious condition by which pardon is procured, but, on the contrary, asserting our absolute desti-

tution of merit by enjoining humiliation and contrition of spirit, in opposition to everything like an attempt to render a compensation to God. The man of broken spirit is one who has been emptied of all vain-glorious confidence, and brought to acknowledge that he is nothing. The contrite heart abjures the idea of merit, and has no dealings with God upon the principle of exchange. Is it objected, that faith is a more excellent sacrifice that that which is here commended by the Psalmist, and of greater efficacy in procuring the Divine favour, as it presents to the view of God that Saviour who is the true and only propitiation? I would observe, that faith cannot be separated from the humility of which David speaks. This is such a humility as is altogether unknown to the wicked. They may tremble in the presence of God, and the obstinacy and rebellion of their hearts may be partially restrained, but they still retain some remainders of inward pride. Where the spirit has been broken, on the other hand, and the heart has become contrite, through a felt sense of the anger of the Lord, a man is brought to genuine fear and self-loathing, with a deep conviction that of himself he can do or deserve nothing, and must be indebted unconditionally for salvation to Divine mercy. That this should be represented by David as constituting all which God desires in the shape of sacrifice, need not excite our surprise. He does not exclude faith, he does not condescend upon any nice division of true penitence into its several parts, but asserts in general, that the only way of obtaining the favour of God is by prostrating ourselves with a wounded heart at the feet of his Divine mercy, and supplicating his grace with ingenuous confessions of our own helplessness.

18. *Do good to Zion in thy good pleasure: build thou the walls of Jerusalem.*[1] From prayer in his own behalf he now pro-

[1] We have already considered Horsley's first objection, founded on the fourth verse, to the authenticity of the title of this psalm. His second and only other objection rests on the 18th verse. He thinks that the prayer, "Build thou the walls of Jerusalem," is more applicable to the time of the Babylonish captivity than to the time of David; and to the former period he refers the psalm. Calmet and Mudge are of the same opinion. Some learned Jewish interpreters, while they assign the psalm

ceeds to offer up supplications for the collective Church of
God, a duty which he may have felt to be the more incumbent upon him from the circumstance of his having done
what he could by his fall to ruin it. Raised to the throne,
and originally anointed to be king for the very purpose of
fostering the Church of God, he had by his disgraceful
conduct nearly accomplished its destruction. Although
chargeable with this guilt, he now prays that God would
restore it in the exercise of his free mercy. He makes no
mention of the righteousness of others, but rests his plea
entirely upon the good pleasure of God, intimating that the
Church, when at any period it has been brought low, must
be indebted for its restoration solely to Divine grace. Jerusalem was already built, but David prays that God would build it
still farther, for he knew that it fell far short of being complete,
so long as it wanted the temple, where he had promised to
establish the Ark of his Covenant, and also the royal palace.
We learn from the passage, that it is God's own work to
build the Church. "His foundation," says the Psalmist elsewhere, " is in the holy mountains," (Ps. lxxxvii. 1.) We are
not to imagine that David refers simply to the Church as a
material structure, but must consider him as having his eye
fixed upon the spiritual temple, which cannot be raised by
human skill or industry. It is true, indeed, that men will not

to the occasion mentioned in the title, conjecture that the 18th and 19th
verses were added by some Jewish bard in the time of the Babylonish
captivity. This opinion is also held by Venema, Green, Street, French
and Skinner. There does not, however, seem to be any sufficient ground
for referring the poem, either in whole or in part, to that period. Neither
the walls of Jerusalem, nor the buildings of Zion, as the royal palace, and
the magnificent structure of the temple, which we know David had already
contemplated for the worship of God, (2 Sam. vii. 1, &c.,) were completed
during his reign. This was only effected under the reign of his son Solomon, (1 Kings iii. 1.) The prayer, then, in the 18th verse, might have a
particular reference to the completion of these buildings, and especially to
the rearing of the temple, in which sacrifices of unprecedented magnitude
were to be offered. David's fears might easily suggest to him that his crimes
might prevent the building of the temple which God had promised should
be erected, (2 Sam. vii. 13.) " The king forgets not," observes Bishop
Horne, " to ask mercy for his people, as well as for himself; that so
neither his own nor their sins might prevent either the building and flourishing of the earthly Jerusalem, or, what was of infinitely greater importance, the promised blessing of Messiah, who was to descend from him, and
to rear the walls of the New Jerusalem."

make progress even in the building of material walls, unless their labour be blessed from above; but the Church is in a peculiar sense the erection of God, who has founded it upon the earth in the exercise of his mighty power, and who will exalt it higher than the heavens. In this prayer David does not contemplate the welfare of the Church for a short period merely, but prays that God would preserve and advance it till the coming of Christ. And here, may it not justly excite our surprise, to find one who, in the preceding part of the psalm, had employed the language of distress and almost of despair, now inspired with the confidence necessary for commending the whole Church to the care of God? How comes it about, may we not ask, that one who so narrowly escaped destruction himself, should now appear as a guide to conduct others to salvation? In this we have a striking proof, that, provided we obtain reconciliation with God, we may not only expect to be inspired with confidence in praying for our own salvation, but may hope to be admitted as intercessors in behalf of others, and even to be advanced to the higher honour still, of commending into the hands of God the glory of the Redeemer's kingdom.

19. *Then shalt thou accept sacrifices of righteousness.* In these words there is an apparent, but only an apparent, inconsistency with others which he had used in the preceding context. He had declared sacrifices to be of no value when considered in themselves, but now he acknowledges them to be acceptable to God when viewed as expressions or symbols of faith, penitence, and thanksgiving. He calls them distinctly *sacrifices of righteousness*, right, warrantable, and such as are offered in strict accordance with the commandment of God. The expression is the same employed in Ps. iv. 5, where David uses it with a tacit condemnation of those who gloried in the mere outward form of ceremonies. We find him again exciting himself and others by his example to the exercise of gratitude, and to the expression of it openly in the solemn assembly. Besides sacrifices in general, two particular kinds of sacrifice are specified. Although some consider כליל, *calil*, and עולה, *olah*, to be both of one signification, others maintain

with more correctness, that the first is to be understood as meaning the priest's sacrifice, because in it the offering was consumed or burnt with fire.[1] In the enumeration which he makes, David designs to teach us that none of all the legal rites can find acceptance with God, unless they be used with a reference to the proper end of their institution. The whole of this verse has been figuratively applied by some to the kingdom of Christ, but the interpretation is unnatural and too refined. Thanksgivings are indeed called by Hosea "the calves of the lips," (Hos. xiv. 2;) but it seems evident that in the passage before us there are conjoined along with the frame or disposition of the heart those solemn ceremonies which constituted part of the ancient worship.

PSALM LII.

This psalm was composed by David at the time when the death of Abimelech and the other priests had spread universal terror among the people, indisposing them for lending any countenance to his cause, and when Doeg was triumphing in the successful issue of his information. Supported, even in these circumstances, by the elevating influence of faith, he inveighs against the cruel treachery of that unprincipled informer, and encourages himself by the reflection, that God, who is judge in heaven, will vindicate the interests of such as fear him, and punish the pride of the ungodly.

¶ To the chief singer. A Psalm of David for instruction; when Doeg the Edomite came and told Saul, and said unto him, that David had come into the house of Abimelech.

I have already had occasion to observe that the term משכיל, *maskil*, is strictly affixed to those psalms in which David makes mention of hav-

---

[1] Ainsworth reads, "the burnt-offering and the whole oblation;" and observes, that "*The whole oblation, the calil,* was a kind of oblation that was wholly and every whit given up in fire unto God, and differed from the *ghnola*, or burnt-offering, which was only of 'beasts or birds,' Lev. i.; whereas the *calil* was also of flour, called the meat-offering, but burned altogether, which the common meat-offerings were not, Lev. vi. 20, 22, 23. It was also of beasts, 1 Sam. vii. 9."

ing been chastised by God, or at least admonished, by some species of affliction, sent, like the rod of the schoolmaster, to administer correction. Of this we have examples in Psalms xxxii. and xlii. As inscribed above the 45th psalm, its meaning is somewhat different. There, it seems designed to intimate to the reader that the song, although breathing of love, was not intended to please a mere wanton taste, but describes the spiritual marriage of Christ with his Church. In this and the following psalms, the term admits of being understood as signifying *instruction*, more particularly such as proceeds from *correction;* and David, by employing it, would evidently insinuate that he was at this time subjected to peculiar trials, sent to instruct him in the duty of placing an absolute trust in God. The portion of history to which the psalm refers is well known. When David had fled to Abimelech in Nob, he obtained provisions and the sword of Goliath from the hands of that priest, having concealed from him the real danger in which he stood, and pretended that he was executing a secret and important business of the king. Doeg, chief of the king's herdsmen, having conveyed intelligence of this to Saul, in expectation of a reward, was the means of drawing down the rage of the tyrant, not only upon that innocent individual, but the whole priesthood.[1] The bloody example which was thus made must have deterred the people from extending to David even the commonest offices of humanity, and every avenue of relief seemed shut upon the miserable exile. As Doeg triumphed in the success of his crime, and others might be tempted, by the reward which he had received, to meditate the ruin of David, we find him in this psalm animating his soul with divine consolations, and challenging his enemies with the audacity of their conduct.

1. *Why boastest thou of thy wickedness, thou mighty man? the goodness of God endureth daily.*
2. *Thy tongue reckons up mischiefs, like a sharp razor, working deceitfully.*
3. *Thou lovest evil more than good, to speak lying rather than righteousness. Selah.*
4. *Thou lovest all words of deceit, O thou guileful tongue!*

1. *Why boastest thou of thy wickedness?* The success which crowned the treachery of Doeg must have tended consider-

---

[1] The history of this transaction is recorded in 1 Sam. xxi. 1-7, and xxii. 9-19. It affords a strong evidence of the hatred which Saul bore to David, and of his savage cruelty to order the execution of eighty-five priests for no crime; and what a monster of iniquity must Doeg have been, who executed this command when not another individual in all Saul's company would do it, and who, in addition to this, " smote the city of the priests with the edge of the sword, both men and women, children and sucklings, and oxen, and asses, and sheep?" " If we are confounded," says Walford, " by the savage ferocity of a prince who could order the

ably to stagger David's faith; and he seems to have adopted the strain of holy defiance with which the psalm commences, in order to arm himself more effectually against this temptation. He begins by charging Doeg with an aggravation of his guilt, in boasting of the power which he had acquired by an act of consummate villany. This power may have been sufficiently considerable to attract the notice which is here taken of it; for although he is only said to have been "master of the king's herdsmen," the designation does not imply that he was personally occupied in herding cattle, but may have been an honorary title; as in modern courts we speak of "The Master of the Horse." He is reminded that there was no reason why he should applaud himself in his greatness, so long as he abused it to purposes of wickedness; nor why he should be vain of any new honour which the king might have conferred upon him in consideration of his late crime, as integrity is the only sure pathway to power and preferment. Any triumph which may be obtained by violence, treachery, or other unjustifiable means, is short-lived. In the second part of the verse, he points at the true cause of the blindness and stupidity that lead men to glory in their wickedness, which is, that they despise the poor and the humble; imagine that God will not condescend to interest himself in their behalf; and therefore embrace the occasion of oppressing them with impunity. They make no account of that providence which God exerts over his own children. David, in the exercise of a holy confidence, challenges such proud boasters with dishonouring the goodness of God; and as the Divine goodness does not always pursue the same even course—occasionally appears to suffer an interruption, and sometimes seems as if it were cut off altogether—David

execution of eighty-five persons of most venerable station, for a crime which existed alone in his disturbed imagination, we shall feel disposed to execrate the ruthless villain who could imbrue his hands in the blood of so many innocent victims; and we shall be ready to draw the conclusion, that both Saul and Doeg were prompted to this deed of atrocious cruelty, not merely by their hatred of David, but by a malevolence, almost without parallel, against the ministers of religion, and which rendered conspicuous their contempt and hatred for God himself. It can excite little surprise to find David saying, as he does, in the next psalm, 'The fool saith in his heart, There is no God.'"

repels any temptation which this might suggest, by asserting that, whatever appearances may say to the contrary, it is daily exercised. This is evidently the meaning which he intends to convey, that any partial obstructions which may take place in the display of it can never prevent its constant renewal. He was confident that he would experience, in the future, what he had found in the past; for God cannot become weary in helping his people, or alleviating their miseries; and although he may suffer them again and again to fall into affliction, he is always equally ready to extend them the deliverance which they need.

2. *Thy tongue reckons up mischiefs.* David is not to be considered as here venting a flood of reproaches against his adversary, as many who have been unjustly injured are in the habit of doing, merely to gratify a feeling of revenge. He brings these charges against him in the sight of God, with a view to encourage himself in the hopefulness of his own cause: for it is plain that the farther our enemies proceed in the practice of iniquity, they proportionally provoke the anger of the Lord, and are nearer to that destruction which must issue in our deliverance. His object, therefore, is not to blacken the character of Doeg in the estimation of the world, but rather to set before his own eyes the divine punishment which the flagrant offences he specifies were certain to draw down upon his head. Amongst these he singles out, as more especially worthy of reprobation, the hidden treachery with which he had been chargeable in accomplishing the destruction of the priesthood. Adverting to his secret and malicious information, he likens *his tongue to a sharp razor*, as elsewhere, Ps. cxx. 4, the tongues of the wicked are compared to "sharp arrows." It is added, *working deceitfully*, which words are considered by some as referring to the razor which cuts subtilely, and not with an open wound like a sword; but perhaps they may be construed with more propriety as applying to the tongue,[1] although there can be no doubt of the reason of the comparison.

[1] According to the first sense, the meaning is, that as a razor cuts so easily, that the wound is at first hardly perceptible, in the same manner,

The term בֶּלַע, *balang*, in verse fourth, which has been translated *destruction*, I prefer understanding in the sense of *hiding* or *concealment*. He seems to allude to the drawing back of the tongue when we swallow; and under this figure, to describe the deceitfulness of Doeg's words, by which he devoured the unsuspecting and the innocent.[1] The great design of David, as I have already remarked in the preceding verses, is to encourage himself in the hope of deliverance by dwelling upon the extreme character of that wickedness which his enemy had displayed.

> 5. God shall likewise destroy thee for ever: he shall take thee away, and pluck thee out of thy dwelling-place, and root thee out of the land of the living. Selah.
> 6. The righteous also shall see, and fear, and shall laugh at him.
> 7. Lo! this is the man that made not God his strength; and trusted in the abundance of his riches, and strengthened himself in his wickedness.

5. *God shall likewise destroy thee for ever.* From these words it is made still more evident that his object in dwelling upon the aggravated guilt of Doeg, was to prove the certainty of his approaching doom, and this rather for his own conviction and comfort, than with a view to alarming the conscience of the offender. Accordingly, he declares his persuasion that God would not allow his treachery to pass unpunished, though he might for a time connive at the perpetration of it. The ungodly are disposed, so long as their prosperity continues, to indulge in undisturbed security; and the saint of God, when he sees the power of which they are possessed, and witnesses their proud contempt of the divine judgments, is too apt to be overwhelmed with unbelieving apprehensions. But in order to establish his mind in the

---

the deceitful tongue works its purposes of mischief before the objects which it means to ruin are conscious of their danger. It is like a sharp razor, that cuts the throat before a man is aware of it. "If, however, we take the words, *thou workest deceitfully*, as being descriptive not of the razor but of the tongue, the sense will be, that such a tongue is capable of inflicting deep and dreadful wounds like a sharp razor."—*Walford.*

[1] "בֶּלַע, *balang*, is *to swallow, to devour*, with the idea of eagerness, greediness."—*Gesenius.*

truth which he announces, it is observable that the Psalmist heaps one expression upon another,—God shall *destroy thee, take thee away, pluck thee out, root thee out,*—as if by this multiplicity of words he would convince himself more effectually, that God was able to overthrow this adversary with all his boasted might and authority.[1] In adding that God would root him out of his *dwelling-place* or *tent,*[2] and *out of the land of the living,* he insinuates that the wicked will be destroyed by God, however securely they may seem to repose in the nest of some comfortable mansion, and in the vain hope of living upon earth for ever. Possibly he may allude, in mentioning a *tent,* to the profession of Doeg, as shepherds have their dwelling in tents.

6. *The righteous also shall see, and fear.*[3] He here adduces, as another reason why the ruin of Doeg might be expected, that an important end would be obtained by it, in so far as it would promote religion in the hearts of the Lord's people, and afford them a refreshing display of the Divine justice.

---

[1] "Wonderful," says Bishop Horne, "is the force of the verbs in the original, which convey to us the four ideas of 'laying prostrate,' 'dissolving as by fire,' 'sweeping away as with a besom,' and 'totally extirpating root and branch,' as a tree eradicated from the spot on which it grew." The second verb, יחתך, *yachtecha,* Bythner explains, "*will snatch thee away,* as one snatches fire from a hearth. From חתה, *chatheh,* he *snatched off live coals or fire from one place to another.*"

[2] There is another interpretation of this expression which may here be stated. It has been thought that the allusion is to God's tabernacle. "מאהל, *meohel,*" says Hammond, "is literally 'from the tabernacle,' not 'from *thy* dwelling-place:' and so the LXX. render it, ''Ἀπὸ σκηνώματος,' 'from the tabernacle;' and though the Latin, and Syriac, and Arabic, have added *tuo, thy,* yet neither will the Hebrew bear, nor do the Chaldee acknowledge it, who read by way of paraphrase, 'He shall cause thee to depart from inhabiting in the place of the Schechina, or tabernacle, the place of God's presence.'" Hammond supposes that the expression is to be understood "of the censure of excommunication, which in the last and highest degree was *Schammatha,* delivering up the offender to the hand of heaven to be cut off, himself and his posterity." "Doeg," says Archbishop Secker, "had no office in the tabernacle; but it seems, by his history, that he frequented it, which he might do to seem a good man. And there seems an opposition between his being plucked out of God's dwelling-place, and David's continuing in the house of God, verse eighth."

[3] French and Skinner read, "The righteous shall see it, and feel reverence;—*feel reverence, i. e.,* in the punishment of this wicked man, find additional reason to reverence God, and to observe his righteous laws."

Should it take place, it would be witnessed by the ungodly as well as by the righteous; but there are two reasons why the Psalmist represents it as being seen especially by the latter. The wicked are incapable of profiting by the judgments of God, being blind to the plainest manifestations which he has made of himself in his works, and it was only the righteous therefore who *could* see it. Besides, the great end which God has in view, when he prostrates the pride of the ungodly, is the comfort of his own people, that he may show to them the care with which he watches over their safety. It is they, therefore, whom David represents as witnessing this spectacle of Divine justice. And when he says that they would *fear*, it is not meant that they would tremble, or experience any slavish apprehension, but that their reverential regard for God would be increased by this proof of his care of their interests. When left exposed to the injurious treatment of their enemies, they are apt to be distressed with doubts as to the concern which he takes in the government of the world. But such illustrations to the contrary have the effect of quickening their discouraged zeal, and promoting that fear which is by no means inconsistent with the joy spoken of in the close of the verse. They are led to reverence him the more when they see that he is the avenger of cruelty and injustice: on the other hand, when they perceive that he appears in defence of their cause, and joins common battle with them against their adversaries, they are naturally filled with the most triumphant joy. The beautiful play upon the words *see* and *fear*, in the Hebrew, cannot be transferred to our language; the form of the expression intimates that they would see, and see effectually.

7. *Lo! this is the man that made not God his strength.* Some think that these words are given as what should afterwards be proverbially applied to Doeg; but they would not appear to have been intended in that restricted signification. They merely express the improvement which the people of God would make of the judgment. It would teach them, on the one hand, to be patient under the insolence of the ungodly, which is so speedily humbled; and, on the other, to

beware of indulging a similarly infatuated spirit themselves. They would laugh at their destruction, yet not in the way of insulting over them, but rejoicing more and more in the confidence of the help of God, and denying themselves more cheerfully to the vain pleasures of this world. This is the lesson to be learned from such dispensations of providence: they should recall our wandering affections to God. The verse is introduced with an exclamation, *Lo! this is the man,* &c.; for David would have us to look upon this one instance as representing to our eyes, in a vivid manner, the end of all who despise the Lord; and it may be remarked, that it is no small point of practical wisdom thus to generalize individual providences. The two clauses, *made not God his strength,* and, *trusted in the abundance of his riches,* stand mutually connected; for none can be said sincerely to repose upon God but he who has been emptied of all confidence in his own resources. So long as men imagine that they have something of their own in which they can boast, they will never resort to God: just in proportion as we arrogate to ourselves do we derogate from him; and it is not only wealth, but any other earthly possession, which, by engrossing our confidence, may prevent us from inquiring after the Lord. The noun הוה, *havah,* which most interpreters have rendered *wickedness,*[1] and some *slaughter* or *destruction,* seems, in this place, rather to mean *substance.*[2] Such repetitions of the same sentiment in different words are common with the Psalmist; and, according to this translation, the verse will flow connectedly, reading, that the man who trusts in his riches, and strengthens himself in his substance, defrauds God of his just glory.

> 8. *But I am like a green olive-tree in the house of God: I have hoped in the goodness of God for ever and ever.*
> 9. *I will praise thee for ever, because thou hast done it: I will wait on thy name, for it is good before thy meek ones.*

[1] If this is the true rendering, there may be a reference to the expectations which Doeg had entertained of increasing his power and influence by maliciously injuring David, as he would thereby obtain, in a high degree, the favour of Saul.

[2] This is the marginal reading in our English Bible. As he was Saul's chief herdsman, it is probable that his riches consisted chiefly in cattle.

8. *But I am like a green olive-tree.*[1] We have seen that David was enabled, by the exercise of faith, to look down upon the worldly grandeur of Doeg with a holy contempt; and now we find him rising superior to all that was presently afflictive in his own condition. Though, to appearance, he more resembled the withered trunk of a tree which rots upon the ground, he compares himself, in the confidence of coming prosperity, to a green olive. I need not say that the destruction of Doeg could only communicate comfort to his mind, in the way of convincing him that God was the avenging judge of human cruelty, and leading him to infer that, as he had punished his wrongs, so he would advance him to renewed measures of prosperity. From his language, it appears that he could conceive of no higher felicity in his condition than being admitted amongst the number of the worshippers of

---

[1] Our English Bible also reads, "like a green olive-tree;" but it would be more correct to translate, "I am like a flourishing, or vigorous olive-tree." The original word, רענן, *raänan*, has no reference to the colour of the tree, but to its fresh, vigorous, and flourishing condition. Hence this word is used, in Ps. xcii. 11, to express "*fresh* oil;" and in Dan. iv. 4, to denote the prosperous condition of Nebuchadnezzar, "I was at rest in mine house, and *flourishing* in my palace." The fact is, that the colour of the olive-tree, so far from being of a bright and lively green, is dark, disagreeable, and yellowish. Travellers, when they have seen this tree, have experienced a feeling of disappointment in not finding it to possess the vivid verdure which they had been led to expect from the description given of it in the Scriptures. An excellent English traveller, Mr Sharpe, writing from Italy, thus expresses himself on this subject: "The fields, and indeed the whole face of Tuscany, are in a manner covered with olive-trees; but the olive-tree does not answer the character I had conceived of it. The royal Psalmist, and some of the sacred writers, speak with rapture of the 'green olive-tree,' so that I expected a beautiful green; and I confess to you I was wretchedly disappointed to find its hue resembling that of our hedges when they are covered with dust." But this disappointment which Mr Sharpe felt arose not from overcharged or exaggerated colouring on the part of the sacred writers, but from his not understanding the meaning of their language. The beauty of the olive-tree is represented in other parts of Scripture as consisting, not in the greenness of its foliage, but in the spread of its branches, (Hosea xiv. 6.) —*Harmer's Observations*, vol. iii. pp. 255-257. The propriety and beauty of the comparison which David here makes appears from the fact that the olive is an evergreen, and is also, considering its size, long-lived. While, in the 5th verse, he had predicted the speedy and total destruction of Doeg, comparing him to a tree plucked up by the roots, he, in contrast with this, represents himself as like a young, vigorous olive-tree, which had long to live and flourish; confidently expecting to obtain that outward peace and prosperity which God had promised him, and, along with this, the enjoyment of all spiritual blessings.

God, and engaging in the exercises of devotion. This was characteristic of his spirit. We have already had occasion to see that he felt his banishment from the sanctuary of God more keenly than separation from his consort, the loss of worldly substance, or the dangers and hardships of the wilderness. The idea of an allusion being here made, by way of contrast, to Doeg, who came to the tabernacle of the Lord merely as a spy, and under hypocritical pretexts, is strained and far-fetched. It is more natural to suppose that David distinguishes himself from all his enemies, without exception, intimating that, though he was presently removed from the tabernacle, he would soon be restored to it; and that they who boasted of possessing, or rather monopolizing, the house of God, would be rooted out of it with disgrace. And here let us engrave the useful lesson upon our hearts, that we should consider it the great end of our existence to be found numbered amongst the worshippers of God; and that we should avail ourselves of the inestimable privilege of the stated assemblies of the Church, which are necessary helps to our infirmity, and means of mutual excitement and encouragement. By these, and our common Sacraments, the Lord, who is one God, and who designed that we should be one in him, is training us up together in the hope of eternal life, and in the united celebration of his holy name. Let us learn with David to prefer a place in the house of God to all the lying vanities of this world. He adds the reason why he should be like the green olive-tree—because *he hoped in the goodness of God;* for the causal particle appears to be understood. And in this he adverts to the contrast between him and his enemies. They might flourish for a time, spread their branches far and wide, and shoot themselves up to a gigantic stature, but would speedily wither away, because they had no root in the goodness of God; whereas he was certain to derive from this source ever renewed supplies of sap and vigour. As the term of his earthly trials might be protracted, and there was a danger that he might sink under their long continuance, unless his confidence should extend itself far into futurity, he declares expressly that he would not presume to prescribe times to God, and that his hopes were stretched into eternity.

It followed that he surrendered himself entirely to God in all that regarded this life or his death. The passage puts us in possession of the grand distinction between the genuine children of God and those who are hypocrites. They are to be found together in the Church, as the wheat is mingled with the chaff on the same threshing-floor; but the one class abides for ever in the stedfastness of a well-founded hope, while the other is driven away in the vanity of its false confidences.

9. *I will praise thee, &c.* He concludes the psalm with thanksgiving, and shows that he is sincere in this, by the special acknowledgment which he makes of the fact that this had been the work of God. Such is the corruption of the human heart, that out of a hundred who profess gratitude to God with their lips, scarcely one man seriously reflects upon the benefits which he has received as coming from his hand. David declares, therefore, that it was entirely owing to the divine protection that he had escaped from the treachery of Doeg, and from all his subsequent dangers, and promises to retain a grateful sense of it throughout the whole of his life. There is no religious duty in which it does not become us to manifest a spirit of perseverance; but we need to be especially enjoined to it in the duty of thanksgiving, disposed as we are so speedily to forget our mercies, and occasionally to imagine that the gratitude of a few days is a sufficient tribute for benefits which deserve to be kept in everlasting remembrance. He speaks of joining the exercise of hope with that of gratitude; for *to wait on the name of God* is synonymous with patiently expecting his mercy even when there is least appearance of its being granted, and trusting in his word, whatever delays there may be in the fulfilment of it. He encourages himself in the belief that his hope will not be vain, by reflecting that the name of God *is good before his saints.* Some read, *because it is good before thy saints;* that is, to hope in the divine name, (Ps. cxviii. 8.) But the other reading appears to me to be the most simple and natural, expressing the truth, that God will not frustrate the expectations of his people, because his goodness towards them is always conspicuous. The name of God may be detested

by the wicked, and the very sound of it be sufficient to strike terror into their hearts; but David asserts it to be a sweet name in the experience of all his people. They are here called his meek ones, because, as I have remarked in commenting upon Ps. xvi. 3, they reflect in their character the kindness and beneficence of their Father in heaven.

PSALM LIII.

This psalm being almost identical with the *fourteenth*, it has not been considered necessary to subjoin any distinct commentary.[1]

¶ To the chief musician upon Mahalath.[2] A Psalm of David for instruction.

1. *The fool hath said in his heart, There is no God: they have become corrupt, they have done abominable works: there is none that doeth good.*
2. *God looked down from heaven upon the children of men, to see if there were any that did understand, that did seek God.*
3. *Every one of them has gone back; they have together become filthy: there is none that doeth good, no, not one.*

---

[1] Some slight differences will be found, on comparison, between this and the 14th psalm; the chief of which is in the 5th verse. For Calvin's explanation of this verse, see vol. i. p. 199. It is not easy to say whether these variations are owing to transcribers, or whether they were made by some prophetic bard, who, during some afflictive period of Jewish history, adapted the 14th psalm, by a few alterations, to circumstances different from those for which it was originally composed. Theodoret is of this last opinion, and refers it to the alarm created by Sennacherib's invasion under the reign of Hezekiah; others think it was written during the captivity—a conjecture which is founded on the last verse, "O that the salvation of Israel were come out of Zion!"

[2] "What מחלת, *mahalath*, signifies, in the title of this and the 88th psalm, must be uncertain, the word not being found elsewhere. It is most probably the name of an instrument on which the psalm was to be sung; and it may fitly be deduced from חלל, *perforavit*, or *incidit*, either from the hollowness of the instrument, or farther, from the holes cut in it; in which respect חליל is ordinarily used for *fistula*, or *tibia, a pipe*."—*Hammond.*

4. *Have the workers of iniquity no knowledge? eating my people as they eat bread:*[1] *they have not called upon God.*
5. *There were they in great fear where no fear was; for God hath scattered the bones of him that encampeth against thee: thou hast put them to shame, because God hath despised them.*
6. *Who shall give the salvation of Israel out of Zion? When God bringeth back the captivity of his people,*[2] *Jacob shall rejoice, and Israel shall triumph.*

PSALM LIV.

David has recorded in this psalm the prayers which he offered up to God when he heard of his having been betrayed by the Ziphites, and was reduced to a situation of extreme danger. It cannot fail to impress us with a high idea of his indomitable faith, thus to find him calling upon the name of God in the immediate prospect of death.

¶ To the chief musician on Neginoth. A Psalm of David for instruction: when the Ziphites came and said to Saul, Doth not David hide himself with us?

We know from the sacred history that David frequently concealed himself in that part of the wilderness which adjoined to the Ziphites. It appears (1 Sam. xxiii. 19; xxvi. 1) that he was betrayed by them on two different occasions; and he takes notice of the particular circumstances in which the psalm was written, to teach us that we should never despair of divine help even in the worst situation. Surrounded as he was by hostile troops, and hemmed in on every side by apparently inevitable destruction, we cannot but admire the rare and heroical intrepidity which he displayed in committing himself, by prayer, to the Almighty. It might have appeared just as credible that God could bring the dead out of the grave, as that he could preserve him in such circumstances; for it seemed impossible that he should escape from the cave where he was concealed with his life.

1. *Save me, O God! by thy name, and judge me by thy strength.*

[1] "C'est, n'en font non plus de conscience, que de manger un morceau de pain."—*Fr. marg.* "That is, they have no more scruple in doing this than in eating a morsel of bread."

[2] "C'est, son peuple captif."—*Fr. marg.* "That is, his captive people."

2. *Hear my prayer, O God! give ear to the words of my mouth.*

3. *For strangers are risen up against me, and the terrible ones have sought after my soul: they have not set God before them. Selah.*

1. *Save me, O God!* As David was at this time placed beyond the reach of human assistance, he must be understood as praying to be saved by the *name* and *the power of God*, in an emphatical sense, or by these in contradistinction to the usual means of deliverance. Though all help must ultimately come from God, there are ordinary methods by which he generally extends it. When these fail, and every earthly stay is removed, he must then take the work into his own hands. It was in such a situation that David here fled to the saints' last asylum, and sought to be saved by a miracle of divine power. By appealing, in the second part of the verse, to God as his judge, he asserts his uprightness. And it must strike us all, that in asking the divine protection it is indispensably prerequisite we should be convinced of the goodness of our cause, as it would argue the greatest profanity in any to expect that God should patronize iniquity. David was encouraged to pray for deliverance by the goodness of his cause and his consciousness of integrity; nor did he entertain a single doubt, that on representing this to God he would act the part of his defender, and punish the cruelty and treachery of his enemies.

2. *Hear my prayer, O God!* The language is expressive of his earnestness. He was led to this fervour of supplication by the extremity of his present circumstances, which is alluded to in the following verse, where he complains of being surrounded by men fierce, barbarous, and unrestrained by a sense of religion. There was no necessity for his informing God of a fact which was already known to him; but he disburdens his own heart by venting the cause of his fear and disquietude. By calling his enemies *strangers*,[1] he seems to

---

[1] For זרים, *zairim, strangers,* upwards of twenty MSS. have זדים, *zoidim, the proud;* and this is the sense given by the Chaldee Paraphrast. As the

refer to their barbarity, whether he applied the name to the Ziphites only, or, in general, to the whole army of Saul. Others consider him, in this term, to advert to their degeneracy as children of Abraham; and it is true that the Jews are repeatedly stigmatized by the prophets under this form of expression, when they had cast themselves out of the Church of God by their profligacy or impiety. But in this passage it seems to be used in a different sense. As even enemies are accustomed, in some measure, to respect the ties of kindred and relationship, David would point out to us the monstrous inhumanity of the men who now surrounded him, by the fact that they assaulted him as *strangers*, as persons who had never known him, or as if he had been born in some distant part of the world. He calls them, also, *terrible ones*,[1] *not mighty*, or *powerful ones*, as some have rendered the word; for that falls short of the meaning intended by David, which was, that they were divested of all humanity, and ready to rush upon him like wild beasts. Hence the fear with which he resorted to the protection of God. He adds, that *they sought after his soul*, to denote that nothing would content their insatiable cruelty but his life. And the better to express the unbridled nature of their fury, he tells us that they had no respect to God. The only thing which could be supposed, in the circumstances, to act as a restraint upon their minds, was the consideration of there being a judge in heaven to whom they were amenable for their conduct; and being insensible to this, what moderation could be expected of them?

4. *Behold! God is my helper; the Lord is with them that uphold my soul.*
5. *He shall reward evil unto mine enemies: cut them off in thy truth.*

Ziphites were Jews, and of the same tribe with David, (Joshua xv. 24,) and therefore not, strictly speaking, "strangers," some think that *the proud* is the true reading. But the Ziphites, as our Author justly observes, may be called "strangers," because they acted towards David the part of strangers and enemies, in seeking to deliver him into the hands of his unjust and cruel persecutor, Saul.

[1] Ainsworth reads, "Daunting tyrants." "*Terrible dismayers*, as Saul and his retinue, whose terror daunted many. See Ps. x. 18."

6. *I will freely sacrifice unto thee : I will praise thy name, O God ! for it is good.*
7. *For he hath delivered me out of all trouble; and mine eye hath seen upon my adversaries.*[1]

4. *Behold ! God is my helper.* Such language as this may show us that David did not direct his prayers at random into the air, but offered them in the exercise of a lively faith. There is much force in the demonstrative adverb. He points, as it were, with the finger, to that God who stood at his side to defend him; and was not this an amazing illustration of the power with which faith can surmount all obstacles, and glance, in a moment, from the depths of despair to the very throne of God ? He was a fugitive amongst the dens of the earth, and even there in hazard of his life—how, then, could he speak of God as being near to him ? He was pressed down to the very mouth of the grave ; and how could he recognize the gracious presence of God ? He was trembling in the momentary expectation of being destroyed ; and how is it possible that he can triumph in the certain hope that Divine help will presently be extended to him ? In numbering God amongst his defenders, we must not suppose that he assigns him a mere common rank amongst the men who supported his cause, which would have been highly derogatory to his glory. He means that God took part with those, such as Jonathan and others, who were interested in his welfare. These might be few in number, possessed of little

[1] The translators of our English Bible have supposed an ellipsis here; and hence they supply " my desire." Calvin, in his translation of the verse, makes no supplement, but understands it in a similar sense, "My eye hath seen punishment upon my adversaries ;" just as it is said in Psalm xci. 8, " With thine eyes shalt thou behold and see *the reward* of the wicked." But if we read the words literally, without any supplement, and as they are rendered by the LXX. and the Syriac, " My eyes beheld, or looked upon mine enemies," they will be susceptible of a very good and natural meaning. David's enemies were not at this time destroyed ; but Saul, when he had reached the farther side of the mountain where David lay concealed, and was about to seize his victim, having heard that the Philistines invaded the land, hastened in confusion to repel the invaders. The meaning of David's language, therefore, may be, that he was so near Saul and his army as to behold them marching away, which may be easily conceived, when it is considered that " Saul went on this side of the mountain Maon, and David and his men on that side of the mountain," (1 Sam. xxiii. 26.)

power, and cast down with fears; but he believed that, under the guidance and protection of the Almighty, they would prove superior to his enemies : or, perhaps, we may view him as referring, in the words, to his complete destitution of all human defenders, and asserting that the help of God would abundantly compensate for all.[1]

5. *He shall reward evil unto mine enemies.* As the verb ישיב, *yashib*, may be rendered *he shall cause to return*,[2] it seems to point not only at the punishment, but the kind of punishment, which would be awarded to his enemies, in the recoiling of their wicked machinations upon their own heads. Some give an optative signification to the verb, understanding the words to express a wish or prayer; but I see no reason why it should not be taken strictly in the future tense, and imagine that David intimates his certain expectation that this favour, which he had already prayed for, would be granted. It is by no means uncommon to find the prayers of the Psalmist intersected with sentences of this kind, inserted for the purpose of stimulating his faith, as here, where he announces the general truth, that God is the righteous judge who will recompense the wicked. With the view of confirming his hopes, he adverts particularly to *the truth* of God ; for nothing can support us in the hour of temptation, when the Divine deliverance may be long delayed, but a firm per-

[1] The phrase, אדני בסמכי, *Adonai besomkey*, which Calvin renders, "The Lord is with them that uphold," is translated by Hammond, "The Lord among the sustainers ;" and he remarks, that this form of expression, which is not unusual among the Hebrews, signifies no more than "God is my upholder ; not one of many upholders, but my only upholder." Thus, when Jephtha (Judges xi. 35) tells his daughter, "Thou art among the troublers of me," or "one of them that trouble me," the meaning simply is, that she very much grieved and troubled him. So Psalm lv. 18, "There were many with me ;" *i. e.*, "God was with me," which is as good as the greatest multitude. This is the sense in which the learned Castellio understands the passage, rendering it, "Dominus is est qui mihi vitam sustentat ;" "The Lord is he who sustains my life ;" and he defends it by the above and like arguments. With this the Septuagint agrees : " Κυριος ἀντιλήπτωρ τῆς ψυχῆς μου," "The Lord is the defender of my soul ;" and also the Syriac, Arabic, and Æthiopic.

[2] French and Skinner read, "May their mischief return upon those who watch me ;" and observe, that *their mischief* in Hebrew is *the evil*, and that the meaning is, the very evil which they devised against me. Compare Ps. vii. 16."

suasion that God is true, and that he cannot deceive us by his divine promises. His confidence of obtaining his request was grounded upon the circumstance that God could no more deny his word than deny himself.

6. *I will freely sacrifice unto thee.* According to his usual custom, he engages, provided deliverance should be granted, to feel a grateful sense of it; and there can be no doubt that he here promises also to return thanks to God, in a formal manner, when he should enjoy an opportunity of doing so. Though God principally looks to the inward sentiment of the heart, that would not excuse the neglect of such rites as the Law had prescribed. He would testify his sense of the favour which he received, in the manner common to all the people of God, by sacrifices, and be thus the means of exciting others to their duty by his example. And he would *sacrifice freely:* by which he does not allude to the circumstance, that sacrifices of thanksgiving were at the option of worshippers, but to the alacrity and cheerfulness with which he would pay his vow when he had escaped his present dangers. The generality of men promise largely to God so long as they are under the present pressure of affliction, but are no sooner relieved than they relapse into that carelessness which is natural to them, and forget the goodness of the Lord. But David engages to sacrifice freely, and in another manner than the hypocrite, whose religion is the offspring of servility and constraint. We are taught by the passage that, in coming into the presence of God, we cannot look for acceptance unless we bring to his service a willing mind. The last clause of this verse, and the verse which follows, evidently refer to the time when the Psalmist had obtained the deliverance which he sought. The whole psalm, it is true, must have been written after his deliverance; but up to this point it is to be considered as recording the form of prayer which he used when yet exposed to the danger. We are now to suppose him relieved from his anxieties, and subjoining a fresh expression of his gratitude : nor is it improbable that he refers to mercies which he had experienced at other periods

of his history, and which were recalled to his memory by the one more immediately brought under our notice in the preceding verses; so that he is to be understood as declaring, in a more general sense, that *the name of God was good, and that he had been delivered out of all trouble.* I have already adverted, in a former psalm, (Ps. lii. 6,) to the sense in which the righteous are said *to see* the destruction of their enemies. It is such a sight of the event as is accompanied with joy and comfort; and should any inquire, whether it is allowable for the children of God to feel pleasure in witnessing the execution of Divine judgments upon the wicked, the answer is obvious, that all must depend upon the motive by which they are influenced. If their satisfaction proceed in any measure from the gratification of a depraved feeling, it must be condemned; but there is certainly a pure and unblameable delight which we may feel in looking upon such illustrations of the divine justice.

PSALM LV.

Many interpreters have thought that this psalm refers to the conspiracy of Absalom, by which David was driven from the throne, and forced to take refuge under circumstances of great distress in the wilderness. But it seems rather to have been written at a period when he was reduced to extreme danger by the persecutions of Saul. It is a prayer, expressive of the deepest distress, and full of fervour, urging every consideration which could be supposed to solicit the compassion of God. After having disburdened his sorrows and given utterance to his requests, the Psalmist contemplates the prospect of deliverance, and offers thanksgivings to God as if he had already obtained it.

¶ To the chief musician on Neginoth. A Psalm of David for instruction.

1. *Give ear to my prayer, O God! and hide not thyself from my supplication.*

2. *Attend unto me, and answer me. I will wail*[1] *in my address,*[2] *and make a noise.*[3]

3. *By reason of the voice of the enemy, under the affliction of the wicked: for they cast iniquity upon me, and in wrath they fight against me.*

1. *Give ear to my prayer, O God!* From the language with which the psalm opens, we may conclude that David at this time was labouring under heavy distress. It could be no ordinary amount of it which produced such an overwhelming effect upon a saint of his distinguished courage. The translation which has been given of אריד, *arid, I will prevail*, does violence to the context, for, so far from boasting of the fortitude which would govern his address, he is anxious to convey an impression of his wretchedness, by intimating that he was constrained to cry out aloud. What is added in the third verse, *By reason of the voice of the enemy*, may be viewed as connected either with the first verse or that immediately preceding, or with both. By the *voice* some understand such a noise as is occasioned by a multitude of men; as if he had said, that the enemy was mustering many troops against him: but he rather alludes to the threatenings which we may suppose that Saul was in the habit of venting upon this innocent prophet. The interpretation, too, which has been given of the *casting of iniquity* upon him, as if it meant that his enemies loaded him with false accusations, is strained, and scarcely consistent with the context. The words are designed to correspond with the succeeding clause, where it is said that *his enemies fought against him in wrath;* and, therefore, *to cast*

---

[1] The verb אריד, *arid,* which Calvin renders, "I will wail," is rendered by Boothroyd, "I am distressed, confused, distracted." Mudge is of opinion that אריד, *arid,* is derived from ירד, *yarad, to tincture, to drop,* &c.; and hence he reads, "While I weep in my complaint."

[2] "Meditation or discoursing, talk, prayer, complaint. The Hebrew *siach* signifieth any large discourse or exercise of the mind or mouth, by busy musing, talking, praying, communing with one's self or others."—*Ainsworth.*

[3] "*Heb.* am in a violent tumultuous agitation, as the waves of the sea."—*Bishop Horne.* The original word הום, *hum,* according to Gesenius, signifies "*to put in motion, throw into commotion, consternation, to agitate;* and *Hiph. to make commotion,* to make a noise, spoken of an unquiet mind, internal commotion, Ps. lv. 3."

iniquity upon him means, in my opinion, no more than to discharge their unjust violence upon him for his destruction, or iniquitously to plot his ruin. If any distinction be intended between the two clauses, perhaps the *fighting against him in wrath* may refer to their open violence, and *the casting of iniquity upon him*[1] to their deceitful treachery. In this case, אָוֶן, *aven*, which I have rendered *iniquity*, will signify hidden malice. The *affliction of the wicked* is here to be understood in the active sense of *persecution*. And in applying the term *wicked* to his enemies, he does not so much level an accusation against them as implicitly assert his own innocence. Our greatest comfort under persecution is conscious rectitude, the reflection that we have not deserved it; for there springs from this the hope that we will experience the help of the Lord, who is the shield and defence of the distressed.

4. *My heart trembles within me, and the terrors of death have fallen upon me.*
5. *Fearfulness and trembling are come upon me, and horror hath overwhelmed me.*
6. *And I said, Who will give me wings like a dove? I will fly away, and be at rest.*
7. *Lo! I will prolong the flight,*[2] *I will repose in the wilderness. Selah.*
8. *I will hasten a deliverance for me,*[3] *from the wind raised by the whirlwind.*

4. *My heart trembles within me.*[4] Here we have additional evidence of the extremity of David's sufferings. He that

---

[1] "Literally *slide iniquity upon me*; *i. e.*, by oblique and artful insinuations they asperse my character. The sentiment of the whole line I take to be this, that the enemies of the Psalmist, by sly insinuations, brought him under the suspicion of the worst enemies, and then wreaked their malice upon him under the colour of a just resentment."—*Horsley.*

[2] "C'est, m'enfuiray bien loin."—*Fr. marg.* "That is, I will flee afar off."

[3] "C'est, hasteroye de m'eschapper."—*Fr. marg.* "That is, I will hasten to escape."

[4] "*My heart is in travail within me.* חִיל, *de tremore* maxime parturientium."—*Fry.* Ainsworth reads, "My heart is pained within me, or trembleth with pain." "The word," says he, "usually meaneth such pains as a woman feeleth in her travail."

uses these words was no soft or effeminate person, but one who had given indubitable proofs of constancy. Nor is it merely of the atrocious injuries inflicted upon him by his enemies that he complains. He exclaims that he is overwhelmed with terrors, and thus acknowledges that his heart was not insensible to his afflictions. We may learn from the passage, therefore, not only that the sufferings which David endured at this time were heavy, but that the fortitude of the greatest servants of God fails them in the hour of severe trial. We are all good soldiers so long as things go well with us, but when brought to close combat, our weakness is soon apparent. Satan avails himself of the advantage, suggests that God has withdrawn the supports of his Spirit, and instigates us to despair. Of this we have an example in David, who is here represented as struggling with inward fears, as well as a complication of outward calamities, and sustaining a sore conflict of spirit in his application to the throne of God. The expression, *terrors of death*, shows that he was on the very eve of sinking unless Divine grace interposed.

6. *And I said, Who will give me wings like a dove?*[1] These words mean more than merely that he could find no mode of

---

[1] This very beautiful image, derived from the flight of the dove, is continued in the two following verses. The defencelessness of the dove, the danger to which it is exposed from birds of prey, the surprising rapidity with which, when pursued by the hawk, it flees to deserts and rocks to hide itself, putting forth its utmost speed, and outstripping its deadly pursuer; all these characteristics of this bird were in the view of the Psalmist on the present occasion. We find an allusion to them in Jer. xlviii. 28: "O ye that dwell in Moab, leave the cities, and dwell in the rock, and be like the dove that maketh her nest in the sides of the hole's mouth." The poets of Greece and Rome make frequent allusions to the rapid flight of the dove :—

"So, when the falcon wings her way above,
To the cleft cavern speeds the gentle dove,
Not fated yet to die."—*Pope's Homer.*

Sophocles, in a passage somewhat similar to this of the Psalmist, says, "O that with the rapid whirlwind flight of a dove I could cleave the etherial clouds!"—(*Œdip. Colon.* 1136.) "Kimshi gives it as the reason why the Psalmist prefers the dove to other birds, that while they become weary with flying, and alight upon a rock or a tree to recruit their strength, and are taken; the dove, when she is fatigued, alternately rests one wing, and flies with the other, and, by this means, escapes from the

escape. They are meant to express the deplorableness of his situation, which made exile a blessing to be coveted, and this not the common exile of mankind, but such as that of the dove when it flies far off to some deserted hiding-place. They imply that he could only escape by a miracle. They intimate that even the privilege of retreat by common banishment was denied him, so that it fared worse with him than with the poor bird of heaven, which can at least fly from its pursuer. Some think that the dove is singled out on account of its swiftness. The Jews held the ridiculous idea that the Hebrew reads *wing* in the singular number, because doves use but one wing in flying; whereas nothing is more common in Scripture than such a change of number. It seems most probable that David meant by this comparison, that he longed to escape from his cruel enemies, as the timid and defenceless dove flies from the hawk. Great, indeed, must have been the straits to which he was reduced, when he could so far forget the promise made to him of the kingdom as, in the agitation of his spirits, to contemplate a disgraceful flight, and speak of being content to hide himself far from his native country, and the haunts of human society, in some solitude of the wilderness. Nay, he adds, as if by way of concession to the fury of his adversaries, that he was willing (would they grant it) *to wander far off*, that he was not proposing terms of truce to them which he never meant to fulfil, merely to gain time, as those will do who entertain some secret and distant hope of deliverance. We may surely say that these are the words of a man driven to the borders of desperation. Such was the extremity in which he stood, that though prepared to abandon all, he could not obtain life even upon that condition. In such circumstances, in the anguish of this anxiety, we must not wonder that his heart was overwhelmed with the sorrows of death. The Hebrew word סוּעָה, *soah*, which I have rendered *raised*, is by

---

swiftest pursuers."—(*Paxton's Illustrations of Scripture*, vol. ii. p. 292.) It is worthy of observation, and it serves to heighten the effect of the Psalmist's comparison, that יוֹנָה, *yonah*, the Hebrew name of the dove, is derived from ינה, *yanah, he hath oppressed by force or fraud*, and seems to have been applied to it from the circumstance of its being particularly defenceless, and exposed to rapine and violence.—*Buxtorf's Lexicon*.

some translated *tempestuous;* and there can be no doubt that the Psalmist means a stormy wind raised by a whirlwind. When he says that this wind *is raised by the whirlwind*,[1] by this circumlocution he means a violent wind, such as compels the traveller to fly and seek shelter in the nearest dwelling or covert.

> 9. Destroy, O Lord! and divide their tongue: for I have seen persecution and strife in the city.
> 10. Day and night they go about it upon the walls thereof: labour[2] also, and sorrow, are in the midst of it.
> 11. Wickedness is in the midst thereof; deceit and guile depart not from her streets.

9. *Destroy,[3] O Lord! and divide their tongue.* Having now composed, as it were, his mind, he resumes the exercise of prayer. Had he indulged longer in the strain of complaint, he might have given his sanction to the folly of those who do themselves more harm than good by the excessive use of this barren species of comfort. There will occasionally escape from the lips of a saint, when he prays, some complaining

---

[1] Whirlwinds are not uncommon in Palestine, and the surrounding countries, and to them we often find allusions in the Sacred Writings. The description of that kind of whirlwind called the Sammiel, which sometimes happens between Egypt and Nubia, will serve to show the propriety with which David made this allusion in his present circumstances of distress and danger. "This wind, which the Arabs call poisonous, stifles on the spot those that are unfortunate enough to breathe in it: so that to guard against its pernicious effects, they are obliged to throw themselves speedily on the ground, with their face close to these burning sands, with which they are surrounded, and to cover their heads with some cloth or carpet, lest, in respiration, they should suck in that deadly quality which everywhere attends it. People ought even to think themselves very happy when this wind, which is always besides very violent, does not raise up large quantities of sand with a whirling motion, which, darkening the air, render the guides incapable of discerning their way. Sometimes whole caravans have been buried by this means under the sand, with which this wind is frequently charged."—Maillet, quoted in *Harmer's Observations,* vol. i. p. 95.

[2] "Malice."—*Fr.*

[3] Hare, Green, and others, conjecture that the first verb in the verse, "destroy," had been originally "divide"—"divide, O Lord! divide their tongues." In Scripture we sometimes meet with an elegant repetition of this kind, as in Psalm lix. 13, "Consume them in wrath, consume them, that they may not be."

exclamations which cannot be altogether justified, but he soon recalls himself to the exercise of believing supplication. In the expression, *divide their tongue,* there seems an allusion to the judgment which fell upon the builders of Babel, (Gen. xxxi. 7.) He means in general to pray that God would break their criminal confederacies, and distract their impious counsels, but evidently with an indirect reference to that memorable proof which God gave of his power to thwart the designs of the wicked by confounding their communication. It is thus that to this day he weakens the enemies of the Church, and splits them into factions, through the force of mutual animosities, rivalries, and disagreements in opinion. For his own encouragement in prayer, the Psalmist proceeds to insist upon the wickedness and malignity of his adversaries, this being a truth never to be lost sight of, that just in proportion as men grow rampant in sin, may it be anticipated that the divine judgments are about to descend upon them. From the unbridled license prevailing amongst them, he comforts himself with the reflection that the deliverance of God cannot be far distant; for he visits the proud, but gives more grace to the humble. Before proceeding to pray for divine judgments against them, he would intimate that he had full knowledge of their evil and injurious character. Interpreters have spent an unnecessary degree of labour in determining whether the *city* here spoken of was that of Jerusalem or of Keilah, for David by this term would appear merely to denote the open and public prevalence of crime in the country. The *city* stands opposed to places more hidden and obscure, and he insinuates that strife was practised with unblushing publicity. Granting that the city meant was the metropolis of the kingdom, this is no reason why we should not suppose that the Psalmist had in his view the general state of the country; but the term is, in my opinion, evidently employed in an indefinite sense, to intimate that such wickedness as is generally committed in secret was at that time openly and publicly perpetrated. It is with the same view of marking the aggravated character of the wickedness then reigning in the nation, that he describes their crimes as going about the walls, keeping sentry or watch, so to speak, upon them. Walls are supposed to protect a city from rapine and incursion, but he complains that this order of things was inverted—that the city, instead of being surrounded with fortifications, was beset with strife and oppression, or that these had possession of the walls, and went about them.¹ I have already commented elsewhere upon the words אָוֶן, *aven*, and עָמָל, *amal*. In announcing that *wickedness was in the midst* of the city, and *deceit and guile* in her streets, he points to the true source of the prevailing crimes; even as it was to be expected that those who were inwardly corrupt, and given to such mischievous devices, would indulge in violence, and in persecuting the poor and defenceless. In general, he is to be considered as adverting in this passage to the deplorable confusions which marked the government of Saul, when justice and order were in a manner banished from the realm. And whether his description were intended to apply to one city or to many, matters had surely reached a portentous crisis in a nation professing the true religion, when any of their cities had thus become a den of robbers. It may be observed, too, that David, in denouncing a curse, as he does in the psalm before us, upon cities of this description, was obviously borne out by what must have been the judgment of the Holy Spirit against them.

> 12. *Of a truth, it was not an enemy that cast reproach upon me, for then I could have borne it :*² *it was not an adversary that did magnify himself against me, for then I would have hid* ³ *myself from him.*

¹ "Violence and Strife" are here personified, as sentinels or patrol, who keep watch over the city; going their rounds upon the walls to guard "labour, sorrow, wickedness, deceit, and guile," which reign in the midst of it, and to exclude happiness, righteousness, and truth. "It is, in fact," says Bishop Mant, "a very fine specimen of that power of personification, or enduing general and abstract ideas with personal qualities; and thus introducing them acting and speaking upon the stage, for which the Hebrew poets are distinguished, equalling therein the most polished writers of other nations in elegance and beauty, and surpassing the most elevated in grandeur and sublimity."

² " C'est, receu et soustenu le coup."—*Fr. marg.* "That is, received and sustained the blow."

³ " C'est, donné garde."—*Fr. marg.* "That is, been on my guard."

13. *But it was thou, a man of mine own order, my leader, and mine acquaintance.*
14. *We sweetly exchanged our most secret thoughts ;*[1] *we walked into the house of God in company.*
15. *Let death seize upon them, let them descend alive into the grave : for wickedness is in their dwelling, and in the midst of them.*

12. *Of a truth, it was not an enemy that cast reproach upon me.* He informs us of one circumstance which added bitterness to the injuries under which he suffered, that they came from the hands not only of his professed enemies, but of such as pretended to be his friends. Those mistake the meaning of נשׂא, *nasa,* who interpret it as if David had said, that he *could patiently have borne* the reproach of an open enemy. What he says is, that had an open enemy reproached him, he could then have *met it,* as one meets and parries off a blow which is aimed at him. Against a known foe we are on our watch, but the unsuspected stroke of a friend takes us by surprise. By adopting this view of the word, we shall find that the repetition in the verse is more perfect; reading in the one member, *I would have met it;* and in the other, *I would have hidden myself.* When he speaks of the enemy *magnifying himself against him,* he does not simply mean that he used insulting language, but in general, that he summoned all his violence to overthrow him. The sum of David's complaint in this passage is, that he was assailed by treachery of that secret description which rendered self-defence impossible. With regard to the individual whom he had particularly in view, when he preferred this accusation, I do not imagine that it was Ahitophel, for the psalm itself would not appear to have been written upon the persecution of Absalom. Whether it may have been some notorious traitor in the city of Keilah, it is impossible to determine. Not the least probable conjecture is, that it may have been some great man at court, whose intimacy with David was generally known. Possibly he may have had more than one in his eye, courtiers who had sacrificed former friendship to a

---

[1] " The phrase, נמתיק סוד, will literally be read, ' We made our secret sweet.' And so it may be an elegance to signify the pleasure of his friendship, or of communicating secrets to him."—*Hammond.*

desire of rising in the royal favour, and lent their influence to destroy him. These, with some more eminent person at their head, may be the parties aimed at. At any rate, we are taught by the experience of David, as here represented to us, that we must expect in this world to meet with the secret treachery of friends, as well as with undisguised persecution. Satan has assaulted the Church with sword and open war, but he has also raised up domestic enemies to injure it with the more secret weapons of stratagem and fraud. This is a species of foe which, as Bernard expresses it, we can neither fly from nor put to flight. Whoever might be the individual referred to, David calls him a man *of his own order*, for so the term עֶרֶךְ, *erach*, should, in my opinion, be translated, and not as by some, *his equal in estimation*, or as by others, *a man esteemed by him to be his second self*.[1] He complains of the violation of the common bond of fraternity, as none needs to be told that there are various bonds, whether of relationship, profession, or office, which ought to be respected and held sacred. He makes mention also of his having been his *leader* and commander, of their having enjoyed sweet interchange of secret counsel together, and of their having frequented the religious assemblies in company,—all of which he adverts to as circumstances which lent an additional aggravation to his treachery. The term רֶגֶשׁ,[2] *regesh*, does not seem to signify here *the stir attending the convention of an assembly*, but rather *company*, intimating, that he was his close companion when they went to the house of God. Thus he would inform us, that he was betrayed by one who had been his intimate associate, and to whom he had looked up as a leader, in matters not only secular but religious. We are taught by the Spirit to reverence all the natural ties which bind us together in society. Besides the common and universal one of humanity, there are others of a more sacred kind, by which we should feel ourselves attached to men in proportion as they are more

---

[1] This is the sense put upon the Hebrew word עֶרֶךְ, *erach*, by the LXX., who read, "Σὺ δὲ ἄνθρωπε ἰσόψυχε." "But thou, a man whom I love and esteem as I do my own soul;" the word ἰσόψυχος signifying ἴσος ἐμῇ ψυχῇ, *equal to my soul*.

[2] "Properly 'a noisy crowd;' hence, genr. *crowd, multitude.*"— *Gesenius*. It is from רָגַשׁ, *ragash, to rage, to make a noise, tumult;* of nations, Ps. ii. 1.

nearly connected with us than others by neighbourhood, relationship, or professional calling, the more as we know that such connections are not the result of chance, but of providential design and arrangement. Need I say that the bond of religious fellowship is the most sacred of all?

15. *Let death seize upon them.* He now denounces the whole faction, not the nation generally, but those who had taken a prominent part in the persecution of him. In imprecating this curse he was not influenced by any bad feeling towards them, and must be understood as speaking not in his own cause but in that of God, and under the immediate guidance of his Spirit. This was no wish uttered in a moment of resentment or of reckless and ill-considered zeal, and which would justify us in launching maledictions against our enemies upon every trivial provocation. The spirit of revenge differs widely from the holy and regulated fervour with which David prays for the judgment of God against wicked men, who had already been doomed to everlasting destruction. The translation, *Let death condemn them,* is forced, and so also is another which has been suggested, *Let him appoint death a creditor over them.*[1] That which we have given is the most obvious and simple. In praying that his enemies *may descend alive into the grave,* it has been well observed, that he seems to allude to the punishment of Korah, Dathan, and Abiram; though I conceive that in imprecating sudden and unexpected ruin upon them, he adverts to the proud persuasion which they cherished in their prosperity, that they would escape the stroke of death. " Lord," as if he had said, " in the infatuation of their pride they consider themselves to be exempted from the ordinary lot of mortality, but let the earth swallow them up alive—let nothing prevent their being dragged down with all their pomp to the destruction which they deserve." The cause which he assigns for his prayer in the latter part of the

---

[1] This is the sense in which Horsley understands the passage. He observes, that " the image here is not sufficiently expressed by the English word *seize,* though it is not impossible that our translators might intend to allude to the seizure of a debtor. But this is rather a kindred image than the same. The precise image in the original is the exaction of payment, not the seizure of the person." His rendering is, " Let death exalt his claim upon them."

verse, is another proof that he was not influenced by any personal resentment against his enemies, but simply denounced the just judgments of God upon such as persecuted the Church. *Wickedness,* he adds, *is in their dwelling.* By this he meant that it could not but dwell where they dwelt and this he expresses still more fully when he adds, *in the midst of them;* intimating, that they inwardly cherished their wickedness, so that it was their inseparable companion, and dwelt with them under the same roof.

16. *I will call upon God, and Jehovah shall save me.*
17. *Evening, and morning, and at noon, will I pray, and cry aloud; and he shall hear my voice.*
18. *He hath redeemed my soul into peace from the battle which was against me: for they were in great numbers with me.*
19. *God shall hear, and afflict them,[1] even He who sitteth from ancient time.[2] Selah. Because they have no changes, and fear not God.*

16. *I will call upon God.* In translating this verse I have retained the future tense of the verb, as the Psalmist does not refer to something already done, but rather excites himself to the duty of prayer, and to the exercise of hope and confidence. Though there was no apparent method of escape, and he stood on the brink of immediate destruction, he declares his resolution to continue in prayer, and expresses his assurance that it would be successful. In the verse which follows he engages more particularly to show perseverance in prayer. He does not content himself with saying that he will pray, for many do this in a perfunctory manner, and soon become wearied with the exercise; but he resolves to display both assiduity and vehemency. From the particular mention he makes of *evening, morning,* and *noon,* we are left to infer that these must have been the stated hours of prayer amongst the godly at that period. Sacrifices were offered daily in the temple morning and evening, and by this they were taught to engage privately in prayer within their own houses. At noon also it was the practice to offer additional sacrifices. As

---

[1] " C'est, leur respondra."— *Fr. marg.* " That is, will answer them."
[2] Ainsworth reads, " from antiquity;" Boothroyd, " from eternity."

we are naturally indisposed for the duty of prayer, there is a danger that we may become remiss, and gradually omit it altogether, unless we restrict ourselves to a certain rule. In appointing particular fixed hours to be observed for his worship, there can be no doubt that God had respect to the infirmity of our nature, and the same principle should be applied to the secret as to the public services of devotion, as appears from the passage now before us, and from the example of Daniel, (chap. ix. 3.) Sacrifices are no longer to be observed in the Church, but as there remains the same indisposition on our part to the duty, and an equal need of incitements to overcome it, we should still prescribe certain hours to ourselves to be observed in prayer. He adds, that he would *cry aloud,* to denote vehemency of supplication, under the grief and anxiety of mind to which he was subjected. He intimates, that no extremity of present trouble would prevent him from directing his complaint to God, and cherishing a confident hope of deliverance.

18. *He hath redeemed my soul into peace.* Those who read the two preceding verses in the perfect instead of the future tense, are apparently led to this by considering that David here proves his former prayers to have been answered, from the fact of deliverance having been granted. But there is no difficulty involved in adopting the other reading. We may suppose that either he was so confident of being delivered that he speaks as if he actually were so already, or that he inserts what was the substance of his meditations at different times; it being sufficiently common, when mention is made of prayers, to subjoin a statement of the event which followed from them. Having spoken, then, of his prayers, he adverts to the result of them, with the view of expressing his thankfulness for the mercy which he had received. He says that he had been *redeemed into peace*—a strong expression, signifying the danger to which he had been exposed, and the almost miraculous manner in which he had been delivered from it. What is added, *they were in great numbers with me,* admits of a double meaning. Some understand him as referring to enemies; *with me* being, according to them, equivalent to

against me. He represents himself as having been beset by a host of adversaries, and commends the goodness manifested by God in accomplishing his deliverance. Others think that he refers to the angels, whose hosts are encamped round about those that fear the Lord, (Ps. xxxiv. 7.) The letter ב, *beth*, which I have rendered *in*, they consider to be here, as in many other places, merely expletive;[1] so that we may read the words, *great numbers were with me.* The last of these interpretations conveys a comfortable truth, as God, although he cannot stand in need of auxiliaries, has seen fit, in accommodation to our infirmity, to employ a multitude of them in the accomplishment of our salvation. But David would appear rather to speak of enemies, and to refer to the number of them, with the view of magnifying the deliverance which he had received.[2]

19. *God shall hear, and afflict them.* As the verb ענה, *anah*, which I have rendered *afflict*, signifies, occasionally, *to testify,* some understand David to say that God would rise up as a witness against them. The syntax of the language will scarcely, however, admit of this, as, in Hebrew, the letter ב, *beth*, is generally subjoined in such a case. There seems no doubt that the word signifies here *to afflict* or *punish*, although this is rather its signification implicitly and by a species of irony; for, most commonly, ענה, *anah*, means *to answer.* Having said that God would hear him, he adds that he would answer him, in the way of avenging his cause, in the

---

[1] Rogers is of this opinion; and observes, that "in the Appendix to the first volume of Glassius, many instances are adduced of the redundancy of the prefix ב; as Exod. xxxii. 22; Ps. lxviii. 5; Ezra iii. 3."

[2] Walford renders the sentence, "Though multitudes be in opposition to me." "The sense," says he, "which is here given, is evidently required, and is fairly deducible from the Hebrew text." Bishop Horsley's rendering is, "For they who stood on my side told for many;"—"they who stood on my side," denoting the Divine assistance described under the image of numerous auxiliaries. See 2 Kings vi. 16; 1 John iv. 4. Bishop Mant is satisfied that this is the Psalmist's meaning, and he accordingly turns the verse thus :—

> " And he shall hear me, he shall shield,
> And he with peace shall crown;
> My guardian in the battle-field,
> An host himself alone."

punishment of his enemies. The epithet, or descriptive title, which he applies to God, is one calculated to comfort the pious mind in times of trouble and confusion. Much of that impatience into which we are hurried arises from not elevating our thoughts to the eternity of God. Can anything be more unreasonable than that poor mortals, who pass away like a shadow, should measure God by their feeble apprehensions, which is to cast him down from his eternal throne, and subject him to the fluctuations of a changing world? As חלף, *chalaph,* may signify *to cut off* as well as *to change,* some have supposed that David here complains of the destruction of the wicked having been too long deferred; but this is not a probable interpretation. The term has been more properly rendered *changes.* But even those who have adopted this rendering have varied in the sense of the passage.[1] Some understand it to mean that no change to the better was to be expected in their character; that they were so bent upon evil as to be inflexible to repentance; so entirely under the influence of a cruel disposition, as never once to incline to humanity or mercy. Others, with more reason, consider that he refers, in the language of complaint, to the uninterrupted flow of their prosperity, which was such that they seemed exempt from the common vicissitudes of life. He represents them as being corrupted by this indulgence, and casting off from their minds every principle of fear, as if they were privileged with immunity from mortal ills. The copulative particle will thus carry the force of a consequence— *they have no changes, and therefore they fear not God.*[2] It is

---

[1] The reason of this difference arises from the ambiguity of the meaning of the original word, which signifies *change* simply, without reference to the kind of change. Of the two senses which our Author proceeds to state, the first is that adopted by the Chaldee, which reads, "Wicked men, who change not their very evil course, and fear not the sight of God, shall perish." Dathe, while he admits the ambiguity of the word, follows the Chaldee. Gesenius gives the same interpretation. "But," says Walford, "this reduces the passage nearly to an identical proposition; so that the probable meaning is, vicissitudes of fortune. These men had enjoyed great prosperity, and been subjected to few trials; they were therefore enamoured of this world and its pleasures, and gave themselves little regard about the will and authority of God. See Ps. lxxiii. 5, 6."

[2] "That is," says Williams, "they suppose they also shall live for ever; or, at least, that things will go on the same for ever. See 2 Peter iii. 4."

an undeniable truth, that the longer the wicked are left in the enjoyment of their pleasures, they are only hardened the more in their evil courses; and that where pride has the ascendancy in the heart, the effect of the Divine indulgence is to make us forget that we are men. In the connection between the two parts of the verse there is an implied censure of the infatuation of those who are led by their exemption from adversity to conclude that they are a species of demigods; for, how insignificant is the course of human life when compared with the eternity of God? We have need to be upon our guard when under prosperity, lest we fall into the secure spirit which the Psalmist here alludes to, and even carry our exultation to the extent of a defiance of the Almighty.

20. *He hath sent his hands against those that were at peace with him :*[1] *he hath broken his covenant.*
21. *The words of his mouth were smoother than butter, and his heart war: his words were softer than oil, yet were they darts.*
22. *Cast thy giving*[2] *upon Jehovah, and he shall feed thee: he shall not suffer the righteous always to stagger.*[3]
23. *Thou, O God! shalt cast them into the pit of corruption: bloody and deceitful men shall not live out half their days: but I will hope in thee.*

20. *He hath sent his hands against those that were at peace with him.* He afterwards speaks in verse 23d in the plural number, but here it is probable that he begins by addressing the leader and head of the wicked conspiracy. He accuses him of waging war in the midst of peace, and being thus guilty of a breach of faith. He had neither suffered provocation, nor had he announced in an open manner his intention to give battle, but had commenced the attack unexpectedly

---

[1] "Misit manus in paces suas."—*Lat.* On the margin of the French version, "paces suas" is thus explained: "C'est, ses alliez et gens qui vivoyent paisiblement avec luy."

[2] "Ou, ta charge."—*Fr. marg.* "Or, thy burden."

[3] "Ou, tombe."—*Fr. marg.* "Or, fall." Fry reads, "He will not permit for ever the displacing, moving, tossing, or slipping of the righteous."

and with treachery. The same charge is insisted upon still further, when it is added, that butter and oil were in his lips, while war was in his heart, and his words themselves were darts. To appearance they were soft and agreeable, but they covered a hidden virulence and cruelty which wounded like a sword or like darts,[1] according to the common proverb, that deceivers carry on their lips poison besmeared with honey. It is well known how many fair promises and flatteries Saul addressed to David with a view to entrap him, and we may conjecture that the same arts were practised by his courtiers. It is one special trial of the Lord's people, that they are exposed to such attempts on the part of crafty men to seduce them into destruction. Here the Holy Spirit puts a mark of reprobation upon all subtilty of this kind, and particularly upon treacherous flatteries, exhorting us to cultivate simplicity of intention.

22. *Cast thy giving upon Jehovah.* The Hebrew verb יהב, *yahab,* signifies *to give,* so that יהבך, *yehobcha,* according to the ordinary rules of grammar, should be rendered *thy giving,* or *thy gift.*[2] Most interpreters read *thy burden,* but they assign no reason for this rendering. The verb יהב, *yahab,* never denotes *to burden,* and there is no precedent which

---

[1] In the figurative language of the East, severe, unfeeling, and injurious words are often compared to swords, daggers, arrows, &c. Thus it is said in Psalm lix. 7, "Swords are in their lips ; for who, *say they,* doth hear?" and in Prov. xii. 18, "There is that speaketh like the piercings of a sword." In our own language, a similar figure of speech is quite common, as when we speak of *keen, cutting,* and *piercing* words, and of the wounds which they inflict. "I will speak daggers to her."—*Hamlet.*

[2] "What thou desirest to have given thee," according to the Chaldee, which renders the word *thy hope ; i. e.,* that which thou hopest to receive. On the margin of our English Bibles it is, *thy gift,* which Williams explains by "allotment." "*Cast thy allotment upon the Lord,*" says he, "on which we may remark, that whatever allotment we receive from God, whether of prosperity or adversity, it is our duty to refer it back to him: 'He that giveth to the poor lendeth to the Lord, and he will repay him ;' or if our lot be adverse, 'he will sustain' under every burden, and 'never suffer the righteous to be moved' from his foundation." In like manner Rogers understands the word. "*Cast upon Jehovah what he allots you ; i. e.,* commit to Jehovah your destiny. Supply אשר before יהבך."—*Book of Psalms in Hebrew,* vol. ii. p. 210. The Septuagint reads, μέριμνάν σου, *thy care ;* in which it is followed by the apostle Peter, (1 Epis. chap. v. 5.) The reading of the Vulgate, Syriac, Æthiopic, and Arabic versions is the same.

might justify us in supposing that the noun deduced from it can mean *a burden.* They have evidently felt themselves compelled to invent that meaning from the harshness and apparent absurdity of the stricter translation, *Cast thy gift upon Jehovah.* And I grant that the sentiment they would express is a pious one, that we ought to disburden ourselves before God of all the cares and troubles which oppress us. There is no other method of relieving our anxious souls, but by reposing ourselves upon the providence of the Lord. At the same time, I find no example of such a translation of the word, and adhere therefore to the other, which conveys a sufficiently important instruction, provided we understand the expression *gift* or *giving* in a passive sense, as meaning all the benefits which we desire God to give us. The exhortation is to the effect that we should resign into the hands of God the care of those things which may concern our advantage. It is not enough that we make application to God for the supply of our wants. Our desires and petitions must be offered up with a due reliance upon his providence, for how many are there who pray in a clamorous spirit, and who, by the inordinate anxiety and restlessness which they evince, seem resolved to dictate terms to the Almighty. In opposition to this, David recommends it as a due part of modesty in our supplications, that we should transfer to God the care of those things which we ask, and there can be no question that the only means of checking an excessive impatience is an absolute submission to the Divine will, as to the blessings which should be bestowed. Some would explain the passage: Acknowledge the past goodness of the Lord to have been such, that you ought to hope in his kindness for the future. But this does not give the genuine meaning of the words. As to whether David must be considered as here exhorting himself or others, it is a question of little moment, though he seems evidently, in laying down a rule for his own conduct, to prescribe one at the same time to all the children of God. The words which he subjoins, *And he shall feed thee,* clearly confirm that view of the passage which I have given above. Subject as we are in this life to manifold wants, we too often yield ourselves up to disquietude and anxiety.

But David assures us that God will sustain to us the part of a shepherd, assuming the entire care of our necessities, and supplying us with all that is really for our advantage. He adds, that *he will not suffer the righteous to fall,* or *always to stagger.* If מוֹט, *mot,* be understood as meaning *a fall,* then the sense will run: God shall establish the righteous that he shall never fall. But the other rendering seems preferable. We see that the righteous for a time are left to stagger, and almost to sink under the storms by which they are beset. From this distressing state David here declares, that they shall be eventually freed, and blessed with a peaceful termination of all their harassing dangers and cares.

23. *Thou, O God! shalt cast them into the pit of corruption.* He returns to speak of his enemies, designing to show the very different end which awaits them, from that which may be expected by the righteous. The only reflection which comforts the latter, when cast down at the feet of their oppressors, is, that they can confidently look for a peaceful issue to the dangers which encompass them; while, on the other hand, they can discern by faith the certain destruction which impends the wicked. The Hebrew word שׁחת, *shachath,* signifies *the grave,* and as there seems an impropriety in saying that they are cast into the *pit of the grave,* some read in preference *the pit of corruption,*[1] the word being derived from שׁחת, *shachath, to corrupt,* or *destroy.* It is a matter of little consequence which signification be adopted; one thing is obvious, that David means to assert that they would be overtaken not only by a temporary, but everlasting destruction. And here he points at a distinction between them and the righteous. These may sink into many a deep pit of worldly calamity, but they arise again. The ruin which awaits their enemies is here declared to be deadly, as God will cast them into the grave, that they may rot there. In calling them *bloody men,*[2] he adverts to a reason which confirmed the assertion he had made. The vengeance of God is certain to overtake the cruel and the deceitful; and this being the

[1] The Chaldee explains it, "the deep Gehenna."
[2] Heb. "men of blood and deceit."

character of his adversaries, he infers that their punishment would be inevitable. "But does it consist," may some ask, "with what passes under our observation, that *bloody men live not half their days?* If the character apply to any, it must with peculiar force to tyrants, who consign their fellow-creatures to slaughter, for the mere gratification of their licentious passions. To such very evidently, and not to common murderers, does the Psalmist refer in this place; and yet will not tyrants, who have butchered their hundreds of thousands, reach frequently an advanced period of life?" They may; but notwithstanding instances of this description, where God has postponed the execution of judgment, the assertion of the Psalmist is borne out by many considerations. With regard to temporal judgments, it is enough that we see them executed upon the wicked, in the generality of cases, for a strict or perfect distribution in this matter is not to be expected, as I have shown at large upon the thirty-seventh psalm. Then the life of the wicked, however long it may be protracted, is agitated by so many fears and disquietudes, that it scarcely merits the name, and may be said to be death rather than life. Nay, that life is worse than death which is spent under the curse of God, and under the accusations of a conscience which torments its victim more than the most barbarous executioner. Indeed, if we take a right estimate of what the course of this life is, none can be said to have reached its goal, but such as have lived and died in the Lord, for to them, and them alone, death as well as life is gain. When assailed, therefore, by the violence or fraud of the wicked, it may comfort us to know that their career shall be short,—that they shall be driven away, as by a whirlwind, and their schemes, which seemed to meditate the destruction of the whole world, dissipated in a moment. The short clause which is subjoined, and which closes the psalm, suggests that this judgment of the wicked must be waited for in the exercise of faith and patience, for the Psalmist rests in hope for his deliverance. From this it appears that the wicked are not cut off so suddenly from the earth, as not to afford us hope for the exhibition of patience under the severity of long-continued injuries.

PSALM LVI.

In this psalm David mixes complaint with prayer, and assuages the distress of his mind by meditation upon the mercy of God. He prays that he may experience the divine help under the persecutions to which he was subjected by Saul, and his other enemies; and expresses his confidence of success. It is possible, however, that the psalm may have been written after the dangers to which he alludes were past, and in thanksgiving for a deliverance which he had already received.

¶ To the chief musician upon the silent dove in distant places,[1] Michtam of David, when the Philistines took him in Gath.

The portion of history referred to in the title is recorded in 1 Sam. xxi. Being driven from every hiding-place in which he had hitherto found safety, he fled to King Achish. He speaks here of having been apprehended; and that he was so, may be gathered from the inspired narrative, where Achish is represented as saying, "Lo, ye see the man is mad; wherefore, then, have ye brought him to me?" It is probable that they suspected him of some sinister design in the visit. He escaped upon that occasion by feigning madness; but this psalm proves that he must have been engaged in fervent supplication, and that faith was secretly in exercise even when he betrayed this weakness. He would not appear to have been under that inordinate agitation of mind, which instigates men to adopt methods of relief which are positively sinful; but in the desperate emergency to which he was reduced, he was compelled through fear to employ an artful device, which might save his life, although it would lower his dignity in the eyes of the world. If he lost the praise of magnanimity, it is at least apparent from this psalm, what a strenuous contest there was between faith and fear in his heart. The words, *upon the silent dove*, are supposed by some to have formed the commencement of a song well known at the time. Others have thought that David is here compared to a dove; and this conjecture is borne out by the propriety of the metaphor in his present circumstances,[2]

---

[1] "The late learned Editor of Calmet, from comparing this title with verse 6 of the psalm preceding, had a suspicion that it is here misplaced, and belonged originally to that psalm."—*Williams' Cottage Bible*.

[2] Harmer is of opinion, that the *dove dumb in distant places* is simply the name of the psalm. In support of this view, he quotes the titles of several Eastern books; a Persian metaphysical and mystic poem, called the

especially as it is added, *in distant places*, for he had been driven to an enemy's country by the fury of his persecutors. The meaning which some have attached to the word, translating it *a palace*, is far-fetched. I have already given my views of the term *Michtam*.¹ I would not pretend to say anything dogmatically on a point upon which even Hebrew interpreters are not agreed in opinion ; but the probability is, that it was a particular kind of tune, or a musical instrument.

1. *Be merciful unto me, O God ! for man swallows me up: he fighting against me,² daily oppresseth me.*
2. *Mine enemies daily swallow me up: surely they be many³ that fight against me, O Most High !*⁴
3. *In the day that I was afraid, I did put my trust in thee.*
4. *In God I will praise his word ; in God I have put my trust : I will not fear what flesh can do unto me.*

1. *Be merciful unto me, O God! for man swallows me up.*⁵ It would be difficult to determine whether he speaks here of foreign or domestic enemies. When brought to King Achish

Rose Bush ; a collection of Moral Essays, the *Garden of Anemonies ;* and a poem in which the Arabian prophet is celebrated for having given sight to a blind person, which is entitled the *Bright Star.* "The ancient Jewish taste," he remarks, "may reasonably be supposed to have been of the same kind. Every one that reflects on the circumstances of David at the time to which the 56th psalm refers, and considers the Oriental taste, will not wonder to see that psalm entitled the *Dove dumb in distant places.*"—*Observations*, vol. iii. p. 147-149.

¹ See vol. i. p. 215.¹
² " Ou, me mangeant."—*Fr. marg.* " Or, eating me."
³ " Ou, des puissans et robustes."—*Fr. marg.* " Or, they be mighty and strong."
⁴ The original word מרום, *marom*, here rendered " O Most High !" is literally *loftily.* Dathe, Berlin, and Gesenius, render it *superbe, proudly.* Cresswell, following Le Clerc, reads, *from the highest places*, and considers the meaning to be, that the foes of David made an incursion upon him, descending from the mountains, and forcing him again to supplicate Achish. Compare 1 Sam. xxvii. 1, 2, 3. Horsley and Dr Adam Clarke read, " from on high ; " by which the latter critic understands from " the place of *authority*, the court and cabinet of Saul." He observes, on the word מרום, *marom*, " I do not think that this word expresses any attribute of God, or, indeed, is at all addressed to him." " In Micah vi. 6, however," says Dr Morrison, " מרום seems to express the perfections of the divine character." Calvin's translation agrees with that of the Chaldee, of Aquila, and of our English Bible.
⁵ The verb here translated *swallows me up*, is rendered by French and Skinner, *panteth after me.* It is literally *draweth in the air.* It thus implies the intense desire of David's enemies to get him into their hands, and to destroy him.

he was as a sheep between two bands of wolves, an object of deadly hatred to the Philistines on the one hand, and exposed to equal persecutions from his own fellow-countrymen. He uses the indefinite term *man* in this verse, though in the next he speaks of having many enemies, the more forcibly to express the truth that the whole world was combined against him, that he experienced no humanity amongst men, and stood in the last necessity of divine help. The term *daily* would suggest that he refers more immediately to Saul and his faction. But in general, he deplores the wretchedness of his fate in being beset with adversaries so numerous and so barbarous. Some translate שָׁאַף, *shaäph, to regard,* but it is more properly rendered *to swallow up,* a strong expression, denoting the insatiable rage with which they assailed him. I have adhered to the common translation of לָחַם, *lacham,* though it also signifies *to eat up,* which might consist better with the metaphor already used in the preceding part of the verse. It is found, however, in the sense *to fight against,* and I was unwilling to depart from the received rendering. I shall only observe in passing, that those who read in the second member of the verse, *many fighting with me,* as if he alluded to the assistance of angels, mistake the meaning of the passage; for it is evident that he uses the language of complaint throughout the verse.

3. *In the day that I was afraid, &c.* In the Hebrew, the words run in the future tense, but they must be resolved into the præterite. He acknowledges his weakness, in so far as he was sensible of fear, but denies having yielded to it. Dangers might distress him, but could not induce him to surrender his hope. He makes no pretensions to that lofty heroism which contemns danger, and yet while he allows that he felt fear, he declares his fixed resolution to persist in a confident expectation of the divine favour. The true proof of faith consists in this, that when we feel the solicitations of natural fear, we can resist them, and prevent them from obtaining an undue ascendancy. Fear and hope may seem opposite and incompatible affections, yet it is proved by observation, that the latter never comes into full

sway unless there exists some measure of the former. In a tranquil state of the mind, there is no scope for the exercise of hope. At such times it lies dormant, and its power is only displayed to advantage when we see it elevating the soul under dejection, calming its agitations, or soothing its distractions. This was the manner in which it manifested itself in David, who feared, and yet trusted, was sensible of the greatness of his danger, and yet quieted his mind with the confident hope of the divine deliverance.

4. *In God I will praise his word.* Here he grows more courageous in the exercise of hope, as generally happens with the people of God. They find it difficult at first to reach this exercise. It is only after a severe struggle that they rise to it, but the effort being once made, they emerge from their fears into the fulness of confidence, and are prepared to grapple with the most formidable enemies. *To praise,* is here synonymous with glorying or boasting. He was now in possession of a triumphant confidence, and rejoiced in the certainty of hope. The ground of his joy is said to be *the divine word;* and this implies, that however much he might seem to be forsaken and abandoned by God, he satisfied himself by reflecting on the truthfulness of his promises. He would glory in God notwithstanding, and although there should be no outward appearance of help, or it should even be sensibly withdrawn, he would rest contented with the simple security of his word. The declaration is one that deserves our notice. How prone are we to fret and to murmur when it has not pleased God immediately to grant us our requests! Our discontent may not be openly expressed, but it is inwardly felt, when we are left in this manner to depend upon his naked promises. It was no small attainment in David, that he could thus proceed to praise the Lord, in the midst of dangers, and with no other ground of support but the word of God. The sentiment contained in the latter clause of the verse might seem at first glance to merit little consideration. What more obvious than that God is able to protect us from the hand of men, that his power to defend is immensely greater than their power to injure? This may be true, but

we all know too well how much of that perverse unbelief there is in our hearts, which leads us to rate the ability of God below that of the creature. It was no small proof, therefore, of the faith of David, that he could despise the threatenings of his enemies. And it would be well if all the saints of God were impressed with such a sense of his superiority to their adversaries as would lead them to show a similar contempt of danger. When assailed by these, it should never escape their recollection, that the contest is in reality between their enemies and God, and that it were blasphemous in this case to doubt the issue. The great object which these have in view is to shake our faith in the promised help of the Lord; and we are chargeable with limiting his power, unless we realize him standing at our right hand, able with one movement of his finger, or one breath of his mouth, to dissipate their hosts, and confound their infatuated machinations. Shall we place him on a level with mortal man, and measure his probable success by the numbers which are set against him? "But how," may it be asked, "are we to account for this sudden change in the exercise of David? A moment before, he was expressing his dread of destruction, and now he bids defiance to the collected strength of his enemies." I reply, that there is nothing in his words which insinuate that he was absolutely raised above the influence of fear, and every sense of the dangers by which he was encompassed. They imply no more than that he triumphed over his apprehensions, through that confident hope of salvation with which he was armed. Men he terms in this verse *flesh,* to impress the more upon his mind the madness of their folly in attempting a contest so infinitely above their strength.

5. *Every day my words vex me; all their thoughts are against me for evil.*
6. *They gather themselves together, they hide themselves, they watch my heels, because they seek my soul.*[1]
7. *After their mischief they think to escape: in thine anger cast down the peoples, O God!*

[1] "Ou, ne demandent qu'a m'oster la vie."—*Fr. marg.* "Or, they want only to take away my life."

8. *Thou hast taken account of my wandering ; put thou my tears into thy bottle : are they not in thy register?*

5. *Every day my words vex me.* The first part of this verse has been variously rendered. Some understand *my words* to be the nominative in the sentence, and with these I agree in opinion. Others suppose a reference to the enemies of David, and translate, *they calumniate my words,* or, *they cause me grief on account of my words.* Again, יעצבו, *yeatsebu,* has been taken in the neuter sense, and translated, *my words are troublesome.* But עצב,[1] *atsab,* commonly signifies *to affect with grief,* and in *Pihel* is always taken transitively ; nor does there seem any reason in this place to depart from the general rule of the language. And the passage flows more naturally when rendered, *my words affect me with grief,* or *vex me,* than by supposing that he refers to his enemies. According to this translation, the verse contains a double complaint, that, on the one hand, he was himself unsuccessful in everything which he attempted, his plans having still issued in vexatious failure ; while, on the other hand, his enemies were devising every means for his destruction. It may appear at first sight rather inconsistent to suppose that he should immediately before have disclaimed being under the influence of fear, and now acknowledge that he was not only distressed, but in some measure the author of his own discomfort. I have already observed, however, that he is not to be considered as having been absolutely divested of anxiety and fear, although enabled to look down with contempt upon his

[1] Horsley observes, that the primary meaning of the verb עצב, *atsab,* is " perhaps *to do a thing with great labour, to take pains about it ;* if, indeed, its primary meaning be not *to distort.* Hence it may signify to affect the mind with any unpleasing passion or sensation, grief, vexation, anger ; for every perturbation is a sort of distortion of the mind. יעצבו עלי דברי —' torquent contra me verba mea,'—' torquent, *i. e.,* laboriose fingunt in mentem alienam et sensum alienum.'—Pagninus after Aben Ezra and R. D."—*Horsley.* Hammond, after stating that עצב, *atsab,* signifies primarily *to grieve,* or *be in pain,* and that by metonomy it is used for the laborious framing or forming of any thing, says, " Here, being applied to another's words or speeches, it seems to denote the depraving them, labouring and using great art and diligence to put them into such a form as may be most for the disadvantage of the speaker, turning and winding them to his hurt, putting some odious gloss upon them, and so, according to sense, may most fully be rendered *depraving.*"

enemies from the eminence of faith. Here he speaks of the circumstances which tried him, which his faith certainly overcame, but at the same time could not altogether remove out of the way. He confesses his own lack of wisdom and foresight, shown in the abortive issue of every plan which he devised. It aggravated the evil, that his enemies were employing their united counsels to plot his ruin. He adds, that *they gathered themselves together;* and this made his case the more calamitous, matched as he was, a single individual, against this numerous host. In mentioning that they *hide themselves,* he adverts to the subtile devices which they framed for surprising him into destruction. The verb יִצְפֹּנוּ, *yitsponu,* by grammatical rule ought to have the letter ו, *vau,* in the middle; from which the general opinion is, that the י, *yod,* is as it were the mark of *Hiphil,* denoting that the enemies of David came to the determination of employing an ambush, with the view of surrounding him. He tells us that they pressed upon him in every direction, and as it were trod upon his heels, so that he had no respite. And he points at their implacable hatred as the cause of their eager pursuit of him; for nothing, he informs us, would satisfy them but his death.

7. *After their mischief they think to escape.* The beginning of this verse is read by some interrogatively, *Shall they escape in their iniquity ?*[1] But there is no necessity for having recourse to this distant meaning. It is much better to understand the words in the sense which they naturally suggest when first read, That the wicked think to escape in their iniquity, but that God will cast them down. He alludes to the fact that the ungodly, when allowed to proceed without interruption in their evil courses, indulge the idea that they have a license to perpetrate the worst wickedness with impunity. In these our own times, we see many such profane characters, who display an unmeasured audacity under the assurance that God's hand can never reach them. They not only look to go

---

[1] French and Skinner read, "Shall they escape after their wickedness?" and observe, that the Hebrew is, "Is there escape for them?" the meaning being, that they assuredly will not escape, because of their wickedness.

unpunished, but found their hopes of success upon their evil deeds, and encourage themselves to farther wickedness, by cherishing the opinion that they will contrive a way of escape from every adversity. David has no sooner stated this vain confident persuasion of the wicked, than he refutes it by an appeal to the judgment of God, declaring his conviction that, however proudly they might exalt themselves, the hour of vengeance would come when God would *cast down the peoples.* He makes use of the plural number, to fortify his mind against fear, when he reflected upon the array of his enemies. Let us remember, when our enemies are many, that it is one of the prerogatives of God to cast down the people, and not one nation of foes merely, but the world.

8. *Thou hast taken account of my wanderings.* The words run in the form of an abrupt prayer. Having begun by requesting God to consider his tears, suddenly, as if he had obtained what he asked, he declares that they were written in God's book. It is possible, indeed, to understand the interrogation as a prayer; but he would seem rather to insinuate by this form of expression, that he stood in no need of multiplying words, and that God had already anticipated his desire. It is necessary, however, to consider the words of the verse more particularly. He speaks of his *wandering* as having been noted by God, and this that he may call attention to one remarkable feature of his history, his having been forced to roam a solitary exile for so long a period. The reference is not to any one wandering; the singular number is used for the plural, or rather, he is to be understood as declaring emphatically that his whole life was only one continued wandering. This he urges as an argument to commiseration, spent as his years had been in the anxieties and dangers of such a perplexing pilgrimage. Accordingly, he prays that God might *put his tears into his bottle.*[1] It was

[1] Some think that there is here an allusion to an ancient custom of putting the tears of mourners into lachrymal urns or bottles. In the Roman tombs there are found small vials, or bottles of glass or pottery, usually called *ampullæ*, or *urnæ lachrymales*, which, it has been supposed, contained tears shed by the surviving relatives and friends, and were deposited in the sepulchres of the deceased as memorials of affection and

usual to preserve the wine and oil in bottles : so that the words amount to a request that God would not suffer his tears to fall to the ground, but keep them with care as a precious deposit. The prayers of David, as appears from the passage before us, proceeded upon faith in the providence of God, who watches our every step, and by whom (to use an expression of Christ) " the very hairs of our head are numbered," (Matth. x. 30.) Unless persuaded in our mind that God takes special notice of each affliction which we endure, it is impossible we can ever attain such confidence as to pray that God would put our tears into his bottle, with a view to regarding them, and being induced by them to interpose in our behalf. He immediately adds, that he had obtained what he asked : for, as already observed, I prefer understanding the latter clause affirmatively. He animates his hope by the consideration that all his tears were written in the book of God, and would therefore be certainly remembered. And we may surely believe, that if God bestows such honour upon the tears of his saints, he must number every drop of their

sorrow. If in this passage there is a reference to this custom, it must have existed at an early period among the Hebrews. It may however be doubted, whether there is any such allusion. " It is only a modern conjecture that these bottles 'found in the Roman tombs' have been deposited there for such a purpose, and there is no trace of such a custom in ancient writings or sculptures. Some think they were intended to contain the perfumes used in sprinkling the funeral pile. On some of them there is the representation of one or two eyes, and this seems to favour the former view."—*Illustrated Commentary on the Bible.* Let it also be observed, that the word נאד, *nod*, here translated *bottle*, means a sort of bottle which had no resemblance to these Roman urns. It was made of a goat's or kid's skin, and was used by the Hebrews for keeping their wine, their milk, and their oil. Compare 1 Sam. xvi. 20 ; Josh. ix. 13 ; Judges iv. 19 ; Matth. ix. 17. " Besides," as Bishop Mant remarks, " the treasuring up of the Psalmist's tears shed by him during his own sufferings, seems a very different thing from the offering up of the tears of surviving relations or friends, as memorials on the tomb of a deceased person." The expression, " Put thou my tears into thy bottle," may be viewed as simply meaning, Let not my tears fall unnoticed ; let my distress and the tears which it has wrung from me be ever before thee, excite thy compassion, and plead with thee to grant me relief. As the choicest things, such as wine and milk, were put into bottles, the Psalmist may also be understood as praying that his tears might not only be noted by God, but prized by him. The נאד, *nod*, was of large capacity, and used for churning as well as for wine. It may therefore contain a reference to the large quantity of tears which David's affliction forced from him.—*Harmer's Observations*, vol. ii. pp. 121, 122.

blood which is shed. Tyrants may burn their flesh and their bones, but the blood remains to cry aloud for vengeance; and intervening ages can never erase what has been written in the register of God's remembrance.

9. *When I cry, then shall mine enemies turn back : this I know, for God is with me.*
10. *In God will I praise his word; in Jehovah will I praise his word.*
11. *In God have I hoped : I will not be afraid what man can do unto me.*

9. *When I cry, then shall mine enemies turn back.* Here he boasts of victory with even more confidence than formerly, specifying, as it were, the very moment of time when his enemies were to be turned back. He had no sensible evidence of their approaching destruction; but from the firm reliance which he exercised upon the promise, he was able to anticipate the coming period, and resolved to wait for it with patience. Though God might make no haste to interpose, and might not scatter his enemies at the very instant when he prayed, he was confident that his prayers would not be disappointed: and his ground for believing this was just a conviction of the truth, that God never frustrates the prayers of his own children. With this conviction thoroughly fixed in his mind, he could moderate his anxieties, and calmly await the issue. It is instructive to notice, that David, when he would secure the obtainment of his requests, does not pray in a hesitating or uncertain spirit, but with a confident assurance of his being heard. Having once reached this faith, he sets at defiance the devil and all the host of the ungodly.

10. *In God will I praise his word.* In the original the pronoun is not expressed, but we are left to infer, from the parallel verse which went before, that it is understood. The repetition adds an emphasis to the sentiment, intimating, that though God delayed the sensible manifestation of his favour, and might seem to deal hardly in abandoning him

to the word—giving him nothing more, he was resolved to glory in it with undiminished confidence. When in a spirit such as this we honour the word of God, though deprived of any present experience of his goodness or his power, we "set to our seal that God is true," (John iii. 33.) The repetition amounts to an expression of his determination that, notwithstanding all circumstances which might appear to contravene the promise, he would trust in it, and persist in praising it both now, henceforth, and for ever. How desirable is it that the Lord's people generally would accustom themselves to think in the same manner, and find, in the word of God, matter of never-failing praise amidst their worst trials! They may meet with many mercies calling for the exercise of thanksgiving, but can scarcely have proceeded one step in life before they will feel the necessity of reliance upon the naked promise. A similar reason may be given for his repetition of the sentiment in the 11th verse—*In God have I hoped,* &c. We shall find men universally agreed in the opinion that God is an all-sufficient protector; but observation proves how ready we are to distrust him under the slightest temptation. When exposed to the opposition of assailants formidable for strength, or policy, or any worldly advantages, let us learn with David to set God in opposition to them, and we shall speedily be able to view the mightiest of them without dismay.

12. *Thy vows are upon me, O God! I will pay thy praises.*
13. *For thou hast delivered my soul from death: hast thou not delivered my feet from falling headlong? that I may walk before God in the light of the living.*

12. *Thy vows are upon me, O God!* I hinted, from the outset, that it is probable this psalm was written by David after he had escaped the dangers which he describes; and this may account for the thanksgiving here appended to it. At the same time, we have evidence that he was ever ready to engage in this exercise even when presently suffering under his afflictions. He declares that *the vows of God were upon him;* by which he means, that he was bound to pay them,

as, among the Romans, a person who had obtained what he sought, under engagement of a vow, was said to be *voti damnatus—condemned of his vow.* If we have promised thanks, and our prayers have been heard, an obligation is contracted. He calls them the vows of God—*thy vows;* for the money in my hand may be said to be my creditor's, being, as I am, in his debt. He views his deliverance as having come from God; and the condition having been performed, he acknowledges himself to be burdened with the vows which he had contracted. We learn from the second part of the verse what was the nature of the vows to which he adverts, and, by attending to this, may preserve ourselves from the mistake of imagining that he sanctions any such vows as those which are practised among Papists. He says that he would render *praises,* or *sacrifices of praise;* for the word is applied to sacrifices, which were the outward symbols of thanksgiving. David knew well that God attached no value to sacrifices considered in themselves, or irrespectively of the design and spirit of the person offering them; but we may believe that he would not neglect the sacred ceremonies of the Law which was imposed upon the Church at that time; and that he speaks of some solemn expression of gratitude, such as was customary among the Jews upon the reception of a signal Divine favour.

13. *For thou hast delivered my soul from death.* This confirms the truth of the remark which I have already made, that he considered his life as received from the hands of God, his destruction having been inevitable but for the miraculous preservation which he had experienced. To remove all doubt upon that subject, he speaks of having been preserved, not simply from the treachery, the malice, or the violence of his enemies, but from death itself. And the other form of expression which he employs conveys the same meaning, when he adds, that God had kept him back with his hand when he was on the eve of rushing headlong into destruction. Some translate מדחי, *middechi, from falling;* but the word denotes here a violent impulse. Contemplating the greatness of his danger, he considers his escape as nothing less than

miraculous. It is our duty, when rescued from any peril, to retain in our recollection the circumstances of it, and all which rendered it peculiarly formidable. During the time that we are exposed to it, we are apt to err through an excessive apprehension; but when it is over, we too readily forget both our fears and the Divine goodness manifested in our deliverance. *To walk in the light of the living* means nothing else than to enjoy the vital light of the sun. The words, *before God,* which are interjected in the verse, point to the difference between the righteous, who make God the great aim of their life, and the wicked, who wander from the right path and turn their back upon God.

PSALM LVII.

This psalm consists of two parts. In the first, David gives expression to the anxiety which he felt, imploring Divine assistance against Saul and his other enemies. In the second, he proceeds upon the confident expectation of deliverance, and stirs up his soul to the exercise of praise.

¶ To the chief musician, Al-tascheth,[1] Michtam of David, when he fled from the face of Saul in the cave.

We are left entirely to conjecture as to the meaning of the word *Michtam;* and equal uncertainty prevails among interpreters regarding the reason of the inscription given to the psalm, *Al-tascheth, i. e., destroy not.* Some are of opinion that this formed the commencement of a song well known at the time; others take it to be an expression uttered by David in the desperate exigency to which he was reduced, *O God! destroy me not.* Others conceive that the word is inscribed upon the psalm in praise of the high principle shown by David when he prevented Abishai from slaying Saul, and are confirmed in their opinion by the fact, that this is the very expression which the inspired historian represents him as having used, (1 Sam. xxvi. 9.) But as the prayers which follow must have been offered up before he gave any such injunction to

---

[1] The words, אל־תשחת, *al-tascheth,* are found in the titles of three other psalms, the 58th, 59th, and 75th.

Abishai, this explanation is not satisfactory; and we are left to adopt one or other of the two former suppositions, either that the psalm was composed to the air of some song generally known at the time, or that the word expresses a brief prayer, which David notes down as having been uttered in memorable circumstances, and in circumstances of great danger.

1. *Be merciful unto me, O God! be merciful unto me, for my soul trusteth in thee; and in the shadow of thy wings will I hope,*[1] *until wickedness*[2] *pass over.*
2. *I will cry unto God most High, to God that performeth all things for me.*
3. *He shall send from heaven, and save me from the reproach of him that would swallow me up.*[3] *God shall send forth his mercy and his truth.*

1. *Be merciful unto me, O God!* The repetition of the prayer proves that the grief, the anxiety, and the apprehension, with which David was filled at this time, must have been of no common description. It is noticeable, that his plea for mercy is, his having hoped in God. His *soul* trusted in him; and this is a form of expression the force of which is not to be overlooked: for it implies that the trust which he exercised proceeded from his very innermost affections,—that it was of no volatile character, but deeply and strongly rooted. He declares the same truth in figurative terms, when he adds his persuasion that God would cover him with the shadow of his wings. The Hebrew word חסה, *chasah*, which I have translated *to hope,* signifies occasionally *to lodge,* or *obtain shelter,* and in this sense it may be understood with great propriety in the passage before us, where allusion is made

---

[1] "Ou, hebergeray."—*Fr. marg.* "Or, will lodge."
[2] The original word, הוות, *ha-uoth,* for *wickedness,* the Septuagint here renders *sin*—"Until sin pass away." Symmachus explains it in Psalm lv. 12, by επηρεια, *insulting injury.* "Simon, from Schultens, has, I think, given the true meaning. הוה, *barathrum—est desiderium,* idque *pravum.* v. c. cupiditas devorandi—*cupiditas* dicitur profundum quod, *barathrum,* quod expleri non potest."—*Fry.* French and Skinner read, "until their mischief pass away;" "the mischief," they observe, "now directed against me by my enemies."
[3] "Ou, a la confusion de celuy qui m'a guetté."—*Fr. marg.* "Or, to the confusion of him who hath laid wait for me." See note on Psalm lvi. 1, where the same original word is used.

to the shadow of wings. David had committed himself, in short, entirely to the guardianship of God; and now experienced that blessed consciousness of dwelling in a place of safety, which he expresses in the beginning of the ninetieth psalm. The divine protection is compared to the shadow of wings, because God, as I have elsewhere observed, the more familiarly to invite us to himself, is represented as stretching out his wings like the hen, or other birds, for the shelter of their young. The greater our ingratitude and perversity, in being so slow to comply with such an endearing and gentle invitation! He does not merely say, in general, that he would hope in God, and rest under the shadow of his wings, but, particularly, that he would do so at the time when wickedness should pass over him, like a storm or whirlwind. The Hebrew word הוה, *hovah*, which I have rendered *wickedness*, some translate *power*. Be that as it may, it is evident he declares that God would prove his refuge, and the wings of God his shelter, under every tempest of affliction which blew over him. There are seasons when we are privileged to enjoy the calm sunshine of prosperity; but there is not a day of our lives in which we may not suddenly be overtaken by storms of affliction, and it is necessary we should be persuaded that God will cover us with his wings. To hope he adds prayer. Those, indeed, who have placed their trust in God, will always direct their prayers to him; and David gives here a practical proof of his hope, by showing that he applied to God in his emergencies. In addressing God, he applies to him an honourable title, commending him as the God who performed whatsoever he had promised, or (as we may understand the expression) who carries forward to perfection the work which he has begun.[1] The Hebrew word גמר, *gomer*, here employed, would seem to be used in the same sense as in Psalm cxxxviii. 8, the scope of both passages being the same. It materially confirms and sustains our hope to reflect that God will never forsake the workmanship of his own hands,—that he will perfect the salvation of his people, and continue his divine guidance until

---

[1] Horsley reads the last clause of the verse, "Upon God, who will bring things to a conclusion for me."

he have brought them to the termination of their course. Some read, *to God, who rewards me;* but this fails to bring out the force of the expression. It would be more to the purpose, in my judgment, to read, *God, who fails me;* in which case the sentence would, of course, require to be understood adversatively: That though God failed him, and stretched not out his hand for his deliverance, he would still persist in crying to him. The other meaning, which some have suggested, *I will cry to God, who performs, or exerts to the utmost, his severity against me,* is evidently forced, and the context would lead us to understand the word as referring to the goodness of God, the constancy of which in perfecting his work when once begun, should ever be present to our remembrance.

3. *He shall send from heaven, and save me.* David, as I have repeatedly had occasion to observe, interlaces his prayers with holy meditations for the comfort of his own soul, in which he contemplates his hopes as already realized in the event. In the words before us, he glories in the divine help with as much assurance as if he had already seen the hand of God interposed in his behalf. When it is said, *he shall send from heaven,* some consider the expression as elliptical, meaning that he would send *his angels;* but it seems rather to be an indefinite form of speech, signifying that the deliverance which David expected was one not of a common, but a signal and miraculous description. The expression denotes the greatness of the interposition which he looked for, and *heaven* is opposed to earthly or natural means of deliverance. What follows admits of being rendered in two different ways. We may supply the Hebrew preposition מ, *mem,* and read, *He shall save me from the reproach;* or it might be better to understand the words appositively, *He shall save me, to the reproach of him who swallows me up.*[1] The latter expression

---

[1] In this all the ancient versions agree. They make חרף, *chereph,* a verb, and not a noun, regarding it as applicable to God, and conveying the idea that He would deliver David, having put to shame, or to reproach, his enemies. Thus, in the Septuagint, it is "ἔδωκεν εἰς ὄνειδος," and in the Vulgate, "dedit in opprobrium," "he gave to reproach;" and in like manner in the Chaldee, Syriac, Arabic, and Ethiopic versions.

might be rendered, *from him who waits for me.* His enemies gaped upon him in their eagerness to accomplish his destruction, and insidiously watched their opportunity; but God would deliver him, to their disgrace. He is said to strike his enemies with shame and reproach, when he disappoints their expectations. The deliverance which David anticipated was signal and miraculous; and he adds, that he looked for it entirely from the mercy and truth of God, which he represents here as the hands, so to speak, by which his assistance is extended to his people.

4. *My soul is among lions;*[1] *and I lie even among them that are set on fire,*[2] *even the sons of men, whose teeth are spears and arrows, and their tongue a sharp sword.*
5. *Exalt thyself, O God! above the heavens: let thy glory be above all the earth.*
6. *They have prepared a net for my steps; my soul is bowed down: they have digged a pit before me, into the midst whereof they are fallen themselves.*

4. *My soul is among lions.* He again insists upon the cruelty of his enemies as a plea to prevail with God for his speedier interposition. He compares them to lions, speaks of them as inflamed with fury or implacable hatred, and likens their teeth to spears and arrows. In what he says of their tongue, he alludes to the virulent calumnies which are vended by the wicked, and which inflict a deeper wound

---

[1] " Mudge translates literally, ' I lie with my soul amidst lionesses.' " —*Arch. Secker.* This agrees with the opinion of Bochart, who thinks that the animals here intended are lionesses, properly when giving suck to their young, a time when they are peculiarly fierce and dangerous. " Nor need we wonder," he observes, " that the lioness is reckoned among the fiercest lions; for the lioness equals, or even exceeds, the lion in strength and fierceness;" and this he proves from the testimonies of ancient writers.

[2] Fry reads, " I lay down among children of men, who are flaming fire, or breathing flames." Ainsworth reads, " I lie among inflamers;" " meaning," says he, " fiery, fierce, and raging persons, that flamed with wrath and envy, and inflamed others. Of such David did complain to Saul, 1 Sam. xxiv. 40." French and Skinner read, " *men of fiery spirit;* and observe, that the Hebrew is *flaming sons of men, i. e.,* violent men urging on my destruction." Mant observes, that it may either be " *persons set on fire,* that is, with rage and malice; or, perhaps, *setters on fire,* kindlers of mischief, incendiaries."

than any sword upon the innocent party who suffers from them. David, as is well known, encountered no heavier trial than the false and calumnious charges which were levelled against him by his enemies. When we hear of the cruel persecution of different kinds which this saint was called upon to endure, we should account it no hardship to be involved in the same conflict, but be satisfied so long as we may bring our complaints to the Lord, who can bridle the false tongue, and put an arrest upon the hand of violence.

To him we find David appealing in the words that follow, *Exalt thyself, O God! above the heavens: let thy glory be above all the earth.* To perceive the appropriateness of this prayer, it is necessary that we reflect upon the height of audacity and pride to which the wicked proceed, when unrestrained by the providence of God, and upon the formidable nature of that conspiracy which was directed against David by Saul, and the nation in general, all which demanded a signal manifestation of divine power on his behalf. Nor is it a small comfort to consider that God, in appearing for the help of his people, at the same time advances his own glory. Against it, as well as against them, is the opposition of the wicked directed, and he will never suffer his glory to be obscured, or his holy name to be polluted with their blasphemies. The Psalmist reverts to the language of complaint. He had spoken of the cruel persecution to which he was subjected, and now bewails the treachery and deceit which were practised against him. His soul he describes as being *bowed down*, in allusion to the crouching of the body when one is under the influence of fear, or to birds when terrified by the fowler and his nets, which dare not move a feather, but lie flat upon the ground. Some read, *He has bowed down my soul.* But the other is the most obvious rendering, and the verb כפף, *caphaph*, is one which is frequently taken with the neuter signification. Although the Hebrew word נפש, *nephesh*, rendered *soul*, is feminine, this is not the only place where we find it with a masculine adjunct.

7. *My heart is prepared, O God! my heart is prepared : I will sing, and give praise.*
8. *Awake up, my tongue : awake, psaltery and harp : I myself shall be awaked*[1] *at dawn of day.*
9. *I will praise thee, O Lord! among the peoples : I will sing unto thee among the nations.*
10. *For thy mercy is great unto the heavens, and thy truth unto the clouds.*
11. *Be thou exalted, O God! above the heavens : let thy glory be above all the earth.*

7. *My heart is prepared, O God!*[2] Some read *fixed*, or *confirmed*, and the Hebrew word נכון, *nacon*, bears that signification as well as the other. If we adopt it, we must understand David as saying that he had well and duly meditated upon the praises which he was about to offer; that he did not rush into a hurried and perfunctory discharge of this service, as too many are apt to do, but addressed himself to it with stedfast purpose of heart. I prefer, however, the other translation, which bears that he was ready to enter upon the service with all cheerfulness and cordiality. And although, wherever this spirit is really felt, it will lead to stedfastness of religious exercise, it is not without importance that the reader should be apprised of the force of the word which is here employed in the Hebrew. The ready heart is here opposed by David to the mere lip-service of the hypocrite, on the one hand, and to dead or sluggish service, on the other. He addressed himself to this voluntary sacrifice with a sincere fervour of spirit, casting aside sloth, and whatever might prove a hinderance in the duty.

8. *Awake up, my tongue.* David here expresses, in poetical terms, the ardour with which his soul was inspired. He calls upon tongue, psaltery, and harp, to prepare for the celebra-

---

[1] " Ou, me resueilleray."—*Fr. marg.* " Or, I will awake."
[2] This psalm consists of two parts. The preceding verses, which contain the first part, express deep distress and extreme danger, and are of a plaintive and imploring strain. But here, where the second part commences, there is an elegant transition suddenly made to the language of exultation and triumph, which continues to the close of the psalm.

tion of the name of God. The word כָּבוֹד, *cabod*, which I have translated *tongue*, some have rendered *glory;* but although this is its more common signification, it bears the other in the sixteenth psalm, and in numerous places of Scripture. The context proves this to be its signification here, David intimating that he would celebrate the praises of God both with the voice and with instrumental music. He assigns the first place to the heart, the second to declaration with the mouth, the third to such accompaniments as stimulate to greater ardour in the service. It matters little whether we render the verb אָעִירָה, *äirah, I will be awaked,* or transitively, *I will awake myself by dawn of day.*[1] But one who is really awaked to the exercise of praising God, we are here taught will be unremitting in every part of the duty.

9. *I will praise thee, O Lord! among the peoples.* As the *nations* and *peoples* are here said to be auditors of the praise which he offered, we must infer that David, in the sufferings spoken of throughout the psalm, represented Christ. This it is important to observe, as it proves that our own state and character are set before us in this psalm as in a glass. That the words have reference to Christ's kingdom, we have the authority of Paul for concluding, (Rom. xv. 9,) and, indeed, might sufficiently infer in the exercise of an enlightened judgment upon the passage. To proclaim the praises of God to such as are deaf, would be an absurdity much greater than singing them to the rocks and stones; it is therefore evident that the Gentiles are supposed to be brought to the knowledge of God when this declaration of

---

[1] Hammond reads, "I will awaken the morning." Dr Geddes, Archbishop Secker, Street, and Fry, give a similar version. "The verb אעירה." says Street, "is in the Hiphil conjugation; and therefore transitive; and the word השחר is the objective case after it." As to translating שחר, *early,* Archbishop Secker says, "שחר is not elsewhere used adverbially, nor, I believe, with an ellipsis of ב;" and he observes, that "'I will awaken the morning' is more grammatical and poetical." A similar thought frequently occurs in poetry. Thus Ovid says, "Non vigil ales ibi cristati cantibus oris evocat auroram." "The cock by crowing calls not up the morning there." And in Milton's Allegro we meet with the following couplet:—

> "Oft listening how the hound and horn
> Cheerly rouse the slumbering morn."

his name is addressed to them. He touches briefly upon what he designed as the sum of his song of praise, when he adds, that the whole world is full of the goodness and truth of God. I have already had occasion to observe, that the order in which these divine perfections are generally mentioned is worthy of attention. It is of his mere goodness that God is induced to promise so readily and so liberally. On the other hand, his faithfulness is commended to our notice, to convince us that he is as constant in fulfilling his promises as he is ready and willing to make them. The Psalmist concludes with a prayer that God would arise, and not suffer his glory to be obscured, or the audacity of the wicked to become intolerable by conniving longer at their impiety. The words, however, may be understood in another sense, as a prayer that God would hasten the calling of the Gentiles, of which he had already spoken in the language of prediction, and illustrate his power by executing not only an occasional judgment in Judea for the deliverance of distressed innocence, but his mighty judgments over the whole world for the subjection of the nations.

PSALM LVIII.

The following psalm consists of two parts. In the commencement, David vindicates his personal integrity from the calumnies cast upon him by his enemies. Having expressed his sense of the grievous injuries which they had inflicted, their cruelty and their treachery, he concludes by an appeal to the judgment of God, and by praying that they might be visited with deserved destruction.

¶ To the chief musician, Destroy not, Michtam of David.

1. *Do ye indeed speak righteousness? O congregation! do ye judge uprightly? O ye sons of men!*
2. *Yea, rather in heart ye plot wickedness; your hands weigh out violence upon the earth.*
3. *They are estranged, being wicked from the womb: they went astray as soon as they were born, speaking lies.*

4. *Their poison is like the poison of a serpent: they are like the deaf adder that stoppeth her ear:*

5. *Which will not hearken to the voice of the enchanter, charm he never so wisely.*

1. *Do ye indeed speak righteousness?* In putting this question to his enemies, by way of challenge, David displays the boldness of conscious rectitude. It argues that the justice of our cause is demonstratively evident when we venture to appeal to the opposite party himself; for were there any ground to question its justice, it would show an absurd degree of confidence to challenge the testimony of an adversary. David comes forward with the openness of one who was supported by a sense of his integrity, and repels, by a declaration forced from their own lips, the base charges with which they blackened his character in the estimation of such as were simple enough to believe them. "Ye yourselves," as if he had said, "can attest my innocence, and yet persecute me with groundless calumnies. Are you not ashamed of such gross and gratuitous oppression?" It is necessary, however, to determine who they were whom David here accuses. He calls them *a congregation,* and again, *sons of men.* The Hebrew word אלם, *elem,* which I have rendered *congregation,* some consider to be an epithet applied to *righteousness,* and translate *dumb;*[1] but this does not express the meaning of the Psalmist. Interpreters differ as to what we

---

[1] "אלם. There is some difficulty in ascertaining the sense of this word. Gesenius derives it from אלם, *to be silent: Is justice indeed silent?* But this breaks the parallelism, which requires צדק תדברון, 'will ye speak righteousness?' in the first line, to correspond with מישרים תשפטו, 'will ye judge uprightness?' in the second. Dathe agrees with Bishop Lowth, &c., who propose to point the word אלם, or *plene,* אלים, *judices,* 'O ye judges, or rulers!' See Exod. xxii. 27; Psalm lxxxii. 1. But this reading, though it makes a very good sense, receives no support from the MSS., or ancient versions. Diodati and De Rossi agree with our translators in taking the word in the sense of *assembly, congregation.* So Schindler אלם, *collegatio hominum,* congregation, multitudo cœtus, ab אלם, *ligavit,* colligavit. This is probably the true sense. LXX. Vulg. Æth. and Ar., seem to have read אולם, or אלם."—(*Rogers' Book of Psalms,* vol. ii. p. 212.) Walford prefers Dathe's version.

should understand by the term *congregation*. Some think that he adverts, by way of accusation, to the meetings which his enemies held, as is usual with those who entertain wicked designs, for the purpose of concerting their plans. I rather incline to the opinion of those who conceive that he here gives (although only in courtesy) the usual title of honour to the counsellors of Saul, who met professedly to consult for the good of the nation, but in reality with no other intention than to accomplish his destruction. Others read, *in the congregation*—a translation which gives the same meaning to the passage we have already assigned to it, but is not supported by the natural construction of the words. The congregation which David addresses is that assembly which Saul convened, ostensibly for lawful objects, but really for the oppression of the innocent. The term, *sons of men*, which he immediately afterwards applies to them—taking back, as it were, the title of courtesy formerly given—would seem to be used in contempt of their character, being, as they were, rather a band of public robbers than a convention of judges. Some, however, may be of opinion, that in employing this expression, David had in his eye the universality of the opposition which confronted him—almost the whole people inclining to this wicked faction—and that he here issues a magnanimous defiance to the multitude of his enemies. Meanwhile, the lesson taught us by the passage is apparent. Although the whole world be set against the people of God they need not fear, so long as they are supported by a sense of their integrity, to challenge kings and their counsellors, and the promiscuous mob of the people. Should the whole world refuse to hear us, we must learn, by the example of David, to rest satisfied with the testimony of a good conscience, and with appealing to the tribunal of God. Augustine, who had none but the Greek version in his hands, is led by this verse into a subtle disquisition upon the point, that the judgment of men is usually correct when called to decide upon general principles, but fails egregiously in the application of these principles to particular cases,[1] through

---

[1] " Argute hic disputant, hominibus rectum esse judicium in generalibus principiis: sed ubi ad hypothesin ventum est, hallucinari," &c. The

the blinding and warping influences of their evil passions. All this may be plausible, and, in its own place, useful, but proceeds upon a complete misapprehension of the meaning of the passage.

2. *Yea, rather, in heart ye plot wickedness.* In the former verse he complained of the gross shamelessness manifested in their conduct. Now he charges them both with entertaining wickedness in their thoughts, and practising it with their hands. I have accordingly translated the Hebrew particle אף, *aph, yea, rather*—it being evident that David proceeds, after first repelling the calumnies of his enemies, to the further step of challenging them with the sins which they had themselves committed. The second clause of the verse may be rendered in two different ways, *ye weigh violence with your hands,* or, *your hands weigh violence;* and as the meaning is the same, it is immaterial which the reader may adopt. Some think that he uses the figurative expression, *to weigh,* in allusion to the pretence of equity under which he was persecuted, as if he were a disturber of the peace, and chargeable with treason and contumacy towards the king. In all probability, his enemies glossed over their oppression with plausible pretences, such as hypocrites are never slow to discover. But the Hebrew word פלס, *phalas,* admits of a wider signification, *to frame* or *set in order;* and nothing more may be meant than that they put into shape the sins which they had first conceived in their thoughts. It is added, *upon the earth,* to denote the unbridled license of their wickedness, which was done openly, and not in places where concealment might have been practised.

3. *They are estranged, being wicked from the womb.* He adduces, in aggravation of their character, the circumstance, that they were not sinners of recent date, but persons born to commit sin. We see some men, otherwise not so depraved in disposition, who are drawn into evil courses through levity

---

French translation runs—" Dispute yci subtilement que les hommes ont un jugement droit et entier és principes generaux, mais quand ce vient à la particularité, que leur raison defaut," &c.

of mind, or bad example, or the solicitation of appetite, or other occasions of a similar kind; but David accuses his enemies of being leavened with wickedness from the womb, alleging that their treachery and cruelty were born with them. We all come into the world stained with sin, possessed, as Adam's posterity, of a nature essentially depraved, and incapable, in ourselves, of aiming at anything which is good; but there is a secret restraint upon most men which prevents them from proceeding all lengths in iniquity. The stain of original sin cleaves to the whole human family without exception; but experience proves that some are characterized by modesty and decency of outward deportment; that others are wicked, yet, at the same time, within bounds of moderation; while a third class are so depraved in disposition as to be intolerable members of society. Now, it is this excessive wickedness—too marked to escape detestation even amidst the general corruption of mankind—which David ascribes to his enemies. He stigmatizes them as monsters of iniquity.

4. *Their poison is like the poison of a serpent: they are like the deaf adder.*[1] He prosecutes his description; and, though he might have insisted on the fierceness which characterized their opposition, he charges them more particularly, here as elsewhere, with the malicious virulence of their disposition. Some read, *their fury;*[2] but this does not suit the figure, by which they are here compared to serpents. No objection can be drawn to the translation we have adopted from the etymology of the word, which is derived from *heat.* It is well known, that while some poisons kill by cold, others consume the vital parts by a burning heat. David then asserts of his enemies, in this passage,

---

[1] The פתן, *phethen,* rendered *adder,* is generally supposed by interpreters to be the kind of serpent called by the ancients the aspic, and to which there are frequent allusions in Scripture. Deut. xxxiii. 33; Job xx. 14, 16; Isa. xi. 8. It is the פתן, *bœten,* of the Arabians, which M. Forskal (*Descript. Anim.* p. 15) describes as spotted with black and white, about one foot in length, nearly half an inch thick, oviparous, and its bite almost instant death; and which is called "the aspic" by the literati of Cyprus, though the common people give it the name of κουφη, *deaf.*

[2] This is the reading of the Septuagint, the Vulgate, and of Jerome. Sept. "Θυμός." Vulg. and Jer. "Furor."

that they were as full of deadly malice as serpents are full of poison. The more emphatically to express their consummate subtlety, he compares them to deaf serpents, which shut their ears against the voice of the charmer—not the common kind of serpents, but such as are famed for their cunning, and are upon their guard against every artifice of that description. But is there such a thing, it may be asked, as enchantment? If there were not, it might seem absurd and childish to draw a comparison from it, unless we suppose David to speak in mere accommodation to mistaken, though generally received opinion.[1] He would certainly seem, however, to insinuate that serpents can be fascinated by enchantment; and I can see no harm in granting it. The Marsi in Italy were believed by the ancients to excel in the art. Had there been no enchantments practised, where was the necessity of their being forbidden and condemned under the Law? (Deut. xviii. 11.) I do not mean to say that there is an actual method or art by which fascination can be effected. It was

[1] That the serpent tribe may be charmed is a well-attested fact, and one of the most curious and interesting in natural history. It is often mentioned by the Greek and Roman classics, by Hebrew and Arabic writers; to the last of whom the different species of serpents were well known. It is also supported by the testimony of many modern travellers. Some serpents are delighted with the sounds of vocal and instrumental music, and by it may be disarmed of their fury and rendered innoxious, (Eccles. x. 11.) In the East it is not uncommon to make use of pipes, flutes, whistles, or small drums, to draw them from their hiding-places and to subdue their ferocity; and when they are tame ones, the charmer makes them dance and keep time with the notes of music, twists them round his body, and handles them without any harm, although the fangs are not broken or extracted. But in some cases the charmer's art fails; and, notwithstanding his incantations, the serpent will fasten on the arm, or some other part of the body, and inflict, with its poisoned fangs, a deadly wound, (Jer. viii. 17.) In this case it "will not listen to the voice of the charmer." It is not necessary to suppose that the "deaf adder" means a species of serpent naturally deaf, and which it is impossible for the charmer ever to fascinate. Nothing more may be meant but that his incantations sometimes fail of success; that some adders are so stubborn that the sound of music makes no impression upon them; and they are like creatures who are destitute of hearing, or whose ears are stopped. The manner in which the "deaf adder stoppeth its ear" is described by Bochart to be this :—" The reptile lays one ear close to the ground, and with its tail covers the other, that it cannot hear the sound of the music; or it repels the incantation by hissing violently." So impenetrable are the wicked here represented to be to persuasion: they will not be wrought upon to forsake their wicked courses, and gained to the ways of God, by his most persuasive entreaties.

doubtless done by a mere sleight of Satan,[1] whom God has suffered to practise his delusions upon unbelieving and ignorant men, although he prevents him from deceiving those who have been enlightened by his word and Spirit. But we may avoid all occasion for such curious inquiry, by adopting the view already referred to, that David here borrows his comparison from a popular and prevailing error, and is to be merely supposed as saying, that no kind of serpent was imbued with greater craft than his enemies, not even the species (if such there were) which guards itself against enchantment.

6. *Break their teeth, O God! in their mouth : break the jaws of the lions.*
7. *Let them flow away like waters, let them depart : let them bend their bow, and let their arrows be as broken.*[2]
8. *Let him vanish like a snail, which melts away; like the untimely birth of a woman, which does not see the sun.*
9. *Before your pots*[3] *can feel the fire of the thorns, a whirlwind shall carry him away, like flesh yet raw.*

6. *Break their teeth, O God! in their mouth.*[4] From this part of the psalm he assumes the language of imprecation,

---

[1] The power which charmers had over serpents was probably ascribed by them to the agency of invisible beings, although it might be the natural effect of the music which they used.

[2] There is nothing in the original for, "Let their arrows be ;" it is a supplement made by Calvin in the French version. There is some difficulty in the last member of the verse. Many interpreters refer it to God, who bends his bow against the ungodly. This agrees with the Septuagint, Vulgate, Chaldee, Syriac, and Arabic versions. But Symmachus and others refer it to ungodly men, who study, indeed, to hurt the godly, but without effect. "This seems," says Dathe, "to be the most natural connection : in the 6th verse the sacred writer addresses God himself in the second person ; and there is here described the unsuccessful issue of the endeavours of the wicked against the righteous." "I am persuaded," says Rogers, "that some word, the name of something with which the wicked, perishing under the Divine vengeance, were compared, is lost in the Hebrew."—*Book of Psalms in Hebrew*, vol. ii. p. 213.

[3] "Ou, vos espines."—*Fr. marg.* "Or, your thorns."

[4] "Break their teeth in their mouth" is most probably a continuation of the metaphorical illustration taken from serpents and adders immediately before, whose poison is contained in a bag at the bottom of one of their teeth, and who are disarmed by being deprived of this tooth which conveys the poison. This the charmer sometimes does after he has brought them out of their retreats by music. When the serpent makes its appearance, he seizes it by the throat, draws it forth, shows its poisoned fangs, and beats them out. To this beating out there seems to be here an allu-

and solicits the vengeance of God, whose peculiar prerogative it is to repel oppression and vindicate injured innocence. It is necessary, however, that we attend to the manner in which this is done. He does not claim the judgment or patronage of God to his cause, until he had, in the first place, asserted his integrity, and stated his complaint against the malicious conduct of his enemies; for God can never be expected to undertake a cause which is unworthy of defence. In the verse before us, he prays that God would crush the wicked, and restrain the violence of their rage. By their *teeth*, he would intimate that they resembled wild beasts in their desire to rend and destroy the victims of their oppression; and this is brought out more clearly in the latter part of the verse, where he likens them to *lions*. The comparison denotes the fury with which they were bent upon his destruction.

In the next verse, and in the several succeeding verses, he prosecutes the same purpose, employing a variety of apt similitudes. He prays that God would make them *to flow away like waters*, that is, swiftly. The expression indicates the greatness of his faith. His enemies were before his eyes in all the array of their numbers and resources; he saw that their power was deeply rooted and firmly established; the whole nation was against him, and seemed to rise up before him like a hopeless and formidable barrier of rocky mountains. To pray that this solid and prodigious opposition should melt down and disappear, evidenced no small degree of courage, and the event could only appear credible to one who had learnt to exalt the power of God above all intervening obstacles. In the comparison which immediately follows, he prays that the attempts of his adversaries might be frustrated, the meaning of the words being, that their arrows might fall powerless, as if broken, when they bent their bow. Actuated as they were by implacable cruelty, he requests that God would confound

sion. "This mention of teeth," says Hammond, "fairly introduces that which follows concerning the lion, whose doing mischief with that part is more violent and formidable, and so signifies the open, riotous invader, the violent and lawless person; as the serpent's teeth, the more secret, indiscernible wounds of the whisperer or backbiter, which yet are as dangerous and destructive as the former, by the smallest puncture killing him on whom they fasten."

their enterprises, and in this we are again called to admire his unshaken courage, which could contemplate the formidable preparations of his enemies as completely at the disposal of God, and their whole power as lying at his feet. Let his example in this particular point be considered. Let us not cease to pray, even after the arrows of our enemies have been fitted to the string, and destruction might seem inevitable.

8. *Let him vanish like a snail, which melts away.* The two comparisons in this verse are introduced with the same design as the first, expressing his desire that his enemies might pass away quietly, and prove as things in their own nature the most evanescent. He likens them to *snails*,[1] and it might appear ridiculous in David to use such contemptible figures when speaking of men who were formidable for their strength and influence, did we not reflect that he considered God as able in a moment, without the slightest effort, to crush and annihilate the mightiest opposition. Their power might be such as encouraged them, in their vain-confidence, to extend their schemes into a far distant futurity, but he looked upon it with the eye of faith, and saw it doomed in the judgment of God to be of short continuance. He perhaps alluded to the suddenness with which the wicked rise into power, and designed to dash the pride which they are apt to feel from such an easy advance to prosperity, by reminding them that their destruction would be equally rapid and sudden. There is the same force in the figure employed in the end of the verse where they are compared to *an abortion.* If we consider the length of time to which they contemplate in their vain-confidence that their life shall extend,[2] they may be said

---

[1] The original word for *snail* occurs only in this instance in the whole Bible. The LXX. render it ὡσεὶ κηρός, *as wax,* and the Syriac and Vulgate follow them. But the Chaldee reads "as a reptile," interpreting the word as meaning some creeping thing, which affords an eminent example of melting, and this seems to apply to the snail, which, in its progress from its shell, leaves a slime in its tract till it altogether melts away and dies. Comp. Job iii. 16.

[2] "Si reputamus quantum temporis inani fiducia devorent," &c. Literally, "If we consider how much time they devour in their vain-confidence," &c. The French version adheres to this translation of the mere words. "Si nous regardons combien ils devorent de temps par leur vaine confiance."

to pass out of this world before they have well begun to live, and to be dragged back, as it were, from the very goal of existence.

9. *Before your pots can feel the fire of your thorns.* Some obscurity attaches to this verse, arising partly from the perplexed construction, and partly from the words being susceptible of a double meaning.[1] Thus the Hebrew word

We have hazarded the more free translation given in the text, because this seems one of those instances where the brevity of the Latin idiom demands explanation, in order that the idea may be intelligible in any other language.

[1] This verse has been deemed one of the most difficult passages in the Psalter, and has greatly perplexed commentators. Bishop Horsley reads—

"Before your pots feel the bramble,
In whirlwind and hurricane he shall sweep them away."

He supposes that the language is proverbial, and that the Psalmist describes the sudden eruption of the divine wrath; sudden and violent as the ascension of the dry bramble underneath the housewife's pot.

Walford reads—

"Before your cooking vessels feel the fuel;
Both the green and the dry a whirlwind shall scatter."

The passage is supposed by this author and others to contain an allusion to the manners of the Arabs, who, when they want to cook their food, collect bushes and brambles, both green and withered, with which they kindle a fire in the open air. But before their culinary vessels are sensibly affected with the heat, a whirlwind not unfrequently arises and scatters the fuel. And this strikingly expresses the sudden and premature destruction of the wicked.

Fry gives a somewhat different explanation. He reads—

"Sooner than your vessels can feel the *blazing* thorn,
The hot blast shall consume them, as well the green as the dry."

And he observes, that " שׂעיר, or סעיר, no doubt expresses the action of the hot wind of the desert." This wind is eminently destructive, and has not unfrequently been known to entomb and destroy whole caravans. Sidi Hamet, describing his journey across the great desert to Tombuctoo with a caravan consisting of above one thousand men and four thousand camels, relates that, "after travelling upwards of a month they were attacked by the Shume, the burning blast of the desert, carrying with it clouds of sand. They were obliged to lie for two days with their faces on the ground, only lifting them occasionally to shake off the sand and obtain breath. Three hundred never rose again, and two hundred camels also perished." —(*Murray's Discoveries in Africa*, vol. i. pp. 515, 516.) Estius gives this sense: "Before your thorns shall arrive to their full growth into a bush, the rage of a tempest shall snatch them away, as it were, in the flower of their age and growing to maturity." The words כמו־חי, *kemo-chai*, which Calvin renders *flesh yet raw*, are used in this sense in Lev. xiii. 16, and 1 Sam. xi. 15.

סִירוֹת, *siroth*, signifies either *a pot* or *a thorn*. If we adopt the first signification, we must read, *before your pots feel the fire which has been kindled by thorns;* if the second, *before your thorns grow to a bush*, that is, reach their full heighth and thickness. What, following the former sense, we have translated *flesh yet raw*, must be rendered, provided we adopt the other, *tender, or not yet grown*. But the scope of the Psalmist in the passage is sufficiently obvious. He refers to the swiftness of that judgment which God would execute upon his enemies, and prays that he would carry them away as by a whirlwind, either before they arrived at the full growth of their strength, like the thorn sprung to the vigorous plant, or before they came to maturity and readiness, like flesh which has been boiled in the pot. The latter meaning would seem to be the one of which the passage is most easily susceptible, that God, in the whirlwind of his anger, would carry away the wicked like flesh not yet boiled, which may be said scarcely to have felt the heat of the fire.

10. *The righteous shall rejoice when he seeth*[1] *the vengeance; he shall wash his hands in the blood of the wicked.*[2]
11. *And a man shall say, Verily there is a reward* [literally *fruit*[3]] *for the righteous; verily there is a God that judgeth in the earth.*

10. *The righteous shall rejoice when he seeth the vengeance.* It might appear at first sight that the feeling here attributed to the righteous is far from being consistent with the mercy which ought to characterize them; but we must remember, as I have often observed elsewhere, that the affection which David means to impute to them is one of a pure and well-regulated kind; and in this case there is nothing absurd in supposing that believers, under the influence and guidance of the Holy Ghost, should rejoice in witnessing the execution of divine

---

[1] " Ou, pource qu'il aura veu."—*Fr. marg.* " Or, because he seeth."
[2] " The similitude is taken from fierce battles, in which the effusion of blood is so great as to moisten the feet of the victors in the conflict."—*Walford*. See Appendix.
[3] Reward is the fruit of obedience, Isaiah liii. 10.

judgments. That cruel satisfaction which too many feel when they see their enemies destroyed, is the result of the unholy passions of hatred, anger, or impatience, inducing an inordinate desire of revenge. So far as corruption is suffered to operate in this manner, there can be no right or acceptable exercise. On the other hand, when one is led by a holy zeal to sympathize with the justness of that vengeance which God may have inflicted, his joy will be as pure in beholding the retribution of the wicked, as his desire for their conversion and salvation was strong and unfeigned. God is not prevented by his mercy from manifesting, upon fit occasions, the severity of the judge, when means have been tried in vain to bring the sinner to repentance, nor can such an exercise of severity be considered as impugning his clemency; and, in a similar way, the righteous would anxiously desire the conversion of their enemies, and evince much patience under injury, with a view to reclaim them to the way of salvation: but when wilful obstinacy has at last brought round the hour of retribution, it is only natural that they should rejoice to see it inflicted, as proving the interest which God feels in their personal safety. It grieves them when God at any time seems to connive at the persecutions of their enemies; and how then can they fail to feel satisfaction when he awards deserved punishment to the transgressor?

11. *So that a man shall say, Verily there is a reward.* We have additional evidence from what is here said of the cause or source of it, that the joy attributed to the saints has no admixture of bad feeling. It is noticeable from the way in which this verse runs, that David would now seem to ascribe to all, without exception, the sentiment which before he imputed exclusively to the righteous. But the acknowledgment immediately subjoined is one which could only come from the saints who have an eye to observe the divine dispensations; and I am, therefore, of opinion that they are specially alluded to in the expression, *And a man shall say, &c.* At the same time, this mode of speech may imply that many, whose minds had been staggered, would be established in the faith. The righteous only are intended, but the indefinite form of speak-

ing is adopted to denote their numbers. It is well known how many there are whose faith is apt to be shaken by apparent inequalities and perplexities in the divine administration, but who rally courage, and undergo a complete change of views, when the arm of God is bared in the manifestation of his judgments. At such a time the acknowledgment expressed in this verse is widely and extensively adopted, as Isaiah declares, " When thy judgments are in the earth, the inhabitants of the world will learn righteousness," (Isaiah xxvi. 9.) The Hebrew particle אך, *ach*, which we have translated *verily*, occasionally denotes simple affirmation, but is generally intensitive, and here implies the contrast between that unbelief which we are tempted to feel when God has suspended the exercise of his judgments, and the confidence with which we are inspired when he executes them. Thus the particles which are repeated in the verse imply that men would put away that hesitancy which is apt to steal upon their minds when God forbears the infliction of the punishment of sin, and, as it were, correct themselves for the error into which they had been seduced. Nothing tends more to promote godliness than an intimate and assured persuasion that the righteous shall never lose their reward. Hence the language of Isaiah, " Say ye to the righteous, that it shall be well with him; for they shall eat the fruit of their doings," (Isaiah iii. 10.) When righteousness is not rewarded, we are disposed to cherish unbelieving fears, and to imagine that God has retired from the government of the world, and is indifferent to its concerns. I shall have an opportunity of treating this point more at large upon the seventy-third psalm.

There is subjoined the reason why the righteous cannot fail to reap the reward of their piety, because *God is the judge of the world;* it being impossible, on the supposition of the world being ruled by the providence of God, that he should not, sooner or later, distinguish between the good and the evil. He is said more particularly to judge *in the earth*, because men have sometimes profanely alleged that the government of God is confined to heaven, and the affairs of this world abandoned to blind chance.

PSALM LIX.

The title, which immediately follows, informs us upon what occasion this psalm was written, which bears a considerable resemblance to the preceding. He begins by insisting upon the injustice of that cruel hostility which his enemies showed to him, and which he had done nothing to deserve. His complaint is followed up by prayer to God for help; and afterwards, as his hopes revive in the exercise of devout meditation, he proceeds to prophesy their calamitous destruction. At the close, he engages to preserve a grateful remembrance of his deliverance, and to praise the goodness of God.

¶ *To the chief musician, Al-taschith, [destroy not,] Michtam of David, when Saul sent, and they watched the house to kill him.*

The incident in David's history, here referred to, is one with which we are all familiar, (1 Sam. xix. 11.) Besieged in his own house by a troop of soldiers, and having no opportunity of egress from the city, every avenue to which was taken possession of by Saul's guards, it seemed impossible that he could escape with his life. He was indebted instrumentally for his deliverance to the ingenuity of his wife, but it was from the divine goodness that he looked for safety. Michal may have contrived the artifice which deceived the soldiers sent by her father, but he never could have been saved except through the wonderful preservation of God. We are told in the words of the title that his house was watched, and this amounts, in the circumstances, to its being said that he was shut up to certain destruction; for the emissaries of Saul were sent with orders not only for his apprehension, but his death.

1. *Deliver me from mine enemies, O my God! lift me up from the reach of them that rise up against me.*
2. *Deliver me from the workers of iniquity, and save me from bloody men.*
3. *For, lo! they lie in wait for my soul: the mighty are gathered against me; not for my transgression, nor for my sin, O Jehovah!*
4. *They run and prepare themselves without my fault: awake to hasten for my help, and behold.*
5. *And thou, O Jehovah, God of Hosts! the God of Israel, awake to visit all the nations: be not merciful to any wicked transgressors. Selah.*

1. *Deliver me from mine enemies, O my God!* He insists upon the strength and violence of his enemies, with the view of exciting his mind to greater fervour in the duty of prayer. These he describes as *rising up* against him, in which expression he alludes not simply to the audacity or fierceness of their assaults, but to the eminent superiority of power which they possessed; and yet he asks that he may be lifted up on high, as it were, above the reach of this overswelling inundation. His language teaches us that we should believe in the ability of God to deliver us even upon occasions of emergency, when our enemies have an overwhelming advantage. In the verse which follows, while he expresses the extremity to which he was reduced, he adverts at the same time to the injustice and cruelty of his persecutors. Immediately afterwards, he connects the two grounds of his complaint together: on the one hand, his complete helplessness under the danger, and, on the other, the undeserved nature of the assaults from which he suffered. I have already repeatedly observed, that our confidence in our applications to a throne of grace will be proportional to the degree in which we are conscious of integrity; for we cannot fail to feel greater liberty in pleading a cause which, in such a case, is the cause of God himself. He is the vindicator of justice, the patron of the righteous cause everywhere, and those who oppress the innocent must necessarily rank themselves amongst his enemies. David accordingly founds his first plea upon his complete destitution of all earthly means of help, exposed as he was to plots on every side, and attacked by a formidable conspiracy. His second he rests upon a declaration of innocency. It may be true that afflictions are sent by God to his people as a chastisement for their sins, but, so far as Saul was concerned, David could justly exonerate himself from all blame, and takes this occasion of appealing to God on behalf of his integrity, which lay under suspicion from the base calumnies of men. They might pretend it, but he declares that they could charge him with no crime nor fault. Yet, groundless as their hostility was, he tells us that they *ran*, were unremitting in their activity, with no other view than to accomplish the ruin of their victim.

4. *Awake to hasten for my help, and behold.* In using this language, he glances at the eagerness with which his enemies, as he had already said, were pressing upon him, and states his desire that God would show the same haste in extending help as they did in seeking his destruction. With the view of conciliating the divine favour, he once more calls upon God to be the witness and judge of his cause, adding, *and behold.* The expression is one which savours at once of faith and of the infirmity of the flesh. In speaking of God, as if his eyes had been hitherto shut to the wrongs which he had suffered, and needed now for the first time to be opened for the discovery of them, he expresses himself according to the weakness of our human apprehension. On the other hand, in calling upon God *to behold* his cause, he shows his faith by virtually acknowledging that nothing was hid from his providential cognizance. Though David may use language of this description, suited to the infirmity of sense, we must not suppose him to have doubted before this time that his afflictions, his innocence, and his wrongs, were known to God. Now, however, he lays the whole before God for examination and decision.

He prosecutes the same prayer with still greater vehemency in the verse which succeeds. He addresses God under new titles, calling him *Jehovah, God of Hosts, and the God of Israel,* the first of which appellations denotes the immensity of his power, and the second the special care which he exerts over the Church, and over all his people. The manner in which the pronoun is introduced, *and Thou, &c.,* is emphatical, denoting that it was as impossible for God to lay aside the office of a judge as to deny himself, or divest himself of his being. He calls upon him *to visit all the nations :* for although the cause which he now submitted was of no such universal concernment, the wider exercise of judgment would necessarily include the lesser; and on the supposition of heathens and foreigners being subjected to the judgment of God, it followed that a still more certain and heavy doom would be awarded to enemies within the pale of the Church, who persecuted the saints under the guise of brethren, and overthrew those laws which were of divine appointment. The opposition which David encountered might not embrace *all nations;* but if these were judicially visited by God, it was absurd to imagine that those within the Church would be the only enemies who should escape with impunity. In using these words, it is probable also that he may have been struggling with a temptation with which he was severely assailed, connected with the number of his enemies, for these did not consist merely of three or four abandoned individuals. They formed a great multitude; and he rises above them all by reflecting that God claims it as his prerogative, not only to reduce a few refractory persons to submission, but to punish the wickedness of the whole world. If the judgments of God extended to the uttermost parts of the earth, there was no reason why he should be afraid of his enemies, who, however numerous, formed but a small section of the human race. We shall shortly see, however, that the expression admits of being applied without impropriety to the Israelites, divided, as they were, into so many tribes or peoples. In the words which follow, when he deprecates the extension of God's mercy to wicked transgressors, we must understand him as referring to the reprobate, whose sin was of a desperate character. We must also remember, what has been already observed, that in such prayers he was not influenced by mere private feelings, and these of a rancorous, distempered, and inordinate description. Not only did he know well that those of whom he speaks with such severity were already doomed to destruction, but he is here pleading the common cause of the Church, and this under the influence of the pure and well-regulated zeal of the Spirit. He therefore affords no precedent to such as resent private injuries by vending curses on those who have inflicted them.

6. *They will return at evening; they will make a noise like a dog, and go round about the city.*[1]

[1] "Ou, ils iront et viendront."—*Fr. marg.* "*Or, they go and come.*" "He here describes the ceaseless pursuit of him in which his enemies were engaged: all the day they were seeking him in vain in more distant places; in the evening they came again into the city, and continued their search, while their execrations and curses resembled the angry howling of a dog." —*Walford.*

7. *Behold, they will prate*[1] *with their mouth ; swords are in their lips : for who (say they) will hear ?*
8. *But thou, O Jehovah ! shalt laugh at them ; thou shalt have all the nations in derision.*
9. *I will put in trust his strength with thee ;*[2] *for God is my fortress.*

6. *They will return at evening.* He compares his enemies to famished and furious dogs which hunger impels to course with endless circuits in every direction, and under this figure accuses their insatiable fierceness, shown in the ceaseless activity to which they were instigated by the desire of mischief. He says that *they return in the evening,* to intimate, not that they rested at other times, but were indefatigable in pursuing their evil courses. If they came no speed through the day, yet the night would find them at their work. The barking of dogs aptly expressed as a figure the formidable nature of their assaults.

In the verse which follows, he describes their fierceness. The expression, *prating,* or *belching out with their mouth,* denotes that they proclaimed their infamous counsels openly, and without affecting concealment. The Hebrew word נבע, *nabang,* means, metaphorically, *to speak,* but properly, it signifies *to gush out,*[3] and here denotes more than simply speaking. He would inform us, that not content with plotting the destruction of the innocent secretly amongst themselves, they published their intentions abroad, and boasted of them. Accordingly, when he adds, that *swords were in their lips,* he means that

---

[1] " Ou, bouilloneront."—*Fr. marg.* " Or, will belch out."

[2] " Ou, sa force est à toy, je me tiendray coy : ou, ma force est à toy," &c.—*Fr. marg.* " Or, his strength is with thee, I will keep myself quiet : or, my strength is with thee," &c.

[3] Ainsworth reads, " *to utter* or *well out,* as from a fountain ; *belch* or *babble,* as Prov. xv. 2, 28, ' As a fountain casteth out her waters, so she casteth out her malice.' " " Le mot Hebrieu signifie *se répandre en paroles,* &c. ;" *i. e.,* " The Hebrew word signifies *to break out in words,* and it here denotes the oft repeated and passionate expressions which proceed from the mouth of persons actuated by hatred and rage, as in Psalm xciv. 4. To it the word *bark* answers very well, which is borrowed from dogs, and expresses the noise made by these animals ; and this word is here the more apposite, that David in the preceding verse compares his enemies to dogs which incessantly run about and do nothing but bark."—*Martin.*

they breathed out slaughter, and that every word they spoke was a sword to slay the oppressed. He assigns as the cause of their rushing to such excess of wickedness, that they had no reason to apprehend disgrace. It may be sufficiently probable, that David adverts here, as in many other places, to the gross stupidity of the wicked, who, in order to banish fear from their minds, conceive of God as if he were asleep in heaven; but I am of opinion that he rather traces the security with which they prosecuted their counsels, and openly proclaimed them, to the fact, that they had long ere now been in possession of the uncontrolled power of inflicting injury. They had succeeded so completely in deceiving the people, and rendering David odious by their calumnies, that none had the courage to utter a word in his defence. Nay, the more atrociously that any man might choose to persecute this victim of distress, from no other motive than to secure the good graces of the king, the more did he rise in estimation as a true friend to the commonwealth.

8. *But thou, O Jehovah! shalt laugh at them.* In the face of all this opposition, David only rises to greater confidence. When he says that God would *laugh* at his enemies, he employs a figure which is well fitted to enhance the power of God, suggesting that, when the wicked have perfected their schemes to the uttermost, God can, without any effort, and, as it were, in sport, dissipate them all. No sooner does God connive at their proceedings, than their pride and insolence take occasion to manifest themselves: for they forget that even when he seems to have suspended operation, he needs but nod, and his judgments shall be executed. David, accordingly, in contempt of his adversaries, tells them that God was under no necessity to make extensive preparations, but, at the moment when he saw fit to make retribution, would, by a mere play of his power, annihilate them all. He in this manner conveys a severe rebuke to that blind infatuation which led them to boast so intemperately of their own powers, and to imagine that God was slumbering in the heavens. In the close of the verse, mention is made of *all nations*, to intimate, that though they might equal the whole

world in numbers, they would prove a mere mockery with all their influence and resources. Or the words may be read—EVEN AS *thou hast all the nations in derision.* One thing is obvious, that David ridicules the vain boasting of his enemies, who thought no undertaking too great to be accomplished by their numbers.

9. *I will intrust his strength to thee.* The obscurity of this passage has led to a variety of opinions amongst commentators. The most forced interpretation which has been proposed is that which supposes a change of person in the relative *his*, as if David, in speaking of himself, employed the third person instead of the first, *I will intrust* MY *strength to thee.* The Septuagint, and those who adopt this interpretation, have probably been led to it by the insufficient reason, that in the last verse of the psalm it is said, *I will ascribe with praises* MY *strength to thee,* or, MY *strength is with thee, I will sing, &c.* But on coming to that part of the psalm, we will have occasion to see that David there, with propriety, asserts of himself what he here in another sense asserts of Saul. There can be no doubt, therefore, that the relative is to be here understood of Saul. Some consider that the first words of the sentence should be read apart from the others— *strength is his*—meaning that Saul had the evident superiority in strength, so as at the present to be triumphant. Others join the two parts of the sentence, and give this explanation: Although thou art for the present moment his strength, in so far as thou dost sustain and preserve him on the throne, yet I will continue to hope, until thou hast raised me to the kingdom, according to thy promise. But those seem to come nearest the meaning of the Psalmist who construe the words as one continuous sentence: *I will put in trust his strength with thee;* meaning that, however intemperately Saul might boast of his strength, he would rest satisfied in the assurance that there was a secret divine providence restraining his actions. We must learn to view all men as subordinated in this manner, and to conceive of their strength and their enterprises as depending upon the sovereign will of God. In my opinion, the following version is the best—*His strength is with*

thee,[1] *I will wait.* The words are parallel with those in the end of the psalm, where there can be no doubt that the nominative case is employed, *My strength is with thee; I will sing.* So far as the sense of the passage is concerned, however, it does not signify which of the latter interpretations be followed. It is evident that David is here enabled, from the eminence of faith, to despise the violent opposition of his enemy, convinced that he could do nothing without the divine permission. But by taking the two parts of the sentence separately, in the way I have suggested,—*His strength is with thee, I will wait,*—the meaning is more distinctly brought out. First, David, in vindication of that power by which God governs the whole world, declares that his enemy was under a secret divine restraint, and so entirely dependent for any strength which he possessed upon God, that he could not move a finger without his consent. He then adds, that he would wait the event, whatsoever it might be, with composure and tranquillity. For the word which we have translated, *I will intrust,* may here be taken as signifying *I will keep myself,* or quietly wait the pleasure of the Lord. In this sense we find the word used in the conjugation *Niphal,* Isaiah vii. 4. Here it is put in the conjugation *Kal,* but that is no reason why we may not render it, " I will silently wait the issue which God may send." It has been well suggested, that David may allude to the guards which had been sent to besiege his house, and be considered as opposing to this a watch of a very different description, which he himself maintained, as he looked out for the divine issue with quietness and composure.[2]

[1] In the Latin edition, from which we now translate, it reads, "Fortitudo *mea* ad te." This is evidently a mistake of the printer for "*fortitudo ejus,*" and has misled the former English translators. This is the more wonderful, as they thus make the Author adopt the very transposition of person which he had immediately before rejected. Of course, the French version reads, " *Sa* forte est à toy : je garderay."

[2] Hammond translates, " His strength I will ward, or avoid, or beware, or take heed of at thee." And the amount of his explanation is : Saul having sent a party to guard, that is, to besiege the house in which David was, in order to kill him, as is mentioned in the title of the psalm, David resolves to guard, or look to, or beware of the strength of his persecutor, by fleeing to God as his refuge.

10. *The God of my mercy will prevent me : God shall let me see my desire upon mine enemies.*
11. *Slay them not, lest my people forget : scatter them by thy power ; and bring them down, O Lord ! our shield.*
12. *The sin of their mouth, the words of their lips ; let them be taken in their pride : and let them speak of cursing and lying.*

10. *The God of my mercy will prevent me.* In the Hebrew, there is the affix of the third person, but we have the point which denotes the first.[1] The Septuagint has adopted the third person, and Augustine too ingeniously, though with a good design, has repeatedly quoted the passage against the Pelagians, in proof that the grace of God is antecedent to all human merit. In the same manner, he has again and again cited the preceding verse, to refute the arrogancy of those who boast of the power of free-will. " *I will put in trust my strength with thee,*" he says ; " that is, men must subject themselves with all modesty and humility to God, as having no strength but that with which he supplies them." Now, it may be said with great plausibility, that the man *puts his strength in trust with God,* who declares that he has no strength but what comes from him, and who depends entirely upon his help. The sentiment inculcated is also, without all doubt, a pious and instructive one ; but we must be ever on our guard against wresting Scripture from its natural meaning. The Hebrew word קדם, *kidem,* means no more than *to come forward seasonably;* and David simply intimates that the divine assistance would be promptly and opportunely extended.[2] The scope of the words is, that God will interpose at the very moment when it is required, however much he may retard or defer his assistance. Were it not that we are hurried on by the excessive eagerness of our own wishes, we would

---

[1] " We have חַסְדּוֹ, *his mercy,* with the points חַסְדִּי, *my mercy,* the *keri* being for the one, and the *kethib* for the other. And, accordingly, of the interpreters, some read the one, some the other, both certainly meaning the same thing : the Chaldee, ' the God of my grace, *or* goodness, *or* mercy ;' but the LXX. ' Ὁ Θεός μου τὸ ἔλεος αὐτοῦ,' ' My God his mercy,' and so the Latin."—*Hammond.* Green translates, " My God shall prevent me with his loving-kindness."

[2] Horsley reads, " God shall give me ready help."

sufficiently recognise the promptness with which God hastens to our help, but our own precipitance makes us imagine that he is dilatory. To confirm his faith, he calls him *the God of his mercy,* having often proved him to be merciful; and the experience of the past afforded him good hopes of what he might expect in the future. The idea of some, that David uses the word in an active sense, and praises his own mercy, is poor and unnatural. Its passive use is quite common.

11. *Slay them not, lest my people forget.* David very properly suggests this to his own mind, as a consideration which should produce patience. We are apt to think, when God has not annihilated our enemies at once, that they have escaped out of his hands altogether; and we look upon it as properly no punishment, that they should be gradually and slowly destroyed. Such being the extravagant desire which almost all, without exception, have, to see their enemies at once exterminated, David checks himself, and dwells upon the judgment of God to be seen in the lesser calamities which overtake the wicked. It is true, that were not our eyes blinded, we would behold a more evident display of divine retribution in cases where the destruction of the ungodly is sudden; but these are so apt to fade away from our remembrance, that he had good reason to express his desire that the spectacle might be one constantly renewed, and thus our knowledge of the judgments of God be more deeply graven upon our hearts. He arms and fortifies himself against impatience under delays in the execution of divine judgment, by the consideration that God has an express design in them, as, were the wicked exterminated in a moment, the remembrance of the event might speedily be effaced. There is an indirect censure conveyed to the people of Israel for failing to improve the more striking judgments of God. But the sin is one too prevalent in the world even at this day. Those judgments which are so evident that none can miss to observe them without shutting his eyes, we sinfully allow to pass into oblivion; so that we need to be brought daily into that theatre where we are compelled to perceive the divine hand. This we must never forget when we see God subjecting his

enemies to a gradual process of destruction, instead of launching his thunders instantly upon their head. He prays that God would *make them to wander,* as men under poverty and misery, who seek in every direction, but in vain, for a remedy to their misfortunes. The idea is still more forcibly described in the word which follows, *make them descend,* or, *cast them down.* He wished that they might be dragged from that position of honour which they had hitherto occupied, and thrown to the ground, so as to present, in their wretchedness and degradation, a constant illustration of the wrath of God. The word בחילך, *becheylcha,* which we have translated, *in thy power,* some render, *with thy army,* understanding the people of God. But it is more probable that David calls to his assistance *the power* of God for the destruction of his enemies, and this because they deemed themselves invincible through those worldly resources in which they trusted. As a further argument for obtaining his request, he intimates in the close of the verse that he was now pleading the cause of the whole Church, for he uses the plural number, *O God* OUR *shield.* Having been chosen king by divine appointment, the safety of the Church stood connected with his person. The assault made upon him by his enemies was not an assault upon himself merely as a private individual, but upon the whole people, whose common welfare God had consulted in making choice of him. And this suggested another reason why he should patiently submit to see the judgments of God measured out in the manner which might best engage their minds in assiduous meditation.

12. *The sin of their mouth, the words of their lips.* Some interpreters read, *for,* or, *on account of the sin of their mouth,*[1] supplying the causal particle, that the words may be the better connected with the preceding verse. And there can be no doubt that the reason is stated here why they deserved to be subjected to constant wanderings and disquietude. The words as they stand, however, although abrupt and elliptical,

[1] This is the reading adopted by Jerome, and also by Horsley, who remarks, that in Jerome's copies the words, "sin" and "discourse," had certainly the preposition ב prefixed.

well express the meaning which David would convey; as if he had said, that no lengthened proof was necessary to convict them of sin, which plainly showed itself in the mischievous tendency of their discourse. Wickedness, he tells us, proceeded from their mouth.[1] They vomited out their pride and cruelty. That this is the sense in which we are to understand the words, is confirmed by what immediately follows—*Let them be taken in their pride.* He here points to the source of that insolence which led them with such proud and contumelious language, and in such a shameless manner, to oppress the innocent. He then specifies the sin of their lips, adding, that *they spoke words of cursing and falsehood.* By this he means that their mouth was continually filled with horrid imprecations, and that they were wholly addicted to deceit and to calumniating. Those have mistaken the meaning of David who give a passive signification to the word which I have translated *to speak,* and understand him as saying that the wicked would be accounted examples of divine vengeance, the plain and notorious marks of which were written upon them.

13. *Consume, consume them in wrath, that they may not be, and let them know unto the ends of the earth that God ruleth in Jacob. Selah.*

14. *And at evening they will return; they will make a noise like a dog, and go round about the city.*

15. *They will wander up and down to eat;*[2] *if they be not satis-*

---

[1] The Syriac translation of the first part of the verse is, " The discourse of their mouth is the sin of their lips." That is, whatever their lips speak is sin; so many words, so many sins.

[2] "The literal translation, *to eat, i. e.,* to devour, may be best."—*Archbishop Secker.* From the great attention which is paid to external purity in the East, and in consequence of dogs being reckoned unclean, as they were by the Jews under the law, the inhabitants do not admit them into their houses, and even carefully avoid touching them in their streets, by which they would consider themselves defiled. But though not there domesticated as with us, dogs are to be found in great numbers, and crowd the streets. They are not attached to any particular person or family, nor accounted the property of any one; and though it is not uncommon for some of the inhabitants, from motives of superstition, to give money weekly or monthly to butchers and bakers to feed them at stated times, and though some even leave legacies at their death for the same purpose, yet they must necessarily subsist in a great measure on what they can seize or steal; and, being very numerous, they are perpetually wandering about

fied,¹ *they will even lodge all night long.* 16. *But I will sing of thy power, I will praise thy mercy in the morning;*² *for thou hast been my fortress and refuge in the day of my trouble.*

17. *My strength is with thee, I will sing psalms ; for God is my defence, the God of my mercy.*

13. *Consume, consume them in wrath, that they may not be.* David may seem to contradict himself in praying for the utter destruction of his enemies, when immediately before he had expressed his desire that they might not be exterminated at once.³ What else could he mean when he asks that God would consume them in wrath, but that he would cut them off suddenly, and not by a gradual and slower process of punishment? But he evidently refers in what he says here to a different point of time, and this removes any apparent inconsistency, for he prays that when they had been set up for a sufficient period as an example, they might eventually be devoted to destruction. It was customary with the victorious Roman generals, first to lead the captives which had been kept for the day of triumph through the city, and afterwards, upon reaching the capital, to give them over to the lictors for execution. Now David prays that when God had, in a similar manner, reserved his enemies for an interval sufficient to illustrate his triumph, he would upon this consign them to summary punishment. The two things are not at

in large troops seeking for something to devour.—(*Harmer's Observations*, vol. i. p. 344.) To these circumstances the Psalmist clearly alludes in the 14th and 15th verses, when he compares the behaviour of his enemies to that of dogs. He repeats what he had said in the 5th verse ; but here he intends to convey a different idea. " Let them do what they may ;" as if he had said, " I am safe under the protection of God."

¹ " C'est, combien qu'ils ne soyent."—*Fr. marg.* " That is, though they be not satisfied."

² " *In the morning.* It should seem this hath a relation to Saul's servants watching for him in the morning to kill him, (1 Sam. xix. 11 ;) meaning, At that time when those people imagine to have me in their hands I shall be in safety, and have cause to praise and bless thee for my deliverance." —*Annotations on the Bible by English Divines.*

³ Williams observes, that the Hebrew rendered *consume* "literally means *to finish*, bring to an end ; namely, the *banditti*. The Psalmist, verse 11, prays, ' Slay them not ;' *i. e.*, take not away their lives as individuals, but put an end to the conspiracy."

all inconsistent; first, that the divine judgments should be lengthened out through a considerable period, to secure their being remembered better, and that then, upon sufficient evidence being given to the world of the certainty with which the wicked are subjected in the displeasure of God to the slower process of destruction, he should in due time bring them forth to final execution, the better to awake, by such a demonstration of his power, the minds of those who may be more secure than others, or less affected by witnessing moderate inflictions of punishment. He adds, accordingly, *that they may know, even to the ends of the earth, that God ruleth in Jacob.* Some would insert the copulative particle, reading, *that they may know that God rules in Jacob, and in all the nations of the world,* an interpretation which I do not approve, and which does violence to the sense. The allusion is to the condign nature of the judgment, which would be such that the report of it would reach the remotest regions, and strike salutary terror into the minds even of their benighted and godless inhabitants. He was more especially anxious that God should be recognised as ruling *in the Church,* it being preposterous that the place where his throne was erected should present such an aspect of confusion as converted his temple into a den of thieves.

14. *And at evening they shall return.* It is of no consequence whether we read the words in the future tense or in the subjunctive, understanding it to be a continuance of the preceding prayer. But it seems more probable that David, after having brought his requests to a close, anticipates the happy issue which he desired. And he makes an apt allusion to what he had already said of their insatiable hunger. The words which he had formerly used he repeats, but with a different application, ironically declaring that they would be ravenous in another sense, and that matters would issue otherwise than they had looked for. Above he had complained that they made a noise like dogs, adverting to the eagerness and fierceness with which they were bent upon mischief; now he derides their malicious efforts, and says, that after wearying themselves with their endless pursuit all day,

they would go disappointed of their purpose. He uses no longer the language of complaint, but congratulates himself upon the abortive issue of their activity. The Hebrew word which I have translated, *if not*, in the close of the fifteenth verse, is by some considered to be the form of an oath. But this is an over-refined interpretation. Others would have the negation repeated, reading, *if they shall not have been satisfied, neither shall they lodge for the night.* But this also is far-fetched. The simple and true meaning suggests itself at once, that, although they might not be satisfied, they would be forced to lay themselves down, and the misery of their hunger would be aggravated, by the circumstance that they had passed the whole day in fruitless application, and must lie down for the night empty, wearied, and unsatisfied.[1]

16. *But I will sing of thy power.* By this he does not mean merely that he would have occasion to sing at some future period, but prepares himself presently for the exercise of thanksgiving; and he proceeds to acknowledge that his deliverance would be at once an illustrious effect of Divine power, and conferred of mere grace. It may be true, that David escaped at this time from the hands of his enemies without stir, and with secrecy, through the dexterity of his wife; still, by means of this artifice, God disappointed the preparations and forces of Saul, and may, therefore, with propriety be said to have exerted his power. We may suppose, however, that David takes occasion, from this particular instance, to look further back, and embrace, in his view, the various Divine interpositions which he had experienced.

17. *My strength is with thee, I will sing psalms.* He expresses still more explicitly the truth, that he owed his safety

---

[1] Street translates, "If they be not satisfied, they spend the night in howling;" and observes, that there seems to be a word lost after the original verb לון, *lun*, which he renders, *they spend the night;* and he supplies it by the words, *in howling*. The meaning of the verb לון, *lun*, is ambiguous. It signifies both *to continue all night*, and *to growl*, or *murmur*. Either sense will be appropriate in this passage. The Chaldee and Syriac understand it in the former sense; and the Septuagint in the latter.

entirely to God. Formerly he had said that the strength of his enemy was with God, and now he asserts the same thing of his own. The expression, however, which admits of two meanings, he elegantly applies to himself in a different sense.[1] God has the strength of the wicked in his hands, to curb and to restrain it, and to show that any power of which they boast is vain and fallacious. His own people, on the other hand, he supports and secures, against the possibility of falling, by supplies of strength from himself. In the preceding part of the psalm, David had congratulated himself upon his safety, by reflecting that Saul was so completely under the secret restraint of God's providence as to be unable to move a finger without his permission. Now, weak as he was in himself, he maintains that he had strength sufficient in the Lord; and accordingly adds, that he had good reason to engage in praise, as James the inspired apostle exhorts those who are merry to sing psalms, (chap. v. 13.) As to the reading which some have adopted, *I will ascribe my strength with praises unto thee*, the reader cannot fail to see that it is forced. It is clear that the two clauses must be taken separately, as I have already observed.

PSALM LX.

David, who was now settled upon the throne, and had gained several signal victories, tending to confirm him in the kingdom, in this psalm exalts the goodness of God, that he might at once express his gratitude, and, by conciliating the favour of such as still stood out against his interests, unite the community, which had been rent into factions. Having first adverted to the clear indications of the Divine favour, which proved that God had chosen him to be king, he more particularly calls the attention of the faithful to the oracle itself, in order to convince them that they could only comply with the mind of God, by

---

[1] " Sed eleganter ambiguam locutionem diverso sensu ponit."—*Lat.* In the French version, " Mais c'est une bonne rencontre et qui a grace, quand il met deux fois un propos ambigu, mais en divers sens."

yielding their consent and approbation to the anointing which he had received from Samuel. Prayers also are offered up throughout the psalm, urging God to perfect what he had begun.

¶ To the chief musician upon Shushan-eduth, Michtam[1] of David, to teach; when he strove with the Syrians of Mesopotamia, and with the Syrians of Zoba, and when Joab returned, and smote of the Edomites in the valley of Salt twelve thousand.

Of the first part of this title I have spoken in another place, and shall not insist upon it further than to repeat, that *Shushan-eduth, the lily of witness*,[2] or *of beauty*, seem to have been the first words of some song which was commonly known at the time. It is added, *to teach;* and this, as some have thought, because the psalm was given to the Levites, that they might learn it. But others have very properly rejected this idea, as we cannot suppose that a title, which is equally applicable to all the psalms, would have been here used as a term of distinction. More probably it points at a particular instruction or doctrine, which would be taught by the following psalm. We may suppose that David, who had gained so many decisive victories, but had not the satisfaction, as yet, of seeing the kingdom finally settled under him, employs the word to denote that he had a special lesson to enforce, which was, the duty of all who had hitherto opposed him to put an end to factions, and, after such convincing evidences, acknowledge that he was their divinely-appointed king. Let experience, at least, as if he had said, prove that the sovereignty which I hold meets with the approbation of God, crowned, as it is, in the eyes of all, with so many tokens of his favour. The psalm is described as being a kind of triumphal song for victories obtained over the Syrians and other allied nations. As the Jews reckon Mesopotamia, and other countries, to be included in Syria, which they call Aram, they are forced subsequently to distinguish it into different parts, as here we find *Syria Naharim* put for Mesopotamia, which some of the Latins have named Interamnis, (or, *between two rivers,*) following the Greek etymology; for Mesopotamia in Greek means between two rivers, that is, between the Tigris and Euphrates.[3] Next, we have *Syria Soba* mentioned, which some have considered upon good grounds to be Sophene, because adjacent to the bank of the Euphrates; and David is said (2 Sam. viii. 3) to have smitten Rehob, king of Soba, as he went to recover his border at the river. In the same passage, we read of a third Syria, that of Damascus,

---

[1] *Michtam* is prefixed to six psalms, of which this is the last. The others are, the 16th, 56th, 57th, 58th, and 59th.

[2] What that means it is not easy to ascertain : from the lily being a six-leaved flower, it has been supposed that the word may also mean a six-stringed instrument.

[3] We have here adopted the French version, which is fuller than the Latin, " laquelle aucuns des Latins à l'imitation des Grecs (car Mesopotamie en Grec signifie entre les fleuves, pource qu'elle est entre Tigris et Euphrates) ont nommee Interamnis."

nearer to Judea, and almost touching upon it. Syria is, in other places of Scripture, represented as still more extensive, and has epithets attached to it according to the different territories which are meant to be pointed out. As David had war with the more adjacent part of Syria, and routed the army which had come out from it to the assistance of the Ammonites, it may be asked why he speaks only of the inhabitants of Mesopotamia and Soba. I think it probable that he specifies the more distant nations, as being the most formidable, and as affording a more illustrious proof of the Divine favour which accompanied his arms. For this reason, he passes over the more neighbouring nations, and mentions those which were situated at a distance, the terror of which was known only by report, and whose overthrow was something unheard of, and almost incredible. In the inspired history, two-and-twenty thousand are said to have been slain,[1] (1 Chron. xviii. 12,) in the title of this psalm only twelve thousand; but the apparent inconsistency is easily explained. It is Abishai whom the history represents as defeating the forces, which are here said to have been overthrown by Joab. We are to consider that the army was divided between the two brothers. Abishai being inferior in rank and authority, we need not wonder that the praise of the victory is ascribed to him who was the chief commander, although both had a share in gaining it; as in 1 Sam. xviii. 7, David is described as having the whole honour of the victory, because he was the individual under whose auspices it had been accomplished. It is probable that about half the number mentioned in the history fell during the main engagement, and that the rest having fled from the field, were put to the sword by Joab in their retreat.[2]

1. *O God! thou hast cast us off; thou hast scattered us; thou hast been displeased: O turn thyself to us again!*
2. *Thou hast made the earth* [or *the land*] *to tremble; thou hast caused it to open wide: heal the breaches thereof; for it shaketh.*
3. *Thou hast showed thy people hard things: thou hast made us drunk with the wine of astonishment.*

[1] It should be eighteen thousand.
[2] There is another way in which this difference as to number may be reconciled besides that in which Calvin attempts to do it. "If the Hebrew numbers here," says Street, "have been ever expressed by letters used as numerals, the variation might be accounted for; ב‎י being twelve, and י‎ח being eighteen, and many instances being to be found of the corruption of ח into ב.—See *Dr Kennicott's Dissertation* on 1 Chron. xi. page 96, where it is plainly shown that many errors in numbers have arisen from the numbers having been expressed by letters, and one letter having been mistaken for another."
[3] The three first verses, which complain of calamities and distresses, seem not to correspond to the title of the psalm, from which we would naturally expect the expressions of joy and praise for the victory obtained. Hare conjectures that these three verses have accidentally changed place

1. *O God! thou hast cast us off.* With the view of exciting both himself and others to a more serious consideration of the goodness of God, which they presently experienced, he begins the psalm with prayer; and a comparison is instituted, designed to show that the government of Saul had been under the divine reprobation. He complains of the sad confusions into which the nation had been thrown, and prays that God would return to it in mercy, and re-establish its affairs. Some have thought that David here adverts to his own distressed condition: this is not probable. I grant that, before coming to the throne, he underwent severe afflictions; but in this place he evidently speaks of the whole people as well as himself. The calamities which he describes are such as extended to the whole kingdom; and I have not the least doubt, therefore, that he is to be considered as drawing a comparison which might illustrate the favour of God, as it had been shown so remarkably, from the first, to his own government. With this view, he deplores the long-continued and heavy disasters which had fallen upon the people of God under Saul's administration. It is particularly noticeable, that though he had found his own countrymen his worst and bitterest foes, now that he sat upon the throne, he forgets all the injuries which they had done him, and, mindful only of the situation which he occupied, associates himself with the rest of them in his addresses to God. The *scattered* condition of the nation is what he insists upon as the main calamity. In consequence of the dispersion of Saul's forces, the country lay completely exposed to the incursions of enemies; not a man was safe in his own house, and no relief remained but in flight or banishment. He next describes the confusions which reigned by a metaphor, representing

---

with Ps. lxxxv. 2, 3, 4. Archbishop Secker observes, that this conjecture "is bold, but otherwise very ingenious and plausible; and this change would make each psalm more consistent, and reconcile this psalm to its title very well; for the historical books mention no distress in the war to which the title refers." Dr Adam Clarke considers this conjecture well founded; but others think the apparent discrepancy may be removed by supposing that the psalm was written after some of the battles of which mention is made in the title, and that the Author does not restrict himself to those events, but takes in a wider range, so as to embrace the afflictive condition both of Israel and Judah during the latter part of Saul's life, and the former years of David's reign.

the country as *opened*, or *cleft asunder;* not that there had been a literal earthquake, but that the kingdom, in its rent and shattered condition, presented that calamitous aspect which generally follows upon an earthquake. The affairs of Saul ceased to prosper from the time that he forsook God; and when he perished at last, he left the nation in a state little short of ruin. The greatest apprehension must have been felt throughout it; it was become the scorn of its enemies, and was ready to submit to any yoke, however degrading, which promised tolerable conditions. Such is the manner in which David intimates that the divine favour had been alienated by Saul, pointing, when he says that God was *displeased*, at the radical source of all the evils which prevailed; and he prays that the same physician who had broken would heal.

3. *Thou hast showed thy people hard things.* He says, first, that the nation had been dealt with severely, and then adds a figure which may additionally represent the grievousness of its calamities, speaking of it as drunk with the wine of stupor or astonishment. Even the Hebraist interpreters are not agreed among themselves as to the meaning of תרעלה, *tarelah*, which I have rendered *astonishment*. Several of them translate it *poison*. But it is evident that the Psalmist alludes to some kind of poisoned drink, which deprives a person of his senses, insinuating that the Jews were stupified by their calamities.[1] He would place, in short, before their

---

[1] It was customary among the Hebrews to make their wine stronger and more inebriating by the addition of hotter and more powerful ingredients; such as honey, spices, *defrutum*, (*i. e.*, wine inspissated by boiling it down to two-thirds or one-half of the quantity,) mandrakes, opiates, and other drugs. Such were the stupifying ingredients which the celebrated Helen is represented, in Homer's Odyssey, as mixing in the bowl, together with the wine, for her guests oppressed with grief, to raise their spirits; and such is probably the wine to which there is here an allusion. The people were stupified by the heavy judgments of God, like a person stupified with wine which had been rendered more intoxicating by the deleterious drugs with which it had been mingled. This highly poetical language is not unfrequently employed to express the divine judgments; as in Isaiah li. 17, 20-22, and Jeremiah xxv. 15, 16. The original word תרעלה, *tarelah*, means properly *trembling*, from the verb רעל, *raäl*, from which the English word *reel* is perhaps derived. We might therefore read, "the wine of trembling."

eyes the curse of God, which had pressed upon the government of Saul, and induce them to abandon their obstinate attempts to maintain the interests of a throne which lay under the divine reprobation.

> 4. *Thou hast given a banner to them that fear thee, that it may be displayed before the truth. Selah.*
> 5. *That thy beloved may be delivered,[1] save with thy right hand, and hear me.*
> 6. *God hath spoken in his holiness; I will rejoice: I will divide Shechem, and mete out the valley of Succoth.*
> 7. *Gilead is mine, and Manasseh is mine; Ephraim also is the strength of my head; Judah is my lawgiver.*[2]
> 8. *Moab is my washpot; over Edom will I cast my shoe: Palestina, triumph over me.*

4. *Thou hast given a banner to them that fear thee.* Some interpreters would change the past tense, and read the words as if they formed a continuation of the prayers which precede —*O that thou wouldst give a banner to them that fear thee!*[3] But it is better to suppose that David diverges to the language of congratulation, and, by pointing to the change which had taken place, calls attention to the evident appearances of the divine favour. He returns thanks to God, in the name of all the people, for having raised a standard which might at once cheer their hearts, and unite their divided numbers.[4] It is a

---

[1] " Ou, que tes bien-aimez soyent delivrez."—*Fr. marg.* " Or, let thy beloved be delivered."

[2] " Ou, gouverneur."—*Fr. marg.* " Or, governor."

[3] Boothroyd gives a translation similar to this, and thinks that this is required by the connection. But see note 3, p. 397.

[4] Harmer has given a very ingenious explanation of this passage, derived from the manners of the East. "It seems," says he, "that the modern Eastern people have looked upon the giving them a *banner* as a more sure pledge of protection 'than that given by words.' So Albertus Aquensis tell us, that when Jerusalem was taken in 1099, about three hundred Saracens got upon the roof of a very lofty building, and earnestly begged for quarter, but could not be induced, by any promises of safety, to come down, until they had received the banner of Tancred [one of the chiefs of the Crusade army] as a pledge of life. It did not, indeed, avail them, as that historian observes; for their behaviour occasioned such indignation that they were destroyed to a man. The event showed the faithlessness of these zealots, whom no solemnities could bind; but the Saracens surrendering themselves upon the delivery of a standard to them, proves in what a strong light they looked upon the giving them a banner; since it induced them to trust it when they would not trust any promises.

poor and meagre interpretation which some have attached to the words, *before the truth,* that God showed favour to the Jews because he had found them true-hearted, and sound in his cause. Those in the higher ranks had, as is well known, proved eminently disloyal; the common people had, along with their king, broken their divine allegiance: from the highest to the lowest in the kingdom all had conspired to overthrow the gracious purpose of God. It is evident, then, that David refers to the truth of God as having emerged in a signal manner, now that the Church began to be restored. This was an event which had not been expected. Indeed, who did not imagine, in the desperate circumstances, that God's promises had altogether failed? But when David mounted the throne, his truth, which had been so long obscured, again shone forth. The advantage which ensued extended to the whole nation; but David intimates that God had a special respect to his own people, whose deliverance, however few they might be in number, he particularly contemplated.

Perhaps the delivery of a banner was anciently esteemed, in like manner, an obligation to protect, and the Psalmist might consider it in this light, when, upon a victory gained over the Syrians and Edomites, after the public affairs of Israel had been in a bad state, he says, 'Thou hast showed thy people hard things, &c.; thou hast given a banner to them that fear thee.' Though thou didst for a time give up thine Israel into the hands of their enemies, thou hast now given them an assurance of thy having received them under thy protection."—*Observations,* vol. iii. pp. 496, 497. Harmer supposes that our translation, which speaks of *a banner displayed,* is inaccurate; observing, that it is most probable that the Israelites anciently used only a spear, properly ornamented to distinguish it from a common one—a supposition which he founds on the fact, that a very long spear, covered all over with silver, and having a ball of gold on the top, was the standard of the Egyptian princes at the time of the Crusade wars, and was carried before their armies. He proposes to read, "Thou hast given an ensign or standard [נס, *nes*] to them that fear thee, that it may be lifted up." But Parkhurst considers the radical meaning of the Hebrew word נס, *nes,* to be *a banner* or *ensign,* from its *waving* or *streaming* in the wind; in other words, *a streamer.* See his Lexicon on נס. Mant's explanation of the phrase is similar to that of Calvin. "In this place," says he, "it may mean no more than that God had united his people under one head, and so enabled them to meet their enemies by repairing to the standard of their sovereign." "The banner, or standard of an army," says Walford, "is the object of constant attention to soldiers: so long as it is safe and elevated, so long courage, hope, and energy, are maintained. The poet uses this symbol to express his hope that God himself would be the source of their valour and success, in order that *the truth,* the promise made to David, might be accomplished."

He next proceeds to address God again in prayer; although, I may observe in passing, the words which follow, *that thy beloved may be delivered*, are read by some in connection with the preceding verse. I am myself inclined to adopt that construction; for David would seem to magnify the illustration which had been given of the divine favour, by adverting to the change which had taken place,[1] God having inspirited his people so far as to display a banner; whereas, formerly, they were reduced to a state of extremity, from which it seemed impossible to escape without a miracle. In the previous verse he calls them *fearers* of the Lord, and now his *beloved;* implying that, when God rewards such as fear and worship him, it is always with a respect to his own free love. And prayer is subjoined: for however great may be the favours which God has bestowed upon us, modesty and humility will teach us always to pray that he would perfect what his goodness has begun.

6. *God hath spoken in his holiness; I will rejoice.* Hitherto he has adverted to the proofs which had come under their own observation, and from which they might easily see that God had manifested his favour in a manner new, and for many years unprecedented. He had raised the nation from a state of deep distress to prosperity, and had changed the aspect of affairs so far, that one victory was following another in rapid succession. But now he calls their attention to a point of still greater importance, the divine promise—the fact that God had previously declared all this with his own mouth. However numerous and striking may be the practical demonstrations we receive of the favour of God, we can never recognize them, except in connection with his previously revealed promise. What follows, although spoken by David as of himself individually, may be considered as the language adopted by the people generally, of whom he was the political head. Accordingly, he enjoins them, pro-

---

[1] The Latin is here concise—"Nam in ipsa varietate David magnitudinem gratiæ commendat." Accordingly, the French version amplifies the passage—"Car David en proposant la diversité et la changement d'un temps a l'autre, magnifie," &c.

vided they were not satisfied with the sensible proofs of divine favour, to reflect upon the oracle by which he had been made king in terms the most distinct and remarkable.[1] He says that God had spoken *in his holiness,* not *by his Holy Spirit,* as some, with an over-refinement of interpretation, have rendered it, nor *in his holy place, the sanctuary;*[2] for we read of no response having been given from it to the prophet Samuel. It is best to retain the term *holiness,* as he adverts to the fact of the truth of the oracle having been confirmed, and the constancy and efficacy of the promise having been placed beyond all doubt by numerous proofs of a practical kind. As no room had been left for question upon the point, he employs this epithet to put honour upon the words which had been spoken by Samuel. He immediately adds, that this word of God was the chief ground upon which he placed his trust. It might be true that he had gained many victories, and that these had tended to encourage his heart; but he intimates, that no testimony which he had received of this kind gave him so much satisfaction as the word. This accords with the general experience of the Lord's people. Cheered, as they unquestionably are, by every expression of the divine goodness, still faith must ever be considered as holding the highest place—as being that which dissipates their worst sorrows, and quickens them even when dead to a happiness which is not of this world. Nor does David mean that he merely rejoiced himself. He includes, in general, all who feared the Lord in that kingdom. And now he proceeds to give the sum of the oracle, which it is observable that he does in such a way as to show, in the very narration of it, how firmly he believed in its truth: for he speaks of it as something which admitted of no doubt whatsoever, and boasts that he would do what God had promised. *I will divide Shechem,* he says, *and mete out the valley of Succoth.*[3]

[1] " Cum præclaris elogiis."—*Lat.* Amplified in the French version as follows:—"l'ornant de titres excellens, et lui faisant des promesses authentiques."
[2] This is the reading of Mudge, Street, Archbishop Secker, and Morrison. " Should not the word be read, *in his sanctuary?* whence the divine oracles were issued forth. David, having received a favourable answer, perhaps by Urim and Thummim, delivers himself in a strain of the fullest confidence of victory over his enemies."—*Dimock.*
[3] Shechem lay in Samaria, and, therefore, by it the whole of Samaria

The parts which he names are those that were more late of coming into his possession, and which would appear to have been yet in the hands of Saul's son, when this psalm was written. A severe struggle being necessary for their acquisition, he asserts that, though late of being subdued, they would certainly be brought under his subjection in due time, as God had condescended to engage this by his word. So with *Gilead and Manasseh*.[1] As *Ephraim* was the most populous of all the tribes, he appropriately terms it *the strength of his head*, that is, of his dominions.[2] To procure the greater credit to the oracle, by showing that it derived a sanction from antiquity, he adds, that *Judah* would be *his lawgiver*, or *chief*; which was equivalent to saying, that the posterity of Abraham could never prosper unless, in agreeableness to the prediction of the patriarch Jacob, they were brought under the government of Judah, or of one who was sprung from that tribe. He evidently alludes to what is narrated by Moses, (Gen. xlix. 10,) " The sceptre shall not depart from Judah, nor a lawgiver from between his feet, until Shiloh come." The same word is there used, מחוקק, *Mechokek*, or legislator. It followed, that no government could stand which was not resident in the tribe of Judah, this being the decree and the good pleasure of God. The words are more appropriate in the mouth of the people than of David; and, as already remarked, he does not speak in his own name, but in that of the Church at large.

8. *Moab is my wash-pot.* In proceeding to speak of foreign-

may be intended. The valley of Succoth, or booths, received its name from Jacob's making booths, and feeding his cattle there. (See Gen. xxxiii. 17, 18.) It lay beyond the Jordan, and it may be employed to designate the whole of that district of country. Though Samaria, and the country beyond the Jordan, were now in the hands of the enemy, yet David anticipates the time when he would gain complete and absolute possession of them, which he expresses by *dividing*, and *meting them out*. The allusion is to the dividing and measuring out of land; and it was a part of the power of a king to distribute his kingdom into cities and provinces, and to place judges and magistrates over them.

[1] Gilead and Manasseh were beyond the Jordan. The tribe of Gad, which was in Gilead, was distinguished for its warlike valour.

[2] This tribe was also distinguished for its valour. (Deut. xxxiii. 17; Ps. lxxviii. 9; see also Gen. xlviii. 19.)

ers, he observes a wide distinction between them and his own countrymen. The posterity of Abraham he would govern as brethren, and not as slaves; but it was allowable for him to exercise greater severities upon the profane and the uncircumcised, in order to their being brought under forcible subjection. In this he affords no precedent to conquerors who would inflict lawless oppression upon nations taken in war; for they want the divine warrant and commission which David had, invested as he was not only with the authority of a king, but with the character of an avenger of the Church, especially of its more implacable enemies, such as had thrown off every feeling of humanity, and persisted in harassing a people descended from the same stock with themselves. He remarks, in contempt of the Moabites, that they would be a vessel in which he should wash his feet, the washing of the feet being, as is well known, a customary practice in Eastern nations.[1] With the same view he speaks of casting his shoe over Edom. This is expressive of reproach, and intimates, that as it had once insulted over the chosen people of God, so now it should be reduced to servitude.[2] What follows

[1] This office of washing the feet was in the East commonly performed by slaves, and the meanest of the family, as appears from what Abigail said to David when he took her to wife, " Behold, let thine handmaid be a servant to wash the feet of the servants of my lord," 1 Sam. xxv. 41; and from the fact of our Saviour washing his disciples' feet, to give them an example of humility, John xiii. 5. The word νιπτήρ, used in this last passage, signifies in general *a washing-pot*, and is put for the word ποδονιπτρον, the term which the Greeks, in strict propriety of speech, applied to a vessel for washing the feet. As this office was servile, so the vessels employed for this purpose were a mean part of household stuff. Gataker and Le Clerc illustrate this text from an anecdote related by Herodotus, concerning Amasis, king of Egypt, who expressed the meanness of his own origin by comparing himself to a pot for washing the feet in, (Herod. Lib. ii. c. 172.) When, therefore, it is said, " Moab is my washing-pot," the complete and servile subjection of Moab to David is strongly marked. This is expressed not by comparing Moab to a slave who performs the lowest offices, as presenting to his master the basin for washing his feet, but by comparing him to the mean utensil itself. See 2 Sam. viii. 2; 1 Chron. xviii. 1, 2, 12, 13.

[2] Edom or Idumea was inhabited by the Edomites, or posterity of Edom, that is, Esau, (the elder brother of Jacob,) who, on account of his profanity in selling his birthright for a mess of red pottage—called in Hebrew *Edom*—had this name imposed upon him to the perpetual disgrace of himself and his posterity, (Gen. xxv. 30; xxxvi. 8, 9; Heb. xii. 16.) The expression, "Over Edom will I cast my shoe," has been differently explained by interpreters. Some, as Gataker and Martin, read, " To Edom

concerning Palestina is ambiguous. By some the words are taken ironically, as if David would deride the vain boastings of the Philistines, who were constantly assaulting him with all the petulance which they could command.[1] And the Hebrew verb רוע, *ruang,* though it means in general *to shout with triumph,* signifies also to make a tumult, as soldiers when they rush to battle. Others, without supposing any ironical allusion, take the words as they stand, and interpret them as meaning servile plaudits: that much and obstinately as they hated his dominion, they would be forced to hail and applaud him as conqueror. Thus in Psalm xviii. 44, it is said, " The sons of the strangers shall feign submission to me."[2]

---

will I cast my shoe;" and suppose that the reference is to the custom which then prevailed, of the master employing his meanest servant to untie, take off, and cleanse his shoes, (Matth. iii. 11; Luke iii. 16;) and that David intimates, that the Edomites would become his menial slaves, who would perform to him the lowest offices. "And the prophet," observes Martin, "uses the word *throw,* which marks an action done in a passionate and angry manner, in allusion to the circumstance that masters, when employing their servants with whom they are displeased to take off their shoes, hold out their feet to them with violence, as if they would thrust their feet against them." The LXX. and Vulgate read, "will extend my shoe." And Bishop Horne is of opinion, that the meaning is, "extending his shoe," that is to say, putting his feet upon them; and this, it is well known, was the manner in which Eastern conquerors were wont to treat their captives. But there is another ancient custom to which others suppose the passage refers. The ancients were wont to throw their shoes and sandals, when soiled with dirt, into some obscure corner before they sat down to meat, and many might possibly have some mean place in their houses into which they commonly threw them; and, therefore, the throwing of the shoe *over* or *on* Edom might mean, as Bucer expounds it, " Edom will be as the place into which I cast my shoe." But whatever may be the precise allusion, the meaning conveyed undoubtedly is, that David would make a complete conquest of Edom, that he would reduce it to the lowest subjection. And such was actually the case, as we learn from 2 Sam. viii. 14. "Abu Walid would have נעל here to signify *a fetter,*—' I will cast my fetter or chain on him:' and so Kimchi, in his roots; though in his comment here he interpret it in the notion of a shoe."—*Hammond.*

[1] "The apostrophe to Philistia is the language of irony and of defiance. —' Philistia, triumph thou over me!' as if he had said, ' Thou hast been used to insult and triumph over me; but circumstances are now reversed, and it is my turn to shout and triumph over thee.' See Ps. cviii. 9."—*Williams' Cottage Bible.*

[2] "*Philistia, be thou glad of me,* rather, *Philistia, welcome me* (as thy conqueror) *with shouts;* a hard task for the vanquished to perform."—*Cresswell.* Bishop Horne reads, " Over Philistia give a shout of triumph." Horsley reads, " Over Philistia is my shout of triumph." " I take," says he, "התריעי for a noun substantive, with the pronoun of the first person suffixed."

9. *Who will bring me into the fortified city ? who will lead me into Edom ?*
10. *Wilt not thou, O God! who hadst cast us off, and thou, O God! who didst not go out with our armies?*
11. *Give us help from trouble : for vain is the help of man.*[1]
12. *Through God we shall do valiantly : for he it is that shall tread down our enemies.*

9. *Who will bring me into the fortified city?* Anticipating an objection which might be alleged, he proceeds to state that he looked to God for the accomplishment of what remained to be done in the capture of the fortified places of his enemies, and the consolidation of his victories. It might be said, that as a considerable number continued to resist his claims, the confident terms which he had used were premature. God, however, had pledged his word that every nation which set itself in opposition to him would be brought under his power, and in the face of remaining difficulties and dangers he advances with certainty of success. By the *fortified city*,[2] some understand Rabbah, the capital of the Moabites. Others, with more probability, consider that the singular is used for the plural number, and that David alludes in general to the different cities under protection of which his enemies were determined to stand out. He declares, that the same God who had crowned his arms with victory in the open field would lead him on to the siege of these cities. With a view to prove his legitimate call to the government, he amplifies a second time the marks of the divine favour which it had received, by contrasting it with that which preceded. "The God," he says, "who had formerly cast us off, and abandoned

---

[1] " C'est, la salut que l'homme peut apporter."—*Fr. marg.* "That is, the help which man can bring."

[2] Literally, " the strong city," or " the city of strength." The Chaldee makes it Tyre, the capital of Phœnicia. Mudge and others think Petra, the capital of Idumea, is meant. Viewed as referring to that remarkable city, which was hewn out of the rock, and deemed impregnable, (Obadiah, 3d verse,) and with which Burckhardt, Laborde, Stephens, and other modern travellers, have made us so minutely acquainted; the language of the Psalmist is very appropriate, illustrating the strength of his faith, and magnifying the greatness of the divine aid. *Who will bring me into the fortified city?* it is impossible for me, by my own strength, or by mere human aid, to occupy this stronghold, unless God interpose in my behalf, assist, and prosper my attempts.

us to unsuccessful warfare, will now lay open before me the gates of hostile cities, and enable me to break through all their fortifications."

11. *Give us help from trouble: for vain is the help of man.* Again he reverts to the exercise of prayer, or rather is led to it naturally by the very confidence of hope, which we have seen that he entertained. He expresses his conviction, that should God extend his help, it would be sufficient of itself, although no assistance should be received from any other quarter. Literally it reads, *Give us help from trouble, and vain is the help of man.* "O God," as if he had said, " when pleased to put forth thy might, thou needest none to help thee; and when, therefore, once assured of an interest in thy favour, there is no reason why we should desire the aid of man. All other resources of a worldly nature vanish before the brightness of thy power." The copulative in the verse, however, has been generally resolved into the causal particle, and I have not scrupled to follow the common practice. It were well if the sentiment expressed were effectually engraven upon our hearts. Why is it almost universally the case with men that they are either staggered in their resolution, or buoy themselves up with confidences, vain, because not derived from God, but just because they have no apprehension of that salvation which he can extend, which is of itself sufficient, and without which, any earthly succour is entirely ineffectual? In contrasting the help of God with that of man, he employs language not strictly correct, for, in reality, there is no such thing as a power in man to deliver at all. But, in our ignorance, we conceive as if there were various kinds of help in the world, and he uses the word in accommodation to our false ideas. God, in accomplishing our preservation, may use the agency of man, but he reserves it to himself, as his peculiar prerogative, to deliver, and will not suffer them to rob him of his glory. The deliverance which comes to us in this manner through human agency must properly be ascribed to God. All that David meant to assert is, that such confidences as are not derived from God are worthless and vain. And to confirm this position, he declares in the last verse of the psalm, that as, on the one hand, we can do nothing without him, so,

on the other, we can do all things by his help. Two things are implied in the expression, *through God we shall do valiantly;*[1] first, that if God withdraw his favour, any supposed strength which is in man will soon fail; and, on the other hand, that those whose sufficiency is derived from God only are armed with courage to overcome every difficulty. To show that it is no mere half credit which he gives God, he adds, in words which ascribe the whole work to him, that *it is he who shall tread down our enemies.* Thus, even in our controversy with creatures like ourselves, we are not at liberty to share the honour of success with God; and must it not be accounted greater sacrilege still when men set free will in opposition to divine grace, and speak of their concurring equally with God in the matter of procuring eternal salvation? Those who arrogate the least fraction of strength to themselves apart from God, only ruin themselves through their own pride.

PSALM LXI.

This psalm begins with prayer, or, at any rate, with the brief record of a prayer, which David had preferred to God in a season of deep distress. It is chiefly occupied, however, with the praises of God, expressing his thankfulness for a miraculous deliverance which he had experienced from some imminent danger, and for his establishment upon the throne.

¶ To the chief musician upon Neginoth, A Psalm of David.

[1] Street supposes that this psalm was composed before the battle of Helam, which is recorded in 1 Chron. xix. 16, where David beat the Syrians of Mesopotamia and the Syrians of Zobah; and, farther, that this psalm might have been sung by the armies of Israel when they were marching out to that battle, triumphantly commemorating their former victories, and avowing their hopes of gaining another by the help of the Almighty. On this verse he observes: "It was a constant practice among the bravest nations of the Greeks, for the troops to advance to battle chanting some kind of song." And, after quoting some lines which were sung by the Spartan soldiery, he adds, "The Grecian poet avails himself of the love of glory, and the ties of domestic affection, to animate his troops; but the Hebrew makes use of the more powerful stimulus of religious enthusiasm."

1. *Hear my cry, O God! attend unto my prayer.*
2. *From the end of the earth will I cry unto thee, when my heart is vexed: thou shalt lead me to the Rock which is too high for me.*[1]
3. *For thou hast been my hope, a tower of strength from the face of the enemy.*
4. *I will abide in thy tabernacle for ever; I will be safe under the covert of thy wings. Selah.*

1. *Hear my cry, O God!* It is not exactly ascertained at what time this psalm was composed; but there seems to be some probability in the conjecture, that David had been for a considerable period in possession of the throne before he fell into the circumstances of distress which are here mentioned. I agree with those who refer it to the time of the conspiracy of Absalom;[2] for, had he not been an exile, he could not speak, as in the second verse, of crying from the ends of the earth. By using the term *cry*, he would intimate the vehemency of his desire; and it is a word which expresses inward fervency of spirit, without reference to the fact whether he may have prayed aloud, or in a low and subdued tone. The repetition which is employed denotes his diligence and perseverance in prayer, and teaches us that we should not faint and become discouraged in this exercise, because God may not have immediately and openly testified his acceptance of our petitions. There can be no question that, by *the ends of the earth*, he refers to the place of his banishment, as being cut off from access to the temple and the royal city. By some, indeed, the words have been understood figuratively, as meaning, that he prayed from the lowest deeps of distress; but I can see no foundation for this. In a subsequent part of the psalm, he calls himself King, a title never assumed by him before the death of Saul, and from this circumstance we may at once infer, that the time referred to was that when he fled in trepidation from the fury of his son Absalom, and hid himself in the wilderness of Mahanaim, and

---

[1] He represents himself as like a man climbing to get up into a place of safety, but who wants strength to get to it.

[2] It is generally agreed that this psalm refers to the history recorded in 2 Sam. xvii. 22, 24.

places of a similarly solitary description. Mount Zion was the place where the ark of the covenant had been deposited, and it was the seat of royalty; and David, when banished from this, which was the principal and most eligible locality, speaks as if he had been driven to the uttermost parts of the earth. Living, though he did, under the shadows of a legal dispensation, he did not cease to pray, because removed to a distance from the temple; and how inexcusable must our conduct be, privileged as we are of God, and called to draw near by the way which has been opened through the blood of Christ, if we break not through every hinderance which Satan presents to our communications with heaven? Let those who may have been deprived of the hearing of the word, and the dispensation of the sacraments, so as, in a manner, to be banished out of the Church, learn from the example of David to persevere in crying to God, even under these solitary circumstances. He adverts, in what follows, to his grief and anguish. He adds the fact of his being shut up from every method of escape, that the grace of God might be made more apparent in his deliverance. The Hebrew word עֲטֹף, *ataph*, which I have translated *vexed*, means occasionally *to cover*, or *involve*, which has led some to render the clause, *while my heart is turned about;* that is, tossed hither and thither, or agitated. This is a harsh translation. Others read with more propriety, *while my heart is involved in cares and troubles, or overwhelmed.*[1] I have adopted a simpler rendering, although I would not be understood as denying the metaphor, to which they suppose that there is an allusion. The clause, there can be no question, is inserted to intimate that he was not prevented by trouble from having recourse to God. Notice was taken already of the outward trial to which he was subjected, in distance from the sanctuary, and of his rising above this, so as to direct his cry to God; and in the words before us, we have his confession that he was far from being stoically insensible, being conscious of a severe inward struggle with grief and perplexity of mind. It is the duty, then, of believers, when oppressed with heaviness and spirit-

---

[1] This last translation is omitted in the French version, perhaps through inadvertency.

ual distress, to make only the more strenuous efforts for breaking through these obstacles in their approaches to God. His prayer is, that God would bring him to that safety from which he seems to be excluded. By a *rock* or *citadel,* he means, in general, secure protection, from which he complains of being shut out, as it was impossible to reach it unless he were raised by the hand of God. In looking round him, it seemed as if every place of shelter and safety were lifted up above his head and rendered inaccessible. He was cut off from all help, and yet, hopeless as deliverance appeared, he had no doubt of his safety, should God only extend his hand for interposition. This is the plain meaning of the passage, when divested of figure, that God was able to rescue him from danger, though all other help should be withdrawn, and the whole world should stand between him and deliverance; a truth which we would do well to consider seriously. In looking for deliverance from God, we must beware of yielding to the suggestions of sense; we should remember that he does not always work by apparent means, but delivers us when he chooses by methods inscrutable to reason. If we attempt to prescribe any one particular line of procedure, we do no less than wilfully limit his almighty power.

3. *For thou hast been my hope.* Here we may suppose, either that he calls to his remembrance such benefits as he had formerly received, or that he congratulates himself upon deliverance which he had presently experienced. There is much probability in either supposition. Nothing animates our hopes more than the recollection of the past goodness of God, and, in the midst of his prayers, we frequently find David indulging in reflections of this kind. On the other hand, the remainder of the psalm is occupied with returning praise to God for his present goodness; and there is no reason why we should not suppose, that these words before us form the commencement of the thanksgiving. In that case, the Hebrew particle, which we have rendered *for* or *because,* may be understood rather in an affirmative sense, *surely* or *certainly.*

In the verse which follows, he expresses the confidence which he had that he would dwell from this time forth in the sanctuary of the Lord. I cannot altogether agree with those who think that David was still in his state of exile from his native country when this was written, and is merely to be understood as promising to himself the certainty of his return. He would seem rather to be rejoicing in restoration already obtained, than assuaging his grief by anticipation of it in the future; and this will be still more apparent, when we come to consider the immediate context. It is noticeable, that now when he was returned from his banishment, and established within his own palace, his heart was set more upon the worship of God than all the wealth, splendour, and pleasures of royalty. We have his testimony in other parts of his writings, that in the worst calamities which he endured, he experienced nothing which could be compared to the bitterness of being shut out from the ordinances of religion; and now he accounts it a higher pleasure to lie as a suppliant before the altar, than to sit upon the throne of a king. By the words which immediately follow, he shows that he did not, like too many uninformed persons, attach a superstitious importance to the mere externals of religion, adding, that he found his safety *under the shadow of God's wings*. Ignorant persons might conceive of God as necessarily confined to the outward tabernacle, but David only improved this symbol of the Divine presence as a means of elevating the spiritual exercises of his faith. I would not deny that there may be an allusion to the cherubim when he speaks of the shadow of God's wings. Only we must remember, that David did not rest in carnal ordinances, the elements of the world,[1] but rose by them and above them to the spiritual worship of God.

> 5. *For thou, O God! hast heard my vows: thou hast given inheritance to those*[2] *fearing thy name.*
> 6. *Thou shalt add days upon days to the king, and his years as generation upon generation.*

[1] "Non fuisse retentum in mundi elementis."—*Lat.* "David ne s'est point arreté aux elemens du monde, (comme Sainct Paul appelle les ceremonies prises charnellement et quant à l'exterieur,") &c.—*Fr.*
[2] "Ou, l'heritage de ceux."—*Fr. marg.* "Or, the inheritance of those."

7. *He shall abide before the face of God for ever : prepare mercy and truth ; let them keep him.*
8. *So will I sing unto thy name for ever, that I may daily perform my vows.*

5. *For thou, O God! hast heard my vows.* He here shows the grounds upon which he had spoken of his abiding under the wings of God. The sudden joy which he experienced arose from the circumstance of God's having heard his prayers, and made light to spring out of darkness. By his *vows* we must understand his prayers, according to a common figure of speech by which the part is taken for the whole, having made vows when he prayed. In general, he would acknowledge himself indebted for his restoration entirely to an interposition of Divine power, and not to any dexterity which he had shown in gaining time for the collection of his forces,[1] nor to any assistance which he had derived, either from the favour of the priests or the exertions of his soldiers. Had the letter ל, *lamed*, been prefixed to the Hebrew word יראי, *yirey*, which is rendered *fearing*, there would have been no reason left to doubt that the words which follow were of the nature of a general assertion, to the effect, that God has given the inheritance to those who fear him. As it is, they may be construed to mean, that God had given David the inheritance of those who fear him. Still I prefer attaching the more general sense to the words, and understand them as intimating that God never disappoints his servants, but crowns with everlasting happiness the struggles and the distresses which may have exercised their faith. They convey an implied censure of that unwarrantable confidence which is indulged in by the wicked, when favoured, through the Divine forbearance, with any interval of prosperity. The success which flatters them is merely imaginary, and speedily vanishes. But *inheritance*—the word here employed by David—suggests that the people of God enjoy a species of prosperity more solid and enduring; their momentary and

---

[1] " Quamvis prudenter colligendis viribus tempus sumpsisset," &c.—*Lat.* " Combien qu'il eust usé de prudence a donner ordre à son affaire, et prendre temps pour amasser forces," &c.—*Fr.*

short-lived troubles having only the effect of promoting their eternal welfare. He praises God that those who fear his name are not left to the poor privilege of rejoicing for a few days, but secured in a permanent heritage of happiness. The truth is one which cannot be questioned. The wicked, having no possession by faith of the divine benefits which they may happen to share, live on from day to day, as it were, upon plunder. It is only such as fear the Lord who have the true and legitimate enjoyment of their blessings.

6. *Thou shalt add days upon days to the king, &c.*[1] David cannot be considered as using these words of gratulation with an exclusive reference to himself. It is true that he lived to an extreme old age, and died full of days, leaving the kingdom in a settled condition, and in the hands of his son, who succeeded him; but he did not exceed the period of one man's life, and the greater part of it was spent in continued dangers and anxieties. There can be no doubt, therefore, that the series of years, and even ages, of which he speaks, extends prospectively to the coming of Christ, it being the very condition of the kingdom, as I have often remarked, that God maintained them as one people under one head, or, when scattered, united them again. The same succession still subsists in reference to ourselves. Christ must be viewed as living in his members to the end of the world. To this Isaiah alludes, when he says, " Who shall declare his generation or age?"—words in which he predicts that the Church would survive through all ages, notwithstanding the incessant danger of destruction to which it is exposed through the attacks of its enemies, and the many storms assailing it. So here David foretells the uninterrupted succession of the kingdom down to the time of Christ.

7. *He shall abide before the face of God for ever.* This is only a simpler way of expressing what he had said before, *I will abide in thy tabernacle for ever.* He refers to the security

---

[1] In the Chaldee it is: "Thou shalt add days to the days of the King Messiah; his years shall be as the generation of this world, and of the world to come."

and peace which he would enjoy under the protection of God, who would effectually preserve his life. By *the face of God*, must be meant the fatherly care and providence which he extends to his people. So numerous are the dangers which surround us, that we could not stand a single moment, if his eye did not watch over our preservation. But the true security for a happy life lies in being persuaded that we are under divine government. There follows a prayer that God would *appoint mercy and truth* for preserving the king. And this admits of two meanings. As clemency and truth are the best safeguards of a kingdom, it would not be altogether unreasonable to suppose that David prays here to be endued with these dispositions, as a means of establishing his throne. But the other meaning is perhaps preferable, that God would gird himself with clemency and truth in order to the preservation of the king. The Hebrew term מנה, *manah*, signifies not only *to prepare*, but *to set over*, or *appoint;* and he speaks as if the true defence of the kingdom was only to be found in the mercy and faithfulness of God. He uses the expression *prepare*, or *command*, to intimate how easily God can provide the means necessary for preserving his people. In the concluding words, he expresses his resolution to persevere in the constant celebration of the praises of God, with a view to fulfilling the vows which he had contracted—and this again may lead us to remark the agreement which ought ever to subsist between the two parts of invocation: for David, while he applied to God for help, under the pressure of calamity, showed himself uniformly grateful when he had experienced deliverance.

PSALM LXII.

The greater part of this psalm is occupied with meditations, in which David encourages himself and others to hope in God, and fortifies his mind against the assaults of temptation. And as we are ever prone to be drawn away from God by the influence which worldly objects exert over our senses, perishing and evanescent as these are, occasion is taken to show the folly of this, and bring us to a single and entire dependence upon God.

¶ *To the chief musician upon Jeduthun, A Psalm of David.*

The fact being ascertained that there was one of the chief singers who bore the name of Jeduthun, some have thought that this psalm was committed into his hands to be sung, (1 Chron. ix. 16; xvi. 38, 41; and xxv. 1.) In the title to Psalm xxxix., it is sufficiently probable that the allusion is to some musician of that family. But this would not seem to be the case here; for the psalm is not said to be given *to*, but *upon* Jeduthun. This has led to the opinion that it formed the beginning of some song commonly known at that time. Still the Hebrew particle על, *al*, which we have rendered *upon*, means frequently *for*, *to*, or *before;* and it will consist with the words to suppose, that this psalm was put into the hands of the posterity of Jeduthun.[1]

1. *Nevertheless, my soul is silent towards God : from him is my salvation.*
2. *Nevertheless, he himself is my rock and my salvation, my high tower : I shall not be greatly moved.*

1. *Nevertheless, my soul is silent towards God.* Should the translation I have followed be adopted, the psalm is to be considered as beginning abruptly, in the usual style of compositions of an impassioned kind.[2] Of this we have an instance in Ps. lxxiii., where the prophet, who had been agitated with doubts, as we shall see more particularly afterwards, suddenly brings his mind to a fixed decision, and, in the way of cutting off all further subject of debate, exclaims, " *Yet* God is good to Israel." And so it is, I conceive, in the psalm before us. We know that the Lord's people cannot always reach such a measure of composure as to be wholly

---

[1] Jeduthun was first chosen to be one of the chief musicians in conducting the praises of the Jewish sanctuary when the ark was brought from Obed-edom to mount Zion. His sons were also appointed to preside over different departments of the vocal and instrumental worship in the tabernacle. He had six sons who were thus employed. Jeduthun and his family appear to have been eminent for their piety, and to have been endued with the spirit of prophecy.

[2] " Sicuti patheticæ sententiæ ut plurimum defectivæ sunt."—*Lat.*
" Comme nous sçavons que les propos dits de quelque affection vehemente, le plus souvent sont imparfaits."—*Fr.*

exempt from distraction. They would wish to receive the word of the Lord with submission, and to be dumb under his correcting hand; but inordinate affections will take possession of their minds, and break in upon that peace which they might otherwise attain to in the exercise of faith and resignation. Hence the impatience we find in many; an impatience which they give vent to in the presence of God, and which is an occasion to themselves of much trouble and disquietude. The Hebrew particle אך, *ach,* is often used in an exclusive sense, and has been rendered by some, *only;* it is also employed in an affirmative sense, and has been rendered *truly,* or *certainly.* But in order to arrive at its full meaning, we must suppose that David felt an inward struggle and opposition, which he found it necessary to check. Satan had raised a tumult in his affections, and wrought a degree of impatience in his mind, which he now curbs; and he expresses his resolution *to be silent.*[1] The word implies a meek and submissive endurance of the cross. It expresses the opposite of that heat of spirit which would put us into a posture of resistance to God. The silence intended is, in short, that composed submission of the believer, in the exercise of which he acquiesces in the promises of God, gives place to his word, bows to his sovereignty, and suppresses every inward murmur of dissatisfaction. The Hebrew word דומיה, *dumiyah,* which I have rendered *is silent,* some consider to be the noun; and it is of little consequence which translation we adopt.

The particle אך, *ach,* in the second verse, I would render

---

[1] The import of the Hebrew word is "patient silence." The Septuagint reads, Ουχι τῷ Θεῷ ὑποταγήσεται ἡ ψυχή μου? "Shall not my soul be subject to God?" And doubtless the Psalmist intended to say that his soul was quiet, submissive, and subject; the rebellious affections being tamed and subdued. With respect to the translation of our English Bible, "Truly my soul waiteth upon God," Dr Adam Clarke remarks, "I do not think that the original will warrant this translation." He reads, "Surely to God only is my soul dumb;" which he thus explains: "I am subject to God Almighty. He has a right to lay on me what He pleases; and what He lays on me is much less than I deserve; therefore am *I dumb* before God. The Vulgate, and almost all the versions, have understood it in this sense: 'Nonne Deo subjecta erit anima mea? Shall not my soul be subject to God?'" With this agree the version and interpretation of Calvin.

in the same way as in the first. The believer triumphs in one encounter with temptation only to enter upon another; and here David, who appeared to have emerged from his distress, shows that he had still to struggle with remaining difficulties. We meet with the same particle no fewer than six times throughout the psalm. This, too, may explain the many titles which he applies to God, each of which is to be considered as a foil by which he would ward off the attacks of the tempter. The expression in the close of the verse, *I shall not be greatly moved*, implies his persuasion that he might be overtaken with afflictions, (for he was well aware that he could claim no exemption from the common lot of humanity,) but his conviction, at the same time, that these would not overwhelm him, through the good help of God. We shall find him saying afterwards, in so many words, *I shall not fall;* perhaps because he felt, as he advanced in prayer, that he had greater boldness in despising affliction. Or the expressions may be taken as synonymous in the two places. The truth itself is unquestionable. The believer may be overthrown for a time; but as he is no sooner cast down than he is raised up again by God, he cannot properly be said to fall. He is supported by the Spirit of God, and is not therefore really prostrated and overcome.

3. *How long will ye continue mischief against a man?*[1] *ye shall be slain all of you: as a bowing wall shall ye be, and a fence which has been struck.*
4. *Yet they consult to cast him down from his elevation: they delight in lies: they bless with their mouth, and curse inwardly. Selah.*
5. *Nevertheless, my soul, be thou silent before God: for my expectation is from him.*
6. *Nevertheless, he is my rock and my salvation: my high tower; I shall not fall.*

3. *How long will ye continue mischief?* The Hebrew

---

[1] " Ou, courrez-vous sus l'homme?"—*Fr. marg.* " Or, will ye make assaults upon a man?"

word תְּהוֹתְתוּ, *tehotethu*,[1] which I have translated *continue*, or *lengthen out, mischief*, is rendered by some, *to meditate*, or *imagine mischief*, while others suppose an allusion to the putting forth of the tongue in sign of mockery. It has been rendered also, *to rush upon*, or *assault*. The sense of the passage seems to be, How long will ye meditate evil against a man, and persist in mischievous devices for accomplishing his ruin? He has in view the obstinate malice of his enemies, moving every stone for his destruction, and forming new plans daily for effecting it. The instruction to be learned from his experience is, that we should exercise patience, even when our enemies show unwearied cruelty in their attempts to destroy us, and are instigated by the devil to incessant artifices for our persecution. We may just advert to the meaning of the figure which is subjoined. Some think that the wicked are compared to a *bowing wall*, because it threatens every moment to fall to the ground, and they, upon every sin which they commit, tend more and more downwards, till they are precipitated into destruction. But it would seem as if the allusion were somewhat different. A wall, when ill built, bulges out in the centre, presenting the appearance of nearly twice its actual breadth; but, as it is hollow within, it soon falls to ruins. The wicked, in like

[1] Hammond observes, that this verb " is but once used in the Scriptures, and so will not be easily interpreted but either by the notion which we find put upon it by the ancient interpreters, or else by the Arabic use of it." The Chaldee renders it, *raise tumults;* the Syriac, *stir up, instigate, incite*, or *provoke;* the Septuagint and Vulgate, *assail*, or *rush upon;* and the Arabic, *use violence or injustice*. Gesenius gives the sense of the Septuagint. Kimchi and Aben Ezra read, *pravitatis cogitabitis*. " Abu Walid compares תְּהוֹתְתוּ with the Arabic תְּהַתְתַן, with *t*, not with *th*, which signifies *to multiply words;* and so he would have it, according to the use of it in that tongue, to signify speaking much against, backbiting, defaming, spreading evil reports of, lashing out with your tongues against, for hurt. What he thus observes of תְּהוֹתְתוּ, with *t*, not *th*, may have place also with the word, as we have it; for the root with ת, *th*, also in Arabic signifies *mentiri, to lie*, and *confusion, injustice, violence;* which as well agree to his sense as that of the root with *t*." When David says, *against a man*, and uses also the third person in the fourth verse, it is of himself that he speaks. "*Against a man; i. e.*, against me, a man like yourselves, whom common humanity obliges you to pity; a single man, who is no fit match for you."—*Poole's Annotations*.

manner, are dilated with pride, and assume, in their consultations, a most formidable appearance; but David predicts that they would be brought to unexpected and utter destruction, like a wall badly constructed, and hollow in the interior, which falls with a sudden crash, and is broken by its own weight into a thousand pieces.[1] The word גדר, *gader*, which I have rendered, *a fence*, means, properly, an enclosure built of slight and insufficient materials;[2] and an epithet is added still more to express the violence and impetuosity of their fall. The Psalmist, then, would teach us that, high as our enemies may appear to stand, and proud and swelling as their denunciations may be, they shall be suddenly and signally overthrown, *like a smitten wall*.

4. *Yet they consult to cast him down from his elevation.* I still would interpret the particle אך, *ach*, in an adversative sense. David, on the one hand, encouraged himself by determining to rest stedfastly upon the promise of divine favour; but, upon the other, he had before him the machinations of his enemies, characterized by cruelty, audacity, pride, and deceit. By all their attempts, as if he had said, they do nothing but precipitate their own fall; still such are the frenzy and the fury by which they are actuated, that they persist in their intrigues against me. He insinuates that their attacks were directed, not so much against himself as against God—agreeably to the picture which is given us

---

[1] Isaiah has also made use of this image to express sudden and utter destruction, (chap. xxx. 13.)

[2] In the East it is common for the inhabitants to enclose their vineyards and gardens with hedges, consisting of various kinds of shrubs, and particularly such as are armed with spines. They have also mounds of earth-walls about their gardens. Rawwolff describes the gardens about Jerusalem as surrounded by mud-walls, not above four feet high, easily climbed over, and washed down by rain in a very little time. Stone-walls are also frequently used. Thus Egmont or Heyman, describing the country about Saphet, a celebrated city of Galilee, tells us, "The country round it is finely improved, the declivity being covered with vines, supported by low walls."—*Harmer's Observations*, vol. ii. pp. 216–219. Doubdan describes some of these in the Holy Land as built of loose stones, without any cement to join them. The original word probably means some such "fence" as this. Indeed, it always appears to denote a wall of stones: sometimes in express contradistinction to the hedge, or thorny fence. See *Parkhurst's Lexicon*, on גדר.

of impiety by the poets in their fable of the Giants.¹ Nothing will satisfy the enemies of God but setting themselves above the heavens. David is to be understood as primarily speaking here of himself in the third person, but of himself as elevated expressly by the divine hand. Accordingly, though we might consider that God is the party directly intended, the scope of the words rather intimates that they aimed at the overthrow of one whom God had exalted, and desired to establish in honour. In thus attempting to thwart his purpose, they were really fighting against God. The clause which follows, *they delight in lies,* has reference to the same thing. Refusing to acknowledge his divine vocation, they persevered in following such corrupt designs, as could only recoil upon them to their own confusion, as the Psalmist exclaims, (Ps. iv. 2,) " O ye sons of men! how long is my glory made matter of your reproach? how long will ye love vanity, and seek after leasing? Selah." Or the expression may denote the hidden and deceitful measures which they adopted in their persecution of this saint of God; for it is immediately added, that *they blessed with their mouth, but cursed inwardly.* Whatever may be the meaning, it is evident that David, contemplating all the treachery, intrigues, and wickedness of his enemies, supports himself by the single consideration, that his help was in God, and that every opposing instrumentality was therefore vain.

5. *Nevertheless, my soul, be thou silent before God.* Here there may appear to be a slight inconsistency, inasmuch as he encourages himself to do what he had already declared himself to have done. His soul was silent before God; and where the necessity of this new silence, as if still under agitation of spirit? Here it is to be remembered, that our minds can never be expected to reach such perfect composure as shall preclude every inward feeling of disquietude, but are, at the best, as the sea before a light breeze, fluctuating sensibly,

¹ " Les Poëtes profanes ont dit que les Geans delibererent de prendre les plus hautes montagnes et les mettans l'une sur l'autre, monter jusques au ciel, pour arracher Jupiter de son siege."—*Fr. marg.* "It was said by the profane poets that the Giants formed a design of taking the highest mountains which they could find, piling them one above another, scaling the heavens, and taking Jupiter by storm."

though not swollen into billows. It is not without a struggle that the saint can compose his mind; and we can very well understand how David should enjoin more perfect submission upon a spirit which was already submissive, urging upon himself farther advancement in this grace of silence, till he had mortified every carnal inclination, and thoroughly subjected himself to the will of God. How often, besides, will Satan renew the disquietudes which seemed to be effectually expelled? Creatures of such instability, and liable to be borne away by a thousand different influences, we need to be confirmed again and again. I repeat, that there is no reason to be surprised though David here calls upon himself a second time to preserve that silence before God, which he might already appear to have attained; for, amidst the disturbing motions of the flesh, perfect composure is what we never reach. The danger is, that when new winds of troubles spring up, we lose that inward tranquillity which we enjoyed, and hence the necessity of improving the example of David, by establishing ourselves in it more and more. He adds the ground of his silence. He had no immediate response from God, but he confidently hoped in him. *My expectation*, he says, *is from God*. Never, as if he had said, will he frustrate the patient waiting of his saints; doubtless my silence shall meet with its reward; I shall restrain myself, and not make that false haste which will only retard my deliverance.

7. *In God is my salvation and my glory; the rock of my strength, and my hope, is in God.*
8. *Hope in him at all times; ye people, pour out your heart before him: God is our hope. Selah.*
9. *Nevertheless, the sons of Adam are vanity, and the children of men*[1] *a lie:*[2] *when they ascend in the scales, they are found*

---

[1] בני אדם, *beney Adam, the sons of Adam.* בני איש, *beney ish, the sons of substance,* or children of substantial men, as Dr Adam Clarke renders the phrase. "*Adam*," says he, "was the name of the first man when formed out of the *earth: Ish* was his name when united to his wife, and they became one flesh. *Before*, he was the incomplete man; *after*, he was the *complete* man." The phrases are rendered in our English version, *men of low degree,* and *men of high degree.*—See note, p. 236, of this volume; and vol. i. note 1, p. 100.

[2] "Because they promise much, and rouse men's expectations upon con-

*together lighter than vanity.*¹ 10. *Trust not in oppression and robbery, and be not vain: if riches increase, set not your heart upon them.*

7. *In God is my salvation.* One expression is here heaped upon another, and this apparently because he wished to rein that infirmity of disposition which makes us so prone to slide into wrong exercise. We may throw out a passing and occasional acknowledgment, that our only help is to be found in God, and yet shortly display our distrust in him by busying ourselves in all directions to supplement what we consider defective in his aid. The various terms which he employs to express the sufficiency of God as a deliverer, may thus be considered as so many arguments to constancy, or so many checks which he would apply to the waywardness of the carnal heart, ever disposed to depend for support upon others rather than God. Such is the manner in which he animates his own spirit; and next, we find him addressing himself to others, calling upon them to enter upon the same conflict, and reap the same victory and triumph. By the *people,* there seems little doubt that he means the Jews. The Gentiles being yet unvisited by the true religion and divine revelation, it was only in Judea that God could be the object of trust and religious invocation; and it would appear, that by distinguishing the chosen people of the Lord from the surrounding heathen, he insinuates how disgraceful it would be in them not to devote themselves entirely to God,

---

sideration of their great power and dignity, but are not able to perform, and generally deceive those who trust in them. In which respect lying is ascribed to *a fountain,* Jer. xv. 18; to *wine,* Hos. ix. 2; to *the olive,* Habak. iii. 17; when they do not give what they promise."—*Poole's Annotations.*

¹ הבל, *hebel.* The radical meaning of the term is, *a breath.* The same word occurs in the first clause, intimating, that men of low degree are as unsubstantial as a breath; and here men of low degree, and men of high degree, when both are united, are described as lighter than a breath. See p. 78 of this volume, note 1. "Taking the infinitive with ל, *lamed,* to stand for the future, as it often does, the latter part may be literally translated, 'They will ascend together in the balance more than vanity.'" —*Arch. Secker.* This strongly expresses how unavailing it is to trust in man. If men of low degree and men of high degree are put both together in one scale, and vanity in the other, the scale of vanity will preponderate.

being, as they were, the children of Abraham, favoured with the discovery of his grace, and specially taken under his divine protection. The expression, *at all times,* means both in prosperity and adversity, intimating the blameworthiness of those who waver and succumb under every variation in their outward circumstances. God tries his children with afflictions, but here they are taught by David to abide them with constancy and courage. The hypocrites, who are loud in their praises of God so long as prosperity shines upon their head, while their heart fails them upon the first approach of trial, dishonour his name by placing a most injurious limitation to his power. We are bound to put honour upon his name by remembering, in our greatest extremities, that to Him belong the issues of death. And as we are all too apt at such times to shut up our affliction in our own breast—a circumstance which can only aggravate the trouble and imbitter the mind against God, David could not have suggested a better expedient than that of disburdening our cares to him, and thus, as it were, *pouring out our hearts before him.* It is always found, that when the heart is pressed under a load of distress, there is no freedom in prayer.[1] Under trying circumstances, we must comfort ourselves by reflecting that God will extend relief, provided we just freely roll them over upon his consideration. What the Psalmist advises is all the more necessary, considering the mischievous tendency which we have naturally to keep our troubles pent up in our breasts till they drive us to despair. Usually, indeed, men show much anxiety and ingenuity in seeking to escape from the troubles which may happen to press upon them; but so long as they shun coming into the presence of God, they only involve themselves in a labyrinth of difficulties. Not to insist farther upon the words, David is here to be considered as exposing that diseased but deeply-rooted principle in our nature, which leads us to hide our griefs, and ruminate upon them, instead of relieving ourselves at once by pouring out our prayers and complaints before God. The consequence is,

---

[1] " Cependant que nostre cœur est enserré et comme estouppé de douleur, jamais il n'en sort de prieres naifves et franchement faites."—*Fr.*

that we are distracted more and more with our distresses, and merge into a state of hopeless despondency. In the close of the verse, he says, in reference to the people generally, what he had said of himself individually, that their safety was to be found only under the divine protection.

9. *Nevertheless, the sons of Adam are vanity.* If we take the particle אך, *ach*, affirmatively, as meaning *surely* or *certainly*, then this verse contains a confirmation of the truth expressed in the preceding verse; and David argues by contrast,[1] that as men are lighter than vanity, we are shut up to the necessity of placing all our expectation upon God. It would agree well, however, with the contrast to suppose that, under an impression of the little effect which the truth he had announced was calculated to have upon the people, (ever disposed to build upon fallacious hopes,) he exclaims with a degree of holy fervour, *Nevertheless, &c.* According to this view, he is here administering a reproof to the blind infidelity so prevalent amongst men, and which leads them to deceive themselves with lying vanities rather than trust in the infallible promises of Jehovah. Having had occasion to discover such a large amount of vanity in the chosen seed of Abraham, he does not scruple to speak of the whole human family in general as being abandoned to lying delusions. The adverb יחד, *yachad, together,* intimates that all, without exception, are ready to find an occasion of turning aside. Such is the sweeping condemnation passed, not upon a few individuals, but upon human nature, declaring men to be lighter than vanity; and may we not ask what in this case becomes of boasted reason, wisdom, and free-will? It is of no avail to object, that believers are delivered from the deceit which is here condemned. If they owe their exemption from lying and vanity to the regeneration of the Spirit, this is to grant that they were subject to these in their natural state. The first man was created by God upright, but drew us by his fall into such a depth of corruption, that any light which

---

[1] "*A repugnantibus ostendet David.*"—*Lat.* Explained in the French version thus—"Montrera par un argument prins des choses repugnantes."

was originally bestowed has been totally obscured. Is it alleged that there still remain in man such gifts of God as are not to be despised, and as distinguish him from all the other creatures, this is easily answered, by remembering, that however great these may be, he is tainted by sin, and therefore nothing to be accounted of. It is only when allied with the knowledge of God that any of the endowments conferred upon us from above can be said to have a real excellency;—apart from this, they are vitiated by that contagion of sin which has not left a vestige in man of his original integrity. With too much justice, then, might David say that all men are vanity and nothingness.

10. *Trust not in oppression and robbery.* We are here taught that there can be no real trusting in God until we put away all those vain confidences which prove so many means of turning us away from him. The Psalmist bids us remove whatsoever would have this tendency, and purge ourselves of every vicious desire that would usurp the place of God in our hearts. One or two kinds of sin only are mentioned, but these are to be understood as representing a part for the whole, all those vain and rival confidences of which we must be divested before we can cleave to God with true purpose and sincerity of heart. By *oppression and robbery* may be understood the act itself of abstracting by violence, and the thing which has been abstracted. It is obviously the design of the passage to warn us against the presumption and hardihood of sin, which is so apt to blind the hearts of men, and deceive them into the belief that their evil courses are sanctioned by the impunity which is extended to them. Interpreters have differed in their construction of the words of this verse. Some join to each of the nouns its own verb, reading, *Trust not in oppression, and be not vain in robbery : if riches increase, set not your heart upon them.*[1] Others connect the words *oppression and robbery* with the first verb, and make the second to stand apart by itself in an indefinite sense. It is of very little consequence which of the constructions we adopt, since both express the main

[1] The words are thus connected in our English version.

sentiment; and it is evident that the Psalmist, in condemning the infatuated confidence of those who boast in robbery, appropriately terms it a mere illusion of the mind, with which they deceive or amuse themselves. Having denounced, in the first place, those desires which are plainly evil and positively wicked, he proceeds immediately afterwards to guard against an inordinate attachment even to such riches as may have been honestly acquired. To *set the heart* upon riches, means more than simply to covet the possession of them. It implies being carried away by them into a false confidence, or, to use an expression of Paul, " being high-minded." The admonition here given is one which daily observation teaches us to be necessary. It is uniformly seen that prosperity and abundance engender a haughty spirit, leading men at once to be presumptuous in their carriage before God, and reckless in inflicting injury upon their fellow-creatures. But, indeed, the worst effect to be feared from a blind and ungoverned spirit of this kind is, that, in the intoxication of outward greatness, we be left to forget how frail we are, and proudly and contumeliously to exalt ourselves against God.

> 11. *God hath spoken once; twice have I heard this, that power belongeth unto God.*
> 12. *Also unto thee, O Lord! belongeth mercy; thou wilt certainly render to every man according to his work.*

11. *God hath spoken once.* The Psalmist considered that the only effectual method of abstracting the minds of men from the vain delusions in which they are disposed to trust, was bringing them to acquiesce implicitly and firmly in the judgment of God. Usually they are swayed in different directions, or inclined at least to waver, just as they observe things changing in the world;[1] but he brings under their notice a surer principle for the regulation of their conduct, when he recommends a deferential regard to God's Word. God himself " dwells in the light which is inaccessible," (1 Tim. vi. 16;) and as none can come to him except by

---

[1] " Ad varias mundi inclinationes."—*Lat.* " Selon les divers changemcnts qu'on voit au monde."—*Fr.*

faith, the Psalmist calls our attention to his word, in which he testifies the truth of his divine and righteous government of the world. It is of great consequence that we be established in the belief of God's Word, and we are here directed to the unerring certainty which belongs to it. The passage admits of two interpretations; but the scope of it is plainly this, that God acts consistently with himself, and can never swerve from what he has said. Many understand David to say that God had spoken once and a second time; and that by this explicit and repeated assertion of his power and mercy, he had confirmed the truth beyond all possibility of contradiction. There is a passage much to the same effect in the thirty-third chapter of the book of Job, and fourteenth verse, where the same words are used, only the copulative is interposed. If any should prefer it, however, I have no objections to the other meaning—*God has spoken once; twice have I heard this.* It agrees with the context, and suggests a practical lesson of great importance; for when God has once issued his word he never retracts: on the other hand, it is our duty to ponder on what he has said, long and deliberately; and the meaning of David will then be, that he considered the Word of God in the light of a decree, stedfast and irreversible, but that, as regarded his exercise in reference to it, he meditated upon it again and again, lest the lapse of time might obliterate it from his memory. But the simpler and preferable reading would seem to be, that God had spoken once and again. There is no force in the ingenious conjecture, that allusion may be made to God's having spoken once in the Law, and a second time in the Prophets. Nothing more is meant than that the truth referred to had been amply confirmed, it being usual to reckon anything certain and fixed which has been repeatedly announced. Here, however, it must be remembered, that every word which may have issued forth from God is to be received with implicit authority, and no countenance given to the abominable practice of refusing to receive a doctrine, unless it can be supported by two or three texts of Scripture. This has been defended by an unprincipled heretic among ourselves, who has attempted to subvert the doctrine of a free election, and of a secret providence. It was not the intention of David to say that God was tied down to the necessity of repeating what he might choose to announce, but simply to assert the certainty of a truth which had been declared in clear and unambiguous terms. In the context which follows, he exemplifies himself that deferential reverence and regard for the word of God which all should, but which so few actually do, extend to it.

We might just put together, in a connected form, the particular doctrines which he has singled out for special notice. It is essentially necessary, if we would fortify our minds against temptation, to have suitably exalted views of the power and mercy of God, since nothing will more effectually preserve us in a straight and undeviating course, than a firm persuasion that all events are in the hand of God, and that he is as merciful as he is mighty. Accordingly, David follows up what he had said on the subject of the deference to be yielded to the word, by declaring that he had been instructed by it in the power and goodness of God. Some understand him to say, that God is possessed of power to deliver his people, and of clemency imbuing him to exercise it. But he would rather appear to mean, that God is strong to put a restraint upon the wicked, and crush their proud and nefarious designs, but ever mindful of his goodness in protecting and defending his own children. The man who disciplines himself to the contemplation of these two attributes, which ought never to be dissociated in our minds from the idea of God, is certain to stand erect and immoveable under the fiercest assaults of temptation; while, on the other hand, by losing sight of the all-sufficiency of God, (which we are too apt to do,) we lay ourselves open to be overwhelmed in the first encounter. The world's opinion of God is, that he sits in heaven an idle and unconcerned spectator of events which are passing. Need we wonder, that men tremble under every casualty, when they thus believe themselves to be the sport of blind chance? There can be no security felt unless we satisfy ourselves of the truth of a divine superintendence, and can commit our lives and all that we have to the hands of God. The first thing which we must look to is his power, that we may have a thorough conviction of his being a sure refuge to such as cast themselves upon his care. With this there must be conjoined confidence in his mercy, to prevent those anxious thoughts which might otherwise rise in our minds. These may suggest the doubt—What though God govern the world? does it follow that he will concern himself about such unworthy objects as ourselves?

There is an obvious reason, then, for the Psalmist coupling these two things together, his power and his clemency. They are the two wings wherewith we fly upwards to heaven; the two pillars on which we rest, and may defy the surges of temptation. Does danger, in short, spring up from any quarter, then just let us call to remembrance that divine power which can bid away all harms, and as this sentiment prevails in our minds, our troubles cannot fail to fall prostrate before it. Why should we fear—how can we be afraid, when the God who covers us with the shadow of his wings, is the same who rules the universe with his nod, holds in secret chains the devil and all the wicked, and effectually overrules their designs and intrigues?

The Psalmist adds, *Thou wilt certainly render to every man according to his work.* And here he brings what he said to bear still more closely upon the point which he would establish, declaring that the God who governs the world by his providence will judge it in righteousness. The expectation of this, duly cherished, will have a happy effect in composing our minds, allaying impatience, and checking any disposition to resent and retaliate under our injuries. In sisting himself and others before the great bar of God, he would both encourage his heart in the hope of that deliverance which was coming, and teach himself to despise the insolent persecution of his enemies, when he considered that every man's work was to come into judgment before Him, who can no more cease to be Judge than deny himself. We can therefore rest assured, however severe our wrongs may be, though wicked men should account us the filth and the offscourings of all things, that God is witness to what we suffer, will interpose in due time, and will not disappoint our patient expectation. From this, and passages of a similar kind, the Papists have argued, in defence of their doctrine, that justification and salvation depend upon good works; but I have already exposed the fallacy of their reasoning. No sooner is mention made of works, than they catch at the expression, as amounting to a statement that God rewards men upon the ground of merit. It is with a very different design than to encourage any such opinion, that the Spirit promises a reward to our works—it is to animate us in the ways of obedience, and not to inflame that impious self-confidence which cuts up salvation by the very roots. According to the judgment which God forms of the works of the believer, their worth and valuation depend, first, upon the free pardon extended to him as a sinner, and by which he becomes reconciled to God; and, next, upon the divine condescension and indulgence which accepts his services,[1] notwithstanding all their imperfections. We know that there is none of our works which, in the sight of God, can be accounted perfect or pure, and without taint of sin. Any recompense they meet with must therefore be traced entirely to his goodness. Since the Scriptures promise a reward to the saints, with the sole intention of stimulating their minds, and encouraging them in the divine warfare, and not with the remotest design of derogating from the mercy of God, it is absurd in the Papists to allege that they, in any sense, merit what is bestowed upon them. As regards the wicked, none will dispute that the punishment awarded to them, as violators of the law, is strictly deserved.

PSALM LXIII.

The following psalm cannot so properly be said to consist of prayers as of a variety of pious meditations, which comforted the mind of David under dangers, anxieties, and troubles of a severe description. It

[1] " D'une pure douceur et support debonnaire dont il use, il fait qu'icelles soyent acceptees de lui," &c.—*Fr.*

contains the vows too which he made to God in the distress occasioned by the alarming circumstances in which he was placed.

¶ A Psalm of David, when he was in the wilderness of Judah.[1]

1. O God! thou art my God; early will I seek thee: my soul has thirsted for thee, my flesh has longed for thee in[2] a desert and thirsty[3] land, where no water is.
2. Thus have I beheld thee in the sanctuary, to see thy power and thy glory.
3. Because thy mercy is better than life, my lips shall praise thee.
4. Thus will I bless thee while I live: I will lift up my hands in thy name.

1. *O God! thou art my God.* The wilderness of Judah, spoken of in the title, can be no other than that of Ziph, where David wandered so long in a state of concealment. We may rely upon the truth of the record he gives us of his exercise when under his trials; and it is apparent that he never allowed himself to be so far overcome by them, as to cease lifting up his prayers to heaven, and even resting, with a firm and constant faith, upon the divine promises. Apt as

---

[1] David was often compelled to flee into the remote deserts which lay in the tribe of Judah, to escape the fury of Saul. In tracing his steps, when eagerly sought after by this relentless persecutor, we find him in the forest of Hareth, and in the wildernesses of Ziph, Maon, and Engedi, all in the tribe of Judah. See 1 Sam. xxii. 5; xxiii. 14, 24, 25; xxiv. 1; and Joshua xv. 55, 62. The only objection which can be made to referring the occasion of the composition of this psalm to David's persecution by Saul is, that in the 11th verse, David is called king; whereas Saul still swayed the sceptre over Israel. But, as Calvin observes on that verse, David may have called himself by this title to express his confident persuasion that God would raise him to the throne in fulfilment of his promise; and his followers might call him king even during Saul's lifetime, though he was not acknowledged to be sovereign by any tribe till after Saul fell at Gilboa. It is, however, supposed by some that the psalm was written during the rebellion of his son Absalom, when he was under the necessity of quitting Jerusalem, and escaping into the wilderness, 2 Sam. xv. 23; xvi. 2; and xvii. 29.

[2] The Syriac, and several MSS., read כְּאֶרֶץ, *ke-erets, as a land,* instead of בְּאֶרֶץ, *be-erets, in a land,* like the parallel text of Ps. cxliii. 6. The two letters, כ, *caph,* and ב, *beth,* may be easily mistaken for each other, differing less than the Roman letters c and g.

[3] The Hebrew word עָיֵף, *ayeph,* here rendered *thirsty,* is literally *weary;* "that is," says Horsley, "a land that creates weariness by the roughness of the ways, the steepness of the hills, and the want of all accommodations." He reads, "dry and inhospitable."

we are, when assaulted by the very slightest trials, to lose the comfort of any knowledge of God we may previously have possessed, it is necessary that we should notice this, and learn, by his example, to struggle to maintain our confidence under the worst troubles that can befall us. He does more than simply pray; he sets the Lord before him as his God, that he may throw all his cares unhesitatingly upon him, deserted as he was of man, and a poor outcast in the waste and howling wilderness. His faith, shown in this persuasion of the favour and help of God, had the effect of exciting him to constant and vehement prayer for the grace which he expected. In saying that *his soul thirsted, and his flesh longed*, he alludes to the destitution and poverty which he lay under in the wilderness, and intimates, that though deprived of the ordinary means of subsistence, he looked to God as his meat and his drink, directing all his desires to him. When he represents his soul as thirsting, and his flesh as hungering, we are not to seek for any nice or subtile design in the distinction. He means simply that he desired God, both with soul and body. For although the body, strictly speaking, is not of itself influenced by desire, we know that the feelings of the soul intimately and extensively affect it.

2. *Thus in the sanctuary, &c.* It is apparent, as already hinted, that God was ever in his thoughts, though wandering in the wilderness under such circumstances of destitution. The particle *thus* is emphatic. Even when so situated, in a wild and hideous solitude, where the very horrors of the place were enough to have distracted his meditations, he exercised himself in beholding the power and glory of God, just as if he had been in the sanctuary. Formerly, when it was in his power to wait upon the tabernacle, he was far from neglecting that part of the instituted worship of God. He was well aware that he needed such helps to devotion. But now, when shut out, in the providence of God, from any such privilege, he shows, by the delight which he took in spiritual views of God, that his was not a mind engrossed with the symbols, or mere outward ceremonial of religion. He gives evidence how much he had profited by the devotional exer-

cises enjoined under that dispensation. It is noticeable of ignorant and superstitious persons, that they seem full of zeal and fervour so long as they come in contact with the ceremonies of religion, while their seriousness evaporates immediately upon these being withdrawn. David, on the contrary, when these were removed, continued to retain them in his recollection, and rise, through their assistance, to fervent aspirations after God. We may learn by this, when deprived at any time of the outward means of grace, to direct the eye of our faith to God in the worst circumstances, and not to forget him whenever the symbols of holy things are taken out of our sight. The great truth, for example, of our spiritual regeneration, though but once represented to us in baptism, should remain fixed in our minds through our whole life,[1] (Tit. iii. 5; Ephes. v. 26.) The mystical union subsisting between Christ and his members should be matter of reflection, not only when we sit at the Lord's table, but at all other times. Or suppose that the Lord's Supper, and other means of advancing our spiritual welfare, were taken from us by an exercise of tyrannical power, it does not follow that our minds should ever cease to be occupied with the contemplation of God. The expression, *So have I beheld thee to see,* &c., indicates the earnestness with which he was intent upon the object, directing his whole meditation to this, that he might see the power and glory of God, of which there was a reflection in the sanctuary.

3. *Because thy mercy is better than life, &c.* I have no objections to read the verse in this connected form, though I think that the first clause would be better separated, and taken in with the verse preceding. David would appear to be giving the reason of his earnestness in desiring God. By *life* is to be understood, in general, everything which men use for their own maintenance and defence. When we think ourselves well provided otherwise, we feel no disposition to

---

[1] "Suivant cela, nous devons toute notre vie porter engravé en notre entendement le lavement spirituel, lequel Christ nous a une fois representé au baptesme."—*Fr.*

have recourse to the mercy of God. That *being* (to speak so) which we have of our own, prevents us from seeing that we live through the mere grace of God.[1] As we are too much disposed to trust in aids of a carnal kind, and to forget God, the Psalmist here affirms that we should have more reliance upon the divine mercy in the midst of death, than upon what we are disposed to call, or what may appear to be, life. Another interpretation has been given of the words of this verse, but a very meagre and feeble one,—That the mercy of God is better than life itself; or, in other words, that the divine favour is preferable to every other possession. But the opposition is evidently between that state of secure prosperity, in which men are so apt to rest with complacency, and the mercy of God, which is the stay of such as are ready to sink and perish, and which is the one effectual remedy for supplying (if one might use that expression) all defects.

The word which I have rendered *life*, being in the plural number in the Hebrew, has led Augustine to assign a meaning to the sentence which is philosophical and ingenious, but without foundation, as the plural of the word is quite commonly used in the singular signification. He considered that the term *lives* was here used in reference to the truth, That different men affect different modes of life, some seeking riches, and others pleasure; some desiring the luxuries, and some the honours of this world, while others are given to their sensual appetites. He conceived that there was an opposition stated in the verse between these various kinds of life and eternal life, here by a common figure of speech called *mercy*, because it is of grace, and not of merit. But it is much more natural to understand the Psalmist as meaning, that it was of no consequence how large a share men possess of prosperity, and of the means which are generally thought to make life secure, the divine mercy being a better foundation of trust than any life fashioned out to ourselves, and than all other supports

---

[1] " Denique nostrum esse, ut ita loquar, perstringit nobis oculos, ne cernamus sola Dei gratia nos subsistere."—*Lat.* " Brief, notre Etre, si ainsi faut parler, nous eblouit les yeux, tellement que nous ne voyons pas que c'est par la seule grace de Dieu que nous subsistons."—*Fr.*

taken together.¹ On this account the Lord's people, however severely they may suffer from poverty, or the violence of human wrongs, or the languor of desire, or hunger and thirst, or the many troubles and anxieties of life, may be happy notwithstanding; for it is well with them, in the best sense of the term, when God is their friend. Unbelievers, on the other hand, must be miserable, even when all the world smiles upon them; for God is their enemy, and a curse necessarily attaches to their lot.

In the words which follow, David expresses his consequent resolution to praise God. When we experience his goodness, we are led to open our lips in thanksgiving. His intention is intimated still more clearly in the succeeding verse, where he says that *he will bless God in his life*. There is some difficulty, however, in ascertaining the exact sense of the words. When it is said, So *will I bless thee*, &c., the *so* may refer to the good reason which he had, as just stated, to praise God, from having felt how much better it is to live by life communicated from God, than to live of and from ourselves.² Or the sense may be, *so*, that is, *even in this calamitous and afflicted condition:* for he had already intimated that, amidst the solitude of the wilderness, where he wandered, he would still direct his eye to God. The word *life*, again, may refer to his life as having been preserved by divine interposition; or the sense of the passage may be, that he would bless God *through the course of his life*. The former meaning conveys the fullest matter of instruction, and agrees with the context; he would bless God, because, by his goodness, he had been kept alive and in safety. The sentiment is similar to that which we find elsewhere, " I shall not die, but live, and declare the works of the Lord;" and again ;—" The dead shall not praise the Lord, neither any that go down into silence, but we who live will bless the Lord," (Ps. cxviii. 17 ; cxv. 17, 18.) In *the lifting up of hands*,³ in the second clause of the verse,

---

¹ " Thy loving-kindness, חסדך, *chasdeca*, thy effusive mercy is better, מחיים, *me-chayim*, than LIVES: it is better, or good beyond, countless ages of human existence."—*Dr Adam Clarke.*

² " Melius esse nobis vivificari ab ipso quam apud nos vivere."

³ " The practice of lifting up the hands in prayer towards heaven, the supposed residence of the object to which prayer is addressed, was anciently used, both by believers, as appears from various passages in the Old Tes-

allusion is made to praying and vowing; and he intimates, that besides giving thanks to God, he would acquire additional confidence in supplication, and be diligent in the exercise of it. Any experience we may have of the divine goodness, while it stirs us up to gratitude, should, at the same time, strengthen our hopes of the future, and lead us confidently to expect that God will perfect the grace which he has begun. Some understand by the *lifting up of his hands*, that he refers to praising the Lord. Others, that he speaks of encouraging himself from the divine assistance, and boldly encountering his enemies. But I prefer the interpretation which has been already given.

5. *My soul shall be satisfied as with marrow and fatness; and my mouth shall praise thee with joyful lips.*
6. *I shall surely[1] remember thee upon my couch: I will meditate upon thee in the night watches,[2]*
7. *Because thou hast been my help: and I will rejoice in the shadow of thy wings.*
8. *My soul has cleaved hard after thee: thy right hand will uphold me.*

5. *My soul shall be satisfied as with marrow, &c.* In accordance with what was said in the foregoing verse, David expresses his assured persuasion of obtaining a rich and abundant measure of every blessing that could call for thanksgiving and praise. At the period of composing this psalm, he may have been already in the enjoyment of ease and plenty; but there is reason to believe that he cherished the persuasion referred to, even when wandering in the wilderness in a state of poverty and destitution. If we would

tament, and by the heathen, agreeably to numerous instances in the classical writers. Parkhurst, considering the 'hand' to be the chief organ or instrument of man's power and operations, and properly supposing the word to be thence used very extensively by the Hebrews for power, agency, dominion, assistance, and the like, regards the lifting up of men's hands in prayer as an emblematical acknowledging of the *power*, and imploring of the *assistance* of their respective gods. Is it not, however, rather the natural and unstudied gesture of earnest supplication?"—Mant.

[1] " Ou, quand," &c.—*Fr. marg.* " Or, when I shall remember thee."
[2] Among the Hebrews the night was divided into portions of three or four hours each, which were denominated vigils or watches.

evidence a strong faith, we must anticipate the divine favour before it has been actually manifested, and when there is no present appearance of its forthcoming. From the instance here set before us, we must learn to be on our guard against despondency, in circumstances when we may see the wicked wallowing and rioting in the abundance of the things of this world, while we ourselves are left to pine under the want of them. David, in the present pressure to which he was exposed, might have given way to despair, but he knew that God was able to fill the hungry soul, and that he could want for nothing so long as he possessed an interest in his favour. It is God's will to try our patience in this life, by afflictions of various kinds. Let us bear the wrongs which may be done us with meekness, till the time come when all our desires shall be abundantly satisfied. It may be proper to observe, that David, when he speaks in figurative language of being *filled with marrow and fatness*, does not contemplate that intemperate and excessive indulgence to which ungodly men surrender themselves, and by which they brutify their minds. He looks forward to that moderate measure of enjoyment which would only quicken him to more alacrity in the praises of God.

6. *I shall surely remember thee, &c.* It may be read also, WHEN, or, AS OFTEN AS *I remember thee, I will pray in the night watches.* But as the Hebrew particle here used is occasionally taken for an adverb of affirmation, as well as of time, I have adhered to the commonly received translation. In this case, his *remembering* God is to be understood as the same thing with his meditating upon him; and the one clause contains just a repetition of the sentiment expressed in the other. If the particle be taken in the different sense formerly mentioned, the words intimate, that as often as the name of God recurred to his mind, he would dwell upon it with pleasure, and speak of his goodness. He particularly mentions *the night watches*, as, when retired from the sight of our fellow-creatures, we not only revert to what may have given us anxiety, but feel our thoughts drawn out more freely to different subjects. We have next the reason

assigned for the engagement or declaration he has just made, which is, that he owed to God his preservation. The experience of the divine goodness should dispose us to prayer as well as praise. "I will come into thy house," says the Psalmist in another place, "in the multitude of thy mercy," (Ps. v. 7.) The second part of the seventh verse is expressive of the lively hope with which he was animated. He was resolved to rejoice and triumph under the shadow of God's wings, as feeling the same peace and satisfaction in reliance upon his protection as he could have done had no danger existed.

8. *My soul has cleaved hard after thee.* The Hebrew verb means also *to apprehend*, or *follow*, especially when in construction with the preposition which is here joined to it, and therefore we might very properly render the words, *My soul shall press or follow after thee.*[1] But even should the other translation be retained, the sense is, that David's heart was devoted to God with stedfast perseverance. The phrase, *after thee*, is emphatical, and denotes that he would follow with unwearied constancy, long as the way might be, and full of hardships, and beset with obstacles, and however sovereignly God might himself seem to withdraw his presence. The latter clause of the verse may be taken as referring simply to the deliverance which he had previously mentioned as having been received. He had good reason to persevere, without fainting, in following after God, when he considered that he had been preserved in safety, up to this time, by the divine hand. But I would understand the words as having a more extensive application, and consider that David here speaks of the grace of perseverance, which would be bestowed upon him by the Spirit. To say that he would cleave to God, with an unwavering purpose, at all hazards, might have sounded like the language of vain boasting, had he not qualified the assertion by adding, that he

---

[1] Dr Adam Clarke renders, "My soul cleaves, or is glued after thee." "This phrase," says he, "not only shows the *diligence* of the pursuit, and the *nearness* of the attainment, but also the *fast hold* he had got of the mercy of his God."

would do this in so far as he was sustained by the hand of God.

9. *And they, whilst they seek my soul to destroy it, shall go into the lowest parts of the earth.*
10. *They shall cast him out*[1] *to the edge of the sword: they shall be a portion for foxes.*
11. *But the king*[2] *shall rejoice in God; and every one who swears by him shall glory: for the mouth of them that speak lies shall be stopped.*

9. *And they, whilst they seek, &c.* Here we find David rising to a more assured confidence, and triumphing as if he had already obtained the victory. And there is every reason to believe, that though he had escaped his difficulties, and was in circumstances of peace and prosperity when he wrote this psalm, yet he only expresses what he actually felt at the critical period when his life was in such imminent danger. He declares his conviction that the enemies who eagerly sought his life would be cut off; that God would cast them headlong into destruction; and that their very bodies should be left without burial. To be *the portion of foxes*,[3] is the same thing with being left to be torn and de—

---

[1] "יגירהו," here rendered, *they shall cast him out,* " from נגר, signifies in *Hiphil, they shall cause to be poured out,* or *shall pour out.* The word is ordinarily applied to water, 2 Sam. xiv. 14; Lam. iii. 49. But here, by the immediate mention of the sword, it is restrained to the effusion of blood; and being in the third person plural, in the active sense, it is, after the Hebrew idiom, to be interpreted in the passive sense, ' They shall pour out by the hand of the sword;' *i. e.,* ' They shall be poured out by the sword,' the *hand* of *the sword* being no more than the edge of the sword."—*Hammond.* Dr Adam Clarke gives the same version: " *They shall be poured out by the hand of the sword.* Heb. That is, their life's blood shall be shed either in war, or by the hand of justice." But נגר, *nagar,* also signifies metaphorically *to give over into one's hands, to give up,* as in the phrase, הגיר על ידי חרב, " to deliver any one up to the sword." See Ezek. xxxv. 5; Jer. xviii. 21. And the Septuagint, Syriac, Vulgate, Æthiopic, and Arabic versions, Gesenius and Hare here read, " They shall be delivered to the sword." Horsley translates, " They would shed it ;" and observes, that *it* signifies " *my life;* for נפש, which is of the doubtful gender, is the antecedent of the masculine suffix הו."

[2] "I, who am king by God's anointing, 1 Sam. xv. 12, 13."—*Ainsworth.*

[3] Under the Hebrew word שועל, *shual,* here rendered *fox,* was comprehended, in common language, *the jackal,* or *Vulpes aureus, golden wolf,* so called in Latin because its colour is a bright yellow; and in this sense

voured by the *beasts of the field.* It is often denounced as one judgment which should befall the wicked, that they would perish by the sword, and become the prey of wolves and of dogs, without privilege of sepulture. This is a fate which the best of men have met with in the world,—for good as well as bad are exposed to the stroke of temporal evil;—but there is this distinction, that God watches over the scattered dust of his own children, gathers it again, and will suffer nothing of them to perish, whereas, when the wicked are slain, and their bones spread on the field, this is only preparatory to their everlasting destruction.

11. *But the king will rejoice in God.* The deliverance

שׁוּעל, *shual,* has been generally interpreted here, because the jackal is found in Palestine, and feeds on carrion. Both of these circumstances are, however, also applicable to the fox, and, moreover, Bochart has made it probable that the specific name of the jackal (the $θώς$ of the Greeks) in Hebrew was אי, *aye, the howler,* being so called from the howling cry which he makes particularly at night. The term occurs in Isaiah xiii. 22; xxxiv. 14; and Jer. l. 39; where אִיִּים, *ayim,* is rendered, in our version, "the wild beasts of the islands," an appellation very vague and indeterminate. At the same time, it is highly probable that *shual* generally refers to the jackal. Several of the modern oriental names of this animal, as the Turkish *chical,* and the Persian *sciagal, sciachal,* or *schachal*—whence the English jackal—from their resemblance to the Hebrew word *shual,* favour this supposition; and Dr Shaw, and other travellers, inform us, that while jackals are very numerous in Palestine, the common fox is rarely to be met with. We shall, therefore, be more correct, under these circumstances, in admitting that the jackal of the East is the Hebrew *shual.* These animals never go alone, but always associate in packs of from fifty to two hundred. They are known to prey on dead bodies; and so greedy are they of human carcases, that they dig them out of their graves, and devour them, however putrescent. They have been seen waiting near the grave at the time of a funeral, eagerly watching their opportunity of digging up the body almost as soon as it was buried. "I have known several instances," says a traveller quoted by Merrick, "of their attacking and devouring drunken men, whom they have found lying on the road, and have heard that they will do the same to men that are sick and helpless. I have seen many graves that have been opened by the jackals, and parts of the bodies pulled out by them." They visit the field of battle to prey upon the dying and the dead, and they follow caravans for the same purpose. It is usual with the barbarous nations of the East to leave the bodies of their enemies, killed in battle, in the field, to be devoured by jackals and other animals. When the Psalmist, therefore, says that his enemies would become *a portion for foxes,* the meaning is, that they would be denied the rites of sepulture, which was deemed a great calamity,—that they should be left unburied, for jackals and other wild beasts to prey upon and devour.

which David received had not been extended to him as a private person, but the welfare of the whole Church was concerned in it, as that of the body in the safety of the head, and there is therefore a propriety in his representing all the people of God as rejoicing with him. Nor can we fail to admire his holy magnanimity in not scrupling to call himself king, overwhelming as the dangers were by which he was surrounded, because he laid claim to that honour by faith, though yet denied him in actual possession. In saying that *he would rejoice in God,* he refers to the gratitude which he would feel; at the same time, in extolling the divine goodness shown to him, he views it as it affected the common body of the faithful.[1] As was already remarked, the safety of God's chosen people, at that time, was inseparably connected with the reign of David and its prosperity—a figure by which it was the divine intention to teach us, that our happiness and glory depend entirely upon Christ. By those who *swear in the name of the Lord,* he means in general all his genuine servants. The act of solemnly calling upon God to witness and judge what we say, is one part of divine worship: hence an oath, by the figure of speech called synecdoche, is made to signify the profession of religion in general. We are not to imagine from this that God reckons all those to be his servants who make mention of his name. Many take it into their lips only to profane it by the grossest perjury; others outrage or slight it by entering into trifling and unnecessary oaths; and hypocrites are chargeable with wickedly abusing it. But those whom David refers to are such as swear by the Lord, considerately and with reverence, and whose hearts respond to what they declare. This appears more clearly from the contrast which follows in the verse, where he opposes those who swear by the name of God to those *who speak lies,* understanding by that term, not only treacherous and deceitful men, but men who profane the name of God by falsehoods of a sacrilegious kind.

[1] "Sed extollit Dei gratiam, quia ad piorum omnium conservationem pertineat."—*Lat.* "Mais il exalte et magnifie la grace de Dieu envers lui, d'autant qu'elle s'etendoit à la conservation de tous les fideles."—*Fr.*

PSALM LXIV.

This psalm expresses the language of complaint and prayer. David, in order that he may incline God to compassionate his case, dwells upon the injustice and cruelty, the intrigues and deceitfulness of his enemies. At the close, his eyes are directed to God, in the anticipation of a joyful deliverance from their hands.

¶ *To the chief musician. A Psalm of David.*

1. *Hear my voice, O God! in my prayer: preserve my life from fear of the enemy.*
2. *Hide me from the counsel of the wicked; from the assembly of the workers of iniquity.*
3. *For they have whetted their tongue like a sword; they have directed* [or *aimed*[1]] *for their arrow a bitter word,* [or *report.*]
4. *To shoot in secret at the perfect; suddenly will they shoot, and not fear.*
5. *They assure themselves in an evil work, they commune of laying snares privily; they say, Who shall see them?*
6. *They have searched out iniquities, they have accomplished a diligent search,* [lit. *a search searched out,*] *both the inward part of each of them, and the heart, is deep.*

1. *Hear my voice, O God!* He begins by saying that he prayed earnestly, and with vehemence, stating, at the same time, what rendered this necessary. The voice is heard in prayer, proportionally to the earnestness and ardour which we feel. He condescends upon the circumstances of distress

---

[1] The original word דרך, *darach*, signifies *to go, to send out, direct,* and is used in different senses, according to the objects to which it is applied. "But most especially it is used of a bow or arrows. If of קשת, *a bow,* then it is *to bend it;* if of חצים, *arrows,* then it is not so properly *to shoot* as *to prepare,* or *direct* them. So Psalm lviii. 7, 'He directeth or prepareth his arrows;' so here, 'they direct, or aim, or make ready their arrows.' Parallel to which is that of Jer. ix. 3, where being applied to the tongue, as to a bow that shoots out lying words, as arrows, it must be rendered *bend;* but here applied to words as arrows, *direct,* and not *bend.*"—*Hammond.*

in which he was presently placed, and takes notice of the dangers to which his life was exposed from enemies, with other points fitted to excite the favourable consideration of God. His praying that God would protect his life, proves that it must have been in danger at this time. In the second verse, he intimates that his enemies were numerous; and that, without divine assistance, he would be unable to sustain their attacks. Some difficulty attaches to the words, from their being susceptible of two meanings. The Hebrew term סוֹד, *sod*, which signifies *a secret*, is understood by some to refer here to the secret plots of the wicked, and by others, to denote their meeting together for consultation. In translating it, I have employed a word which admits of either interpretation. The term רִגְשַׁת, *rigshath*, used in the second part of the verse, may also be rendered in two ways, as meaning either an *assembly* of men, or *noise* and *uproar*. It comes from רָגַשׁ, *ragash*, a root signifying *to make a tumult*. This would suggest that the word סוֹד, *sod*, in the former clause, might refer to the clandestine plots of the wicked, and רִגְשַׁת, *rigshath*, in the latter, to their open violence; and that David prayed to be protected, on the one hand, from the malicious purposes of his enemies, and, on the other, from the forcible measures by which they proceeded to put them into execution. But the meaning first given, and which I have adopted, seems the most simple and natural, That he solicits the compassion of God, by complaining of the number that were banded against him. Still his language implies that he looked upon the protection of heaven as amply sufficient against the greatest combination of adversaries. I may add, that there is an implied plea for strengthening his cause in prayer, in what he says of the malice and wickedness of those who were opposed to him; for the more cruel and unjust the conduct of our enemies may be, we have proportionally the better ground to believe that God will interpose in our behalf.

3. *For they have whetted their tongue like a sword.* His enemies, in their rage, aimed at nothing less than his life, and yet what he complains of, more than all beside, is the poison with which their words were imbued. It is probable that he

refers to the calumnious reports which he knew to be falsely spread to his discredit, and with a view of damaging his reputation with the people. *Their tongues* he likens to *swords; their bitter and venomous words* to *arrows*.[1] And when he adds, that *they shoot against the upright and innocent*, he is to be considered as contrasting his integrity with their unprincipled conduct. It inspired him with confidence in his religious addresses, to know that he could exonerate his own conscience from guilt, and that he was the object of undeserved attack by worthless and abandoned men. In mentioning that *they shoot secretly* and *suddenly*, he refers to the craft which characterised them. They were not only eagerly bent upon mischief, and intent in watching their opportunities, but so expert and quick in their movements, as to smite their victim before he could suspect danger. When we hear that David, who was a man in every respect so much more holy and upright in his conduct than ourselves, suffered from groundless aspersions upon his character, we have no reason to be surprised that we should be exposed to a similar trial. This comfort, at least, we always have, that we can betake ourselves to God, and obtain his defence of the upright cause. He takes particular notice of another circumstance, that

---

[1] *They have directed for their arrow a bitter word.* There may be, in these words, an allusion to the practice of fixing letters on arrows, and shooting or directing them where it was designed they should fall and be taken up. Thus the Jews say, Shebna and Joab sent letters to Sennacherib, acquainting him that all Israel were willing to make peace with him; but Hezekiah would not suffer them. Timoxenus and Artabazus sent letters to one another in this way at the siege of Potidæa. See Gill, *in loco*. The *word* which they are said to direct as their arrow is called מר, *mar*, *bitter*, and this probably contains an allusion to poisoned arrows. The Chaldee paraphrast has "bending the bow and anointing the arrows," plainly intimating a conviction that such an allusion is implied. Poisoned arrows appear, from Job vi. 4, to have been of very ancient use in Arabia. They were also used by many other nations in different parts of the world. Homer says of Ulysses, that he went to Ephyre, a city of Thessaly, in order to procure deadly poison for smearing his deadly-pointed arrows, Odyssey, Lib. i. l. 335-345. Virgil describes one of his heroes as eminently skilful in anointing the dart, and arming its steel with poison, Æn. Lib. ix. l. 771. And Horace mentions the *venenatæ sagittæ*, *the poisoned arrows* of the ancient Moors in Africa, Lib. i. Ode 22, l. 3. Wherever this practice has prevailed, the poison employed has been of the most deadly kind, the slightest wound being followed by certain and almost instant death. This makes the language here strikingly expressive. David compares the calumnies his enemies launched against him to poisoned arrows.

they shot their empoisoned arrows from their lips *without fear,* or shame. This self-secure spirit argued a degree of abandoned presumption, in so far as they could persist in obstinately pursuing the conduct in which they had been repeatedly detected, and renew their desperate attempts, to the disregard of all fear of God or worldly shame.

5. *They assure themselves in an evil work.* He proceeds to complain of the perverse determination with which they pursued their wickedness, and of their combinations amongst themselves; remarking, at the same time, upon the confidence with which they stirred one another up to the most daring acts of iniquity. In this there can be little doubt that they were encouraged by the present state of weakness to which David was reduced in his circumstances, taking occasion, when they found him in poverty and exile, and without means of resistance, to persecute him with the greater freedom. Having adverted to them as being beyond hope of amendment, and incapable of any impressions of humanity, he speaks of their meeting together to plot his destruction; and, in connection with this, of the unbounded confidence which they were led to display, from a belief that their designs were not seen. It is well known that one circumstance which strengthens the false security of the wicked, and encourages them to triumph in their crafty policy towards the simple and upright in heart, is their thinking that they can cover their crimes by such pretexts as they have always at hand. *They say, Who shall see them?* The word למו, *lamo, them,* may refer either to the workers of iniquity themselves, or to the snares spoken of in the preceding clause. The first seems the preferable meaning. They run recklessly, and without restraint, in the ways of sin, blinded by their pride, and influenced neither by the fear of God nor a sense of shame.

In the verse which follows, he animadverts severely upon the deceit which they practised. He speaks of their having exhausted all the arts of mischief, so as to have left nothing in this department to be discovered. The *search* referred to has relation to the secret methods of doing evil. He adds, that their malice was deep. By the *inward part* and *the heart*, which was *deep*, he means the hidden devices to which the wicked have recourse for concealment. Some, instead of translating the words, *the inward part of each, &c.*, give a more indefinite sense to איש, *ish*, and read, *the inward part, and deep heart,* OF EVERY ONE, *is found in them;* that is, his enemies contrived to comprise in themselves all that men have ever displayed in the shape of craft and subtilty. Either rendering may be adopted; for it is evidently David's meaning that his enemies practised secret stratagem as well as open violence, to compass his ruin, and showed themselves to be possessed of the deepest penetration in discovering dark and unimagined methods of doing mischief.

> 7. And God shall shoot an arrow at them; suddenly shall they be wounded.
> 8. And they shall make their own tongue to fall upon themselves: and all that see them shall flee away.[1]
> 9. And all men shall see, and shall declare the work of God, and shall understand[2] what he hath done.
> 10. The righteous shall be glad in Jehovah, and shall hope in him; and all the upright in heart shall glory.

7. *And God shall shoot an arrow at them.* The Psalmist now congratulates himself in the confident persuasion that his prayers have not been without effect, but already answered. Though there was no appearance of God's approaching judgment, he declares that it would suddenly be executed; and in this he affords a remarkable proof of his faith. He saw the wicked hardening themselves in their prosperity, and presuming upon impunity from the divine connivance and forbearance; but instead of yielding to discouragement, he was borne up by the belief that God, according to his usual mode of procedure with the wicked, would visit them at an unexpected moment, when they were flattering themselves with having escaped, and indulging in extravagant confidence. It is a consideration which should

---

[1] "Ou, trembleront."—*Fr. marg.* "Or, shall tremble."

[2] "Ou, feront entendre."—*Fr. marg.* "Or, shall cause to understand."

comfort us, when subjected to long-continued trial, that God, in delaying to punish the ungodly, does so with the express design of afterwards inflicting judgments of a more condign description upon them, and when they shall say, "Peace and safety," overwhelming them with sudden destruction, (Jer. viii. 11.[1])

8. *And they shall make their own tongue to fall upon themselves.* Pursuing the same subject, he remarks, that the poison concocted in their secret counsels, and which they revealed with their tongues, would prove to have a deadly effect upon themselves. The sentiment is the same with that expressed elsewhere by another figure, when they are said to be caught in their own snares, and to fall into the pit which they have digged themselves, (Ps. lvii. 6.) It is just that Heaven should make the mischiefs which they had devised against innocent and upright men to recoil upon their own heads. The judgment is one which we see repeatedly and daily exemplified before our eyes, and yet we find much difficulty in believing that it can take place. We should feel ourselves bound the more to impress the truth upon our hearts, that God is ever watching, as it were, his opportunity of converting the stratagems of the wicked into means just as completely effective of their destruction, as if they had intentionally employed them for that end. In the close of the verse, to point out the striking severity of their punishment, it is said that *all who saw them should flee away.* The judgments of God are lifted above out of the sight of an ignorant world, and ere it can be roused to fear and dismay, these must be such as to bear signal marks indeed of a divine hand.

9. *And all men shall see, and shall declare the work of God.* He insists more fully upon the good effects which would result from the judgment executed in leading such as had formerly overlooked a Divine Providence altogether, to catch a spirit of inquiry from the singularity of the spectacle, and acquaint themselves with, and speak one to another of a subject

---

[1] In the French version the reference is changed to 1 Thess. v. 3.

hitherto entirely new to them. He intimates, that the knowledge of what God had so signally wrought would extend far and wide—for he says, *all men,* &c. The Hebrew verb שכל, *shachal,* employed, admits either of the neuter signification, *they shall understand,* or of the active, *they shall cause others to understand.* But as it is usual with David to repeat the same thing twice, perhaps the latter or transitive sense is preferable. Another desirable consequence which would flow from the deliverance granted is mentioned in the last verse, that it would afford matter of joy, hope, and holy triumph to the saints, who would be confirmed in expecting the same help from God which he had extended to his servant David. Those formerly called the *righteous* are now styled *the upright in heart,* to teach us, that the only righteousness which proves acceptable is that which proceeds from inward sincerity. This truth I have insisted upon at large elsewhere.

PSALM LXV.

This psalm is composed both of petition and thanksgiving. It contains a prediction of the Gentiles being called to the common faith, but is principally occupied with praising God for the fatherly care which he exercises over his Church, and the benefits which flow from it. The Psalmist prays particularly that God would continue his former kindness to the Jewish people. Two instances of the Divine goodness are specified,—the powerful defence extended to their land, and the enriching of it with so many blessings.

¶ To the chief musician, a Psalm of David.[1]

[1] The title of this psalm does not inform us on what particular occasion it was written. Mudge is of opinion that it was " composed by a person just come to Jerusalem from some very distant parts, where, upon his prayers and vows, he had been signally delivered from the fury of the sea, and uproar of the natives ; which leads him into a general acknowledgment of the Divine Providence which extended itself to the end of the earth." It is thought by others to be a thanksgiving to God for having graciously sent to the land of Judea a copious rain, after it had been previously suffering from the effects of a long-continued drought ; and that it

1. *Praise waiteth*[1] *for thee, O God! in Zion ; and unto thee shall the vow be performed.*
2. *O thou that hearest prayer! unto thee shall all flesh come.*
3. *Words of iniquity have prevailed against me : our transgressions thou shalt purge away.*[2]

1. *Praise waiteth for thee, O God! in Zion.* Literally it runs, *Praise is silent to thee,* but the verb דמיה, *dumiyah,* has been metaphorically rendered first, *to be at rest,* then *to wait.* The meaning of the expression is, that God's goodness to his people is such as to afford constantly new matter of praise. It is diffused over the whole world, but specially shown to the Church. Besides, others who do not belong to the Church of God, however abundantly benefits may be showered upon them, see not whence they come, and riot in the blessings

---

probably relates to the three years of famine that followed some time after the rebellion of Absalom, (2 Sam. xxi.,) which, being alleviated by some plenteous showers of rain, called forth this hymn of thanksgiving. Dr Morrison supposes that David wrote it for the feast of tabernacles, as it seems to contain an expression of public thanksgiving for the fruits of the earth, which had been safely gathered in. All these, however, are only conjectures. Nor is it material for us to know the occasion of its composition, embracing, as it does, such general topics as may form a suitable theme for contemplation at all times and in all circumstances.

[1] In our English version it is also *waiteth,* and in the margin *is silent.* "Waiteth as a servant, whose duty it is to do what thou commandest."—*Boothroyd.* "The allusion in this verse is beautiful, when we remember that Eastern servants wait in silence, watching their lords, waiting for the signs of their will."—*Edwards.*

[2] The Hebrew word here rendered, "Thou shalt purge them away," is תכפרם, *techapperem;* properly, "thou wilt make atonement for them." It is from the verb כפר, *kaphar,* which signifies *to cover, to draw over;* and "which in the conjugation *pihel,* acquired the signification *to forgive,* (as it were *to cover* an offence,) and *to do any act* which shall be the *cause* or *occasion* of forgiveness; and thence, by a further process in the flow of ideas, *to compensate, to expiate, to propitiate,* and to accept an expiation." See Dr Pye Smith on *The Sacrifice of Christ,* pp. 339, 340. The covering of the ark was called כפרת, *happoreth,* Ex. xxv. 17; in Greek ἱλαστήριον, that is, *the propitiatory* or *mercy-seat ;* for upon it the blood of expiation, typical of the blood of Christ, was sprinkled on the great day of atonement; and from it God revealed his grace and will to his ancient people. The name ἱλαστήριον is in Rom. iii. 25, given by Paul to Christ, who was the true propitiation for our sins, 1 John ii. 2. The words of the Psalmist, then, without doubt, have a reference to the expiatory sacrifices under the law, and consequently to Him who, "in the end of the ages, hath appeared *to put away sin* by the sacrifice of himself."

which they have received without any acknowledgment of them. But the main thing meant to be conveyed by the Psalmist is, that thanksgiving is due to the Lord for his goodness shown to his Church and people. The second clause of the verse is to the same effect, where he says, *unto thee shall the vow be performed;* for while he engages on the part of the people to render due acknowledgment, his language implies that there would be ever remaining and new grounds of praise.

With the verse which we have been now considering, that which follows stands closely connected, asserting that God hears the prayers of his people. This forms a reason why the vow should be paid to him, since God never disappoints his worshippers, but crowns their prayers with a favourable answer. Thus, what is stated last, is first in the natural order of consideration. The title here given to God carries with it a truth of great importance, That the answer of our prayers is secured by the fact, that in rejecting them he would in a certain sense deny his own nature. The Psalmist does not say, that God has heard prayer in this or that instance, but gives him the name of the hearer of prayer, as what constitutes an abiding part of his glory, so that he might as soon deny himself as shut his ear to our petitions. Could we only impress this upon our minds, that it is something peculiar to God, and inseparable from him, to hear prayer, it would inspire us with unfailing confidence. The power of helping us he can never want, so that nothing can stand in the way of a successful issue of our supplications. What follows in the verse is also well worthy of our attention, that *all flesh shall come* unto God. None could venture into his presence without a persuasion of his being open to entreaty; but when he anticipates our fears, and comes forward declaring that prayer is never offered to him in vain, the door is thrown wide for the admission of all. The hypocrite and the ungodly, who pray under the constraint of present necessity, are not heard; for they cannot be said to come to God, when they have no faith founded upon his word, but a mere vague expectation of a chance issue. Before we can approach God acceptably in prayer, it is necessary that his promises should be made known to us, without which we can have no access to him, as is evident from the words of the apostle Paul, (Eph. iii. 12,) where he tells us, that all who would come to God must first be endued with such a faith in Christ as may animate them with confidence. From this we may infer, that no right rule of prayer is observed in the Papacy, when they pray to God in a state of suspense and doubt. Invaluable is the privilege which we enjoy by the Gospel, of free access unto God. When the Psalmist uses the expression, *all flesh*, he intimates by these few words that the privilege which was now peculiar to the Jews, would be extended to all nations. It is a prediction of Christ's future kingdom.

3. *Words of iniquity have prevailed against me.*[1] He does

[1] In our English Bible it is, "Iniquities prevail against me;" and on the margin, "Words or matters of iniquity," &c. Calvin gives the same meaning which is naturally suggested by our English version, although from his translating the Hebrew text by *words of iniquity*, we would at first view be apt to suppose that he would explain them as referring to the evil reports, the calumnies and slanders, which David's enemies propagated against him to ruin his reputation. Dr Adam Clarke understands the words in this sense, and gives a translation equivalent to Calvin's, "Iniquitous words have prevailed against me," or, "The words of iniquity are strong against me." He thinks the reading of our English Bible " is no just rendering of the original;" observing, that "this verse has been abused to favour Antinomian licentiousness;" and that "the true and correct translation of the former clause will prevent this." But we cannot see how the verse, as it stands in our English Bible, can with justice be viewed as tending to give encouragement to sin, it being no more than the confession of a repentant sinner, accompanied with hope in the mercy of God, founded on the glad tidings announced in the Gospel, that God is willing to pardon the most guilty who believe in his Son, and repent of their sins. The old Scottish version of this verse—

"Iniquities, I must confess,
 Prevail against me do :
 And as for our transgressions,
 Them purge away wilt thou,"

which this learned author terms "most execrable" and "abominable doggrel"—and at hearing which he supposes David would feel chagrin, if such a feeling could affect the inhabitants of heaven—is, it must be admitted, ill expressed, feeble, and easily susceptible of an Antinomian sense. But not so, we think, the revised version, now in very general use in Scotland, which, by the alteration of a single word in the beginning of the third line, has made the verse at the same time more correct and more nervous :—

"*But* as for our transgressions,
 Them purge away shalt thou :"

not complain of the people being assailed with calumny, but is to be understood as confessing that their sins were the cause of any interruption which had taken place in the communication of the divine favour to the Jews. The passage is parallel with that in Isaiah lix. 1,—"The ear of the Lord is not heavy that it cannot hear, but our iniquities have separated betwixt us and him." David imputes it to his own sins and those of the people, that God, who was wont to be liberal in his help, and so gracious and kind in inviting their dependence upon him, had withdrawn for a time his divine countenance. First, he acknowledges his own personal guilt; afterwards, like Daniel, (ix. 5,) he joins the whole nation with himself. And this truth is introduced by the Psalmist with no design to damp confidence in prayer, but rather to remove an obstacle standing in the way of it, as none could draw near to God unless convinced that he would hear the unworthy. It is probable that the Lord's people were at that time suffering under some token of the divine displeasure, since David seems here to struggle with some temptation of this kind. He evidently felt that there was a sure remedy at hand, for no sooner has he referred to the subject of guilt, than he recognises the prerogative of God to pardon and expiate it. The verse before us must be viewed in connection with the preceding, and as meaning, that though their iniquities merited their being cast out of God's sight, yet they would continue to pray, encouraged by his readiness to be reconciled to them. We learn from the passage that God will not be entreated of us, unless we humbly supplicate the pardon of our sins. On the other hand, we are to believe firmly in reconciliation with God being procured through

thus implying at once a deep sense of the evil of sin, and a confident reliance on the forgiving mercy of God—two subjects on which it is of the highest importance for us to entertain just views in drawing near to God in prayer.

Dr Morrison gives the following rendering :—

" *Our* iniquities prevail against us;
But thou art he who blotteth out our transgressions."

Horsley's version is :—

"The account of iniquities is too great for me :
Thou shalt expiate our crimes."

gratuitous remission. Should he at any time withdraw his favour, and frown upon us, we must learn by David's example to rise to the hope of the expiation of our sins. The reason of his using the singular number, in the confession which he makes of sin, may be, that as king he represented the whole people, or that he intended, like Daniel, to exhort them each to an individual and particular examination and confession of his own guilt. We know how apt hypocrites are to hide their personal sin, under a formal acknowledgment of their share in the general transgression. But David, from no affectation of humility, but from deep inward conviction, begins with himself, and afterwards includes others in the same charge.

4. *Blessed is the man whom thou hast chosen, and hast brought near thee; we shall be satisfied with the goodness of thy house, even of the sanctuary of thy palace.*
5. *Terrible things in righteousness wilt thou answer to us, O God of our salvation! the hope of all the ends of the earth, and the far off places of the sea.*[1]
6. *By his strength setting fast the mountains, being girded with power.*[2]
7. *Stilling the noise of the seas, the noise of their waves, and the tumult of the nations.*
8. *They also that dwell in the ends of the earth shall fear at thy signs; thou shalt make the outgoings of the evening and morning to rejoice.*

4. *Blessed is the man whom thou hast chosen.* Having already acknowledged that the people had separated themselves

---

[1] ים, *yam, the sea,* is frequently employed to denote the *islands* which are encompassed by the sea, and being here set in opposition to "the ends or extreme parts of the earth," that is, the continent, it signifies the most remote islands of the world. Accordingly, the Chaldee paraphrase is, "And of the islands of the sea which are remote from the continent." The concluding part of this verse is evidently prophetical of that period when all mankind, when people of every tribe and colour and clime, shall be blessed with the knowledge of the gospel, and worship the only true God.

[2] From the length and looseness of the garments of the inhabitants of the East, in ancient times, it was necessary to bind them close with a girdle, when they intended to exert their strength. Hence the expression, "girded with strength." Dr Lowth thinks the allusion is to the vesture of the Aaronical priesthood.—*Lectures on Sacred Poetry,* vol. i. pp. 173-175.

from God by their sins, and forfeited all right to be heard, he now takes refuge in the free grace of God, which secures the remission of sin amongst other blessings. He thus casts an additional light upon what he had said on the point of guilt being purged away, by pointing to the cause of God's being favourable to poor sinners, which can only be found in his fatherly love leading him to welcome them into his presence, however undeserving. That pardon which we daily receive flows from our adoption, and on it also are all our prayers founded. How could the sinner venture into the sight of God, to obtain reconciliation with him, were he not persuaded of his being a Father? In the words before us, David does not speak of the grace of God as reaching to the Gentiles, (which he had done in a preceding part of the psalm,) but in terms which apply only to the times in which he wrote. The Church of God was confined to the Jews, and they only were admitted into the sanctuary; whereas now, when the distinction has been abolished, and other nations called to the same privilege, we are all at liberty to approach him with familiarity. Christ is our peace, (Ephes. ii. 14,) who has united in one those who were far off, and those who were nigh.

What has been now said may show at once the scope of the Psalmist. The Church and chosen people of God being in possession of the promise of the remission of sins, he calls those blessed whom God has included within that number, and introduced into the enjoyment of such a distinguished privilege. His language intimates, that the election did not at that time terminate upon all; for he insists upon it as the special prerogative of the Jews, that they had been chosen by God in preference to the other nations. Were it supposed that man could do anything to anticipate the grace of God, the election would cease to be with God himself, although the right and power of it are expressly ascribed to him.[1] But the Jews had no excellency above others, except in the one point of having enjoyed the distinguishing favour of God. The middle wall of partition is now broken down,

---

[1] "Nam si anteverterent homines Dei gratiam, non resideret penes ipsum electio, cujus potestas et jus ei tribuitur."—*Lat.*

that the Gentiles might be called in. It is evident, however, that all are not alike called; and observation proves the ignorance of those who will assert that the grace of God is extended to all in common, without any choice exerted on his part. Can any reason be imagined why God should not call all alike, except it be that his sovereign election distinguishes some from others? Faith and prayer may be means for procuring us an interest in the grace of God; but the source whence it flows is not within but without us.[1] There is a blessedness in exercising trust upon God, and embracing his promises—a blessedness experienced when, through faith in Christ the Mediator, we apprehend him as our Father, and direct our prayers to him in that character;—but ere this faith and prayer can have any existence, it must be supposed that we who are estranged from God by nature have been brought near by an exercise of his favour. We are near him, not as having anticipated his grace, and come to him of ourselves, but because, in his condescension, he has stretched out his hand as far as hell itself to reach us. To speak more properly, he first elects us, and then testifies his love by calling us. It is noticeable, also, that though God separated the seed of Abraham to be a peculiar people, entitled as the circumcision to a place in his temple, there can be no question that David recognised a distinction even amongst those who were Jews, all not having been the subjects of God's effectual calling, nor yet properly entitled to a place in his temple. The Psalmist alludes, indeed, to the outward sanctuary, when he speaks of the Jews as chosen to approach God; but we must remember (what was brought under our attention, Ps. xv. and xxiv. 3) that all were not real members of the Church who trod the court of the temple, but that the great qualifications necessary were the pure heart and the clean hands. Accordingly, we must understand by those brought near to God, such as present themselves before him in the exercise of genuine faith, and not such as merely occupy a place in his temple as to outward appearance. But, again, the being cho-

---

[1] "Fides quidem et invocatio media sunt, quæ nobis concilient Dei gratiam, sed fons extra nos quærendus est."—*Lat.* "Sont les moyens pour nous faire trouver grace envers Dieu," &c.—*Fr.*

sen, and the being called to approach God, are two things mentioned here together, to correct any such vain idea as that the sheep of God's flock are allowed to wander at will for any length of time, and not brought into the fold.[1] This is one way by which our gratuitous adoption is evidenced, that we come to the sanctuary under the leading of the Holy Spirit.

The Psalmist insists upon the fruit springing out of the blessed privilege of which he had spoken, when he adds, that believers *would be satisfied* with the fulness of his temple. Hypocrites may go there, but they return empty and unsatisfied as to any spiritual blessing enjoyed. It is noticeable, that the person is changed in this part of the verse, and that David associates himself with other believers, preferring to speak upon this subject from personal experience. We are not to understand that believers are fully replenished with the goodness of God at any one moment; it is conveyed to them gradually; but while the influences of the Spirit are thus imparted in successive measures, each of them is enriched with a present sufficiency, till all be in due time advanced to perfection. I might remark here, that while it is true, as stated, (Ps. ciii. 5,) that "God satisfieth our mouth with good things," at the same time it is necessary to remember what is said elsewhere, "Open thy mouth, and I will fill it." Our contracted desires is the reason why we do not receive a more copious supply of blessings from God; he sees that we are straitened in ourselves, and accommodates the communications of his goodness to the measure of our expectations. By specifying particularly the *goodness of the sanctuary*, the Psalmist passes an implied commendation upon the outward helps which God has appointed for leading us into the enjoyment of heavenly blessings. In these former times God could have directly stretched out his hand from heaven to supply the wants of his worshippers, but saw fit to satisfy their souls by means of the doctrine of the law, sacrifices, and other rites and external aids to piety. Similar are the means

[1] "Jam hic vocatio adjungitur electioni, ne quis somniet oves perpetuò vagari, neque unquam colligi in ovile. Nam hoc effectu se ostendit," &c. —*Lat.* "Or la vocation exterieure est yci adjointe à l'election, afin que nul n'imagine que les brebis soyent tousjours errantes sans estre recueillies en la bergerie : car l'adoption gratuite de Dieu se declare," &c.—*Fr.*

which he employs in the Church still; and though we are not to rest in these, neither must we neglect them.

5. *Terrible things*[1] *in righteousness wilt thou answer to us.* He proceeds to illustrate, although in a somewhat different form, the same point of the blessedness of those who are admitted into the temple of God, and nourished in his house. He declares that God would answer his people by miracles or fearful signs, displaying his power; as if he had said, in deliverances as wonderful as those which he wrought for their fathers when they went out of Egypt. It is in no common or ordinary manner that God has preserved his Church, but with terrible majesty. It is well that this should be known, and the people of God taught to sustain their hopes in the most apparently desperate exigencies. The Psalmist speaks of the deliverances of God as specially enjoyed by the Jewish nation, but adds, that he was *the hope of the ends of the earth,* even to the world's remotest extremities. Hence it follows, that the grace of God was to be extended to the Gentiles.

6. *By his strength setting fast the mountains.* For the sake of illustration, he instances the power of God seen in the general fabric of the world. In these times it sounded as a new and strange truth to say that the Gentiles should be called to the same hope with the Jews. To prove that it was not so incredible as they were apt to conceive, the Psalmist very properly adverts to the Divine power apparent in all parts of the world. He instances the mountains rather than the plains, because the immense masses of earth, and the lofty rocks which they present, convey a more impressive idea of

---

[1] The original word for *terrible things* "signifies sometimes *terrible,* sometimes *wonderful things,* anything that exceeds in greatness or quality. In the latter sense we have it, Deut. x. 21, when speaking of God, it is said, ' He is thy praise, and he is thy God, that hath done for thee these great and terrible things,'—*great, exceeding, wonderful things;* and those acts of mercy, and not of justice or punishment ; and so here it appears to signify, being joined with *answering us,* or *granting us, in answer to our prayers,* (so ענה signifies *to answer a request, to hear a prayer,*) and with *in righteousness,* which frequently imports *mercy.* The LXX. accordingly read it θαυμαστός, *wonderful.*"—*Hammond.*

the Godhead. Interpreters are not agreed as to the exact meaning of the verse which follows. Some think that the mark of similitude must be supplied before the first word of the sentence, and that it is meant to be said that God stills the tumults of men when raging in their insolent attempts, *as* he stills the agitations of the sea. Others understand the first part of the verse to be a metaphorical declaration of what is plainly stated in the close. I would take the words simply as they stand, and consider that in the first member of the verse, David adverts to the illustration of the divine power which we have in the sea, and in the second to that which we have in his operations amongst men. His strength is shown in calming the waves and tempestuous swellings of the ocean. It is put forth also in quelling tumults which may have been raised by the people.

8. *They also that dwell, &c.* By the *signs* referred to, we must evidently understand those signal and memorable works of the Lord which bear the impress of his glorious hand. It is true, that the minutest and meanest objects, whether in the heavens or upon the earth, reflect to some extent the glory of God; but the name mentioned emphatically applies to miracles, as affording a better display of the divine majesty. So striking would be the proofs of God's favour to his Church, that, as the Psalmist here intimates to us, they would constrain the homage and wonder of the most distant and barbarous nations. In the latter part of the verse, if we take the interpretation suggested by some, nothing more is meant, than that when the sun rises in the morning, men are refreshed by its light; and again, that when the moon and stars appear at night, they are relieved from the gloom into which they must otherwise have been sunk. Were this interpretation adopted, a preposition must be understood; as if it had been said, Thou makest men to rejoice *on account of*, or *by* the rising of the sun, of the moon, and of the stars. But the words, as they stand, convey a sense which is sufficiently appropriate without having recourse to any addition. It was said, that in consequence of the wonders done by the Lord, fear would spread itself over the uttermost parts of the

earth; and the same thing is now asserted of the joy which they would shed abroad: from the rising to the setting sun, men would rejoice in the Lord, as well as fear him.

9. *Thou hast visited the earth, and watered it : thou hast greatly enriched it; the river of God is full of waters : thou wilt prepare their corn, for so thou hast provided for it.*
10. *Thou dost saturate its furrows, thou makest the rain to fall into them; thou moistenest it with showers; thou blessest the buddings forth of it.*
11. *Thou crownest the year with thy goodness, and thy paths will drop fatness.*
12. *They drop upon the dwellings*[1] *of the wilderness, and the hills shall be girt about with gladness.*[2]
13. *The pastures are clothed with flocks, the valleys are covered with corn; they shout for joy, they also sing.*

9. *Thou hast visited the earth, and watered it.* This and the verbs which follow denote action continually going forward, and may therefore be rendered in the present tense. The exact meaning of the second verb in the sentence has been disputed. Some derive it from the verb שׁוּק, *shuk,* signifying *to desire;* and giving this meaning, that God visits the earth after it has been made dry and thirsty by long drought.[3] Others derive it from the verb שׁקה, *shakah,* signifying *to give drink.* This seems the most natural interpretation—*Thou visitest the earth by watering it.* It suits the connection better, for it follows, *thou plentifully enrichest it,* an expression obviously added by way of amplification. Whether the Psalmist speaks of Judea only, or of the world at large, is a point as to which different opinions may be held. I am disposed my-

---

[1] " Ou, pasturages,"— *Fr. marg.* " Or, pastures."
[2] " Curiously wrought or embroidered girdles are still, as they were of old, an essential part of Eastern finery both to men and women. It is in allusion probably to such sumptuous girdles worn particularly on joyful occasions, that the Psalmist here represents the hills as ' girded with joy.' " —*Mant.*
[3] This is the sense preferred by Aben Ezra and Kimchi. *Thou hast visited in mercy; i. e.,* blessed the earth *or* land, *after thou hast made it dry or thirsty; thou hast* or *dost enrich it greatly; i. e.,* thou, the same God, who hast punished and made thirsty, dost again return in mercy, enriching the land and restoring plenty to it. Thus it was after the three years' famine recorded in 2 Sam. xxi. 1. But the Septuagint, Arabic, Chaldee, and Syriac versions, interpret the word in the sense of *watering.*

self to think, that although what he says applies to the earth generally, he refers more particularly to Judea, as the former part of the psalm has been occupied with recounting the kindness of God to his own Church and people more especially. This view is confirmed by what is added, *the stream* or *river of God is full of water.* Some take the *river of God* to mean a great or mighty river,[1] but such a rendering is harsh and overstrained, and on that supposition, *rivers*, in the plural number, would have been the form of expression used. I consider that he singles out the small rivulet of Siloah,[2] and sets it in opposition to the natural rivers which enrich other countries, intending an allusion to the word of Moses, (Deut. xi. 10,) that the land which the Lord their God should give unto his people would not be as the land of Egypt, fertilized by the overflowings of the Nile, but a land drinking water of the rain of heaven. Or we may suppose that he calls the rain itself metaphorically *the river of God*.[3] The words must, at any rate, be restricted to Judea, as by *the pastures* or *dwellings of the wilderness*, we are also to understand the more dry and uncultivated districts, called in Scripture " the hill country." But while it is the kindness of God

[1] Some think reference is made to the overflowing of the Jordan after a long drought.

[2] This river ran through Jerusalem, the city of God. Bishop Hare, following Simeon de Muis, is of opinion that this river is meant.

[3] " *The stream of God;* i. e., copious rain, according to the Oriental idiom."—*Dr Geddes.* See p. 7, note 1, of this volume. And without supposing this Hebraism, the treasures of water which descend from the clouds may, with great poetical beauty, be termed *the river of God.* He collects them there by the wonderful process of evaporation, and he pours them down. They are entirely in his hand, and absolutely beyond the control of man. " The keys of the clouds," say the Jews, " are peculiarly kept in God's hand, as the keys of life and resurrection." He can employ them as the instruments of his mercy, by pouring down from them upon the earth copious and refreshing showers, to promote vegetation and produce fruitful seasons; and he can also make them when he pleases the instruments of judgment, either by bottling them up, or by pouring from them floods of rain, as in the deluge, and when the harvest is made a heap in the day of grief and desperate sorrow, Isa. xvii. 11. Horsley, instead of פלג, *peleg*, in the singular, proposes to read פלגות, *pelagoth*, in the plural, and translates, " God is he who filleth the rivulets with water." " The word פלג," says he, " as remarked by Archbishop Secker, is very rarely used as a noun in the singular number. Mr Bates, indeed, takes it to be a noun in Psalm lv. 9; but his interpretation of that text is very doubtful. In the plural it never signifies large rivers, but small brooks and rivulets. We have the authority of the Syriac for reading it in the plural."

to his own people which is here more particularly celebrated as being better known, we are bound, in whatever part of the world we live, to acknowledge the riches of the Divine goodness seen in the earth's fertility and increase. It is not of itself that it brings forth such an inexhaustible variety of fruits, but only in so far as it has been fitted by God for producing the food of man. Accordingly, there is a propriety and force in the form of expression used by the Psalmist when he adds, that *corn is provided for man, because the earth has been so prepared by God;*[1] which means, that the reason of that abundance with which the earth teems, is its having been expressly formed by God in his fatherly care of the great household of mankind, to supply the wants of his children.

10. *Thou dost saturate its furrows.* Some take the verbs as being in the optative mood, and construe the words as a prayer. But there can be little doubt that David still continues the strain of thanksgiving, and praises God for moistening and saturating the earth with rains that it may be fitted for producing fruit. By this he would signify to us, that the whole order of things in nature shows the fatherly love of God, in condescending to care for our daily sustenance. He multiplies his expressions when speaking of a part of the divine goodness, which many have wickedly and impiously disparaged. It would seem as if the more perspicacity men have in observing second causes in nature, they will rest in them the more determinedly, instead of ascending by them to God. Philosophy ought to lead us upwards to him, the more that it penetrates into the mystery of his works; but this is prevented by the corruption and ingratitude of our hearts; and as those who pride themselves in their acuteness, avert their eye from God to find the origin of rain in the air and the elements, it was the more necessary to awaken us out of such a spirit.

---

[1] In the Septuagint the last clause reads, "'Οτι οὕτως ἡ ἑτοιμασία," "For thus is the preparation;" that is, the earth was thus prepared. In the Syriac it is, "When thou didst found or establish it;" and in the Chaldee, "Seeing thou hast so founded it."

11. *Thou crownest the year with thy goodness.* [1] Some read—*Thou crownest the year* OF *thy goodness;* as if the Psalmist meant that the fertile year had a peculiar glory attached to it, and were crowned, so to speak, by God. Thus, if there was a more abundant crop or vintage than usual, this would be the crown of the year. And it must be granted that God does not bless every year alike. Still there is none but what is crowned with some measure of excellency; and for that reason it would seem best to retain the simpler rendering of the words, and view them as meaning that the Divine goodness is apparent in the annual returns of the season. The Psalmist further explains what he intended, when he adds, that *the paths of God dropped fatness,*—using this as a metaphorical term for *the clouds,* upon which God rideth, as upon chariots, as we read in Ps. civ. 3.[2] The earth derives its fruitfulness from the sap or moisture; this comes from the rain, and the rain from the clouds. With a singular gracefulness of expression, these are therefore represented as dropping fatness, and this because they are the paths or vehicles of God; as if he had said, that wherever the Deity walked there flowed down from his feet fruits in endless variety and abundance. He amplifies this goodness of God, by adding, that his fatness drops even upon the wilder and more uncultivated districts. The *wilderness* is not to be taken here for the absolute waste where nothing grows, but for such places as are not so well cultivated, where there are few inhabitants, and where, notwithstanding, the Divine goodness is even more illustrated than elsewhere in dropping down fatness upon the tops of

---

[1] This, say some, was probably the year which followed the three years of famine, after Absalom's rebellion.

[2] Some have imagined that instead of *paths* we should render *clouds;* but the former reading is more poetical. The original word מַעְגְּלֶיךָ, for *thy paths*, is derived from עגל, *round, circular, smooth,* because *paths* are made by *cart-wheels turning round* upon them. Accordingly, Horsley renders it, "thy chariot-wheels," and French and Skinner, "the tracts of thy chariot-wheels." God is here represented as driving round the earth, and from the *clouds* the *paths* of his chariot everywhere scattering blessings upon mankind. This is an instance of the bold and sublime imagery for which the Hebrew poetry is so remarkably distinguished. God is elsewhere described as riding on the clouds during a storm of rain or thunder, Ps. xviii. 9, 10, 11. Some read, "thy orbits," and understand all the circling seasons of the year, as ruled by the courses of the heavenly bodies.

the mountains.¹ Notice is next taken of *the valleys* and level grounds, to show that there is no part of the earth overlooked by God, and that the riches of his liberality extend over all the world. The variety of its manifestation is commended when it is added, that *the valleys* and lower grounds *are clothed with flocks*,² as well as with corn. He represents inanimate things as rejoicing, which may be said of them in a certain sense, as when we speak of the fields smiling, when they refresh our eye with their beauty. It may seem strange, that he should first tell us, that they *shout for joy*, and then add the feebler expression, that *they sing;* interposing, too, the intensative particle, אף, *aph, they shout for joy,* YEA, *they also sing*. The verb, however, admits of being taken in the future tense, *they shall sing*, and this denotes a continuation of joy, that they would rejoice, not only one year, but through the endless succession of the seasons. I may add, what is well known, that in Hebrew the order of expression is frequently inverted in this way.

PSALM LXVI.

There may have been one deliverance in particular, which the Psalmist celebrates here in the name of the Church, but he includes the many and various mercies which God had all along conferred upon his chosen people. While he takes notice of the divine interposition in

---

¹ "By desert or wilderness," observes Dr Shaw, "the reader is not always to understand a country altogether barren and unfruitful, but such only as is rarely or never sown or cultivated; which, though it yields no crops of corn or fruit, yet affords herbage, more or less, for the grazing of cattle, with fountains or rills of water, though more sparingly interspersed than in other places."

² The phrase, " the pastures are clothed with flocks," cannot be regarded as the vulgar language of poetry. It appears peculiarly beautiful and appropriate, when we consider the numerous flocks which whitened the plains of Syria and Canaan. In the Eastern countries, sheep are much more prolific than with us, and they derive their name from their great fruitfulness; bringing forth, as they are said to do, "thousands and ten thousands in their streets," Ps. cxliv. 13. They, therefore, formed no mean part of the wealth of the East.

their behalf, in a crisis of great mercy and distress, he suggests it as matter of comfort under trial, that their subjection to the tyranny of their enemies had been designed to prove them as silver in the furnace. At the close, he would appear to speak of himself individually, and adduces it as a proof of his integrity, that God had heard him, for God does not grant acceptance to the wicked.

¶ To the chief musician, the Song of a Psalm.[1]

1. *Shout unto God, all the earth.*
2. *Sing the honour of his name : make glorious his praise.*[2]
3. *Say unto God, How terrible art thou in thy works ! in the greatness of thy power shall thine enemies lie* [or *feign submission*] *unto thee.*
4. *All the earth shall worship thee, and they shall sing unto thee ; they shall sing thy name. Selah.*

1. *Shout unto God, all the earth.* The psalm begins with this general declaration, which is afterwards reduced to particulars.[3] He addresses himself to the whole world, and from this it would seem evident, that he predicts the extent to which the kingdom of God should reach at the coming of Christ. In the second verse the call is repeated with increasing vehemency, to stir up to the praises of God, such as might otherwise be remiss in the service. *To sing the honour of his name,* is an expression sufficiently obvious; meaning, that we should extol his sacred name in a manner suitable to its dignity, so that it may obtain its due and deserved adoration. But the clause which follows is rather ambiguous. Some think that it conveys a repetition of the same idea contained in other

---

[1] "This psalm is anonymous; nor can we, with certainty, determine to what time it relates. Venema refers it to the reign of Hezekiah, and supposes it to celebrate the deliverance which was effected by the destruction of Sennacherib's army. Rudinger is of opinion, that it celebrates the opening of the sacred temple, after the return from Babylon. It must be owned, that we have nothing but conjecture to offer on this subject; yet it appears to me, that the latter of these opinions is the most probable."—*Walford.*

[2] "Ou, mettez gloire a sa louange."—*Fr. marg.* "Or, put glory to his praise."

[3] "Generalis est præfatio, quam mox sequentur hypotheses."—*Lat.* "C'est une preface generale, dont les applications speciales suivent incontinent apres."—*Fr.*

words, and read, *set forth the glory of his praise*.[1] I prefer taking the Hebrew word signifying *praise* to be in the accusative case; rendering the words literally, *make a glory his praise*. And by this I understand him to mean, not as some do, that we should glory exclusively in his praises,[2] but simply, that we highly exalt his praises, that they may be glorious. The Psalmist is not satisfied with our declaring them moderately, and insists that we should celebrate his goodness in some measure proportionably to its excellence.

3. *Say unto God, How terrible art thou in thy works!* Here he proceeds to state the grounds why he would have us to praise God. Many content themselves with coldly descanting to others of his praises, but with the view of awakening and more deeply impressing our hearts, he directs us to address ourselves immediately to God. It is when we hold converse with him apart, and with no human eye to witness us, that we feel the vanity of hypocrisy, and will be likely to utter only what we have well and seriously meditated in our hearts. Nothing tends more to beget a reverential awe of God upon our spirits than sisting ourselves in his presence. What the Psalmist adds is fitted and designed to produce the same feeling, *that through the greatness of God's power, his enemies feign submission to him.* Are they who would perversely and obstinately revolt from his service, forced to humble themselves before him, whether they will it or not, how much more, then, ought his own children to serve him, who are invited into his presence, by the accents of tenderness, instead of being reduced to subjection by terror? There is an implied contrast drawn between the voluntary homage which they yield, as attracted by the sweet influences of grace, and that slavish obedience which is wrung reluctantly from the unbeliever. The Hebrew word here used for *to lie*, signifies to yield such a submission as is constrained, and not free or cor-

---

[1] Hammond's objection to this is, that if כָּבוֹד, *glory*, were in the construct state, governing the noun which follows, and giving this reading, *the glory of his praise*, the vowel should be changed from ־ָ, *kamets*, to ־ֶ, *segol*.

[2] This is Aben Ezra's view. He would read, "Make *your* glory his praise;" that is, let it be your glory to praise him.

dial, as Ps. xviii. 45. Neither the words nor the scope favour the other senses which have been suggested, as, that his enemies would acknowledge themselves to have been deceived in their hopes, or that they would deny having ever intended hostilities against him. There are many ways in which hypocrites may *lie,* but nothing more is meant by the Psalmist here, than that the power of God is such as to force them into a reluctant subjection.

4. *All the earth shall worship thee.* The Psalmist had good reason for insisting upon this one point again and again. Though all tongues were tuned to the praise of God, they never could adequately extol it; and yet such are the negligence and the perversity of men, that they will scarcely lift one feeble note in celebration of a theme which should command their united strength and might. We have another prediction here, of a time being to come when God would be worshipped, not only by the Jews, a small section of the human family, but by all the nations which would be eventually brought under his government. And we are not to consider that he refers to such a worship as would be constrained, and only not withheld, because resistance might be dangerous, but to the sincere homage of the heart—*they shall sing unto thee, they shall sing unto thy name.* Praise is the best of all sacrifices, (as we are told, Ps. l. 14, 23,) and the true evidence of godliness.[1]

> 5. *Come and see the works of God ; he is terrible in his doing towards the children of men.*
> 6. *He turned the sea into dry land ; they went through the flood on foot ; there did we rejoice in him.*
> 7. *He ruleth by his power over the world ; his eyes behold the nations ; rebels[2] shall not exalt themselves.*
> 8. *Bless our God,[3] O ye people ! and resound the voice of his praise.*

[1] "Est enim hoc præcipuum laudis sacrificium, ut habetur, Psalmo l. 14, 23, ac verum etiam testimonium pietatis."—*Lat.* "Car c'est le principal sacrifice, que le sacrifice de louange, &c., et aussi le vray tesmoignage de pieté."—*Fr.*

[2] *Defectores.*—*Lat.* *Apostats.*—*Fr.* The original word is הסוררים, *hassorerim,* from סור, *sur, to turn aside.*

[3] "On this Theodoret remarks, that when men bless God they offer him

9. *Who hath brought our souls unto life, and hath not suffered our feet to fall.*

5. *Come and see the works of God.* An indirect censure is here passed upon that almost universal thoughtlessness which leads men to neglect the praises of God. Why is it that they so blindly overlook the operations of his hand, but just because they never direct their attention seriously to them? We need to be aroused upon this subject. The words before us may receive some explanation by referring to a parallel passage, Ps. xlvi. 8. But the great scope of them is this, that the Psalmist would withdraw men from the vain or positively sinful and pernicious pursuits in which they are engaged, and direct their thoughts to the works of God. To this he exhorts them, chiding their backwardness and negligence. The expression, *Come and see*, intimates that what they blindly overlooked was open to observation; for were it otherwise with the works of God, this language would be inappropriate. He next points out what those works of God are to which he would have our attention directed; in general he would have us look to the method in which God governs the human family. This experimental or practical kind of knowledge, if I might so call it, is that which makes the deepest impression.[1] We find, accordingly, that Paul, (Acts xvii. 27,) after speaking of the power of God in general, brings his subject to bear upon this one particular point, and calls upon us to descend into ourselves if we would discover the proofs of a present God. The last clause of the fifth verse I would not interpret with some as meaning that God was *terrible above the children of men*—superior to them in majesty—but rather that *he is terrible towards them*, evincing an extraordinary providence in their defence and preservation, as we have seen noticed, Ps. xl. 5. Men need look no further, therefore, than themselves, in order to discover

words only; but when God blesses man, it is not in word only, but in deed; an abundance of good things always accompanying the benediction."—*Cresswell.*

[1] "Hæc enim experimentalis (ut ita loquar) notitia magis afficit."—*Lat.* "Car ceste cognoissance d'experience et de prattique esmeut d'avantage."—*Fr.*

the best grounds for reverencing and fearing God. The Psalmist passes next from the more general point of his providence towards mankind at large, to his special care over his own Church, adverting to what he had done for the redemption of his chosen people. What he states here must be considered as only one illustration of many which he might have touched upon, and as intended to remind God's people of the infinite variety of benefits with which their first and great deliverance had been followed up and confirmed. This appears obvious from what he adds, *there we rejoiced in him.* It is impossible that the joy of that deliverance could have extended to him or any of the descendants of the ancient Israelites, unless it had partaken the nature of a pledge and illustration of the love of God to the Church generally. Upon that event he showed himself to be the everlasting Saviour of his people; so that it proved a common source of joy to all the righteous.

7. *He ruleth by his power over the world.* The Hebrew word עוֹלָם, *olam,* which I have translated *the world,* signifies occasionally *an age,* or *eternity;*[1] but the first sense seems to agree best with the context, and the meaning of the words is, that God is endued with the power necessary for wielding the government of the world. What follows agrees with this, *that his eyes behold the nations.* Under the law, Judea was the proper seat of his kingdom; but his providence always extended to the world at large; and the special favour shown to the posterity of Abraham, in consideration of the covenant, did not prevent him from extending an eye of providential consideration to the surrounding nations. As an evidence of his care reaching to the different countries round, he takes

---

[1] Our English version renders the word in this last sense. Hammond, with Calvin, prefers reading "over the world." "That עוֹלָם," says he, "αἰών, as the English *age,* signifies not only *time* and *duration,* but also the *men* that live in any *time,* there is no question. And then מֹשֵׁל עוֹלָם, must here most properly be rendered *ruling the world,* or *over the world;* and so the Chaldee certainly understood, who read, 'who exerciseth dominion over the world;' and so I suppose the LXX. their 'δεσπόζοντι τοῦ αἰῶνος,' 'having dominion over the world,' doth import." The Vulgate, in this instance not following the Septuagint, has "in æternum," "for ever."

notice of the judgments which God executed upon the wicked and the ungodly. He proves that there was no part of the human family which God overlooked, by referring to the fact of the punishment of evil-doers. There may be much in the Divine administration of the world calculated to perplex our conclusions; but there are always some tokens to be seen of his judgments, and these sufficiently clear to strike the eye of an acute and attentive observer.

8. *Bless our God, O ye people!* Although calling upon all, without exception, to praise God, he refers particularly to some Divine interposition in behalf of the Church. He would seem to hint that the Gentiles were destined, at a future period, to share the favour now exclusively enjoyed by God's chosen people. In the meantime, he reminds them of the signal and memorable nature of the deliverance granted, by calling upon them to spread abroad the fame of it. Though he speaks of the Jewish people as having been *brought unto life,* (an expression intended to denote deliverance of a more than ordinary kind,) this means that they had been preserved from approaching danger, rather than recovered from a calamity which had actually overtaken them. It is said that *their feet had not been suffered to fall,* which implies, that, through seasonable help which they had received, they had not fallen, but stood firm. The Psalmist, however, does not take occasion, from the evil having been anticipated and averted, to undervalue it. As they had been preserved safe by an interposition of Divine goodness, he speaks of this as tantamount to having been brought or restored to life.

10. *For thou, O God! hast proved us, thou hast tried us as silver is tried.*
11. *Thou broughtest us into the net, thou laidest restraint upon our loins.*
12. *Thou hast made man to ride over our heads,*[1] *we have come*

[1] *To ride over,* signifies to insult or tyrannize over. But here the image may be taken from the trampling of war-horses in the day of battle. The cavalry, in the field of battle, pay no regard to the fallen, the dying, and the dead, but tread promiscuously upon all that come in their way. " Thou hast permitted us," says Dr Adam Clarke, " to fall under the do-

*into fire and water, and thou hast brought us into a fruitful place.*¹

10. *For thou, O God! hast proved us.* We may read, *Though thou, O God! &c.*, and then the passage comes in as a qualification of what went before, and is brought forward by the Psalmist to enhance the goodness of God, who had delivered them from such severe calamities. But there is another object which I consider him to have in view, and this is the alleviation of the grief of God's people, by setting before them the comfort suggested by the words which follow. When visited with affliction, it is of great importance that we should consider it as coming from God, and as expressly intended for our good. It is in reference to this that the Psalmist speaks of their having been *proved and tried.* At the same time, while he adverts to God's trying his children with the view of purging away their sin, as dross is expelled from the silver by fire, he would intimate, also, that trial had been made of their patience. The figure implies that their probation had been severe; for silver is cast repeatedly into the furnace. They express themselves thankful to God, that, while proved with affliction, they had not been destroyed by it; but that their affliction was both varied and very severe, appears not only from the metaphor, but from the whole context, where they speak of having been cast into the net, being reduced to straits, men riding over their heads, and of being brought through shipwreck and conflagration.² The

minion of our enemies, who have treated us as broken infantry are when the cavalry dashes among their disordered ranks, treading all under their horses' feet."

¹ "In planitiem."—*Lat.* "En lieu plantureux."—*Fr.*

² "Per naufragium et incendium transiisse." The French version reads, "Par l'eau et par le feu;" but it is important to retain the original more closely, as giving what Calvin considered to be the sense of the words in the text. Fire and water, the one of which elements consumes, while the other suffocates, is a proverbial expression, signifying, as our author afterwards states, extreme danger and complicated calamities. "When thou passest through the *waters,* I will be with thee; when thou walkest through the *fire,* thou shalt not be burnt," Isa. xliii. 2. See also Psalm xxxii. 6; Ezek. xvi. 6, 7; Num. xxxi. 23. Those things are said to come into or to pass through the fire, which abide the same, without being consumed; and which, like metals, lose only thereby their dross.

expression, *laying a restraint* [or *chain*] *upon their loins,* is introduced as being stronger than the one which goes before. It was not a net of thread which had been thrown over them, but rather they had been bound down with hard and insolvable fetters. The expression which follows refers to men who had shamefully tyrannized over them, and ridden them down as cattle. By *fire* and *water* are evidently meant complicated afflictions; and it is intimated that God had exercised his people with every form of calamity. They are the two elements which contribute more than any other to sustain human life, but are equally powerful for the destruction of it. It is noticeable, that the Psalmist speaks of all the cruelties which they had most unjustly suffered from the hands of their enemies, as an infliction of Divine punishment; and would guard the Lord's people against imagining that God was ignorant of what they had endured, or distracted by other things from giving attention to it. In their condition, as here described, we have that of the Church generally represented to us; and this, that when subjected to vicissitudes, and cast out of the fire into the water, by a succession of trials, there may at last be felt to be nothing new or strange in the event to strike us with alarm. The Hebrew word רְוָיָה, *revayah,* which I have rendered *fruitful place,* means literally *a well-watered land.* Here it is taken metaphorically for a condition of prosperity, the people of God being represented as brought into a pleasant and fertile place, where there is abundance of pasturage. The truth conveyed is, that God, although he visit his children with temporary chastisements of a severe description, will ultimately crown them with joy and prosperity. It is a mistake to suppose that the allusion is entirely to their being settled in the land of Canaan,[1] for the psalm has not merely reference to the troubles which they underwent in the wilderness, but to the whole series of distresses to which they were subjected at the different periods of their history.

---

[1] Cresswell takes this view. His note on the place is, "'*Into* a wealthy place,' literally *into* an irriguous region, (comp. Judges i. 15,) *i.e.,* into a fertile country, a land of abundance, the promised land: comp. Exod. iii. 8."

13. *I will come into thy house with burnt-offerings; I will pay thee my vows,*
14. *Which my lips have uttered, and my mouth hath spoken, when I was in trouble.*
15. *I will offer unto thee burnt-sacrifices of fatlings, with the incense of rams;*[1] *I will bring bullocks, with goats. Selah.*
16. *Come, hear, I will tell to all them that fear God, what he hath done for my soul.*

13. *I will come into thy house with burnt-offerings.* Hitherto the Psalmist has spoken in the name of the people at large. Now he emphatically gives expression to his own private feelings, and calls upon them, by his example, to engage individually in the exercises of religion, it being impossible that there should be any hearty common consent unless each entered seriously upon the service of thanksgiving for himself and apart. We are taught that when God at any time succours us in our adversity, we do an injustice to his name if we forget to celebrate our deliverances with solemn acknowledgments. More is spoken of in this passage than thanksgiving. He speaks of vows having been contracted by him in his affliction, and these evidenced the constancy of his faith. The exhortation of the Apostle James (chap. v. 13) is worthy of our special notice: "Is any among you afflicted? let him pray. Is any merry? let him sing psalms." How many are there who lavish their hypocritical praises upon God in the career of their good fortune, while they are no sooner reduced to straits than the fervour of their love is damped, or gives place to the violence of fretfulness and impatience. The best evidence of true piety is when we sigh to God under the pressure of our afflictions, and show, by our prayers, a holy

---

[1] Here Calvin, as well as our English Bible, joins *incense* with *rams*, appearing to mean by *incense*, offering by fire, the smoke produced by the sacrifice. But the burning of incense was a distinct offering from that of animal sacrifices; and therefore many critics read the verse so as to make *incense* a distinct offering. Thus Horsley, altering the punctuation, translates,

"Offerings of fatlings I will offer unto thee, with incense;
"I will sacrifice rams, bullocks, and full-grown goats."

This, we think, gives an improved view of the passage. It may be here observed, that the Hebrews were not allowed to sacrifice other animals than these three kinds, rams, bullocks, and goats.

perseverance in faith and patience; while afterwards we come forward with the expression of our gratitude. The words, *which my lips have uttered,* are not an unmeaning addition, but imply that he had never allowed himself to be so far overcome by grief as not to throw his desires into the express form of petition, declaring that he cast himself for safety into the hands of God. On the subject of vows, I may just shortly repeat the remarks which have been given at greater length elsewhere. First, the holy fathers never vowed anything to God but what they knew to be sanctioned by his approval. Secondly, their sole end in vowing was to evidence their gratitude. The Papists, therefore, can find no warrant, from their example, for the rash and impious vows which they practise. They obtrude upon God whatever chances to come first into their lips; the end which they propose to themselves is the farthest removed from the right one; and with devilish presumption they engage themselves to things which are not allowed them.

15. *I will offer unto thee burnt-sacrifices of fatlings.* We must suppose the speaker to be either David or one of the more considerable men of the nation, for none in humbler circumstances could have offered rich sacrifices of this kind. It is probable that David was the author of the psalm, and here he signifies his intention to show a kingly liberality in his offerings. The reason why God ordered victims to be offered as an expression of thanksgiving was, as is well known, to teach the people that their praises were polluted by sin, and needed to be sanctified from without. However we might propose to ourselves to praise the name of God, we could only profane it with our impure lips, had not Christ once offered himself up a sacrifice, to sanctify both us and our services, (Heb. x. 7.) It is through him, as we learn from the apostle, that our praises are accepted. The Psalmist, by way of commendation of his burnt-offering, speaks of its incense or sweet savour; for although in themselves vile and loathsome, yet the rams and other victims, so far as they were figures of Christ, sent up a sweet savour unto God.[1] Now that the

---

[1] "Le Prophete louë yci le perfum de son holocauste, combien qu'il n'en

shadows of the Law have been abolished, attention is called to the true spiritual service. What this consists in, is more clearly brought under our notice in the verse which follows, where the Psalmist tells us, that he would spread abroad the fame of the benefits which he had received from God. Such was the end designed, even in the outward ceremonies under the Law, apart from which they could only be considered as an empty show. It was this—the fact, that they set forth the praises of the divine goodness—which formed the very season of the sacrifices, preserving them from insipidity. In calling, as he does, upon all *the fearers of the Lord,* the Psalmist teaches us, that if we duly feel the goodness of God, we will be inflamed with a desire to publish it abroad, that others may have their faith and hope confirmed, by what they hear of it, as well as join with us in a united song of praise. He addresses himself to none but such as feared the Lord, for they only could appreciate what he had to say, and it would have been lost labour to communicate it to the hypocritical and ungodly.

17. *I cried unto him with my mouth,*[1] *and have extolled him under* [or *with*] *my tongue.*
18. *If I regard iniquity in my heart, the Lord will not hear me.*
19. *But truly God hath heard me; he hath attended to the voice of my prayer.*
20. *Blessed be God! who hath not turned away my prayer, and his mercy from me.*

17. *I cried unto him with my mouth.* He proves that he owed his safety to Divine interposition, from the circumstance of his having prayed, and in consequence, having sensibly ex-

---

peust monter au ciel qu' une odeur puante et infecte : mais il faut noter que les beliers et autres bestes qu'on sacrifioit flairoyent bon devant Dieu, entant que c'estoyent figures de Iesus Christ."—*Fr.*

[1] In the original, the prefix ב, *beth,* for *with,* is omitted, but it is evidently understood. The reading is simply פִּי, *pi, my mouth,* for בְּפִי, *bephi, with my mouth.* It is not uncommon in Hebrew for some word or phrase to be omitted, which must be supplied by the reader, in order to complete the regular or full construction. Thus in Psalm cxiv. 8, to the words אֲגַם־מָיִם, *agam-maim, a pool of waters,* the letter ל, *lamed,* is to be supplied, לְאֲגַם, *laägam, into* a pool of, &c.

perienced his kindness. Answers to prayer serve in no small degree to illustrate the goodness of God, and confirm our faith in it. In saying that he cried to God with his *mouth* and *tongue*, these are terms denoting, as we have seen in a previous part of the psalm, the vehemency and earnestness with which he prayed. Had he not prayed from the heart, he would have been rejected, but he makes mention of the *tongue* also, in token of the ardour of his supplications. Some absurdly imagine, that because the expression *under the tongue* is used, the meaning is *with the heart*. Words are said to come from under the tongue, because they are formed by the flexion of the tongue, as in that passage, " The poison of asps is under their lips," (Ps. cxl. 3.) The term *extol* intimates, that we cannot honour God more in our worship, than by looking upwards to him for deliverance. The Papists rob him of a chief part of his glory, when they direct their prayers to the dead or to images, and make such little account of calling upon the name of the Lord.

The Psalmist next lays down the rule, which must be attended to, if we would pray properly and acceptably; guarding against that presumptuous exercise which overlooks the necessity of faith and penitence. We see with what audacity hypocrites and ungodly men associate themselves with the Lord's people, in compliance with the general calls of the word to engage in prayer. To check this solemn mockery, the Psalmist mentions integrity of heart as indispensable. I am aware that the words may be considered as an assertion of his own personal uprightness of conduct, as we find him frequently vindicating this, by an appeal to the visible and practical proofs which God had shown of his favour to him; but his main object is evidently to enforce by the example of his own exercise, the common propriety of drawing near to God with a pure heart. We have a parallel scripture in John ix. 31, " We know that God heareth not sinners." In one sense, he hears none but sinners; for we must all conform to the great rule of applying to him for the remission of our sins. But while believers make an unreserved confession of guilt before God, by this very thing they cease to be sinners, for God pardons them in answer to their supplications. We are not to forget the words of Paul, "Let every one that nameth the name of Christ depart from iniquity," (2 Tim. ii. 19.) Besides, to *regard iniquity in the heart,* does not mean to be conscious of sin,—for all the Lord's people must see their sins and be grieved for them, and this is rather praiseworthy than condemnable ;—but to be bent upon the practice of iniquity. He particularly refers to the *heart,* intimating that not only were his hands clean, in the sense of his being innocent before men, but that he could appeal to God in proof of his inward integrity. When the heart does not correspond to the outward conduct, and harbours any secret evil intent, the fair exterior appearance may deceive men; but it is an abomination in the sight of God. The Psalmist affirms with emphasis, that his prayers had been answered, and we ought to draw the inference that we shall never be disappointed, if we seek God in sincerity.

20. *Blessed be God! who hath not turned away my prayer.* He concludes the psalm, as he began it, with thanksgiving, and gives the reason of his not having met with a repulse; or, to take the figurative expression which he employs, of God's not having *turned away his prayer.* This was, that he had not withdrawn his mercy. For it is entirely of his free grace that he is propitious, and that our prayers are not wholly ineffectual.

www.ingramcontent.com/pod-product-compliance
Lightning Source LLC
Chambersburg PA
CBHW070300010526
44108CB00039B/1256